Melvin Konner, born in 1946 in New York City, was graduated from Brooklyn College, received his doctorate and taught at Harvard University, and spent two years doing field work among the !Kung San, or Bushmen, hunter-gatherers of Africa's Kalahari. He is the author of *The Tangled Wing: Biological Constraints on the Human Spirit*, which was nominated for the National Book Award. He is the Samuel Candler Dobbs Professor of Anthropology at Emory University, where he is also affiliated with the Department of Psychiatry in the School of Medicine. He is a contributing editor of *The Sciences*, for which he writes a regular column, "On Human Nature," and he also writes a column on health and behavior for *The New York Times Magazine*. His most recent book is *Medicine at the Crossroads: The Crisis in Healthcare*. He is married and has three children.

BECOMING
A DOCTOR

*A Journey of Initiation
in Medical School*

MELVIN KONNER, M.D.

PENGUIN BOOKS

PENGUIN BOOKS
Published by the Penguin Group
Penguin Group (USA) Inc., 375 Hudson Street, New York, New York 10014, U.S.A.
Penguin Group (Canada), 90 Eglinton Avenue East, Suite 700, Toronto,
Ontario, Canada M4P 2Y3 (a division of Pearson Penguin Canada Inc.)
Penguin Books Ltd, 80 Strand, London WC2R 0RL, England
Penguin Ireland, 25 St Stephen's Green, Dublin 2, Ireland (a division of Penguin Books Ltd)
Penguin Group (Australia), 250 Camberwell Road, Camberwell,
Victoria 3124, Australia (a division of Pearson Australia Group Pty Ltd)
Penguin Books India Pvt Ltd, 11 Community Centre, Panchsheel Park, New Delhi – 110 017, India
Penguin Group (NZ), cnr Airborne and Rosedale Roads,
Albany, Auckland 1310, New Zealand (a division of Pearson New Zealand Ltd)
Penguin Books (South Africa) (Pty) Ltd, 24 Sturdee Avenue,
Rosebank, Johannesburg 2196, South Africa

Penguin Books Ltd, Registered Offices: 80 Strand, London WC2R 0RL, England

First published in the United States of America by
Viking Penguin Inc., 1987
Published in Penguin Books 1988

40 39 38 37 36 35 34 33 32 31

Copyright © Melvin Konner, 1987
All rights reserved

Grateful acknowledgment is made for permission to reprint
excerpts from the following material:

"Do Not Go Gentle into That Good Night," from *Poems of Dylan
Thomas*, by Dylan Thomas. Copyright 1952 by Dylan Thomas.
Reprinted by permission of New Directions Publishing Corpora-
tion and J. M. Dent & Sons Ltd.

"Physicians' Reactions to Patients: A Key to Teaching Humanistic
Medicine," by Richard Gorlin, M.D., and Howard Zucker, M.D.,
from the *New England Journal of Medicine*, May 5, 1983, volume
308, pp. 1059–1063. Reprinted with permission of the *New
England Journal of Medicine*.

LIBRARY OF CONGRESS CATALOGING IN PUBLICATION DATA
Konner, Melvin. Becoming a doctor. 1. Konner, Melvin.
2. Medical students—United States—Biography. I. Title.
[R154.K44A3 1988] 610'.92'4 [B] 87–32832
ISBN 0 14 01.1116 6

Printed in the United States of America
Set in Caledonia

To my mother and father,

HANNAH LEVIN KONNER *and* IRVING KONNER,

this book is fondly and gratefully dedicated

I swear by Apollo the physician, by Aesculapius, Hygeia, and Panacea, and I take to witness all the gods, all the goddesses, to keep according to my ability and my judgment the following oath:

To consider dear to me as my parents him who taught me this art; to live in common with him and if necessary to share my goods with him; to look upon his children as my own brothers, to teach them this art if they so desire without fee or written promise; to impart to my sons and the sons of the master who taught me and to the disciples who have enrolled themselves and have agreed to the rules of the profession, but to these alone, the precepts and the instruction. I will prescribe regimen for the good of my patients according to my ability and my judgment and never do harm to anyone. To please no one will I prescribe a deadly drug, nor give advice which may cause his death. Nor will I give a woman a pessary to procure abortion. But I will preserve the purity of my life and my art. I will not cut for stone, even for patients in whom the disease is manifest; I will leave this operation to be performed by specialists in this art. In every house where I come I will enter only for the good of my patients, keeping myself far from all intentional ill-doing and all seduction, and especially from the pleasures of love with women or with men, be they free or slaves. All that may come to my knowledge in the exercise of my profession or outside of my profession or in daily commerce with men, which ought not to be spread abroad, I will keep secret and will never reveal. If I keep this oath faithfully, may I enjoy my life and practice my art, respected by all men and in all times; but if I swerve from it or violate it, may the reverse be my lot.

> Oath of Hippocrates of Kos,
> Fifth century B.C.

Life is short and the art long, the occasion instant, experiment perilous, decision difficult.

> Medical aphorism,
> also attributed to Hippocrates

Something has gone wrong in the practice of medicine, and we all know it.

> Richard Gorlin and Howard D. Zucker,
> "Physicians' Reactions to Patients:
> A Key to Teaching Humanistic Medicine,"
> Special Article, *New England Journal of Medicine*,
> May 5, 1983

Acknowledgments

In an enterprise of this kind, which is as much a matter of life as of art, it is difficult to discern where gratitude begins and ends. The people who helped guide my thinking in the direction of going to medical school and who taught or otherwise helped me during medical school are too numerous to mention by name. They know who they are, I hope, and that I am deeply grateful.

I have made every effort to protect the privacy of the patients, physcians, and other persons who appear in this book, as well as the confidentiality of the proceedings or relations described; names, descriptions, and identifying characteristics have therefore been changed.

Stephan Chorover and Lionel Tiger were among the first to encourage the writing of the book. For advice and support during the writing I am especially indebted to Susanna Konner, Adam Konner, Lawrence Konner, Jerome and Edna Shostak, Irven and Nancy DeVore, Herbert Perluck, Robert Liebman, Earl and Martha Kim, Mark and Susan Shell, Pavel Pisk, Herbert and Hazel Karp, John and Lou Stone, Joseph and Kay Beck, Jerome and Melissa Walker, Boyd and Daphne Eaton, Sylvia Cerel Bowen, Stefan Stein, Robert Green, Michael Cantor, and Sarah Steinhardt. The manuscript was read in its entirety by Peter Brown, John Stone, Stuart Seidman, Misha Ples, and Timothy Harlan, and their comments were particularly helpful. Marian Wood made valuable comments on an early draft of part of the book. The concluding chapter was read by members of the Medicine and Technology discussion group at the Center for Advanced Study in the Behavioral Sciences, including Lawrence Crowley, P. Herbert Leiderman, Julius Moravcik, Robert Rose, Albert Rothenberg, and Robert Scott; and my discussions with them have helped in the preparation of the final draft.

I am deeply indebted to the administration, faculty, and students of Emory University for their practical and spiritual support during the preparation of the book. Particular thanks are due to David Minter, James Laney, John Palms, Robert Paul, Peter Brown, E. O. Smith, Debra Fey, Bernard Holland, Jeffrey Houpt, and

Frederick King. Discussions with John Stone, and the benefit of his friendship, have illuminated for me many aspects of medicine and medical humanism that would otherwise have remained obscure.

The final editing of the book was accomplished at the Center for Advanced Study in the Behavioral Sciences, in Stanford, California. I am grateful to Gardner Lindzey, Robert Scott, Carol Treanor, Julie Schumacher, and other members of the staff of the Center for encouragement and assistance.

My agent, Elaine Markson, and her associate, Geri Thoma, were early supporters of the project, and their warm but practical advice has been keenly appreciated. Elisabeth Sifton, Vice President of Viking Penguin and Publisher of Elisabeth Sifton Books, is any serious author's dream editor. Her devoted professional attention to the project at every level of abstraction and detail has done much to make it succeed as well as it has. The combination of this professionalism with a friendly and supportive personal style has helped make the process a labor of love. Julie Dolin and Elizabeth Arlen in her office are also due a vote of thanks. I am grateful to Sharon Minors for her help in the preparation of the manuscript.

I wish I could name the patients who have taught and guided me during my medical education, and the wish is especially poignant in some cases. Every health care provider learns from patients, but I was trying especially to learn about the human dimensions of patient needs and patient care; for this reason my reliance on what I have learned from them, and on their attitude of tolerance in the midst of their suffering, has been unusually great.

The book is dedicated to my mother and father, Hannah Levin Konner and Irving Konner, who through great sacrifice established in me the sense of responsibility toward life and the world that is the healing stance, and more important, a sense that I might be able to accomplish something in relation to it. I am deeply and permanently grateful to them.

Finally, the most important person in the genesis of this book was Marjorie Shostak. I owe her an immense debt of gratitude for her tolerance, at great personal cost, of my strange career development; for her devotion to my enterprise both in training and in writing; for the lifeline of her supportive conversations at every step of the climb; for her twenty years of friendship; for her love.

Preface

This is a book about an unusual journey.

It is not the usual sort of unusual journey undertaken by an anthropologist—a voyage into an arctic waste or a semiarid wilderness or a dense hot wet tropical forest in search of human or protohuman exotica. I have taken that sort of journey too, and so I can say that the one described here, if less romantic, is no less exotic and is not devoid of drama and palpable danger.

It is a journey I made "in the middle of this pathway of our life," to use Dante's words, through one of the most challenging of common human experiences. Even when undertaken in early youth, the basic training of a physician strains resources—and not just financial ones—talent, intelligence, detachment, perseverance, courage, just as Dante's own marvelous journey did. But undertaken in the midst of the fourth decade of life, it calls, too, upon one's knowledge of the world and of oneself; and, alas, for a suppression of such knowledge.

Of course something must motivate a life choice so out of phase, and here I would name an appetite for experience that exceeds the normal restraints of pride. In this, too, it resembles Dante's journey: one cannot easily imagine Virgil's trembling acolyte as a twenty-year-old. We must think instead of a fully adult man in submission, having in some important sense lost his way. Yet the trials must be worthy of the acolyte, just as he must try to be worthy of them; at best, then, they may lend some degree of dignity to each other in the end.

A decade ago, when I sat down to write this book, I had just finished medical school. I tried to offer exacting, vivid descriptions of an immediate factual world in which technical intricacy gives order to human drama. I tried to recount the challenge of training, but inevitably I had to describe institutions: two leading medical schools and ten or twelve hospitals. I have seen many others since. If there are systems for the hospital training part of medical school that are markedly different from what I saw, they are certainly not common.

Like most people who go into medicine, unconsciously I must have thought I would someday take care of myself and of those I loved most. Little did I realize how full my life would become of opportunities to do this. Two years after I received my M.D. degree, my brother's wife, then forty-four, had a massive brain stem stroke. When her life hung in the balance, I was deeply involved in family decisions about her care, and I have helped guide her rehabilitation ever since. Eight months later, when I had had enough of medical crisis, my wife was diagnosed with breast cancer. Although her prognosis had been good, her cancer came back not once but several times, and at present she is fighting for her life. My mother suffered a large left-brain stroke, and eventually died, but only after months of painful, humbling illness, while we agonized over what she would have wanted. In the meanwhile, I ruptured a couple of lumbar discs and had major surgery; the pain was at times impressive. As if these were not enough life lessons in medicine, my youngest daughter, then four, was bitten by a copperhead when my wife was out of the country. I stayed at her bedside around the clock for a week that included two operations; though it ended well, it was one of the roughest experiences a parent can go through.

So I have been on both sides now. And the things I learned both as a patient and as a family member of patients have, if anything, strengthened the concerns I expressed in this book. I still sympathize with the plight of the doctor, especially today when the doctor is under siege. But medical schools have failed, and continue to fail, to produce graduates who are capable of humane as well as merely scientific medical care. It is this failure more than anything that has put the modern doctor so thoroughly on the defensive. Today's physicians—the medical students of the seventies and eighties—have lost the public trust because they have not cared enough about their patients. Is it surprising that their patients no longer care about them?

I know that we are not supposed to like to say "I told you so," but the fact is I love to, and I will not resist. The chapters of this book detail a set of experiences almost guaranteed to produce doctors who will fail their patients. I don't mean fail scientifically. They succeed as well as possible in that important but limited sphere. But what they cannot do is navigate the much larger sphere of human emotions. Illness brings fear, yearning, rage, grief, pain, and yes, the joy of recovery. It brings rebellion in the form of noncompliance, or an unshakable alliance with the doctor who knows how to forge one. What happens in medical school not only does not adequately prepare young doctors for the emotions that patients have, it prepares them to ignore them. To the doctors who are bewildered that they have lost America's trust, I say: You have lost it because you did not try to keep it, or perhaps because those who were responsible for your training never tried to teach you how.

This book focuses on the clinical portion of medical school. It is not about internship, the first year after medical school, which is at least equally crucial. It is the year of assumption of responsibility, of the true consolidation of efficient, reliable skill. It is when willingness to act, and to accept responsibility, become reflexive. This is the sine qua non of the character development of the physician. But there are now a number of readable, accurate books about internship, while the medical student's very first clinical encounters have been relatively ignored. That year, the third year of medical school, is the year in which all the basic skills are first formed—lancing a boil, diagnosing the source of a fever, calculating a baby's medicine dosage, hearing a heart murmur, ordering a brain scan, dictating an assessment note, talking to the mother of a hopelessly ill child.

A bewildering blizzard of facts has passed through the mind of the student during the first two years—in effect an encyclopedia of medicine committed to memory and then largely forgotten. Now these facts must be reawakened and reinculcated in the harsh light of the clinic, under the aspect of suffering and death. All this scientific learning is disassembled from its carefully crafted order—"microbiology," "neuroanatomy," "respiratory pathophysiology"—and reassembled around the experience of individual patients becoming ill, recovering, or dying.

Above all, for my purposes, it is the year in which the most important phase of socialization is largely completed, when the adoption of the values of physicians is effected. If at the end the acolyte cannot yet act or think like a physician, he or she can and does make moral judgments like a physician; or, to be more precise (and this distinction is important), like a house officer—a hospital resident or intern. This is because it is the house officers to whom, more than anyone else, the student is apprenticed. The process of identification with them takes over the soul of the student not merely because what they can *do* (always the first word in this world, the second being *know*) is so prodigiously impressive, but because the immediate goal is not to become a physician in some general sense but to become—in less than two years—a house officer and to master as quickly as possible their strategies for survival under the inhuman regimes to which house officers are subjected and subject themselves.

The fourth year of medical school is generally viewed as anticlimactic in comparison with the third. Most students find it easy. Many spend a good part of it arranging for further training or in the laboratory. Those who spend it in the clinic refine their basic skills, but since they do not yet assume responsibility, the next critical phase of their training is deferred. The fourth year is one of consolidation, of becoming more comfortable in the new knowledge and role. At the end of it, the acolyte will be addressed—by the teachers, the nurses, the patients, the pharmacist, and the law—as "Doctor." Amazingly, this label (carried literally on the name tag) will not be entirely unjustified.

About this third-year process I might have written at least two different books. It might have been a dry social-science account of becoming a physician: "socialization," or "enculturation" into the social and cultural world of the principal healing profession. This would entail giving a strict account of the social structure of that world, some theoretical foundation for interpreting it, a review of the literature on the sociology of the professions, and an analysis, cast in appropriate psychologese, of the personality changes of the "typical" medical student. There would probably be a profusion of diagrams—a flow chart of the trainee's progress, a pyramid of the hospital bureaucracy, a floor plan of the waiting room or ward or surgical suite. Charts tabulating such subjects as the cost of medical education and the incidence of medical-student suicides would be mandatory. As an anthropologist, I was adept at such writings long before I went to medical school, and I could have done all that. But this is not that book.

The other would have been a sort of medical diary, the kind that might read like a novel, full of true-life adventures, with no pause for comment or reflection—what they call in Hollywood a "punched-up" docudrama. It might even have had some of the quality of television medical fiction, although it would have been nastier and more complex, albeit, palatable and engaging. This is not that book either.

In a sense it is something of both. I have tried to give an account of the process of socialization of young physicians. I am an anthropologist trained to study odd and complex social worlds through the marvelous prism of participant observation—that paradoxical method through which the investigator both lives and watches the progress of a set of more or less exotic customs. Since I have spent two years in Africa engaged in studies of San (or Bushman) hunter-gatherers in the Kalahari Desert—as well as brief sojourns among the Navajo and in a little Spanish village in the Pyrenees—I have anthropological methods in my bones. My experiences in medical school were not at all the same thing. Anthropological participant observation both permits and requires an ultimate detachment to which I cannot in this case pretend. When I was in Africa I certainly tried to immerse myself, but like most anthropologists who bathe in exotic waters, I found that I was not quite born again; or if I was, it was not into the foreign culture but into my own. The virtue of this almost universal failure of anthropologists is that we can then write about our chosen subject with a certain amount of detachment and objectivity.

But, alienated as I may feel from modern American medical practice, little involved as I now may be in clinical work, I am and always will be an American physician in a sense in which I can never be a San. I have aspired to be a doctor since early childhood; it was a profession respected, even revered, by my family and cultural group. It and I belong to one another, and however angry or disenchanted I may be with it, no one will ask or expect that I should leave it. I have joined, to put it bluntly, as I could not have been permitted to join the culture of the San, and in so doing I sacrificed objectivity.

Yet, from the moment that the idea of this book first entered my mind, it was clear to me that it would be critical of American medical training and also of modern medicine. This prospect frightened me. A conversation with a man I greatly respect comes to mind.

It was a happy occasion, a party celebrating the promotion as well as the marriage of a friend. I was then nearing the end of the third year of medical school. I knew I could talk freely with him about this project, especially my doubts about it. He said, "If there is one thing I have learned in life, if there is one thing I would want to impress on my friends . . . it would be that there is nothing more important than our personal experience. There is no greater contribution we have to make—no measurement, no theory, no pretense of objectivity—that can compare in value, in uniqueness, in authenticity, to an account of how we have experienced the world. Such accounts, precisely because of their frank subjectivity, invariably produce the highest truths."

My "truth," such as it is, can neither assume the defensive posture typical of physicians nor upbraid in the shrill tone of their most extreme critics. Rather, like most truths in the world as I understand it, mine stakes out an inevitable, initially uncomfortable but ultimately quite stable middle ground.

Still, this entails enough criticisms of medicine to alienate me from most American doctors. They may claim, among other things, that I had my mind made up before I started; that I never progressed far enough to appreciate the value of my training for "real life"; and that, worst of all, I may never do so. My answer is that I did not have my mind made up, but rather, like most medical students, I revered doctors and wanted to be one as far back as I can remember; that I progressed far enough to identify with and appreciate the anguish of their situation; that I brought years of experience as an anthropologist and educator that ought to count for something; and that the answer to the question of whether I continue in medicine, which to this day I cannot consider without a mixture of fear and longing, depends not so much on my desire to assume responsibility for the care of the ill as on my willingness to undergo years of further training in the existing conditions of the modern system of medical apprenticeship.

It was my hope that I would have not only critics but allies, and this hope was realized. Yet, even if it had not been, I would still have intended this book for another constituency: patients (including doctors who have been sick). This constituency seemed natural to me, not because I had ever been seriously ill, but because throughout my training I identified more with patients than with doctors. Perhaps this was partly because of my age—it is a rare medical student who is not in good physical condition, and even the parents of most medical students are still young and healthy. But it was mostly because I tend to identify with victims, which is no way to get along in the modern hospital.

I frequently found myself watching doctors instead of trying my damnedest to become like them. Most of them didn't notice, but if they had they would have been annoyed, and I wouldn't have blamed them. Medical care and training are not spectator sports. They are hands-on matters of life and death. You are in it or you are out of it; there is no in-between. Or so the arguments go. Yet with all due respect, I *was* in and out of it at one and the same time. That is the paradox of participant observation, and it is also, incidentally, more or less the story of my life. But on the other hand it may have been naive to presume that none of my teachers anticipated my reactions. A decade ago I said to a friend and colleague, "They didn't let me into medical school so I could turn around and criticize their own system of training."

She answered, "Don't underestimate them. How do you know why they let you in?" Her remark turned out to be prescient. When this book first appeared it was given a self-described "rave review" by a revered surgeon-teacher in the *New England Journal of Medicine*, high praise in the *Annals of Internal Medicine* from a leader of the American College of Physicians, and a front-page positive appraisal in *The New York Times Book Review* by the Chief of Medicine at a major medical school, among many other pats on the back from doctors and medical educators. So evidently some of my teachers were subtler and craftier than I thought, and in some ways I may even have been a "plant," designed to send a message to their more conservative colleagues.

Also, I like to think, my respect for doctors did come through in this often critical book. In my Conclusion I call them "healing artisans." Whether healing goes on in this strange world is a matter of some contention; in my opinion, it does. But "artisans" is a puzzling word, requiring explanation. Doctors are not scientists, at least not in their medical roles, because, though they certainly draw on science, what they do is neither objective enough nor oriented to the production of new knowledge—nor should it be. And they are certainly not artists, since aesthetic principles and independent creativity have little or no place in practice, despite everything that has been said about the "art" of medicine. But doctors are craftspeople of the highest order. Sometimes, like engineers, they lean very heavily on science. Sometimes, like diamond cutters, they seem to be coasting along on pure skill. And occasionally, as with glassblowers or goldsmiths, what they do verges on art. But in almost all cases doctors are practical, no-nonsense women and men who have given their lives to this craft of theirs and do not suffer fools gladly. They are as brilliant, hardworking, and dedicated a group as one will find in any profession, and they are more of all three than most. When I talk about what I think is missing I mean accomplishments that would have to be grafted onto an already prodigious set of achievements. I do not want to belittle those achievements when I say that what is missing is at least as important as what is there. But now I am getting far ahead of my story.

—September 1994

Contents

Acknowledgments ix

Preface xi

1. INTRODUCTION: *A Compensatory Pause* 1

2. BASIC CLINICAL SKILLS: *The First Encounters* 23

3. EMERGENCY WARD SURGERY: *No Man's Land* 41

4. ANESTHESIOLOGY: *The Technicians of Sleep* 74

5. WARD SURGERY: *Crossing the Boundary* 92

6. NEUROSURGERY AND NEUROLOGY: *Lesions of the Soul* 125

7. PSYCHIATRY: *The Mind-Body Problem* 154

8. PEDIATRICS: *Suffer the Children* 183

9. OBSTETRICS: *The Anatomical Volcano* 208

10. GYNECOLOGY: *The Machinery of Creation* 229

11.   PATHOLOGY: *The Aspect of Death*   242

12.   MEDICINE I: *A Failure of the Heart*   260

13.   MEDICINE II: *Deathwatches*   278

14.   MEDICINE III: *Healing and Hope*   298

15.   THE FOURTH YEAR: *Highlights and Heroes*   324

16.   CONCLUSION: *Healing Artisans*   360

A Glossary of House Officer Slang   379

BECOMING
A DOCTOR

I

INTRODUCTION

A Compensatory Pause

"New trauma patient to Room One. New trauma patient to Room One."
The desk clerk's deadpan voice came over the Emergency Ward intercom in a characteristic monotone, except for the equally characteristic rising tone on the first "One" and falling tone on the second. This blank ritual chant was always precisely preserved, in a denial of what was really being said: "Here comes a physical and personal disaster, a pathetic human life coming asunder." And "You! You in the white coat! Yes, you! You are responsible!"

I was on my feet reflexively before the repetition, and as I moved out into the hallway two of the house officers were already ahead of me. Room One, one of the two main trauma surgery rooms in the E.W., was both crowded and at its center empty, awaiting the patient's arrival. The clock on the wall said four-fifteen. It was Sunday morning, which meant that it was still the likely arrival time for any human wreckage from an urban Saturday night that had not yet found its way to a hospital. The figures poised or active in preparation or merely nervously ambling in the hallway were the crack trauma surgical team of Galen Memorial Hospital— senior and junior residents in surgery, interns, trauma nurses, medical students, orderlies, and dispatchers. Their conversation concerned both the routines of readiness—the hanging of I.V. fluid bags, the preparation of instruments and supplies, the possible need for transfer to the operating room—and those irrelevancies of a personal, amusing sort that seem to fill in awkward gaps of time.

I walked out into the main part of the admitting lobby, where the desk clerks—almost all gay men—and the triage nurses were sitting. Docs from the medical, pediatric, and other sections of the Emergency Ward were going about their business, indifferent to our urgent expectancy in the surgical section. A hapless medical student from another part of the hospital, who should have been asleep but was obviously preparing for some sort of early morning drilling, sat at a computer terminal. This provided wonderful summaries of patient data—when it worked—but it was crazily poised right next to the main E.W. entrance, so the poor frizzy-haired, pale, gaunt fellow was constantly distracted by incoming patients. At the moment, a well-known junkie was trying to convince a very jaded desk clerk that his girlfriend needed pain medication for a twisted elbow.

The main double doors swung open. The medical student leaped to his feet, the triage nurse got up from her desk, even the junkie stopped short in his anxious monologue. A crowd poured in around a noisy rolling stretcher, the chrome legs and white sheets of which flashed among the uniforms in the moving knot of people—emergency medical technicians in brown, policemen in blue, an intern from Mount Saint Elsewhere in white, and other white jackets from Galen. The E.M.T.'s who, as usual, looked very much in charge, stopped only for the triage nurse, a thin, hard-bitten but basically friendly blond named Jan Striker who had sat behind that desk for seven years.

"This the new T.?" she asked. T. for trauma.*

"Oh my God! Oh my God!" came a woman's screams from the stretcher. No attention was paid.

"Multiple stab wounds," said one of the E.M.T.'s, a medium-sized man with a small brown mustache. He looked up at Jan with his head inclined down, the look of a tough but well-behaved young man who respects his superiors, especially if they are women and they know more than he does.

"Chest?"

"Chest too, yeah. Could be a collapsed lung."

"Oh my God! Oh my God!" came the screams again. Jan was scrawling something on her chart and said at the same time, "Take her right down to Room One." The stretcher had been stopped for about ten seconds.

I stood gingerly aside and began to follow the stretcher as it rolled past, getting my first glimpse of the central figure of the action. She was a young woman in her late teens or early twenties, with dark hair and thick dark

---

*A Glossary of House Officer Slang, listing words and phrases commonly used in the hospital, can be found at the end of this book.

eyebrows. She was small and neither thin nor fat. She was lying on her left side, wearing jeans and a garish, filmy blouse soaked in blood, and she was writhing and moaning softly. "Oh my God he knifed me I can't believe it he knifed me Oh my Oh my God" was about as much as I could interpret from her periodic wailing interjections. Then, "Oh my God I can't breathe."

Nobody seemed much impressed. Right, I thought. She can talk and scream. That means she can breathe, of course. She was pale and in obvious pain but very much alive. On the other hand, nobody was wasting any time. The intern, Freddy Robertson, was grilling an E.M.T. in his obnoxiously self-important way, trying to piece together the story as we all moved down the hallway. My hands had somehow got on to the stretcher, and the young woman lying on it was now a more vivid personal presence; her pain was almost palpable in the air. She had a hand on her chest and was gasping for breath with terror in her eyes.

The hum of conversation around her was constant and confusing. We were now in Room One. Turning my head, I was able to glimpse the triage note Jan Striker had scribbled: Name: Madeline Fine, Age: 21, Complaint: Multiple stab wounds. Madeline Fine was yelling again: "He knifed me my God he did it I can't breathe."

People were moving briskly all around. I had understood that it was my turn to run upstairs with the blood gas sample, but Freddy Robertson had other plans for me, which was all right with me, since I would much rather stay. "You and Margaret get her clothes off. Fast." Margaret was one of the other medical students, a smart, serious, friendly, officious, pleasant-looking blond.

"Everything?" I asked flatly, more or less knowing the answer.

"Everything. Step one is, see what she's got." I went to work on her shoes while Margaret started on her belt buckle. A nurse was already unbuttoning her blouse. Freddy was holding up the needle that he would use to get the blood gas. Mike Bowker, the senior resident, stood at the head of the stretcher, looking at her head and neck, and directing traffic. Another nurse, Charlene, was holding an I.V. line, getting set to place it in an arm vein. This would be Madeline's second line, since one was already in place—I had not even seen who did it, or when or how. Scott Lucas, the junior resident, was inspecting her chest wall, especially one wound that had emerged from under the blood-soaked blouse.

Suddenly Madeline's twisting and writhing shifted into a higher gear, her utterances into a more intense whine. "Oh my God I gotta get outta here, I gotta get outta here, I can't breathe. Oh when is it gonna stop hurting. I gotta get outta here, my mother's goin' to Europe tomorrow, don't you understand, I gotta get up, it hurts so bad."

I realized Mike was beckoning me. Freddy yelled superfluously, "Get up to the head, Mel." Evidently my new job was to hold Madeline down. I stood next to Mike and grabbed firm hold of her shoulders, pressing them down on the stretcher. She continued to writhe and yell. My eye caught a small tattoo, a pretty little rose, on her left shoulder, no more than the size of the eraser on a pencil. Mike saw me looking at it and said, "Ask me about that later." (He told me later that a tattoo like that on a woman was a sure sign of a "street person.")

"What happened?" I asked.

"Boyfriend," he said. It was all the conversation we had time for. Madeline was now completely unclothed and still writhing and yelling, but four or five of us managed to hold her down enough to do the required procedures. Freddy punctured her groin with the blood gas needle and the bright red arterial blood came pulsing up and up on the first try.

"Superficial wounds on the legs and abdomen," Scott said.

"Only the one bad one in the chest?" asked Mike rhetorically.

"Looks like that's it. Should I go ahead with the chest tube?"

"Yep." With this permission Scott, who was still being trained in the procedure, took a syringe and quickly anesthetized an area between two ribs under her shoulder blade. He then took a long surgical clamp in his left hand and a large scalpel in his right.

"Hold her steady now," he said matter-of-factly. He proceeded to insert the scalpel deep into the chest wall, quickly making a second wound that rivaled the one she already had. He stuck the surgical clamp—a long thin pair of pliers, really—into the new wound and pried it open. Then he reached out his other hand and Charlene placed a second clamp holding a rubber tube into it. He put one end of the tube into the hole, and let it close. The other end was already being connected to a suction device, and Scott began sealing the wound.

Madeline practically leaped off the stretcher when the blade went in, screaming and writhing deliriously. Yet in less than a minute she could breathe again; her lung was reinflated, and after that she was calm. I relaxed my hold on her shoulders a bit. Charlene covered her from the waist down. Freddy and Mike were looking at Scott, saying "Really nice" and "Beautiful." Four units of cross-matched blood had already come down and were being hung. Mike got on the phone with the senior in the

O.R., to whom she would momentarily be transferred. Two E.M.T.'s were smiling in the doorway.

As I surveyed this strange, otherworldly scene my mind turned, for the thousandth time, to the long course of events that had led me from my professorial office—where I had followed my thoughts and read and taught and talked quietly with students and colleagues, surrounded by old books —to this world of pain and urgency, of noise and barked orders, of injury, of healing, and all too frequently, of death.

In the clinical study of the heartbeat there is a kind of abnormal rhythm called a "premature ventricular contraction." It consists of a firing of the ventricles—the business part of the heart—at a point in the heart cycle when they are not supposed to fire. Ordinarily these are not very serious, and most of us have them at least occasionally. If we feel one (we usually don't) we often identify it as a "missed heartbeat," but really it is an extra or "interpolated" one. It is generally followed by a "compensatory pause" —a brief rest in the heart cycle before the next beat, a normal one, occurs.

It is very brief, just the sort of slightly lengthened rest a good pianist might take as a small interpretative liberty in a Chopin étude, the sort that might make a music lover almost miss a heartbeat—and be grateful, since the return to the normal flow of things after the rest is over is so wonderfully, so inexplicably, satisfying. In the case of the heart, it is as if that miraculous muscle, which squeezes away like clockwork through a lifetime, needs an extra moment to gather its forces after being disrupted by the beat that has occurred at the wrong time; upon which it can continue squeezing away forever.

This book is a compensatory pause. The "abnormal beat" was a medical education that took place at the wrong time—in my mid-thirties, after I had settled in to another, promising career and also into a marriage and a family. It was as if the electrical stability of my life, the normal rhythm of the soul, was temporarily disrupted; there was a need to gather one's forces for the next normal beat. But, of course, rest—whether of the heart, the body, or the soul—is never merely rest. It is always some kind of reorganization, a regrouping of energies into a clear and usable order. For my somewhat disrupted life—as, perhaps, for the heart—there needed to be a retracing of the strange, awkward, out-of-time path.

I cannot remember a time in my youth when I did not want to be a doctor. This is considered a good sign by medical school admissions officers. It is held to be evidence of "motivation to study medicine." This is something like election in Calvinist theology, as if physicians were born rather than made. Although something happened in college to perturb my motivation, it was present early and steadily throughout my childhood. My parents were handicapped by severe hearing impairment (it is not unusual for children who have contact with illness and handicap to want to become doctors) and they had medical ambitions for me as much as I had them for myself. Their encouragement and their dedication to my education formed the basis of my plans, but I did not get or need pushing. In those days, in a lower-middle-class family and neighborhood in Brooklyn, many bright Jewish boys wanted to be doctors; at so early a stage of life neither persistence nor ability can be fairly challenged, and wishes are open to almost everyone.

I also wanted to be a pilot. I had been named after my mother's favorite nephew, the co-pilot of a B-25, who had been killed during World War II. I thus had at least my share of boyhood warrior fantasies. But he was a dead hero, and all my living heroes were doctors. Uncle Bobby, for instance— his real name was Abraham—was one of the lights of my childhood. He was always smiling or laughing, singing, telling stories, even tap-dancing. He once wrote a love song and sometimes played it on the piano, a sweet plaintive melody. His energetic round face, with eyes framed by rimless spectacles, was a cheerful, life-affirming presence in our little house. He and his wife, my Aunt Marion—a warm, attractive woman who, as my mother's older sister, had a central advisory role—were held up as being —no, they obviously *were*—as fine and elegant as human beings could be. Their commanding presence spoke volumes about the serenities of culture and the advantages of upper-middle-class living.

Uncle Bobby was a general practitioner cast in the old mold. He was trained during World War I and he spent his life serving, in the old way, a poor Brooklyn community that desperately needed his care. More nights than not, he rolled out of bed and dressed and went out—I can picture his cheerful demeanor—to deliver the sort of care that, today, money simply cannot buy. Perhaps he took too much on himself and failed to refer certain problems to specialists more qualified than he. He certainly did not get rich. He and Marion always lived in an apartment, not a house, their children went to public schools, they drove modest automobiles. They had a style in dress and decoration but they did not spend much money supporting it. And the center of both their lives was Bobby's medical practice.

This was the old kind, with the babies being born in the middle of the night and the croupy children with no respect for sleep and the agonal breathing of old men beginning just before dawn. It was a world in which the black bag was no anachronistic symbol but a vessel of magical potions and instruments sharpened against death. My uncle lived between his car and his patients' homes. And my aunt was the classic physician's wife, on first-name terms with his patients, somehow absorbing a medical education by association. Once, years after Uncle Bobby's death, I happened to mention to her that I was studying the anthropology of thalassemia, and she said, "Oh, of course, Cooley's anemia," and spoke with confidence on the course of that chronic illness and on the fate of a patient, an Italian immigrant, whose courage in the face of almost unrelenting misery had brought it repeatedly into her consciousness.

The other medical figure from my childhood was Milton Finkel, the local general practitioner in the neighborhood we lived in. I remember Dr. Finkel at my bedside when I was in pain as a child, not once but many times: his calm demeanor, his fresh medicinal smell, the magical contents of *his* small black bag, and above all, perhaps, his incredibly clean hands. In his office, with the great dissected poster-eye gazing down at me and the seven types of rashes displayed on the opposite wall, I used to watch him wash his clean hands—pink with the wet rubbing of them—again and again and again.

In my high school years, he would talk to me about my desire to be a doctor. He had two daughters, and since it was an era in which only 2 or 3 percent of physicians were women, he did not entertain much hope of their following in his footsteps. I was one boy, probably among several, whom he could try to gentle along into such an ambition. The older I got, the more I realized that he genuinely was satisfied. He talked with an undefensive, wise air of retrospective delight about his days as a motorcycling medical student in prewar Berlin, and about his decades as the physical shepherd of a Brooklyn neighborhood. His office, which was in his home, was a block away from the synagogue, with which he maintained cordial but skeptical relations. The rabbi, who lived to eulogize him, thought the world of him in spite of his virtual atheism, and to me the rabbi's opinion meant almost everything. Dr. Finkel's wife, an elegant Virginian with a graceful Southern drawl, was nearly a match for my Aunt Marion, and his daughters—well, a city block was not enough distance for me to avoid the distraction the thought of them caused me on my way home from the synagogue.

In my last year of high school, through a connection made by one of his daughters, I became a recreation volunteer on the pediatric surgery ward of the Kings County Hospital. There I saw children broken and torn by trauma and illness, the first such experiences in my typically protected modern life. One was a charming thirteen-year-old girl whose occasional cynical hardness was frightening. She had been run over by a truck, and her right arm was grafted to her belly in order to provide its remaining skin with sufficient nourishment. She had been in the hospital for over a year and would not be leaving soon. She and I joked harshly, but it helped her to pass the time.

Another was a black boy about ten who had both legs in casts and who, like many of the other children, called me "Doctor Mel." He loved giving me orders in a lilting, imperious voice, confident of my continued collusion. Another was a nine-year-old black girl with a belly so grossly distended she looked as if she were pregnant. She had cancer—"C.A.," said a nurse who had called me aside conspiratorially, as she shook a pillow into a clean pillowcase—and she would soon die. After weeks of trying, I finally —but unwittingly—got a smile out of her. I'd been leaning on her bed rail when it collapsed under me. I began to laugh at myself when I noticed that a broad smile had spread across her ordinarily grim features, showing a row of fine white teeth.

Subsequently I became involved with mentally ill children, and their severe handicaps struck me as being as bad as the worst chronic diseases of the body. The prospect of helping such children, of alleviating even some of their suffering—as, say, a child neurologist or psychiatrist— seemed the noblest possible goal. My ambition to study medicine was now stronger than ever.

But winds of change were blowing, and not only for me. In my first semester in college, which was in 1963, I took a course in which I confronted an analytic philosopher over the subject of religion every other day. The result for me was a grade of D and a totally changed world view. Sitting beside me in the class was a young woman I was in love with; my unhappy affair with her did not help me adapt. But beyond my little concerns the specters of war, racism, and overpopulation were tossing their ugly heads, and, in response to them, student "revolution." Increasingly, I was drawn to what seemed to me the implicit questions of the time: What was the cause of evil and of folly? Was there such a thing as human nature? Could there be a science of behavior? Would it ever be possible to predict and control the scourges of war, famine, and deliberate oppression—scourges that caused more suffering, and even more death, than any disease in the industrialized world?

These cancers on the human soul proved more compelling to me than any physical illness. I relinquished the stable world order provided by religion, but the consolation of philosophy—analytic philosophy, at least —was too meager to satisfy me. I began to study anthropology, and I found what I was looking for. It was empirical enough and did not ask for any professions of faith. Yet it was not afraid of the whole great sweep of human experience, from the proverbial primordial slime through the course of evolution to the dawn of human consciousness, from the Pre-Raphaelite Madonnas to the baboon mother-infant pairs of the Kenyan savannah, from the New Guinea tribal warrior to the Strategic Air Command. Here, I thought, was a science of human nature that could conceivably alter the diseased course of history.

By my senior year, my heart was no longer in my earlier ambition; although I had the medical school applications on my desk, I never filled them out, and I went off to become an anthropologist. After two or three years of study at Harvard, I'd had a total of more than five years of laying the groundwork for a conception of human nature—not in abstract but in empirical terms. My doctoral thesis was to be on the development of infants among Kalahari Desert hunter-gatherers. This would address origins in two separate realms: in the beginnings of behavior in infancy, and in the most elementary form of human social life.

As I should have known from the big box of medicines my teachers sent along with me, my two-year sojourn in the Kalahari had its practical side —not just with broken trucks and unresponsive campfires, but with illness and healing. Two days' drive from the nearest doctor, we were at the mercy of anything that came up. And the people we were living with and studying, most of whom had never been to a doctor, had only us between them and the tragic mortality curve that was typical of people like them throughout the Third World.

With a clumsily applied drop of antibiotic ointment, I saved the eye of many a child suffering from conjunctivitis or trachoma. With a few pills of chloroquine phosphate, I put an end to the convulsive chills and spiking fevers of malaria. With a few syringes full of ordinary penicillin—I had been taught by a physician friend to inject an orange—I put a stop, for a while at least, to a local epidemic of gonorrhea. And with oral rehydration salts—basically a fancy drugstore version of chicken soup—I saved babies and children with intractable diarrhea from death by relentless dehydration.

None of this was unusual. Anthropologists get involved in this sort of treatment when they are far enough away from the nearest physician, usually under that physician's remote but still more or less watchful eye. Without medical training, and in spare time stolen from research, they do

—I did—more indispensable good in a year or two than many physicians do in a decade.

I also lost a child. I passed a mother and boy on the road and urged her to let me look at him, though she had decided he was "dead." One did not have to be an M.D. to know that this child was dying: his eyes were bulging, his face and limbs flaccid and motionless, the skin over his abdomen paper thin, wrinkled, and dry as old leather, the bones of his chest and shoulders countable from a distance. He was too weak to be taken on the long road to the hospital. I knew that I had to get fluid into him, but he was too weak to take more than a few sips.

As I think back on him now, I can feel my arms trying to form the motions of the insertion of an intravenous line. It is so easy, and my arms and hands now know the routine so well. It would almost certainly have saved him. But at that time it was as remote from my abilities as brain surgery.

Flipping through my few medical books, I learned that I must get the fluid into him by any means possible. As instructed, I injected it into his abdomen, and under the skin of his armpits, which was loose enough to accommodate the fluid. Yellow liquid poured out of his rectum at frequent intervals, nullifying all my paltry ministrations. After he rested for a while, I tried one last time to get him to take something by mouth—an absurd mixture of rehydration salts and chocolate milk. This inept strategem was probably worse than useless. He took a sip or two, weakly, looked at me with uncomprehending sadness in his eyes, and died in my arms.

Still, none of these experiences struck me as a compelling reason to view the practice of medicine as more important than the study of human behavior. That boy should not have been ill to begin with. The "diseases of the soul" were still paramount. The problems of the Third World would not be solved by medicine or even by public health, but only by the accumulation of unprecedented knowledge about what makes human beings tick. As with many of the !Kung San who are ill, the little boy in question was the object of a healing dance—a community effort in which women sing and clap while men dance themselves into a trance soberly and deliberately—that gives them the supposed power to heal. This ritual, for which I had and have the greatest respect (despite, not because of its mysticism), seemed to me closer to what was needed to heal the wounds of the world—with its emphasis on social support and cohesion and on the infinite interdependency of individual human beings—than any Western medicine I could imagine.

I returned to Harvard, where I continued to do research and teach.

Initially I was interested in the evolutionary background of human infancy and in the way ecological demands may constrain early experience. After finishing my doctorate, I studied the effects of different rearing conditions on the brains of rats—in effect a laboratory model of cultural influences. Later I returned to Africa to study the hormonal effects of lactation in relation to fertility and still later tried to study human brain development during the first few years of life, in an effort to help explain cross-cultural universals of psychological development. At various times, I did neurological examinations of neonates, hormone and neurotransmitter studies and nutrition and growth studies. I attended conferences with pediatricians, psychiatrists, neurologists, and other physicians, and even wrote a review essay on Dr. Spock's *Baby and Child Care.* My work was always on the periphery of medicine, and I always felt like—and was—an outsider.

Yet my early ambition to become a physician myself did not wane. Actually it waxed and waned repeatedly, and when it came back it did so with heightened force. At twenty-five, when I received my Ph.D., I had considered going to medical school but laid the issue aside once and for all. I remember talking with a computer scientist in his mid-thirties, an MIT professor, who was in the second year of medical school. We were driving back from a day of rock-climbing, and I told him that I admired what he was doing, but that I had decided against it. He turned and said, "Things change in ways you can't expect. You don't have to finish your life this year." At thirty-three, after six years as a Harvard professor, and at just about the time in life when he had made the same decision, I reviewed my life and decided to apply to medical school.

I made that decision at the end of July in an idyllic Vermont setting, and in order to avoid losing yet another year I would have to take the Medical College Admission Test on September 15. I had my work cut out for me. In six weeks I had to revive my knowledge of college physics, inorganic chemistry, and organic chemistry—subjects I had studied as much as fifteen years earlier—and then compete with bright young people who had studied these subjects that year. Other portions of the exam, such as the biology and the analytic and interpretive selections, would come more easily, but they would not suffice to get me through. I crammed like mad, sitting in the Vermont woods or in a sugar shack near the house, and took practice exams that, like the real thing, went on for six hours.

When the real thing came, I not only passed but, amazingly, scored creditably against broad national competition—even in physics and chemistry. Since about half of those who took the test would in fact be admitted to medical school, my score placed me comfortably in the upper range of the next year's entering class in terms of science aptitude and knowledge. I took this statistic very seriously, for it was the sort of thing I needed to hold onto, to assure myself that I could in fact go through with it. Psychologically, I needed all the help I could get.

I applied to many medical schools—eighteen, I think it was—because I feared that my age and background would tend to keep me out. This fear was unfounded. When I went for interviews, I was received with serious interest. These encounters were varied and instructive. Johns Hopkins was renowned for the superiority of its clinical teaching, descended from the method of great turn-of-the-century physician William Osler. Applicants were treated to a wonderful experience of Southern hospitality and graciousness. I had lunch with a neurologist who wore a tie with the Hopkins motto, *Aequanimitas*, and who spoke in glowing terms of the Osler tradition. I was interviewed officially by a woman younger than I, an endocrinologist who was familiar with my published research. She candidly admitted that this was her first time serving as an interviewer, and she claimed to be more nervous than I.

At Columbia, there was little comparable graciousness. The New York gruffness that I knew well from my youth was much in evidence. Students labored under a biweekly schedule of exams in all courses, and the atmosphere in the first two years seemed rather like a high school. I was interviewed by a harried young surgeon who came an hour late from an emergency repair of someone else's inept heart surgery on a child; he did not know what to make of me.

At Cornell, also in Manhattan, the atmosphere was more pleasant. I was interviewed by a black thoracic surgeon who had army certificates all over the walls of his little office, having served for years in Southeast Asia. When I came in he was on the telephone, turning a grungy pacemaker over and over in his hand, complaining about its failure to the person on the other end of the line. He was a friendly, no-nonsense man, and he and I got along well.

At Yale I came a few minutes late and was asked to sit in the waiting room. After six or eight minutes of catching my breath and composing myself, the distinguished-looking slightly plump middle-aged black man sitting opposite me in the waiting room introduced himself as the obstetric surgeon who was scheduled to interview me. He had been making observations of me in that neutral public setting. (This was the only event that remotely resembled the classic medical school interview horror stories—being asked to open a window that has been nailed shut, or being given a chair with one leg two inches shorter than the other three—setups designed to reveal how you will react to the unexpected.)

I then had a second interview with a distinguished cardiac surgeon. He sat in profile by the window and looked off into the distance as I talked a bit about my vision of medical research. Then he began talking, not to me only, and in the most eloquent way I have heard on the subject before or since. "When I started out it was just after the war. I knew that I was interested in research, but all I really knew how to do was tinker. So I did my surgery like everybody else. But it turned out that there were great discoveries to be made. It wasn't difficult; we didn't know anything. It was like looking out on a vast, uncharted landscape, and walking out slowly, picking up precious jewels just lying there on the ground, one after another after another."

At Harvard I met a neurologist whose work I had revered for years—an authority on brain-mind relations. We had a discursive, marvelous discussion about how the future of psychology and even philosophy must rest in large part on brain science, and how patients with brain injury would be critically important in this future. My second interview was with an authority on childhood leukemia. He had recently traveled in China and been treated royally because he had been called in to consult on the care of a grandchild of a high Communist Party official—so much for social leveling in that "ideal society." He showed me a simple graph of the change in the previous fifteen years in mortality from the main form of childhood leukemia. In the dip of the curve, from a usually deadly disease to one that is 90 percent survivable, was one of the great success stories of modern therapeutics. Near us was a bulletin board covered with scores of pictures of children, children who had every excuse to be dead but who were shown here at birthday after birthday, defying the laws of illness and obeying the laws of medicine.

At Stanford I was interviewed by a student as well as by a professor, a unique arrangement that I thought made good sense. The professor had read my folder carefully, and he was worried for me. He would recommend that I be accepted—that, he said, went without saying. But he was worried about the loss of what I would otherwise do in behavioral science. He understood that I viewed medical training as an expansion of my research purview, and my vision of the scope of human nature—not just the addition of a critically pragmatic dimension to my life. But he wanted to express both a hope and a warning. "It would be terrible if you became a mechanic," he said. His contempt for such an outcome, which I did not want either, was palpable in the air between us.

These encounters, and others like them elsewhere, helped me to clarify what I wanted. But I could not work out exactly what my interviewers had learned about me, though the medical school interview is supposed to be an almost sacred event, its purpose to assess that most mysterious and most central concept, the "motivation to study medicine."

Whatever it was, they evidently thought I had it. I was accepted by many schools, and I chose the Flexner School of Medicine, which was associated with the Galen Memorial Hospital—both world-famous institutions. A few months later, after, as it were, putting my affairs in order, I was ready to begin the preclinical years, the two continuous years of classroom study.

There were few things in medicine or medical education in which I could consider myself expert. But I had done years of college teaching, from introductory lecture courses of more than four hundred students to graduate seminars with six or eight and everything in between. It was almost inevitable that I should have a strong reaction to the preclinical years of medical school, which are pedagogically similar, at least superficially, to college and graduate school education. In almost every medical school endless series of lectures—punctuated, to be sure, by a few laboratory exercises—are delivered by different experts, every one of whom tries to cram as much as is humanly possible into an hour. Often the lectures are good, and it is remarkable how much a good speaker *can* cram into an hour without losing an audience. But there can be as many as six of these a day, in addition to laboratory time, some of which often turns into an opportunity for more lecturing. Rarely if ever is there one mind truly in charge of this knowledge assembly line, which after all is pouring through the one mind of each individual student. No expert on medical education I know of contends that all this material can be absorbed, much less remembered.

Indeed, only a fraction of it is expected to be remembered even a few weeks after its delivery, on a pencil and paper test, and of this fraction it is expected that further decay will be steep. There is no evidence in this pedagogical approach or in the published literature about medical education that anyone has applied what we know from a hundred years of systematic quantitative study of human memory (one of the most impressive research accomplishments in psychology). As for pedagogical skill, it is assumed to be in the bones of academic physicians.

There has been little success in dealing with the implications of the modern medical knowledge explosion, and methods of medical education continue to be the same as they were in "the good old days" when men were men and things were really tough, and when the necessary knowledge for the practice of medicine was, in aggregate and in pace of change, a small percentage of what it is today.

Consider a few of the changes that have occurred just within four years of my first day at medical school. Liver transplants, previously a rarity, have become relatively practical and commonplace. The immunosuppressant cyclosporine has dramatically altered the success rates of all kinds of transplants. Traditional antacid therapy for ulcers has been laid aside in favor of systemic drugs like cimetidine, which within two years of its approval became the most frequently prescribed drug of any kind in the United States. Calcium-channel blockers, a completely new class of drugs, were approved and became a mainstay of cardiology. Noninvasive widening of clogged arteries in the heart began to rival bypass surgery as a treatment method for one of our most common serious illnesses. AIDS, a new and fatal disease, was identified, shown to be taking on dangerous epidemic proportions, and linked to a virus not just of a species but of a whole biological category previously not considered to be among the causes of human illness. Lithium, an extraordinarily simple elemental substance, overtook antischizophrenic drugs as the treatment of choice for intermittent forms of psychosis. Alzheimer's disease was recognized as the leading cause of senile and presenile dementia and a major health problem of our time. The basic science of recombinant DNA became an essential part of every physician's knowledge, promising as it does a vast variety of new and powerful drugs, as well as the imminent prospect of that science-fiction therapy "gene surgery." Magnetic resonance imaging— known also as nuclear magnetic resonance, or N.M.R.—became the gold standard of radiology, promising to replace CAT scanning (itself a quite new modality) in several important areas of diagnosis. And in vitro fertilization made the transition from a science-fiction laboratory technique to a proven and accepted method of treatment for infertility, making hundreds of "test-tube babies" a reality.

These are only a few highlights of the new knowledge discovered or made practical while my graduating class was attending medical school. In most cases they were not, and could not be, taught to the students who graduated the year before we entered. Those students thus had substantially less to learn than we did, although they must have been equally bewildered trying to keep up with discoveries made in their four years and equally suspicious of the validity of textbooks just published. Neither they nor we had an education that taught us in any significant way the skills needed to evaluate and master this always-emerging new knowledge. Medical educators are understandably committed to delivering the most up-to-date version of this knowledge, and to producing graduates who are at least moderately conversant with it. This is easier than teaching the skills involved in keeping abreast of developing knowledge, a pedagogical process more characteristic of graduate school than of medical school.

Of course I learned a lot. Some of my fellow students learned much more than I, being as they were more accustomed to strategies and tactics of teaching that I had last consistently experienced in high school. Also, I discovered to my surprise that they liked it. Probably, some of them were pretending, putting on a show, as I sometimes did myself; it would have been too difficult, otherwise, to persist. But many of them truly enjoyed this style of teaching and learning, and seeing this forced me to ask two questions: Was there something about them that made them more comfortable with it, something other than their youth? Or was there something wrong with me, that I found it so unnatural? My answer was, ultimately, yes to both. Still, even in the most traditional medical schools, even in the lecture halls, there is some effort to achieve clinical exposure in the preclinical years. The lecturers are, after all, talking to future doctors.

Episodes involving four teachers come to mind.

The first occurred during the orientation week, when Dr. Feinstein, the dean, was in charge. Before my admission, he and I were on something like an almost equal footing. He was later to become one of what I call my ambiguous medical heroes. Dr. Feinstein was a tall, slim, handsome Jewish boy from Brooklyn who was now every inch the elite medical-school grandee; the similarity of our backgrounds, while it never came up, made me feel slightly more comfortable with him than I otherwise might have been. During the orientation week I found myself one afternoon on my knees beside a model of a human form, pressing on its rubbery chest in a poor imitation of cardiopulmonary resuscitation, which Dr. Feinstein—brilliantly, I thought—had arranged for us to begin learning right then, on Day One of medical school. Nothing could have dramatized more strongly for me the difference between what I had done before and what I was now about to begin doing. I was out of the ivory tower all right, kneeling down on a dusty floor, simulating the very crux of the physician's functional role. Had this been a person in cardiac arrest, there would have been nothing between life and death except my stupid pair of hands, squeezing death out of the chest seventy times a minute. Feeling unbelievably inept, I looked up to see his distant, smiling, dignified face looking down at me from what seemed a great height. For the first of countless times, I remembered what I had read in introductory sociology: that change or conflict in status and role constitutes one of the most severe forms of psychosocial stress.

Later the same week, Dean Feinstein arranged yet another event, equally illustrative of his pedagogical wisdom. He presented two patients to the assembled class of 165 or so, the first official patient presentations in our medical lives. The first was a two-year-old boy—he could hardly have been more lively or more charming—who had been born with the congenital anomaly of duodenal atresia. This is an obstruction in the upper part of the small intestine owing to an error in intrauterine growth. This boy had been lucky enough to be in the subgroup that has no other associated anomalies; yet he must have lain there for days, a tiny newborn with a distended belly, vomiting frequently, failing to produce the awaited feces, leaving his parents bewildered and terrified. Not many years before, he would have died without treatment; but thanks to what is now routine surgery, he had been unambiguously cured—a miracle of modern medicine, if the term "miracle" has any meaning at all. As he sat on the examining table at the bottom of the great lecture hall, chirping and playing between his mother and his doctor, the most remarkable thing about him was that he was serenely unremarkable.

The other patient presented that day was a seventy-four-year-old woman who had, two years earlier, suffered the loss of her husband of almost fifty years. She had grieved normally and, presumably, had resolved her grief when she presented herself to Dr. Feinstein because she was vomiting large quantities of blood. She was admitted to the hospital not once but several times, and kept there while being probed with the aid of every relevant diagnostic test—and some perhaps irrelevant ones as well. No meaningful diagnosis was ever reached, and no treatment was instituted, except for support relating to loss of blood. After several severe and terrifying episodes, the problem simply went away, and she had now not been troubled by it for over a year. She, too, was cheerful and lively, and offered some fairly obvious and possibly true speculations, but neither she nor her physician pretended to understand.

I later learned to wish that such forbearance were more common. But for now I was satisfied by the juxtaposition: a baby boy who was a miracle of aggressive surgical intervention and had as a result gained a whole life; and an elderly lady who was in effect a mystery of nature, a woman who had suffered badly, become ill, and healed according to principles no one understood. The contrast, and the implied lessons, were nothing short of wonderful.

The next episode occurred during the standard course on microbiology that we took in the second half of the first year. In the competition for the most relentless application of the throw-it-against-the-wall-and-see-if-it-sticks tactics of medical teaching, this course took the prize. (Evidently it is often like that, since Charles LeBaron in *Gentle Vengeance* describes something similar at his medical school.) It was almost unrelentingly pedantic, a microbe-a-day diet with no apparent organizing ideas. The head of the course, known to all as Jerry Kaplan, talked in a condescending whine that, if I closed my eyes, took me right back to junior high school. His idea—and, not surprisingly, that of some of his younger colleagues— of how to relieve the sheer boredom of the lectures, was to make fun of patients and their illnesses. This, I learned, was something one became used to: vulgar jokes about patients are a ubiquitous feature of medical social life, excused (and perhaps excusable) as a "necessary defense mechanism" in the face of illness and death. But he was not an intern shooting the breeze in the middle of the night; he was a physician and scientist talking to a large class of first-year medical students who had not yet had any official experience with patients.

About half way through the course, a vulgar poem was presented, by 35-mm slide projection on a giant screen, and read aloud in its entirety, by a young woman with shoulder-length blond hair who was lecturing on syphilis. (She also posted the poem, for our further entertainment, on the bulletin board in the microbiology teaching lab.) It brutally ridiculed a man with a case of this awful disease and was thought to be useful because it graphically described the symptoms and course of illness. She made a number of other vulgar jokes during her presentation, and it was interesting that Jerry Kaplan, who was sitting in the first row, not only encouraged her but actually played straight man in several exchanges.

Later, however, he himself exceeded even this effortful vulgarity. He was lecturing on plague, an illness the mere mention of which sends shivers up and down the spine of any decent person who has ever read any European history. In the course of a typically tedious lecture on the causative organism, *Yersinia pestis*, he felt an understandable need to entertain. He showed a modern plague victim whose face, enlarged to ten feet in height on the lecture-hall projection screen, was grotesquely misshapen, bulbous, swollen, and deep purple in color. He then proceeded to make lame jokes about this patient and drew peals of laughter from the audience. That swollen, pathetic face is engraved on my mind.

I must add that to my bafflement many students loved Jerry Kaplan. I later saw his name on a list of just a few faculty members—chosen by the students—being considered for the honor of delivering a prestigious commencement address. But to me he represented a low point in medical school teaching. Long since primarily a research physician, he was entrusted with some of the first socializing experiences medical students have in relation to clinical thought and behavior. He used this opportunity to instill a sense of inappropriate humor about things that might well, at this stage, be taken more seriously. Now Dr. Kaplan seems in retrospect a rather amusing figure himself, whining on in his school-teacherly voice, waving his electronic pointer around, straining for jokes like a bad stand-up comic, in the reflected glow of that giant purple face. And I would readily excuse some vulgar remarks about a plague patient made privately between two exhausted and overburdened young physicians—in fact, I might make some. But in a fifty-year-old professor who stands on a platform from which he can influence the emotional response systems and the ethics of scores of future physicians, such remarks seemed inexcusable. More important, they seemed to call for some new hypotheses about what exactly is going on in medical school.

The third episode occurred during a class in neuroscience. We were taken to an academic hospital for a clinical presentation by a world-renowned neurologist, Stephen Wyndham. Because it was early in the fall semester, Dr. Wyndham had the mistaken impression that this was the students' first-ever patient presentation, so he undertook to make a serious little speech, our presumed introduction to clinical medicine, which had three points. First, clinical medicine is an art, not a science, and the sooner we get out of our heads the notion that it is somehow scientific, the sooner we would be on the right track. Second, in encountering any patient one must do whatever is necessary to give the patient the feeling that one is "The Doctor;" if for a particular patient, for example, the doctor is the one who takes the blood pressure, then we must take the blood pressure, even if there is no rational reason for doing it. Third, in dealing with terminal patients—an inevitable experience—we must be prepared to deliver the news of the hopelessness of the case in such a way that the patient will believe us, even if he or she has not believed thirty other doctors who have recently given the same opinion. This would have mainly to do with authority and confidence.

I found Dr. Wyndham difficult to comprehend. I could write off his first remark as the usual defensiveness of the superb clinician who is not much of a scientist. But in the second and third he seemed to encourage a kind of game-playing, even a kind of lying. I later realized that he had delivered himself, however pompously and pedantically, of some important insights into the existential dilemma of the physician, insights quite consistent with everything that anthropologists have learned about the virtually universal features of human healing arts. I also discovered that he was worshipped by his patients—whether recovering, permanently disabled, or terminally ill.

But the most memorable aspect of the episode by far was the patient he presented. He was a man in his forties with amyotrophic lateral sclerosis—A.L.S., or Lou Gehrig's disease—a deterioration of the nerves controlling the muscles, including eventually the nerves controlling breathing; the patient would inevitably succumb within, at most, a couple of years, as had the famous Yankee ballplayer, with his intelligence and awareness intact. It was not difficult to guess who he was—a middle-aged stranger, sitting toward the rear next to his wife. As Dr. Wyndham enunciated his advice about talking to patients with terminal illnesses, I turned to see the patient's own reaction. He sat calmly, smiling easily and comfortably, and full of that glow of satisfaction often (and rightly) felt by patients on display, satisfaction at being uniquely able to perform a critical teaching function. Above all, though, I think he was full of admiration for Dr. Wyndham, who could not do anything else for him except what he was now dramatically doing.

The fourth, last, and happiest episode occurred in a common room, in a small-group lunch-hour discussion that was entirely optional and thus was attended by only a dozen or so of the three hundred students (two classes) explicitly invited. The speaker, David Fleming, was a psychiatrist known for his writings on the subject of dying. He was a gentle and thoughtful man who spoke slowly and comfortingly, with unpretentious confidence. He had been a Jesuit priest before he became a physician, so his calm words about the dreadful subject at hand carried dual authority: he had intimate knowledge, perhaps even mastery, of both the body and the soul.

His theme was that the dying help you to help them, and that if you listen to them they teach you all you need to know. You usually do not need to supply them with bravery since frequently they have more of that than you will be able to muster. He brushed aside the oversimplified schemes for the psychology of the dying patient, with their obligatory sequences of existential moments—moments that in reality no one can predict. He told this story among others.

A hospital house officer was following in his clinic a patient with lung cancer. The question was whether the therapy had succeeded in containing the tumor or whether it would make its final escape from control; if it did, it would be past the point at which further efforts could succeed. Lung cancers being what they are, there was not a great deal of cause for hope.

The young doctor was listening through his stethoscope to the patient's breathing. He was tired, but this was a routine check. He began at the apex of the lungs and went down the chest wall, listening symmetrically on each side until he came to an area near where the tumor had been surgically resected. Under his stethoscope there was a solid mass where there should have been thin air.

"Shit," he said, almost under his breath.

His heart skipped a beat—it was clear that the patient had heard him. Flushed and flustered, he raised his tired head to offer an extremely embarrassed apology that, he knew, would now have to complicate any words of explanation and comfort.

"That's O.K.," the patient said. "It's nice to know you care."

Dr. Fleming ended his talk, unforgettably, with what he called "the four laws of medicine." He smiled coyly and counted on his fingers.

"If it's working, keep doing it.

"If it's not working, stop doing it.

"If you don't know what to do, don't do anything.

"And never call a surgeon." (This last law had a milder form—"Never call a surgeon unless you want an operation.")

I later learned that the most difficult one by far, the one least adhered to in common medical practice, and beyond a doubt the most important one is the third. It is in the inability of teachers to instill that law in the acolytes that modern medical training exhibits what may be one of its most interesting failures.

But that again is getting ahead of the story. For now let these episodes stand as a few vivid examples of preclinical foreshadowing of the clinical experience. First, they came from senior physicians who had long since had their trial by fire, earned their authority. No words spoken to medical students carry the sort of power that is conveyed by those who truly speak from clinical experience. Second, they fell on receptive ears. The first two years of medical school are spent in a state of almost ludicrously keen anticipation, like that of a teenager in love. Against this background of suppressed stormy emotion, the few crumbs of clinical wisdom that are dropped during those years are consumed with a voracious and grateful appetite. Meanwhile, the patient (the object of the longing) and the clinic (the site of the rendezvous) loom larger and larger in the student's imagination, until the poignancy of further delay becomes almost unbearable.

2

BASIC
CLINICAL SKILLS

The First Encounters

For some students in medical school, the ultimate encounter with the patient is not essentially new. This includes the few students who were previously nurses or physician associates and the larger number who have volunteered extensively to work in hospital or other clinical settings. But for many if not most, this experience is the most keenly anticipated and most anxious moment of life as a medical student.

Almost all medical students are young enough so that the naive energy of youth overcomes any natural timidity. To extend the analogy of the adolescent crush, contact with a patient, like marriage, is easier to get into when you are young and, if not foolish, then at least confident, even headstrong. The older you get the more you know, and after a certain point you know too much; you can envision the pitfalls, and you feel embarrassed by what earlier might have been a rough but effective brash éclat. I noticed in myself a level of concern about how I would handle patients, how they would react to me, what I might do wrong that, if not exactly inappropriate, was also not perfectly adaptive. I wanted to be the sort of person who would simply dive in, as so many did all around me.

For example, in a moving clinical exercise during the preclinical years, we visited a rehabilitation hospital for a lecture on the subject of paraplegia by a specialist who was a paraplegic himself—the result of an injury that had taken place within weeks of his graduation from medical school. As might be expected, he remarked on many aspects of day-to-day care, the sort that most physicians prefer to relegate to nurses, with a sensitivity and sympathy that few other physicians could have had. Between the lecture and the patient presentations, we took a break, and as we filed out into the hall to stretch our legs, I saw that one of the patients to be presented—a new quadriplegic—was lying on a portable bed in the hall-way. He could not have been more than twenty-one or twenty-two. He was handsome, healthy-looking—his muscles had not had time to deterio-rate—and had, as the cliché goes, his whole life ahead of him. Yet he had just lost, permanently, the use of his body below the shoulders. I was one of about forty medical students milling around, spilling out of the class-room into the hallway, all healthy, ambitious and strong; and here, uncom-fortably close to me, was a young man about as broken as one could be.

I could not think of anything to say to him. Surely this was a situation in which the wrong words could do damage, and I was highly conscious of the power of my embryonic medical role. I had not been taught the right words, so I was reluctant to say any. Still, the awkwardness of the situation as it was could not be much better than even the wrong words, and I began to grope for some phrases that might be acceptable, that might break the barrier.

During the few seconds that I was preoccupied with this effort, one of my fellow students—a particularly uninspiring athletic type, I thought—walked up to the stretcher, looked down at the crippled young man, and said, "Pretty tough break."

Ouch, I thought. Just the sort of thing I wanted to avoid. "Yeah," said the patient, his face brightening perceptibly.

"How did it happen?" the medical student asked, and they began a conversation in which all the barriers I had envisioned immediately broke down. The emotional topology of the hallway, which for me had been dominated by tension resulting from the lack of communication between the medical students and the patient, had been utterly changed.

I was reminded of the advice I once got as a boy about talking to a girl at a party: if she wants to talk to you, it doesn't much matter what you say first; and if she doesn't want to, it doesn't matter either. Unlike the girls of my youth, however, patients almost always want to be spoken to by doctors (including medical students), but it is not so easy to say the wrong thing. Thus I learned from one of my less inspiring fellow medical students the first lesson of interacting with patients: the doctor is not entitled to be reluctant. However awkward the situation, however discouraging or con-fusing or ugly the disease, however apparently withdrawn the patient, the doctor must step across the barrier in interpersonal space that everyone else must properly respect.

And yet it was plain to see that the result of this forthrightness was not always good. Teachers and students alike "dove in" with a brusque, abrupt style that many patients disliked. The laying on of hands was reduced to the carrying out of procedures, and words exchanged with the patient were basically viewed as tools to make those procedures go more smoothly.

At my medical school it was arranged for first-year students to have preliminary clinical experiences in hospital settings. I was assigned to a small group led by an immigrant physician who happened to be a superb if slightly pompous neurologist. He used to say, "Touch the patient." This, he explained, was a categorical imperative. No matter what, find an excuse to touch the patient, however reluctant you are, however reluctant you imagine the patient is. If necessary, pretend to check for a fever by putting your hand on the patient's forehead. Take an unnecessary pulse. His words made an indelible impression on me.

On this occasion we stepped out of the elevator onto one of the highest floors of a just-finished hospital tower, a surgical ward so new it seemed to glitter. As we turned a corner into the main part of the ward, we saw and became part of a white-coated commotion around a stretcher. My clinical tutor, as the neurologist was called, introduced me to a young woman who was a third-year medical student engaged in her surgical clerkship. Moans were emanating from within the crowd of hospital whites. The medical student narrated the scene in a cheery lilting tone with a bright, fresh expression on her face; but I was riveted by the moans, which were now taking the shape of the word "Mama," pathetically repeated over and over again. The patient was an old-looking woman (I would now characterize her, in retrospect, as merely middle-aged) who was described as an alcoholic and evidently not *compos mentis.* She was undergoing the procedure of placement of a central line—the insertion of a large-bore needle in a major vein below the clavicle—needed for the pouring in of great volumes of fluid, as well as nutrients and drugs.

The woman did not stop moaning, "Mama, Mama, Mama." (I still cannot get those moans out of my mind. One sees terrible things in medicine, and this was far from the worst I saw, but it was my very first encounter as a student in a hospital; I remember it with the vividness that seems to be preserved for first encounters.) She was frail and small, with a long tangle of orange hair. Curled in the fetal position in a faded yellow hospital gown, she kept repeating her epithet like an uncalm mantra. She was surrounded by large sturdy young men, all handsome and strong of voice. They unfolded her brusquely and efficiently from the fetal curl. Her moans became louder and pierced their moderate, if spirited, professional exchanges: "Mama, Mama, Mama, Mama." Glancing off these was the voice of the cheery young medical student whose explanatory commentary I found harder and harder to listen to. I had a thought that I was to have innumerable times over the next few years, although the feeling that went with it would wane: *Why doesn't somebody touch her forehead? Why doesn't somebody take her hand? Why doesn't somebody say, "It's all right"?*

After a deftly conducted struggle in which the woman's resistance was treated as an annoyance and her cries were ignored, the central line was placed and the residents congratulated one another, as they often and properly do. After all, they are learning, and they deserve and need the praise that goes with new achievement. Also, the central line was for this patient a lifeline, and they could breathe that sigh of relief that comes when, as in a movie, we see a drowning person finally grab hold of a rope.

The patient's body recurled into the fetal position, as the young men stepped away from the stretcher. I was close enough so that without being obtrusive (and they were through with her anyway) I could satisfy my strong urge to touch her. At no point did she stop repeating the plaintive cry, "Mama." "It's O.K., dear, it's all right," I said, taking her hand and stroking her hair back away from her forehead. She made no obvious response to these gestures, and I naturally thought they might be useless; but that did not mean I should not be making them. Equally, I didn't know whether the residents' matter-of-fact approach to her entered into her experience in any meaningful sense; in retrospect, with greater knowledge of the neuropsychology of brain damage from alcohol and other causes, I can say with some confidence that they didn't know either.

One could wonder, as I shortly did, whether doctors should not maintain a humane approach to patients not only because of the patients themselves but also because of the students and the residents, always likely to act inhumanely because of the stresses of excessive responsibility, overwork, and sleeplessness; or, for the same reason, because of oneself.

This was before I realized that humane acts not directly affecting "care" —a word meaning neither more nor less than medical and surgical intervention for the purpose of favorably altering the course of an illness—are in short supply in the hospital world; that the patient's mental status is only marginally relevant to the effort at helpful verbal or nonverbal communication; and that far from being embarrassed by brusqueness, residents are more likely to be embarrassed by (and to consider not quite professional) acts and gestures that are other than completely instrumental.

One's shock does not last long, but at that point I was still shocked. When the residents were gone and the nurses had removed the patient with her plaintive cries, I looked to the third-year student for some kind of explanation. "What did you think of that?" I asked her.

"Wasn't that great? You have to see a lot of those before you get a feel for them. I'll probably get to place a couple of central lines myself before the clerkship ends."

"Is it difficult to get used to?"

"Oh, it's great, really. The residents are great to you. As long as you do your scut and keep the patients' labs and everything straight. I love it."

I left with a vision of the brightness in her face and with the lilt of her voice in my ears, but I was deeply disturbed by what I had seen. On the bus on the way home I met a psychiatrist whom I had known before I began medical school. I told her about my experience, and she was moderately sympathetic to my concern. But I was looking for something stronger, some sharing of my "obviously" just and righteous anger. The incident was not a surprise to her, and although she deplored it, she seemed to accept it and to consider my reaction somewhat immature, surprisingly so, given my relatively advanced age.

"That's just the way things are," was about what she had to offer. When I confided that I might decide I couldn't be a part of this, she did not take me very seriously. "You'll get used to it," she said. "You don't have to become like them." She left me with the sensible advice that whatever was going on around you, you could and should be the way you wanted to be. "Light your corner," she said finally and emphatically.

My corner was for a period fairly dark. Some time during my first year a young woman physician in my community committed suicide. She had been in the obstetrics department, and was not only a practitioner but an excellent lecturer and teacher. Her case became a subject of constant discussion centered mainly on feminist issues. I knew these were central —she had been in what was virtually the first substantial cohort of women coming into medicine. She had forgone marriage and motherhood, and her situation must have been professionally oppressive and personally lonely.

But I thought there were more issues at stake than could be effectively subsumed under the feminist banner. She had been highly competent and successful, and she had been in obstetrics, generally considered the most hopeful and cheering of medical subfields. Yet she had judged her life not worth living. I thought that there might be lessons about the nature of modern medicine and the awkwardness of the physician's existential situation. In general, suicide risk is higher for men than for women and much higher for physicians than for the population at large. So the death of this young woman cast a shadow over me, too.

At the end of the first year I sat for Part I of the National Medical Board Examinations, and this experience gave me a considerable jolt. For medical students who elect this route to licensure (generally considered the most difficult one) three examinations are taken, Part I normally after the second year. It consists of two full days of multiple-choice questions covering anatomy, biochemistry, physiology, pathology, microbiology, and behavioral sciences. The questions are not of the straightforward "choose the one best answer" type, but of the more bewildering "Choose A if 1 and 3 are right, B if 2 and 4 are right, C if 1, 2, and 3 are right" type; and there are a thousand of them (about one per minute) over the course of two days. Somewhere between 10 and 15 percent of the students who take this test fail.

I was comfortably above that margin and well above the bottom of my own class's performance—not surprising, since I tended to be just about in the middle of the class on most examinations. But I had found the test extremely stressful and felt chastened by my far-from-impressive score. There were many mitigating factors. I was too old for this sort of thing, I told myself, and during the preclinical years this was made most evident by examinations. I had family responsibilities (my daughter was then two and a half, and I used to take her to a sunny little park in the late afternoons and try to memorize preclinical facts while keeping one eye on her wanderings). I had taken some of the basic courses—notably anatomy and biochemistry—six or seven years earlier. Finally, I was taking the exam at the end of the first instead of the second year, so that I could accelerate into the clinical training part of medical school earlier.

All this helped to explain why I didn't do better—I could tell myself it wasn't stupidity, or sloth—but the lesson of the exam came home to me all the more emphatically: my age, my atypical turn of mind, and my stage of life were showing, and these were not ideal for medical school.

But of course I had made my bed and I was going to lie in it. In at least one sense, the worst of it was over. I still had some preclinical sciences to complete, but I was now empowered to set foot on the hospital floor as a student in Basic Clinical Skills. In my interactions with patients I would now have slightly more than spectator status.

It was also the first setting I experienced in medical school in which the class consisted of a small group of students, and after those lecture theaters, the group was almost oppressively intimate. Yet it was very good to have a group small enough to be intimate at all and to provide the sort of friendship and personal support that is needed for the transition to clinical work. We seemed a rather oddball group: an overweight, slow-moving, pleasant fellow with a wry sense of humor whose father was a psychoanalyst but who wanted himself to be a surgeon; a woman with waist-length straight blond hair, appealing in an anorectic sort of way, who was a marathon runner by avocation as well as by austere personality; a handsome, cheerful, harried jock with a mild speech defect who seemed constantly bemused; a Korean student my own age who was doing pathbreaking research in virology and needed this one course for certification in the United States; and me, a misfit anthropologist who couldn't explain himself even to himself, much less to anyone else. Even if I had wanted to, I could not preserve an alienated stance in this group. We were all going through this together.

We had many good discussions, formal and informal. Our teachers were strongly oriented to clinical work and were concerned about psychological and ethical aspects of the doctor-patient relationship. (I did not grasp at the time how unusual this was, and my appreciation of what I was getting was blunted by the erroneous assumption that it was characteristic of clinical training in general.)

In this setting I learned a lot about myself. For example, in one exercise we were given the following problem. A patient needs a kidney transplant. Family members are immunologically surveyed, and a brother is found who can be a technically successful donor. The brother is confidentially interviewed and refuses. The patient is told that no suitable donor is available, "suitability" being understood to include technical factors as well as willingness to donate. I argued strongly that the patient should have been told that his brother was immunologically eligible and had refused to donate; otherwise seeds of suspicion with respect to the whole family might have been sown in the patient's mind. The brother, I thought, should be made to take the consequences of his refusal.

Later I had second thoughts and decided that I had spoken glibly. Kidney donation is a risky enterprise, and it is not at all clear that one owes such a bodily sacrifice to anyone, even a brother. Also, kidney transplants often do not work, and the potential uselessness of the sacrifice cannot be ignored. I did not change my mind exactly. I simply made the single most important discovery one can make about such problems, confirmed many times since: they have no right answer. My appreciation of that fact increased with further clinical encounters. The proposition has a corollary:

whatever a doctor does in such a situation, it can be viewed from the outside as having been the wrong choice. It is only by living through the anguish of such choices that we come to appreciate the ethical depths they sound.

I also learned things about myself directly. In one exercise we filled out a form designed to assess our state of health, a form that had proved to be superior to a physician's examination in predicting future medical problems. I filled out the form honestly, and at the end was judged to have a "health age" two years older than my chronological age; all the others in the group had a health age younger than their stated age. Either I was in lousy shape or my fellow students were exceptionally vigorous, and either way I was at a disadvantage—for a medical student, the most ironic disadvantage of all.

We had a number of introductory lectures on clinical topics, and the most important of these concerned various aspects of history-taking and physical examination, in support of the complete histories and physicals we were doing regularly. As I had been before, I was a bit diffident in these encounters, finding it hard to cross the conventional barriers to interpersonal interaction that I had built up over half a lifetime. It was especially difficult for me to ask patients questions about their use of alcohol and about their sex lives, subjects we were expected to probe deeply, skeptically, and efficiently. This was all the more difficult since we were not participating in patient care but were there by sufferance; patients had been (quite properly) asked to give their permission to be interviewed and examined by second-year medical students, for the benefit of our education.

My first encounter was comically awkward. Purely by chance, I was assigned to a woman who told me during the brief interview that she was an actress with a local repertory company, the name of which I recognized. She was twenty-two years old, had long auburn hair and large brown eyes, and, although small, carried herself with considerable bearing. She had presence—despite being in the hospital, on a bed, dressed in a drab hospital gown. She was about to be discharged, but her physicians had failed to find the source of the pain she still had, a moderate fluctuating sharp discomfort in the lower left quadrant of her abdomen.

She was not in pain at that moment, and at its worst the pain was not very great, but her poise was noticeably disturbed by worry. She had been talked into letting a student do this examination, and it was the last thing she had to do before leaving the hospital. My charge was to give her a complete *neurological* examination. This was utterly irrelevant to her problem; but it was deemed a good way for me to begin, being the most methodical and meticulous part of the physical examination and the easiest to relate meaningfully to anatomy and physiology. One proceeded literally from head to toe, testing sensation, muscle tone and strength, reflexes, perceptual discrimination and integration, and finally higher coordination of movement and thought.

As in most neurological examinations, there was no reason to intrude on any part of the body ordinarily considered intimate, and of course I did not. But I soon found out that any part of the body is intimate in the sense that it is protected by the customary barriers of interpersonal space. There are cultures where these barriers are fewer or lighter than they are for us, and others where they are more numerous or severe. But they are always definite and somehow are known to every person in the culture, if only subconsciously. A violation of these strictures, subtle as they may seem, can dramatically transform the nature of a relationship—resulting in embarrassment, in ostracism, in legal action, or even in homicide. Anthropologists had discovered that diplomatic and business failures—for example, in Japan or in Arab countries—may sometimes be traced to missteps in the frame of personal space.

Yet the physician is supposed to cross these barriers briskly, with confidence and aplomb. And the medical student crossing them for the first time must pretend to the same confidence, ignoring the force and weight of all the previous years of obscure but strict training with regard to personal space. I certainly did try to pretend, and my task was greatly complicated by the fact that I was doing my very first physical examination on a woman who promptly aroused in me unmistakable if fleeting feelings of romantic tenderness and sexual desire. I could not imagine that she was unaware of this, and so another dimension of intersubjectivity was added to an already complex interaction.

I was desperately trying to produce from memory the obsessive protracted sequence of the neurological examination, trying to appear professional, trying to conceal (at all costs!) the fact that I had never examined a patient before (which was probably transparently obvious), and trying to carry forward a stream of small talk, all the while suppressing ridiculous lustful sentiments. The simplest things—looking into her mouth, testing the suppleness of her neck, pushing down on her knee to test the muscle strength in her thighs, checking the mobility of her ankle joint—seemed almost intolerably intrusive. Touching the neck or the knee of a beautiful woman was something one earned with an appropriate investment of time and sentiment: candlelight dinners, walks in the moonlight, that sort of thing (or at least, in this age of marvels, a couple of drinks in a singles bar). But to the patient, I was just one of a long line of men and women who had come around to poke at her in the service of various obscure hospital purposes. She understood perfectly well that the rules of interpersonal space are totally different in a medical encounter; it was I who had trouble with the contrast. Understandably, there were moments when the poor young woman almost burst out laughing.

Later I confided my feelings to the group, with the encouragement of the doctor who was leading that day's discussion. He was a very well-meaning man who was appropriately sensitive—indeed almost too much so. (People who say "share" more than twice in one conversation are always suspect to me, and he exceeded this limit by some measure.) He was trying rather desperately to elicit some valuable confessions about our first experience of the physical examination and not getting very far, so I decided to help him out—having been a teacher, I was alert for those moments when panic is setting in because of student unresponsiveness. I said rather flatly that I had had to examine a woman who was very attractive, and that this made me uncomfortable. There was no response from any of my fellow students, who looked at me strangely. "Thank you for sharing that with us," Dr. Clark finally said, and went on to the next topic. I now knew that this was not to be a forum for discussion about learning to be a doctor, as had been claimed, but yet another setting in which everything about you, even feelings, would be judged. I became accordingly diffident about my feelings.

As the weeks went by I became comfortable with the ritual of the history and physical. The stethoscope, the penlight, and the reflex hammer still seemed foreign, but I was beginning to learn how to use them. We were getting hands-on individual training with our preceptors. We were practicing everything constantly on each other (with the exception of the two most intimate parts of the physical examination, the rectal and vaginal exams, which we practiced on hired models). Two days each week we spent the afternoon with a patient, then presented the patient to our preceptors, and finally returned to the bedside with them. Some of my patients were pieces of human wreckage on the other shore of life. With them the reluctance to touch was different from what it had been with the actress, but this too I overcame—more readily, in fact.

I realize now that I was absurdly meticulous and lengthy in my approach to those first patients. This is true of most beginning clinical students—the less you know, the less confident you feel about leaving out something that might be pertinent. Since I was not engaged in an aggressive and time-pressured approach to the patients' present illnesses, and since I did not have a large panel of patients to think about at the same time, I was able —in fact I felt required—to treat every health problem as important. Each history and physical took about three hours, and my write-up took even longer, involving me as it did in constant consultation of books for the right word, phrase, or explanation. (In patient write-ups, the order is ritualistic, the phrasing formulaic, and the emphasis and reasoning stringently constrained. If they are not, the already problematic circumstances of medical communication and legal vulnerability become impossible.)

How could this process be reduced to one hour for history and physical and one hour for write-up, which was the standard time spent (at best) by interns in their admission work-ups? Actually, since interns might be required to admit up to eight patients in one day, besides attending lectures and rounds and discharging many other duties, it was easy to see that two hours might not be available. So even as I was making my very first inroads into these basic clinical skills, I began to appreciate how they would have to be compromised.

Some interns and residents I met claimed they could be as thorough in an hour or two as I could in six, and at first I found their arguments convincing. But as I got closer to their stage of training, I could appreciate the corners they were cutting (which I would eventually have to cut as well). They focused more narrowly on the present illness, showed less concern for the patient's or, certainly, the family's general health; paid less attention to behavioral and social factors in the patient's illness; were more abrupt and brusque and less responsive to the patient as a human being. The concept of adequate care was eminently flexible, and the judgment about what was really important to give the patient could become very narrow. Of course, when physicians were constantly beset by demands that they reduce costs, they could not feel encouraged to linger with their patients over details that were not immediately essential. Yet such details could turn out to be life-saving in the near term and highly cost-efficient for the future.

In Basic Clinical Skills I had the luxury (for the last time) of giving each patient the fullest conceivable attention. The patients, almost without exception, seemed grateful, and they provided a very instructive set of experiences. There was a sixty-eight-year-old childless widow who had a forty-five-year history of heavy smoking and was now dying of chronic obstructive pulmonary disease. There was a "morbidly obese"—he weighed 389 pounds—forty-five-year-old man who was hypertensive, diabetic, and suffering from numerous recurring painful abscesses in all the creases of his enormous body. All his illnesses were directly related to obesity. A thirty-two-year-old mother of seven suffered from other problems stemming principally from obesity, although she weighed "only" about two hundred pounds: diabetes resulting in kidney impairment, chronic upper abdominal pain, and hypertension. She also had a thyroid problem and chronic asthma, and she was grieving visibly, although it was years past, over her beloved father's untimely death. Her own children had been fathered by a number of different men, and at the time I met her she said she was living and struggling alone.

Another obese man—he weighed 350 pounds—said, "I'm like an alcoholic on food." In addition he was an alcoholic on alcohol. He was now in the hospital, as he had been many times before, for painful swelling in his feet, and this time also in his testicles. His sleep had been sorely troubled by breathing stoppages that woke him—a common problem in the obese —and left him narcoleptic during the day. This had been cured by the surgical opening of a channel into his trachea. But he had been unable to work for about a year due to depression, and he had begun drinking again.

There was a spry seventy-eight-year-old man with a fine wry sense of humor who had just had his gallbladder removed. He had previously had part of his colon removed because of diverticulosis. There was a thirty-four-year-old admittedly promiscuous homosexual, a musician, with a relapse of hepatitis. There was an eighty-three-year-old obese woman with arthritis, hypertension, and leg swelling who had had a bad fall. She was evidently no longer able to take care of herself at home. There was a thirty-nine-year-old man whose lifelong asthma had been exacerbated severely on the day of his separation from a lover. There were cases of cellulitis, thrombophlebitis, cardiac pain, ulcers, cancer, prostatitis, and much more.

What struck me about these patients, aside from the variety of their illnesses, was that many, perhaps most, were hospitalized because of behavioral problems or predispositions. I was not about to blame them, and I don't believe I ever allowed a hint of disapproval to be communicated to them. They taught me a great deal about illness and its treatment and about how to think and talk and act like a doctor. But treatment for many of them was a Sisyphean task, and for some it was almost a fool's errand. Not only was there often very little that could be done for them; but, even more frustratingly, changes in behavior and other preventive measures could have kept them in excellent health in the first place. It was very unusual for any of them to be referred for psychiatric evaluation or even for social service assistance, so they were trapped in a psychological cycle

—smoking, drinking, overeating, accident-prone motorcycling, or risky sex—that had brought them into the hospital again and again. Fortunes were being spent on their care by third-party payers, yet these same payers did not deem it suitable to pay for preventive measures or for behavior modification. They would thus never find out whether such methods might be cost-effective—to say nothing of whether they might be the best thing that could happen to these patients.

I discussed all this with a psychiatrist I knew—he had actually recommended me for medical school—who was now head of the Institute of Medicine. He was involved just then in a program recommending the investment of more resources in behavioral medicine on a grand national scale. My interpretation of my patients was old news to him. This was to be only one of many encounters in which I learned that the opinions of those at or near the top of American medicine bore no relation—or, rather, bore only an ironic relation—to actual practice in the trenches.

At this time I seemed to be what I came to call "medically accident-prone." Amusingly, ironically, and probably not entirely coincidentally, I found myself in life situations where my nascent skills seemed to be called for. The first time was on the airplane on the way back from Edinburgh, where I had spoken at a World Health Organization conference on breast-feeding. The pilot's voice scratched over the public address system asking if there were a medical doctor among the passengers. I held my breath for a while, then asked a stewardess what was up. A middle-aged passenger had collapsed, and they feared a heart attack. I was certainly no doctor, but I was feeling the squeeze of responsibility. If I opened my mouth would it do more harm than good? Fortunately, I did not have to answer the question: there were two physicians aboard.

A week or so later I had been attending an intolerably tedious anthropological lecture in a stuffy lecture hall. I had been on the way home from the hospital and still had my little bag with me—it was the only time during medical school when we actually carried those bags—and I was trying to hide it under my seat. The lecturer droned and ostentatiously turned his pages. The air in the room was so thick it was difficult to breathe. As we filed out, I noticed a commotion and saw that a young woman had fainted. Some people got her to a bench, and I rolled up her coat and put it under her legs. She was soon awake, complaining of a pain in her eye, which I tried to examine gently. "I'm a second-year medical student," I said. "I'm not going to touch your eye, but if you like I can look at it." She said that when she fainted she had scratched her eye on her glasses. The eye was teary but looked intact, except for what seemed to be a scratch on the surface of the sclera—the membrane covering the white. She said that she had an ophthalmologist in town, and I offered to call him. I told her to stay where she was.

He was not terribly excited by my story. He said he would see her at his office in an hour. I tried to get him to tell me how worried I should be, and he tried to be noncommittal. "Take a history," he said. There was no relevant history, as was obvious from what I had already told him. So I simply stayed with her until she got a ride home with her parents. I had judged that this was not an emergency, and I was right.

The third incident, a week or two after that, involved a "consultation" by the rather reckless twenty-four-year-old son of an old friend of mine. The young man, who in every way still acted like a teenage boy, was using the injectable anesthetic ketamine, not a "conventional" street drug. He wanted me to provide him with information about it. I looked over the package insert, already stunned. What I found out was not at all reassuring. Ketamine had a low therapeutic ratio, which meant that the difference between an effective dose and a lethal dose was not very great. For the dreamlike state and occasional hallucinations that were its incidental side effects, he was risking respiratory depression and potentially fatal cardiac arrhythmias. I warned him strongly about these effects, but he did not seem to take my warning very seriously.

After some thought, I told his father about the episode. The young man was living at home and consistently behaved immaturely. His father was always getting him out of trouble. And he was a close friend. I thought that it was important for him to know.

I discussed all three episodes with my preceptors in Basic Clinical Skills. In their estimation I had done the right thing only once, with the young woman in the lecture hall. On the plane, they said, I should have offered to help in any way I could, introduced myself as a second-year medical student, and described the limitations on my knowledge—ludicrously limited, really. I might have been the closest thing to a doctor on the plane, and I was therefore on the spot. I had to get used to that sense of responsibility.

As for my friend's son, they thought I had taken a serious legal risk. He was an adult and was consulting me about a private medical matter. It was a completely privileged communication. For telling my friend his father about the consultation, he could have sued me, probably successfully.

These events made me understand for the first time that my role in life was going to be permanently changed—no, that it had already been changed. I had to begin to relate to the world as a doctor, because that was the way the world would now be relating to me. That entailed the ready acceptance of heavy responsibility, with all its practical, legal, and social consequences. I was no longer just a passenger, or a member of the audience, or a friend. Within and above all those social roles, I was more and more like a physician.

My first surgical experience made a strong impression on me. I was seeing patients one morning with a general surgeon who was conducting his usual clinic, evaluating patients before surgery or following their progress after it. At around noon he said he had to leave to go to a small hospital on the other side of town where a patient was waiting to have an axillary lymph node biopsy. Since he was coming back afterward, I asked him if he would mind my tagging along, and on the contrary he was pleased. As we rode together he spoke reverentially of the surgeon he had trained under who had inspired him to become a surgeon himself. What had been only a famous name to me now became real, and I felt as if I were in the presence of an authentic, impressive tradition that comprised emotion as well as knowledge and skill.

And ritual. When we arrived at the little hospital, the surgeon—a plump, middle-aged Irishman with no pretensions to the status of his teacher—guided me gently through the procedures of sterile technique. The hand washing was so methodical and repetitive, so exceedingly thorough, that it was like a ritual confirmation of the germ theory, a self-reteaching of that theory, every day. The gowning and gloving were equally ritualistic but more dramatic, since they involved nurses attending the surgeon—and me, his new assistant—like priestesses who, although subordinated, were responsible for the purity of the ritual and who would pounce mercilessly on a technical blemish. I had to put my hands and arms into the gown without letting my fingers contact any part of the front of it. Then I had to plunge my hands, one at a time, into the tight rubber gloves without missing a finger or touching anything or ending up with the fingers too loose. I did my best, as careful as if walking on eggs, and I did not contaminate anything, but the two nurses' pairs of eyes scrutinized me with an unrelenting critical gaze.

The young man on the table was conscious, and his shaved armpit had been prepared with a local anesthetic. I was content to stand and watch, with my rubber-gloved hands gripping each other awkwardly, staying in the sterile area just in front of my chest. The surgeon showed me the lump in the axilla, made his incision, and began quickly and efficiently to explore the wound with his fingers. Suddenly he turned to me. "Put your fingers in and feel it," he said. His own fingers pried the wound open to ease the way for me. There was no avoiding this even if I had wanted to. The young man turned briefly to look at us, but he was not really concerned. I put two fingers of my right hand in and felt in the area where I had seen the shape made by the lump under the skin surface. Timidly, I began to move them around. Finally I felt it, a lump about one centimeter across, smaller than I had expected. I nodded, holding my breath, eye to eye with the surgeon, and removed my hand.

I watched the surgeon take out the offending node and prepare it for pathological study. But that was anticlimactic. I was more interested in the blood on my fingers, the lingering mystery, the feeling in my hand. It was like the feeling or even the smell of a hand used in making love to a woman; my fingers had been inside another person's body, not just in the mouth or the vagina or the rectum, but beneath the protective surface of the skin, the inviolable film set up by millions of years of evolution, the envelope of ultimate individuality. Taking me along with him had been a matter-of-fact random event for the surgeon, but for me it had been an unforgettable experience.

I did not fully appreciate while I was taking Basic Clinical Skills that I was being exposed to two of the best clinical teachers I would encounter in medical school. One was Ross Weinberger, the internist who was my primary supervisor in most of the patient evaluations. He was a socially awkward man with a beak nose and heavy glasses, and an asthenic, slightly stooped frame. He worked for a community health plan with an excellent reputation and he seemed to have no academic ambitions. His general grasp of internal medicine seemed as good as that of anyone I met before or since, but that was not the point really. He was simply *with* the patients in a way I would rarely see again. He had a penetrating gaze that was medically critical yet full of convincing practical warmth—no "sharing" here. He cared, professionally, about the nonmedical aspects of his patients' problems—their characters, their families, their living situations, their incomes. Ignorant as I was, I made the mistake of taking all this for granted. I assumed I had had some bad breaks in certain teaching encounters during the preclinical years, and that now I was embarked on an apprenticeship journey under the command of real doctors. Little did I realize with what longing I would later look back on Dr. Weinberger's simple human decency.

In pediatrics, my supervisor was Ed Gold, who stood out similarly in basic human competence. Pediatricians in general are known for being better people—it sounds silly, but it's true—than most medical specialists. They have accepted the lowest financial status in medicine in exchange for an opportunity to serve in the most nurturant primary care capacity. Ed's touch with children was unsentimental and smooth, but as good as his surname in its ability to calm and even amuse them while he carried out efficiently the necessary examinations and procedures. His handling of parents—the pediatrician's bread and butter—was equally adept. He had worked for a time at the Centers for Disease Control, and he was strongly oriented to preventive medicine.

As a teacher, he managed to confer confidence. He brought out the best in whatever natural skill with children I had, as well as in my experience doing research with children in Africa and my more recent experience as a father. I felt more comfortable with the patients in his consulting room than I had up to then anywhere else in the hospitals and clinics. Toward the end, there was one afternoon when I was closeted for an hour or two with a pair of unusually active ten-year-old twins who were, to use the common expression, bouncing off the walls. I did all that was necessary in interviewing their mother and in observing and examining each of them in turn. I felt in control of the situation and consequently happy.

Ed told me a story that made me appreciate the rigors of internship in a somewhat new and more ominous way. After a long struggle with a deadly illness, he had lost a small child. The parents were grateful to him for the effort—they frequently are—and invited him to their home. They wanted him to be a part of the process of experiencing, and recovering from, their grief. He was touched and was grateful to be with them. They left him alone with a drink in his hand on their living room couch, for a few minutes, while they attended to the dinner they were preparing. He fell asleep, and they left him to sleep, realizing how desperately he needed it.

What struck me was that this unusually sensitive doctor did not have the physical wherewithal to stay awake at such a moment, to serve the function of psychological healing for which he was then badly needed. This was not a man who, in such a situation, would allow himself to fall asleep lightly, and he had felt guilty about it ever since. How bad could the stress of internship be? Worse, evidently, than I had thought.

The parade of exquisitely healthy, normally growing children that came through Ed's clinic, with their usually minor problems, presented a stark contrast to my memory of Africa. That memory in turn made me fear, as it always did, for the health of my own daughter, and of my son who was then soon to be born. Life in general seemed fragile, but children seemed more fragile than anything, and I knew that their basic expectable health and safety was a historical novelty. Not only in Africa but in Europe and the United States a mere century or two before, half of all children could be expected to die.

Near the end of my semester in Basic Clinical Skills, this issue came up in a discussion at the home of a physician who was an expert on public health. He had held a powerful administrative position in internal medicine, and had also made a reputation for himself doing research. But he had given up all that to take a leadership role in the field of public health. People were puzzled, and I, like many others before, gave voice to that puzzlement.

He was forthright, even adamant. Public health measures, not medical care, were responsible for all the important reductions of morbidity and mortality in modern times, he said. This was not news to me and I had little trouble with it, but the vehemence with which he defended this position was surprising. Another physician who joined in the conversation was the designer and implementer of a program for screening newborn infants for hypothyroidism, which if undetected can easily cause profound mental retardation. The two of them insisted not only that public health measures were much more important than medicine, but that medicine had accomplished nothing at all.

I protested. Coronary artery bypass surgery? Appendectomy? Antibiotics? Nothing I mentioned impressed them in the least. The treatments were overrated, the numbers of people saved were trivial compared with the numbers, past and future, saved by preventive measures. I felt like an idiot. Here I was, taking my first steps in clinical work, defending the whole enterprise of clinical medicine in an argument with two men who had spent decades practicing medicine at its best and who had abandoned it and insisted that it was useless. There was no getting around the irony of this exchange, or its implications for the journey on which I had embarked.

3

EMERGENCY WARD SURGERY

No Man's Land

The official first day of my first "rotation"—two months assigned to a specific specialty at the hospital—coincided with my thirty-sixth birthday. Because of some last-minute rearrangements in my program, as my first clinical rotation ever I drew Galen and surgery. Most students like me drew easier assignments: Galen surgery, considered the most rigorous third-year rotation, was for future surgeons, not for students who had definitely ruled it out and were planning careers in other fields, psychiatry or pediatrics, for example. But for two months—with the exception of a week of anesthesiology—I would be working every day and every other night, living, eating, drinking, and breathing with some of the most high-powered surgical residents in the world.

These were people—mostly men—who ate determination for breakfast. They had no use for the slow, the sensitive, the theoretical, or the timid. They thrived on stress and sleeplessness, they were openly proud of their ability to take punishment, and they enjoyed making moment-to-moment, even snap decisions about matters of life and death. They expected to make the toughest decisions quickly, and they expected to be right. Last but not least, they *acted*—in the operating room, in the Emergency Ward, on the recovery wards, and in the outpatient clinics, every hour of every day in every way. This was their reputation, and this was the impression I was to carry away from two months with them. For the present, I was frightened as well as excited. It seemed an ironic and paradoxical birthday present, although certainly a big and fascinating one.

If drawing Galen, and starting the year with it, were not enough, I had the additional luck to start surgery with the Emergency Ward. I opted for three weeks of it instead of two—I really thought that this would be one of the most important experiences in my clinical training and one that would go a long way toward making me feel like a doctor. We were told that we would be on a twenty-four-hours-on, twenty-four-off schedule, the theory being that on the nights on, we would get at most two hours' sleep (in fact, we almost always got none). But since conferences and clinics were planned during the off days, that schedule seemed optimistic. My one piece of good luck was to start my actual duties the day *after* my birthday, which itself was spent in preliminary orientation conferences. I got the evening off to spend with my family, which now included a baby boy as well as a little girl. And, luckily, considering what was to come, I got a good night's sleep.

One encounter that day left an unexpectedly strong impression. The six of us assigned to the E.W.—three on each of the alternating days—were briefly oriented by a young surgeon in charge of the Trauma Surgery Unit. He was arrogant, blustering, gruff, not my sort of man at all. And he seemed to take a dislike to me. Because of my (actually very neat) beard? Because my age was too close to his for comfort? I couldn't say. But he decided to single me out for embarrassment. He pointed under my chair at a cherished if new amulet—a beautiful medical bag made of soft Italian leather that I had bought in Florence the previous spring. "You get rid of that thing," he said, snickering at me. "You'll be a fool if you bring that down to the E.W. It'll be gone in no time. And anyway, it's useless." His advice was right, and I followed it, but something about the way he delivered the message told me that he and I would not get along.

The next day I was in the E.W. at six-thirty in the morning and met the team of residents and nurses. We were given a little tour to establish the layout of the unit—if in addition to our inevitable clumsiness we should be lost, we could be quite dangerous people to have around. Patients could walk (or crawl) in through the double swinging doors that gave onto a hallway only twenty or so steps from the main entrance of the hospital. Directly across the hall was an entry that spilled into the ambulance bay; stretchers could be rolled from there into the E.W. in seconds.

An ambulatory patient would meet the first "wall" just inside the swinging doors, in the guise of a clerk (not medically trained) who would do an informal sort of triage. This clerk's desk was on one side of a large room full of alert and bustling doctors and nurses, and the triage nurse sat at a smaller desk only ten yards or so beyond. She had a clear view of anything coming through the door, and no nurse was put at that desk unless she had the experience to recognize potentially serious problems at that distance with her back turned. Her other function was to decide where to send the patient—to medicine, pediatrics, orthopedics, obstetrics and gynecology, psychiatry, or surgery. This was a major political as well as medical responsibility, since many cases were on border lines between the specialties, and her triage decisions could heavily influence the residents' work load.

In the middle of this large room was the administrative center of the E.W., where records were made and briefly kept, and from which blood and other physiological samples were sent out for analysis. From this big central area several hallways proceeded to the specialty emergency rooms. The minor surgery clinic, where I was to spend most of my shift, was a small shiny room with a few chairs and a writing surface below some wall cabinets in one corner, and three patient "bays" with curtains around them, affording a minimal sort of privacy. On the opposite side of the hall were three partially equipped operating rooms for the care of major trauma victims in the first hour or so after they arrived at the hospital. These rooms were centers of tremendous anticipatory excitement for us. Behind the minor surgery clinic was a dingy, dismal waiting room. Beyond that was the large X-ray unit for the E.W., and beyond that was the overnight ward, an observation unit where patients were temporarily held pending a decision in a day or so whether or not to admit them to the hospital.

Unfortunately the residents would be switching their rotations the following day, so I had only one twenty-four-hour period with this friendly and helpful group. Still, I began my hands-on training immediately. The stream of patients was unrelenting—burns, cuts, partial amputations, abrasions, concussions, fractures, ingestions, unidentified abdominal and chest and back pain, complications of previous surgery, knife and gunshot wounds, and the ubiquitous "lacs" (short for lacerations).

These patients were backed up in the waiting room for waits ranging from two to five hours, hours full of pain and fear. Only the most minimal effort was made to "touch base" with the patients after their arrivals. Many were not seen or talked to, even briefly, for hours. But all of them were screened by a triage nurse as soon as they walked through the door, and the serious emergencies were taken care of immediately. Indeed, these were the cases that most readily mobilized the best and most intelligent energies of the trauma team. Nevertheless, a patient occasionally—albeit rarely—died in the waiting room.

I spent the first day learning the routines of patient contact, cleaning and debriding wounds and burns, taking the cursory histories typical of the E.W., and learning to cut corners wherever possible and safe, to move patients along more quickly. I held the proverbial retractor on a number of minor surgical procedures and began to get some sense of how to sew a laceration. Although I was not quite ready to try one myself, I knew the procedure would soon be one of my major responsibilities.

There was no major trauma that day on the surgical side of the E.W., but as if to introduce me to the nature of emergencies, a medical patient was brought in from an outlying hospital. The surgical residents, sheepish about the lack of action on their side, urged the medical students to go and have a look. When I got to the medical side, the patient had not yet arrived, and the medical residents, nurses, and students were crowding the hallway. Suddenly the E.M.T.'s—the Emergency medical technicians—burst through the doors rolling a stretcher carrying a plump middle-aged man under a white sheet. A handsome young resident from the other hospital—Mount Saint Elsewhere—who had traveled in the ambulance with the patient, came down the hall. He asked who was in charge, was told, and then said, "I'm taking the intubation." He was challenged on this. Suddenly he and the Galen senior resident were standing nose to nose shouting at each other in the hallway about who would intubate the patient who had been rolled in dying. I couldn't believe my eyes and ears—a turf fight at such a moment! The Galen residents got the intubation, and I learned a little more not only about handling emergencies but about medical teaching and its politics. As the day and the night wore on, I was too excited to feel tired, and, more important, things were moving too quickly.

During a short lull on that first night—one finally came around two A.M. —I had a chance to familiarize myself with the layout of the very large and multifaceted E.W. There were many interesting nooks and crannies, including a rest area for nurses where I found myself surprisingly welcome and where I surmised I would learn a great deal. Nothing, however, could have prepared me for two other strange discoveries I made. The first was a bulletin board not far from the nurses' rest area, and just outside a room where certain surgical cases were held for observation. The room was dark and quiet, and the hallway was humming slightly with the minimal level of activity that, I would learn, characterized the E.W. in the middle of the night when nothing was happening. A sign above the bulletin board was headed, in careful handwritten letters, "Case of the Week." It was dated a few days earlier, just before the start of my rotation:

> *Complaint:* ~~FOR~~ CIRCUMCISION
> *Triage Notes:* Self-induced circumcision 48 hrs. ago.
> ō G.U. sx   ō fever

The symbol "ō," I had already learned, meant "without," and "sx" meant "symptoms." So the gist was that there were no genito-urinary symptoms, including infection, and there was no fever. "NKA," meaning "No Known Allergies," was scrawled and circled haphazardly. The time was noted as 6:15, the temperature as "99po"—*"per os,"* Latin for "by mouth." There were no notations in the boxes for Blood Pressure, Pulse, Respirations, or Pupil Size. The last name of the triage nurse was scrawled to the left of a printed "R.N.," and in a space labeled "Assigned to Dr. Southwick" were the letters "M.S." for "Minor Surgery."

This was exactly how a door sheet—so called because it was filled out at the door of the E.W. or frequently hung on the door of a patient's room —would have looked when we pulled one out of the box in minor surgery. This one was a completely typical deadpan triage note, in which the only indication of a missed beat on the part of the nurse was the crossed-out "FOR," probably the beginning of the word "foreskin." The absence of notation of blood pressure, pulse, and so on was baffling, but I later realized that this was a sign of a patient so obviously in the pink of health that these measures did not have to be taken, at least at the triage stage.

After a number of empty lines, under a printed "Start Note Here," flanked by arrows pointing downward, was the note written by the surgical intern who had examined this patient:

> 24 yo w ♂ circumcised himself 2 days ago. Wants to know that it is healing properly.
> Pt. shaved pubic area, excised foreskin with a "sterile" razor. Washed the area with alcohol & wrapped it with gauze.
> Today he unwrapped it, noted healing. Erection this A.M. s̄ complications. Last tetanus shot date unknown.
>
> *PE:* Neat circumferential incision at base of glans, with wound edges separated by 3mm. 1×2cm hematoma under ventral aspect. No erythema, streaking, induration; only mild tenderness. Nl. sensation distally.
>
> *A:* Circumcision, healing, s̄ sign of infection. Wound was treated c̄ bacitracin wrapped in gauze. To be changed 2 X daily. RTSD 8d to R/O infection.

After recovering from my double take, I used my growing knowledge of medical language to interpret the case. A twenty-four-year-old white male had circumcised himself, without complications ("š" was a synonym for "ō"). The patient ("Pt.") had consciously imitated real surgery. The intern's physical examination ("PE") showed a properly healing wound with a small collection of blood underneath the head of the penis (nothing to worry about); absence of the classic signs of infection; and normal ("Nl.") sensation at the tip of the penis beyond the wound, demonstrating that no nerves had been injured. The assessment ("A") was that of a properly healing circumcision wound, and the treatment was topical antibiotic for prophylaxis. "Return to Surgical Dispensary in eight days to rule out infection" was the perfectly bland meaning of the last string of alphabet soup.

Not a hint of surprise was shown. Did they see self-circumcision every day here? No, after all it *was* the case of the week. More interestingly and significantly, the note showed no indication of the mental status of the patient, indeed did not even show that it had been thought of. I had already learned that certain subjects had to be covered in a note for legal reasons, including stock phrases to show that certain problems were absent, proving that they had at least been thought of ("No erythema, streaking, induration"). I had been sent back to rewrite my own notes several times because I had omitted one or more of them. This was a basic lesson of all medical report-writing: in any situation there were certain key symptoms and signs the *absence* of which had to be formally documented; a default led not to the interpretation that the patient was normal in that respect but that that portion of the evaluation had been omitted—an inference that made the doctor (or medical student) a medico-legal sitting duck.

But as I was gradually and painfully to learn, this note showed the stricture did not apply to psychiatric signs and symptoms, unless the patient's mental status was so frankly abnormal as to make even a surgeon realize there was a screw loose. There was no indication that a psychiatric consultation for this patient had been recommended, although the best psychiatric emergency service in the region was located a few yards down the hall; nor was there any formal indication that a consult or a referral to Social Service at least had been suggested. Had the intern even thought of the possibility that a young man who circumcised himself might have some emotional problem? Urological surgeons, I knew, sometimes had to remove pens and other objects from the bladders of psychotic patients who had inserted them through their urethras. Surely *they* called in the Psychiatric Emergency Service? Even the one-line throwaways on mental status—"A & O × 3" (alert and oriented to time, place, and person) or "Responds to questioning with full comprehension"—had not been included. There was merely the surgical intern's tacit admiration ("Neat circumferential incision") for a fellow craftsman. The job had been done well under poor conditions, by an amateur, on himself, and with (no less) appropriate follow-up self-examinations!

I went back to minor surgery where I found Steve Ray, the young and very friendly senior resident. The bays were empty and dark, and he was taking a rest from the cases in the overnight ward, who were probably mostly sleeping. (I did not appreciate until later how unusual it was for a Senior even to enter the minor surgery room.) It was his last night in Emergency Surgery. He was sitting at the desk, playing with his pen, turning it over and over in his hands.

"Did you get a load of that case of the week?" I asked him.

"Which? Oh, you mean the circumcision. That was Jody Wilson's case." He laughed slightly. "I wasn't here, unfortunately."

"They just discharged him?"

"Sure. Why not? He did a good job."

Steve's beeper went off in a piercing repetitive whistle. He was on his feet as the tape recited mechanically "Call . . . Extension . . . seven . . . two . . . seven . . . seven." "That'll be my blood," he said. "Pretty soon, sleep. Maybe." He strolled out jauntily and calmly through the door, stretching his stethoscope rhythmically and jerkily between his hands.

I looked down almost longingly at my own beeper, appropriately but depressingly inactive. Then I realized that the bays were not all empty after all: one was occupied by an intern, John Williams, curled up with a sheet over his head. That was why the room was dark. But there was still enough light to snoop around by. I began quietly to open the closets, trying to sort out where the stream of supplies I had seen all day—bandages, gauze, cotton, scalpel blades, needles—had precisely come from. On the inside of the door a cabinet that held a broad assortment of scalpel blades was a photocopy of a notice typed on official hospital stationery, the name of the director printed at the top:

NOTICE

Beginning January 20, 1982, handguns will be issued to all Emergency Ward personnel, along with the following instructions for their use.

Henceforth, patients may be shot, but only after a careful history has been taken and one or more of the following criteria have been met.

1. Patient was caught committing a violent crime and was not sufficiently beaten by the police.
2. Patient was caught committing RAPE or CHILD MOLESTING and was not adequately injured by victim and family.
3. Patient comes to E.W. by ambulance for suture removal or pain med-prescription refill.

4. Five members of the E.W. staff or two doctors (only one need be licensed to practice) certify the patient is a dirtball.
5. Patient reports to the E.W. at 3:00 A.M. for an injury that occurred more than 6 days ago.
6. Maggot count is numerically higher than blood count.
7. Patient wants a new cast because the old cast melted when 6 bottles of cheap wine spilled on it or it was broken in a fight.
8. Heroin needle broke off in arm.
9. Patient was arrested on outstanding warrants and suddenly remembers an injury that requires immediate hospitalization.
10. Patient requires IMMEDIATE Methadone, but cannot remember dose.
11. Patient speaks NO English until discharged without pain medication, then quotes the PDR [Physician's Desk Reference].
12. Patient insists on pain medication for a nondiscernible injury, then states they are allergic to everything except DEMEROL.

NO PATIENTS ARE TO BE SHOT WITHOUT FIRST NOTIFYING UROLOGY AND OPHTHALMOLOGY FOR POSSIBLE ORGAN DONATIONS.

ALL DIRTBALLS MUST BE SHOT IN THE CONTAMINATION ROOM.

ALL PATIENTS TO BE SHOT MUST FIRST HAVE CHEST TUBE, CUTDOWN, TRACHEOSTOMY AND CENTRAL LINE UNLESS THE RESIDENTS ON CALL HAVE PERFORMED GREATER THAN 3 EACH.

PATIENT MAY BE KEPT IN E.W. LONGER THAN 30 MINUTES BUT NO LONGER THAN 4 HOURS PRIOR TO BEING SHOT.

Below this last typewritten line was a scrawled addition: "All lawyers are dirtballs by definition." And below this, on the bottom, was the printed legend, "A Nonprofit Institution—An Equal Opportunity Employer."

I stood with my jaw slack reading this document. Here was the residents' self-analysis: their hatreds, their fears, the pressures on their lives, and, by inversion, their hopes and dreams for the future. Here was their comment on medicine's way of classifying the human world, on the spectrum of patients—on those who brought problems (including illness and injury) on themselves and deserved what they got and those who were abusive or even dangerous to doctors and other E.W. personnel. Embedded in this document too was the notion that illness and injury were physical, and that behavior belonged wholly to another, moral realm. This latter realm could bring about illness and injury but did not overlap with the vast category of abnormalities for which physicians were held to account. In other words, substance abuse, failure to keep clean, and child molesting were purely moral problems and in no sense medical abnormalities.

I heard footsteps behind me. Frank, the desk clerk on night shift, had come up with a new door sheet in his hand. "Do you want it, or should I drop it in the box?" He smiled coyly when he saw what I was reading. "Better not let a lot of people know about that." I took the sheet and closed the cabinet door.

The new patient was a twenty-six-year-old man with low back pain. No fever, no drugs, no other symptoms, no known allergies. Was I going to wake up poor long-suffering John Williams for this? I knew I would have to, since no one was allowed to depart without seeing an M.D. Besides, after a total of eighteen hours and thirty minutes of surgical experience, I wouldn't have trusted myself to manage a shaving nick or even a mosquito bite. Still, I would have to present the case anyway, so the least I could do was let John sleep until I had made my fumbling first pass.

Mr. Furillo was a vision out of the "patients may be shot" memo. He was sullen, slouched, unkempt, and not very clean, even from a distance. His manner when I questioned him was curt and gruff, with a the-world-owes-me-a-living tone. He did not seem impoverished, intoxicated with alcohol or other drugs, withdrawing from same, confused, tired, or ill. His story was that of a typical chronically recurring mild-to-moderate low back pain syndrome, very much like the one I had had myself for fifteen years. He was able to sit up on the cot, with his legs dangling over the side, talking steadily. He was obviously uncomfortable, but this, I knew, was not low back pain at its worst. More significant, he had had this condition for years, on and off, and this episode had started three days ago. *What brings the patient in now?*, a question drummed into me in Basic Clinical Skills as one of the great illuminators, seemed particularly apt in this case. His answer that it was getting worse did not, somehow, satisfy. The clock said 3:03 A.M.

I strolled out of the half-lit bay and listened to John's snoring on the other side of the curtain. I could imagine his face coming out of its groggy sleep, and then snapping out, saying "Low back pain? *Low fucking back pain? You're waking me up for low fucking back pain?*" Fortunately, at that moment I noticed that Steve Ray was back at his desk, twirling his pen in one hand, leaning on the other hand with his elbow on the table.

Ray was a puzzle to me. He was a third-year surgical resident in one of the best programs of its kind in the world at the almost incredible age of twenty-three. He came from the ultimate in urban Mount Saint Else-where, a medical school based at a nasty big city hospital. To have got where he was at the age he was he must have skipped a couple of grades in grammar or high school and then entered medical school after only two years of college (a possibility in certain six-year programs). He was a walking, breathing challenge to the argument that breadth and maturity are necessary to be a good doctor. He contradicted every cliché about surgeons. Everyone loved him, including patients, other residents, E.W. and O.R. nurses, medical students, even me, and I did not then nor would I ever love many residents. He had done three appendectomies as a medical student—something allowed in certain municipal hospitals—and that was indicative of the clinical experience with which he *began* his residency. He could charm the pinstripes off the chairman of the hospital board or the haze out of a junkie's eyes. Half the nurses were in love with his boyish good looks, and the other half wanted to take care of him. He was said by everyone to be a superb surgeon and, despite not being a scientist, to be destined for great things. Still, a key part of his charm was a distinct *épater les bourgeois:* the brash-young-man image subtly graded into a punk defiance.

His cards, for instance. All residents and medical students carried a pocketful of three-by-five index cards for note-taking of all kinds, and it was said that one goal of a residency was to learn how to put all the key data about a patient on just one card. His cards were printed at the top with a ditty he composed, based on his nickname, "The Ace." (His real name was similar to that of a famous comic book hero with that nickname.) The comic-book "Ace" had dominated the imaginations of two generations of American boys, projecting a hypermasculine aggressive image based on a clean-cut rugged face and a bull-like body. Calling Steve "The Ace" was both hilariously wrong and subtly true. He was certainly masculine, but his masculinity was that of the clever handsome runty guy who makes out like crazy, leaving the big bruiser in his figurative romantic dust. And yet he *was* a hero in the eyes of virtually everyone—and one of the few heroes I would ever encounter in that complex, puzzling world of hospitals. At any rate, he had sat down at the Kardex stamping machine out front, where plastic cards were made up for the new patients with names, addresses, ages, ID numbers and dates of arrival, and had made up a plastic card with raised letters that read:

The Ace says,
And he ain't shittin',
Go fuck yerself,
And do it today.

Using this card, he stamped up his index cards with the ditty at the top, much the way everyone else stamped the patients' data on their index cards. He then inserted a stack of them so that the little quatrain poked up out of the vest pocket of his white jacket, facing out, not far from the pinned-on nameplate that said "Dr. Stephen Ray."

As I drifted out of Mr. Furillo's bay, Steve did not move from his semireclining posture, but he pulled one of the cards out of his pocket, laid it on the table, the pen still in his hand, and said, "What've we got?"

"Low back pain," I said. "Low back pain."

"Loss of sensation?"

"Nope."

"Can he walk?"

"Yep."

"How long?"

"Years, on and off. This time three days."

He laid his pen down on his card. This was not worth writing about.

"Should I wake up John?"

"No, it's O.K., I'll take it."

"Do you realize that this is in clear violation of Principle Number"—I opened the cabinet door—"of Principle Five of the Patients-May-Be-Shot memo?"

Steve smiled tolerantly. I went on, "I don't believe this guy. He comes in at three A.M.—exactly—with low back pain that he's had for days, not to mention having it on and off for years. These guys must think there are shifts here, or something. Like we've been home asleep all day and we just showed up to take over, all fresh like. He's up, so he figures we should—"

"That's the E.W.," was Steve's placid summary interruption. He lifted his head from his hand and his elbow from the table. "Let's see him," he said.

"Hello, Mr. Furillo," he said. "I'm Doctor Ray." Steve shook hands with him. The doctor, pale and thin, with sleepy eyes, looked worse than the patient. He had been operating all day long. "Can you tell me what's been bothering you, sir?" This was not the "sir" that I would soon get used to hearing, the openly contemptuous one, transparent to patient and student alike. This was real.

Mr. Furillo began, "Like I told him . . ." and started again on his story, glad to be seeing a more important doctor but annoyed at having to waste his time repeating himself. He had the same presumptuous tone he had taken with me. Steve went on questioning him in a way that was both polite and gentle, interested and respectful. He said "sir" often. "Sir, can I ask you to step down here? Are you able to do that?" He put a footstool in place and helped Mr. Furillo climb down. He asked him to bend forward a bit and then examined his lower back, pointing out to me the place where the spasm was. Then he helped him back onto the cot and examined the mobility and sensation in his legs.

"Is there anything else you want to tell us, sir, that we might have forgotten to ask about?"

"No. Just if you could give me something for the pain."

"I can't give you anything other than Tylenol for this, sir."

"Well, O.K., I'll take Tylenol. And I need a note? For work tomorrow?"

"What kind of work do you do, sir?"

"Warehouse work. I got a lot of lifting, and I don't see myself doin' it, not in this shape I'm in."

"I'll give you a note, sir."

We walked out of the bay, and Steve remained placid. I could hardly believe my eyes and ears. I had seen patients insulted and mistreated all day under much more favorable circumstances. I thought I'd had the whole brutal system figured out. "How can you be so nice to that guy? What does he want, just pain meds or something?"

"No, it didn't faze him when I said no to that. He wants the note for work. That's why he came in now. Something went wrong at work, and as the night wore on, he couldn't sleep, and he realized he had a good excuse not to go to work tomorrow. The back problem was real enough, but he needed a note. If you want to write the note, I'll write him a scrip for a couple of Valium. What the hell."

"I still don't see how you can stay so calm and be so nice."

"It's the E.W.," he said. "It's the only way to be."

Other residents, I knew, found many other ways to be, none of them nice. Perhaps Steve did not see the gulf between his own bedside manner —somewhere between genuine courtesy and a heartfelt simulation of it —and their listlessness, condescension, or patent fakery. He had devoted his whole young life to achieving excellence as a general surgeon, and yet was reflexively decent to an insolent man who was not really sick and who was wasting his time—and this in a context that encouraged the worst in everyone, in which insult and impudence was the dominant mode. How he managed this—how he had become what he was, in the system as it was —puzzled me for a long time.

Most of what I experienced on the surgical rotation was quite different from what I saw with Steve Ray. For example, the next morning, after the shift changed and our twenty-four hours in the E.W. were over, John Williams and I went to his follow-up clinic. We practically ran over to the ambulatory care wing, and he introduced me to the nurses there; they were having doughnuts and cake to celebrate the residents' last day. We lingered over this for about five minutes and then began the fastest run-through of a dozen or so patients that I had seen before or would see since. He spent just two or three minutes each with most of them. I guess he did what he was supposed to do. He even lanced a boil that had recurred and packed the wound. But how he thought he could truly check up on this varied group of post-minor-surgery patients in such a short time was beyond me. It was not because he was so pressed; he and I and a nurse sat around chatting for half an hour or so after his patients had been put through. During that time the nurse, an overweight, pretty brunette with a pleasantly professional manner, took out the books and announced that John had set an all-time record for monthly earnings by an intern in that clinic. This was proof that his speed was off the scale, but it was no more than an exaggeration of what was expected.

During one encounter that morning, a sixty-year-old man who looked older came in for a check of a leg infection that had been incised and drained. John did the check in less than a minute, since the dressing had already been removed. The leg wound did not look good, but presumably it was better than it had been. The man asked how often he should change the new dressing. "The nurse will explain all that," said John, in a tone that said, Don't let's get involved in such trivia, it's not for tough guys like us, and don't ask me any more questions.

The man said, in a tentative friendly way, "I had this other operation," he said, pointing into his lap. "On my privates. They cut off the end of it," he went on, smiling nervously, trying to formulate his question, using the fingers of his right hand as a scissors to snip off the end of his left forefinger. "So they cut it and—"

I could not believe my eyes. John Williams had turned his back during this and was already out the door. The awkward, intimate, tentative question never quite came out. I put my hand on the man's shoulder. "I'm sorry, but I have to follow him," I said, truly embarrassed for John. "I hope you'll be really well soon." I bolted out so as not to lose John, since I had been told in no uncertain terms that I was to be his shadow, and he was as informative as a bottle of iodine about what he was going to do next. I caught up to him as he zipped past the door of the nurses' conference room, where they were again eating cake and doughnuts. He waved good-bye and said "Thanks," over his shoulder. His hand came up to his mouth in a characteristic gesture. All ten fingernails were bitten below the quick.

At six-thirty on the morning of my next day on, after a good talk with my wife and a good night's sleep, I came into the minor surgery room to find, as expected, a new set of residents. Margaret, Bill, and I, the three medical students, sat down in our corner to fill out forms. There were ten copies each of about six forms: requests for blood and blood products, for urinalysis, for arterial blood gas measurements, for toxicity screens, and for routine biochemical measurements in venous blood, among others. We filled these out in advance so that they would be ready when a trauma patient—like Madeline Fine, the young woman with the collapsed lung who had been repeatedly stabbed by her boyfriend—needed these fluids without delay. No degree of emergency would get us to square one with the labs if we hadn't filled out the forms.

This tedious clerical task done, we awaited the arrival of Jack Parker, the respected and feared Director of Trauma Surgery, the one who had told me to get rid of my Florentine leather medical bag. He arrived on the dot of seven, muscular and well-rested, and sat down and began talking.

"Trauma is a surgical epidemic. There are a hundred and fifty thousand trauma deaths a year in this country, and sixty percent of those didn't have to die. Fifty thousand are motor-vehicle accident cases—more than the number of Americans lost in the whole Korean War. Twenty-five thousand are suicides. In 1965 somebody did a study that showed that fifty percent of U.S. ambulance drivers were morticians.

"You are the first-hour physician. You are not supposed to sit around like that bunch of mopes and fleas upstairs figuring out an analysis. You are supposed to do something and do it damn fast. Now, a lot of times you're going to go blank when the guy hits the door. You can't look it up. You can't stand around thinking while the guy is trying to box.

"But all you have to do is remember your ABC's. If you've got those down pat, you have nothing to worry about. A—" Here he paused for a moment, and I thought he was looking for an answer. As a former teacher,

I tried to help in those situations, and this was so easy that it could not be like showing off—just an expected interaction.

"Airway," I said.

He shot me an unpleasant look, letting me know that my answer had not been called for, and went on with his monologue. "Airway, Breathing, and Circulation. Those are the things you check for first and establish first if they're missing. A, B, C, D, E. Sounds simple, but people forget it every day. D is for Disability, which means neurologic, but *basic*. We're talking level of consciousness here—how much of his brain is blown. E is for Expose. That means, take their clothes off. Every item. Until you've seen every inch of that patient you don't know what it is you've got. A-B-C-D-E. Learn your ABC's and you won't be one of the ones who forget.

"More stupid alphabet soup: AVPU—that's your cursory neurologic exam. A is Alert. V—not alert, but responds to vocal stimuli. P—doesn't respond except to painful stimuli. U—Unresponsive—no nothing, whatever you do. They also stand for Awake, Vomiting, Pupils, Urination. Those four things tell you a lot about your level of brain or spinal cord damage. Learn what they mean.

"X-rays: LCS plus CXR within the first fifteen minutes. That means lateral cervical spine film to rule out broken neck, and chest X-ray to rule out flail chest and mediastinal injury, not to mention a bunch of other things. LCS plus CXR in the first fifteen.

"History: you don't screw around. Remember this: AMPLE. Allergies, Medications, Previous *major* illnesses, Last meal, and Events leading to injury. That's it, that's an AMPLE history. You don't have time to get their life story. Any questions about the alphabet soup?"

I should have recognized this as an offer to pass up. But I said, "How do you handle a c-spine injury with CPR?"

He shot another, nastier look at me and said, "We'll get to that," and went on with his lecture.

I reminded myself of some of my own alphabet soup, learned from a highly successful senior colleague as a faculty-meeting tactic. *K.M.S., you jerk*, I said to myself, as loudly as I could inside my head. KEEP MOUTH SHUT. *At least until you get the lay of the land. Or until you have something indispensable to say.*

I began to realize I was making a fatal mistake. Because the group was small—small groups were rare in medical school during the preclinical years—I had unconsciously acted as though I were in a graduate seminar. That wonderful setting for teaching had been my bread and butter for years, and I had eagerly participated in them for years before that. Their function was to encourage thought, exchange of views, even temporary error. A good graduate seminar became itself like a thoughtful mind, beset with ambiguities, arguing generously with itself, teaching itself, learning. But there was no such thing in medical school. If Dr. Parker's "seminar" could be likened to a single mind, it was a rigid, authoritarian one, intolerant of ambiguities and constantly searching for certainties: reliable rules, unchallengeable procedures, incontrovertible facts. This could not be justified on the grounds that in medicine there was only one right way; it was, rather, that physician-teachers and residents preferred to believe that there was only one right way. The more constricting the rules were, the more easily they could be memorized and, more important, the more comfortable you would feel—regardless of the outcome—when you had followed them.

Out of the corner of my eye I noticed that the door from the waiting room into the minor surgery room had opened about six inches. A man in a dark suit and tie, with black curly hair, was holding his head and looking around tentatively, evidently in pain. Neither Parker nor any of the residents or other students had noticed him, and I wondered if I should speak up. *K.M.S.*, I repeated to myself once again, *K.M.S.*

Half an hour later the man with the hurt head had poked his head into the room three more times. I wrestled with my conscience. Could it really be that none of them had noticed him? It did not seem possible. Yet it seemed equally impossible that they would be ignoring him. Surely one of us could talk to him for a few minutes?

I remembered a time in the first year of medical school when a clinical professor was lecturing on the mechanism of the blood pressure cuff. His beeper rang three times over the course of half an hour, and each time he turned it off and went on lecturing. I remember not being able to concentrate very well on his technical points, wondering instead what problem, what danger, what pain was waiting for his attention at the other end of that persistent, ignored beeper. And if he had had some reason to be *absolutely sure* that he was not really needed (it is hard to imagine what it would be), might it not have been instructive at least to allude to it? Mightn't we otherwise be learning a bad meta-medical lesson?

Despite the evidence that ignoring patients was normative—a fact that I would soon learn beyond any possible doubt—I was too disturbed by the patient's repeated appearances to *K.M.S.* any longer. "There's a patient," I said timidly.

Dr. Parker's response was reflexive and harsh. "I'm gonna have to ask you"—he stabbed the air in my direction with a stiff pointed finger—"If

you're gonna keep interrupting me I'm gonna have to ask you to leave."
His tone, tense, defensive, and shrill, differed dramatically from the ordinary loud, pompous tone of the rest of his lecture.

It was the last message I needed to get from him. *K.M.S.* was from then on not only easy but second nature to me. I faded into the woodwork in every situation. I rarely if ever spoke unless I had been directly addressed. *This is the army,* I thought. *Every time you open your mouth you create complications for yourself.* It was a rule I followed throughout the rest of my medical training; making exceptions only when I was in the presence of the unusual medical teacher who was not overbearingly arrogant, and whom I instinctively felt I could trust.

None of them stirred to see the patient, to speak of or to him, or even to cast a look in the direction of the waiting room. By the time Dr. Parker's talk was over and I went out into the waiting room, the patient had left without treatment. His door sheet indicated that he had had a significant head trauma—he had slammed into the windshield in an automobile accident. The door sheet, signed by a resident, blamed him for leaving "A.M.A."—Against Medical Advice. What medical advice? I wondered. He never saw a doctor. Later in the morning I bumped into Dr. Parker, who gave me one of those "apologies" that people give who are incapable of apologizing—really a repetition of the insult. I was surprised that he even took notice of me enough to remember our exchange. But it didn't matter; I smiled and thanked him. I was already beyond where he could touch me.

My first experience in "the Saturday Night Knife and Gun Club" turned out to be very quiet, yet I got a chance to do some work. Just before nine o'clock a middle-aged woman came in with a painfully swollen finger constricted by her wedding ring and two other rings on the same finger. She had obviously gained a good deal of weight since first putting the rings on, and they were now impossible to remove. The finger was clearly infected, and the tissue under the ring looked ischemic (oxygen-starved); it was purple. She could lose the finger. I injected the local anesthetic Xylocaine at the base of the finger on both sides. Then I went to work sawing at the rings with a small tool expressly designed for that purpose.

It wasn't working. After ten minutes or so I asked the intern, Freddy Robertson, if it was supposed to take that long. "Of course," he said. "You're just afraid of work. Keep turning it. It'll saw through." I was working as hard as I could putting pressure on the instrument. My hands by now hurt badly. The situation was oddly intimate. This very nice, patient, but clearly upset woman, in considerable pain despite the Xylocaine, tried to control her reactions with her face a few inches from my own. There was no visible progress, and after another twenty minutes, I asked Freddy again. He gave me the same assurances, this time even more annoyed with me for bothering him.

When I became thoroughly discouraged, I didn't go to him. I went to Bob McIntyre, the junior resident, who told me to ask the "orthopods"— the orthopedic surgeons—for advice. I went next door and told them the story, which gave them a good laugh. They said, "It ought to take about a minute and a half." One of them opened a drawer and took out an identical but shinier ring-removing tool. Armed with that, I returned to the unfortunate woman, set to work again, and removed the largest ring —the first one, which I was still working on—in about a minute and a half.

I was furious at Freddy, and yet I had learned a lesson. His arrogance was ignorance, and this was true of many residents in many situations. Yet he was every bit as self-assured as if he were talking about something he really knew. The patient had suffered an extra forty-five minutes of unnecessary pain as well as risk of losing a finger, and she would have suffered much more unless I had explicitly disobeyed his order and gone over his head. It was a good lesson to have learned early. After we sent her out, Ted Webster, the senior resident, arrived in a jacket and tie. After checking in briefly, he went off to change. "I didn't recognize him," I said, attempting a lame joke. "How come he looks like that?"

A resident I didn't know said, "That's because he's the senior. When we grow up and get to be the senior, we'll get to look like that too."

There was nothing major until the early morning, but we were kept up all night by small problems. At six A.M. a woman with serious spinal damage was brought in on a stretcher. She had only fallen off a bed, but she had metal rods in place to stabilize her spine from a previous injury; the minor fall had dislodged the rods and severely reinjured her. Ted, who had caught an hour's sleep—he was somewhat the worse for wear as a result of whatever he had been doing in the suit and tie before arriving for work —was staggering toward us down the hall, rubbing his sleepy eyes. He continued to rub them in the trauma room, obviously having some trouble waking up.

I stood near the door beside the policeman and policewoman who had brought the patient in and who were intently watching Ted try to get going. I said, "Two minutes ago he was fast asleep and now he's completely in charge of somebody's life."

The young policewoman, small and slender with blue eyes and blond curls, said, "Better her than me."

As soon as that patient was successfully stabilized, we had our only other major trauma of the night—bad news coming, as it often does, in bunches. A young man had suffered multiple trauma in a motorcycle accident—one of the major sources of the unit's business. He was in moderate shock, pale and cool with low blood pressure. I remembered some aphorisms on shock: *a rude interruption in the machinery of life,* and, even more ominous, *a momentary pause in the act of death.* Following orders, I helped undress him, hung some bags of saline, and ran out with the first arterial blood gas. When I came back there was not much to do but watch and note the unfolding alphabet soup: Airway, Breathing, and Circulation; the cursory neurological exam—I was asked to check periodically on his pupils, which fortunately were equal, round, normal in size, and reactive to light; LCS plus CXR, the X-rays that were done by a technician with a portable machine after gently stabilizing the neck and emptying the room; and the history—what little there was of it—taken from the police.

This was a hands-on lesson in the handling of major trauma, and the fifteen minutes seemed on the one hand like fifteen seconds—there was no time at all to think—and on the other like fifteen hours—time seemed suspended while a life hung in the balance and an incredible amount went on. At one point the lights went out. Ted, now long since awake, said, "Hey! Very dramatic! Just like 'General Hospital.' " The basic life support activity continued without interruption under his smooth supervision, by the light of a separately powered surgical lamp. The ABC's were working for this unfortunate young man, and by the time he was sent up to the O.R. his future looked like something more than a hopeful speculation.

Although I was supposed to leave that morning at seven-thirty, just about the time that the young man was rolled in, I ended up not getting home until late morning.

The subway ride in my hospital whites (I had not yet formed the good habit of changing out of them before leaving) felt strange, even other-worldly. I walked home from the subway on an exhausted high.

My parents happened to be visiting with us, and I found them, my wife, and my children sitting around enjoying a rather sumptuous late Sunday breakfast of fresh rolls, bagels, lox, sable, cheeses, even herring. I told my parents about the unbelievable pace of the work. My father winked, spread some cream cheese on a bagel, and said, "It'll make a man out of you." Aside from the annoyance of the cliché, I could have been angered by the implication that the rest of my life had not yet sufficed to accomplish that goal. But I could not really get angry, since his characterization was uncomfortably close to my own view of why I was dressed in white.

On the way in for my next shift, on Labor Day, I ran into Bill, another of the students on emergency surgery, and we talked while walking up from the subway. He was normally taciturn but now was in a complaining mood. He wondered aloud why we had to be at the hospital so early— before seven—and I said we needed the overlap with the team ending its shift. He also resented the residents' cryptic talk, not the technical jargon, but the inside jokes, slang, and abbreviations they never tried to explain. This I agreed with completely. Then his next complaint was about his loans. He was groaning under their burden. I wondered whether, if he calculated even the lowest income he could be certain of in the future, and the number of years he would have to pay them back, he would realize that it was not really something he had to worry about. Bill did not buy this argument at all. His final point, for emphasis, was, "You know, I'm even beginning to think that my choice of where I'm going to live may have to be conditioned by financial considerations." This stunned me; it said more about the ideas doctors have of their privileges and expectations than any sociological treatise could. What profession's members did *not* have to consider such mundane human matters as money?

When we walked in the three residents were standing around in the minor surgery room making fun of patients. This was a regular part of the morning ritual. Since nothing was happening, they had nothing to do, and instead of policing the overnight ward or waiting for a patient in one of the trauma rooms, they took over our corner in minor surgery. They rarely entered the room to help when patients were piled up outside, but now they usurped the only part of the place that could be considered ours. Ted, the senior, also took my newspaper. I bought another one.

In the late afternoon a charming old Italian woman came in with a nasal fracture after a fall in the street. Her solicitous, handsome husband was with her. She was very worried. She'd been preparing for a party later in the week. Was the nose broken? Would it be reset? Would she still be wearing a bandage by next Thursday? There were many other questions. She and her husband each had an intense and implicit concern: his was to show his love for her and his guilt at having allowed this to happen; hers was more specific and more difficult to discern, but she gradually revealed to me that she was hoping to have a prettier nose after the fracture was corrected and healed. Her two daughters had had elective rhinoplasty as teenagers, she told me, having inherited her rather beakish nose. She wanted keenly to know if the accident might have given her a chance to have a similar alteration.

Her husband, insistently doting, told her several times that he liked her nose "just as it is." I made a point of getting a "roadside," or informal, consultation on this from Steve Ray. It would not be possible, he said, but he would have a talk with her and offer her the rhinoplasty after her recovery from the fracture. This made me a little sad, since I doubted that she would do it then.

At the ten o'clock meal that night—the hospital provided a nightly all-you-can-eat so-called dinner for any staff members in the house—there was grim dinner conversation about patients who had been brought in dead and yet had had to be coded—slang for being put through a full-scale attempt at resuscitation. Each resident had a story. One man was brought in dead and "coded" for half an hour. An elderly woman with a ruptured abdominal aortic aneurysm had been brought in from a distant suburb. Her chances would have been slim even an hour earlier, but now she was dead and cold; still she was coded. A college student had jumped or fallen from a dormitory window and lain dead on the street apparently for hours —a rat had eaten part of his eye; but since the students who had found him in the morning had dutifully started C.P.R.—cardiopulmonary resuscitation—the E.M.T.'s had felt obligated to treat him as a code, and so, in their turn, had the residents. Expensive resources were being lavished on the not-too-recently dead, and the residents, trapped by rules not of their making, could not do anything but laugh.

At around two that morning, a street drunk named Sam Bigelow came in with a report of a head injury. He had been pushed or had fallen down a flight of stairs. He did have a bruise on his head, but it did not look serious. In fact no one thought he needed a skull film. However, he was trembling all over. He was clearly not drunk, and he spoke to me politely, recounting his repeated attempts to get and stay dry. This latest, he said, was two days old, and he somehow convinced me that he wanted to stay with it, that he was not merely looking for a place to spend the night. He was in distress, nauseous, flushed, unable to eat. I spent some time trying to calm him down, and then stalled for a couple of hours so that he could continue to occupy a bay in minor surgery where he could at least lie down. Freddy Robertson and the other surgical residents showed no interest. If his head injury was not serious—and it wasn't—he had to be turfed to the street. If I was serious about treating his withdrawal, I should wake up a psychiatrist.

So, according to protocol, I went to the triage nurse to ask her to page the psychiatrist on call, so that Bigelow could be transferred to their service (and if surgery were quiet enough I could help with his treatment). The nurse, a hard, pretty brunette, looked at me unbelieving. "You want me to wake up a psychiatrist at four A.M. to take care of Sam Bigelow?"

"He's a patient, isn't he? He's sick. He's in withdrawal. The surgeons are going to turf him back to the street. Isn't it the job of the psychiatrists to take care of a patient in withdrawal?"

"Sure, but . . ." Her face softened, and a distant look came into her pretty brown eyes. I later imagined that she had been trying to think back to a time when she had had the sort of faith that I was now demonstrating. "How long have you been here?" she asked. She did not wake the psychiatrist, and I told Sam to come in to the detox clinic the following day. But, through various excuses, I managed to keep him in a bed in minor surgery —there were no patients who needed it, at least not as badly as he did— until after seven o'clock in the morning.

That day was the official day of publication of my book about the biological constraints on human behavior. I dragged myself out of bed after three or four hours' sleep to give a not completely coherent two-hour interview to National Public Radio, focusing on the "dark side of human nature." I was not so tired that the irony was lost on me. Neither my years in Africa nor more than a decade of rather cynical study had quite prepared me for the darkest shadows of the Galen E.W.

The following morning I awoke at five, as usual, but this time, with a clear mind, not wanting to go. As I struggled to figure out whether it was Tuesday or Saturday (it turned out to be Wednesday), I remembered Freddy Robertson's remark on the first day we had met, "You'll forget what day it is." As my train progressed toward the hospital in the dark, I realized that I would miss the superb dawn skies that had greeted me in the past week. Winter was closing in. For the rest of the term I would come to the hospital and leave it—often thirty-six hours later—in the dark, having never seen the light except through a window.

I was able to skip Dr. Carter's lecture that morning, because I had an appointment with a senior surgeon, Dr. Maple, who would be supervising my presentation on breast cancer. I sat for a while in the waiting room of the radiation clinic trying to collect my thoughts. The waiting room was a wonderfully pleasant space, with soft, curved, continuous couches upholstered in a warm dark orange color: they had only round shapes without corners, and even the armrests were soft and round. A wall of handsome fresh red brick, also without corners, rose to a clerestory of glass. Large potted trees stood in several places, and an inoffensive abstract bronze sculpture in the center of a spiral staircase. There was a constant fall of soft natural light through the clerestory.

On the wall high in the atrium was a round naive painting of an exotic tropical bird flying across candy-colored mountains. Around this painting on the frame it said, *Sarah J. Winslow, 1972. These Waiting Rooms Established Through Her Generosity.* Had she done the painting? Had she helped to design the room? Had she been a breast cancer victim herself? I wanted to think all this was true; that she was someone who had really thought, as few people did who were not touched by it, about what it was like to be a woman with that particular disease. This was by far the nicest place I had discovered in the hospital—with the possible exception of the chapel. It was a fit place, if any was, for a woman to sit for a long time, repeatedly, in substantial pain, and to think about disfigurement, deterioration, and death.

Dr. Maple told the two of us who were presenting that week that we should take a day off to prepare properly. "It will be the single most important determinant of your grade in surgery, which will be one of the most important determinants of what residency you get." Knowing that Freddy Robertson would not like our disappearing, I pressed Dr. Maple to make sure he would support me.

"Who's down there?" he asked.

"Freddy Robertson is the intern."

"No. Who's older?"

"Ted Webster is the senior."

"Good. Tell him to come to me if he has any questions." Seeing my uncertainty he added, "You're already developing a medical neurosis. You think you're needed. It's not true." Of course, he was helping to encourage our other neurosis, the one about "the most important determinant . . ."

Webster said, "That's reasonable. Come back tonight if you can. Use your judgment. They'll be glad to have you back if you can get back. Tell Freddy."

I went to find Freddy in the surgical follow-up clinic, where I was supposed to be working with him. Freddy reacted as I knew he would. "When I was a student," he grumbled without looking at me—he was talking about two months ago as if it were ten years—"we had to give presentations without taking days off." But the names of Maple and Webster quieted him. At least my age was worth an understanding of how to make the hierarchy work, if only occasionally, in my favor.

On my way out to the library I ran into Stephanie Walker, an intern who had the same job as Freddy on the same shift but in the other wing of the hospital. I was on good terms with her.

"Where's your medical student?" I asked.

"Not here," she said, sounding surprised. "Does Freddy make you come to his clinic after your shift?"

"You bet. Including days off."

"Days off!" she said. "Tell him to stuff it up his nose." So I learned that there was some variation in the system, that I had not been lucky, and that I might still have some leverage to use against Freddy. I was not bucking for an "Excellent" in surgery. I wanted to finish the course, and to pass, with my mental faculties and my motivation for medicine intact.

The talk on breast cancer epidemiology went very well; I had to have learned something during my years as a professor. At Dr. Carter's conference on my next shift, there was some Monday morning quarterbacking about a couple of patients. One, with a ruptured "triple A" (abdominal aortic aneurysm) had died during the night because of insufficient replacement of lost blood. The residents had called for the usual amounts (ten units of packed red cells, five of fresh frozen plasma, ten of platelets—for which we medical students daily filled out the needed forms). But the blood bank had prepared only a fraction of them, reasoning that the surgeons always call for a lot more than they need. Were the blood bank people responsible or had the surgeons cried wolf too many times? Either way, this territorial second-guessing had cost a life.

The other patient discussed was a "multi-T" (multiple trauma) victim whom the nurses thought they could have handled better than the residents had. The residents had done a belly tap in the wrong place. They had failed to rule out retroperitoneal bleeding—a patient could exsanguinate into this ample space behind the viscera; the blood pressure had not responded to volume replacement, an ominous sign not taken seriously enough; and they had not ruled out a ruptured spleen. These were all good lessons, but there was a key meta-medical one: Ted Webster was called upon to justify his actions in response to criticism from the nurses. This particular aspect of hospital checks and balances was new to me, and I thought it was just fine.

Some time after this conference, around noon, I saw a handsome Irish-immigrant carpenter with a charming, florid brogue. He came in with a hand wound, having come in some days earlier with another. He reported a strange reaction to Keflex, the antibiotic he'd been given—a fifteen-minute powerful "rush" followed by a whole night of auditory hallucinations. He had heard the voices of his friends, he said, who were having a party in a suburb a few miles away. The voices were coming through the chimney, and the unfriendly remarks mostly pertained to him. He was frightened by but also rather proud of these new powers.

I looked up Keflex in the P.D.R. There was nothing remotely like such a side effect. I called the emergency psychiatric service and the psychiatrist agreed that he should be seen. I got him over to her on the pretext of documenting a new side effect of this widely used antibiotic. The psychiatrist, a small, thin, harried woman—her hospital name tag was upside down—with long, frizzy, red-blond hair, gave him a half-hour interview that seemed to me competent, if also dull and lacking in individuality.

Outside in the hall afterward she said, "He's *very* crazy." But she thanked me for "helping to get him plugged into the mental health network." I wasn't absolutely sure that he'd be better off.

We—the medical students—had two conferences back to back that afternoon, one on pathology with the director of the morgue, and one on transplantation with one of the great pioneers in the field. We'd been out of minor surgery for more than three hours, and when we came back we should have begun working as soon as we stepped in the door. Instead I was stopped short by a pretty, dark-haired young woman elegantly dressed in a pink-and-purple party dress, with two different pink-and-purple barrettes—one a flower, one a bow—in her long straight hair. Streaming down from her eyes were two great shiners, each drawing down to a point, the left slightly longer than the right, each a play of pinks and purples like her colorful dress. She was not in a patient bay but in the residents' and students' corner. She was sitting up in a chair, happy and animated, talking to Freddy Robertson in a way that amused him. She was plainly well.

"What happened to you?" I asked her, when she had stopped for a moment and turned toward me.

"You know that stone wall outside the hospital? I drove into it at fifty miles an hour."

"You look pretty good, considering."

"Well, it was a couple of months ago. I've still got these black eyes." She was deliberately charming.

"They're not black. Actually they look nice. Match your dress."

The E.R. manager, a tall handsome Italian, had come in a short while earlier, and I asked him whether he didn't agree. But Freddy Robertson, who had been writing at the desk, said to me quite properly, "Are you gonna socialize or are you gonna work?"

"Work," I said, regretful but ready. "What do you want me to do?"

"See the lady in that bay," he said, pointing across the room. "Hemorrhoids." The patient, an obese person who apparently bathed only rarely, gave off an odor detectable from at least half way across the room.

Later that day, Freddy and I were out in the hall when the nurses' shift changed, and we saw one of the friendlier ones leaving. "You guys are supposed to be back in minor scourge," she said. "What are you doing out here?"

"We came to flirt with you," said Freddy unconvincingly.

"Where's Bob Gross?" Gross was a senior medical resident assigned that month to work with the surgeons—a budding superdoc, humorless, arrogant, self-centered, no doubt destined for the chairmanship of a major department of medicine, someday, somewhere.

"Right over there, on the phone," said the nurse pointing. "Beat him up for me, will you?" She was not smiling.

"Sure," Freddy said. "Should I put your name on the bruises?"

Now she smiled. "Every one," she said and was out the door.

Freddy asked me to check with Gross about a patient, and so I waited the few minutes until he was off the phone. He gave me his answer with his usual contempt for students, as we walked into the "doctors' lounge," an ugly room with a few chairs and a coffee maker. I thanked him, and as I was leaving he said to a junior resident, "Wanna go get a drink?"

"That's right!" the junior reminded himself. "Happy Hour!"

This was news to me. I followed them as they tore out of the "lounge" down the hall. "Wait . . . hold it," I said, in what must have been a comical way, struggling to keep up with them. "Wait, please tell me about this Happy Hour." I didn't need a drink, but I wanted to be included in whatever was going on.

Gross, turning back for a second without breaking his stride, said, "It's for the hospital staff."

"Does that include medical students?" I asked.

He hesitated. "Sure, come on."

"I can't come right now—I have to check back at minor surge. Just tell me where it is, so in case I can get away . . ."

Gross turned back again, just momentarily. "Flagg fifteen," he said matter-of-factly, and they were gone.

There were no patients in the E.W. so I went to the elevators in the Flagg wing of the hospital, where I had not had occasion to go before. I had no intention of drinking, since I would be working all night, but I wanted to be a part of any ritual social gathering and "liver rounds," as I learned these sessions were called, were certainly that. The elevator was a long time in coming, and when I got on I was eager; just possibly, this would be the beginning of my being allowed to *join*. I went for the button. The Flagg wing had only twelve floors.

At the E.W., we were backed up with patients all night, mainly "small stuff," yet a constant stream of blood and pain, and constant pressure for us. Friday night was second only to Saturday night for sheer density of human wreckage in the current of surgical patients. Sleeplessness was beginning to get to me, and I was discouraged by Freddy's dislike.

At around two A.M. a handsome young man came in with a knife wound in his left forearm. He was accompanied by two solicitous, pretty young women. One, with long red hair, was crying. He had been assaulted in the street by two men, one brandishing a gun and the other slashing around with a knife, and had made a running jump over a parked car to escape. I noticed he wore name-brand running shoes.

It was a very deep red wound, with white ends of a cut tendon visible in its recesses. We established by simple examination that he had lost some of the function in his fingers as a result of the severing of the tendon. To my amazement, and without consulting any other resident, Freddy decided to go to work on it himself. It had been my understanding that wounds affecting hand function had to be taken care of, or at least looked at, by more senior residents. Freddy was only two months out of medical school, yet he blithely set to work on a complex problem that could leave permanent impairment.

Well, I thought, I guess rules like that are made to be broken. I did mention to him the possibility of calling Steve Ray, who I knew was in the house and who was an expert on hands. "I'm not gonna bother Steve for this," he said, and went to work, sewing together the two cut ends of the tendon first. After an hour of holding the retractor for him while he grimly and silently went about his work, I was fighting off sleepiness greater than any I could remember. When I dozed off—not for more than a second— neither Freddy nor the patient noticed. I shook myself surreptitiously awake, stunned and embarrassed, hyperalert now. Freddy's intense silence proceeded without interruption. He was never very friendly and on this occasion was no more forthcoming with conversation. But at one point he turned to me, then turned back to the surgical field, and said, "I live for this. I could do this twenty-four hours a day."

The following week my mother had an appointment with Peter Engelmann, a Galen cardiologist who was my adviser in medical school. During minor surgery at a hospital in Florida she had been diagnosed as having evidence of past heart muscle damage and had been placed on a new cardiac drug. I did not have confidence in the hospital or in the physician, who, I gathered, had made the diagnosis on the basis of one routine electrocardiogram. I convinced my mother that we should bring to bear the power of Galen medicine.

But Engelmann was more than just Galen. He was a prince of a man, reserved and formal but generous in the extreme, and he struck me as completely trustworthy. He was a clear and elegant lecturer, a helpful adviser, a capable administrator, and—it went without saying at Galen— a clinical scientist of considerable reputation. He was a Viennese Jew who had come to the United States in the 1930s, and he spoke with a charming accent that, like his bearing and formal courtesy, seemed more Austrian than Jewish.

My mother was handicapped by severe lifelong hearing loss, and so she presented more than the usual challenge to bedside manner. Engelmann was more than I had hoped for. His patience in talking with her, his courtesy, his lengthy, careful history and physical, his personal administration and reading of the electrocardiogram—all this, after weeks at Galen, nearly brought tears to my eyes. He ruled out, or at least failed to confirm, the abnormality identified by the Florida physician; indeed it was very equivocal even in the EKG tracing she had brought with her from there. We threw away her pills, which had had some unpleasant side effects, and she emerged from the mistaken category of cardiac cripple.

At the same time, I emerged for a while from the category of discouraged medical student. Engelmann represented everything I had imagined a doctor could be. Part of me wanted to grab hold of him and insist that he tell me why he and the rest of the faculty assigned us to places like the surgical emergency clinic, when what we needed was to see more of people like him. But instead I wrote him a grateful note calling attention to the contrast; and went back to the grotesque version of medicine that was practiced by Freddy Robertson and the others.

Sunday morning there was little happening, and the residents were sitting around in minor surge chatting and laughing. Freddy said to Ted Webster, who was reading the funny papers, "My dream used to be a Cadillac Eldorado." He paused and then laughed. "Now it's a Porsche. But I have to wait until I get out West. Can't you see me tooling around New Mexico in a Porsche?" This was the first time I had heard him allude to any vision of the future. He had been a prep-school English teacher before entering medicine and was one of those whose humanistic background was supposed to make him a better physician.

Another resident, a smooth Ivy League type with a neat bow tie, a man who often bragged about his investments, was leaning over the shoulder of a new Vietnamese intern, trying to explain an article about financial planning in *Money* magazine. The Vietnamese intern's bafflement was hilarious, even to him.

Meanwhile Freddy and Webster were exchanging stories about security guards they had sicced on patients. Freddy, who I must admit, was funny, did a routine comparing the guards to trained attack dogs: "Whoa! Down boy! That's a good boy!" and after they disposed of a particularly obnoxious "sleaze-ball" he rewarded them "with a slab of raw meat."

Things heated up a bit that Sunday. A young Chinese man, apparently quite crazy, came in with a self-inflicted, moderately serious arm injury. What with the inevitable hours in the waiting room, with cleaning his wound and sewing his arm, with the psych consult that even the surgeons realized was necessary, he was with us from morning until midnight—a regular fixture with intense and wary eyes, a taut thin body, and a suspicious angry voice. Another completely crazy patient came in having swallowed a handful of small sharp pieces of metal (this was soon documented by X-ray). But since no one took the time to talk with him during the hours he spent in the waiting room, he walked out without treatment—a potentially life-threatening circumstance. A third patient was a big, belligerent black man who smelled stalely of whiskey and who had been found unconscious on the street by the E.M.T.'s. He had been badly beaten and was suspected of having a skull fracture. "Don't move, John," Freddy said to him as we wheeled him to X-ray.

"I won't move," he said with a bad slur, "I move for my kids. That's the only thing I move for. I move for my children."

The stream of patients went on all day without a break. At three minutes after midnight a nineteen-year-old named Joseph Mazullo, large, slow-moving, and gentle, came in looking confused and hurt. His door sheet said, "Back injury. No medicines or allergies. Assaulted by pizza trays." It wasn't really funny. He worked in a restaurant, and his boss had assaulted him with pizza trays. But after fifteen hours or so of nonstop patients, no one found it easy to keep a straight face.

After he had been examined and been cleared and left, we finally had a lull. Ted lay on a stretcher in one of the bays, Freddy ate some old yogurt, and Bob McIntyre was reading the funny papers. We sent out for Chinese food. Freddy and Ted did one of their favorite routines, which they called the Wheel of Pain. The Wheel of Pain, like the big wheel on a T.V. game show, would be spun to determine which pain medication would be prescribed. Any sort of patient would do, but addicts and other undesirables who were faking symptoms were especially appropriate.

The imagined wheel, invisible on the wall, was spun. Freddy followed it, building up the suspense. "There it goes, there it goes, Perca-, Perca-, Perca—No, sorry, but you do get a choice: enteric-coated aspirin or Tylenol."

"Can I have Tylenol with codeine, at least?" Ted asked plaintively.

"No sir, you may not. Next. Perca-, Perca-, Perca-, where will it stop? Where will it stop? Yes! Congratulations! You get Percocet! Next! You say you have a terrible pain in your back? Headaches too? Well, let's see what we can do about this! Spin the Wheel of Pain, where it stops nobody— Perca-, Perca-, Perca—No! Sorry sir! You get Pez! That's right, Pez! What a shame, folks! Better luck next time! But you do get your choice of flavors and the handy little dispenser! Enjoy it sir! Next!"

Ted, still on the stretcher, laughed himself literally blue in the face.

A couple of days later at morning conference Dr. Carter took the residents to task for the waits in minor surgery that Sunday. "A five-hour backup in minor surge is not acceptable," he said. Freddy explained that there were some complicated lacs to sew that day—like the Chinese boy's self-inflicted tendon injury.

Carter said, "Those go to plastics. I know that takes away some of your fun, but you're not here to have fun." I wondered what he would have made of the much more complicated tendon surgery Freddy had done a few days earlier. I also knew that five-hour waits were not at all unusual. But I was practicing K.M.S.

That night around two A.M. a beautiful, dark-haired young woman was brought in, her clothes—silk blouse, short shorts, and stockings—soaked with blood. She was conscious, and her boyfriend was with her. Almost as soon as she arrived Freddy had to run off to another case, leaving me to take care of her. She had a six-inch gash on her face, so the first thing I did was to stop it from bleeding. The story was that she had drunk too much at a party, gone to sleep on a couch, and rolled off it in her sleep onto some drinking glasses on the floor. These had broken, cutting her. Whether this unlikely story was true did not seem relevant. I got her boyfriend to help me take off her bloody clothing, and we wiped all the blood off of her, establishing that there was only the one wound.

I cleaned it carefully and was about to call Steve Ray, who was on plastics that month, when Freddy walked in. I told him the story. "Don't wake up Steve for this," he said. "We'll do it."

"Freddy," I said privately, "that's a six-inch gash on the face of a woman who obviously has a lot vested in her looks. It goes from her hairline to her chin, and it passes close to the eyelid. You don't really want to try that yourself."

"You bet I do," he said. "Let's get going."

K.M.S., I reminded myself, and stayed with him—or rather, with her—for three hours while he sewed. I watched the lovely face come slowly back together again—it would be weeks before it was clear how well he had done—and hoped for the best.

On my next shift, in the evening, I looked after a rather grand, upper-class woman in her nineties, who had sustained some leg abrasions after walking into a garbage can. She was a delightful woman, in almost perfect health, courageous and pleasant in the face of pain—a perfect example of the best Yankee tradition—stoical, good-humored, and exquisitely polite as I dressed her leg.

I was shaking my head admiringly as she walked out when a nurse we all knew well walked in, in obvious distress. Her eyes were red and moist, and three residents turned from their patients to converge on her.

"Princess Grace—" she stammered, a sob welling up in her throat. "She's dead! Cerebral hemorrhage . . . fifty-three years old!" She sobbed again.

Ted was mildly sympathetic. "Oh gee, that's really too bad."

Freddy was less concerned than curious. "How'd she get a cerebral hemorrhage?"

The nurse began to explain, but was too moved to continue. She handed Ted a newspaper article describing the accident.

Freddy began his inevitable ribbing. "Did you announce that minor surge is closed to commemorate Princess Grace's demise?"

Ted was reading the article. "She was lucky to live as long as she did," he said, without looking up. "The car fell a hundred twenty feet into a ravine. Some farmer heard a crash and came out and found a car upside down in his garden overlooking the Mediterranean. In the car the two princesses were trapped. The younger was saved first. Boy, this is really dramatic."

"Come on," said the nurse, obviously hurt. "I really feel bad." She turned and walked out.

"Yeah," said Freddy with a look of mock concern. "I really liked some of her movies. Some of 'em were really great."

"I don't get it," I said. "That nurse watches people box around here every night. She never bats an eyelash. Then she reads a newspaper story about Princess Grace and she's crying."

"Sure," said Ted without missing a beat. "It's the difference between a legend and a nobody."

The stream of nobodies continued without abatement. A man had some-how been run over by a truck while eating breakfast and drinking a beer. Another had been shot in the side by a .38 caliber bullet that improbably penetrated almost every abdominal organ. Another had sustained a gar-roting injury—these were common in rural areas where farmers strung wires between trees so that motorbike or snowmobile riders would en-counter them at neck level. Another had come in with a routine diaphrag-matic hernia. "Go upstairs and enjoy it," Dr. Carter had said. "It's easy to fix, and it's fun."

An engineer—tall, fair, handsome, broad-shouldered, with wire-rimmed glasses, confidently friendly—came in with a scrotal lump. Under his arm was a worn and extensively underlined book about cancer. He was convinced that he had the dread disease, though this was not likely, and he was terrified. And a sweet, intelligent old man came in with a broken neck. He had been picking apples and pruning his orchard when he fell out of a tree. He was paralyzed from the shoulders down. He kept trying to reconstruct the event that, he knew, had destroyed his retirement and the rest of his life, the part he had waited fifty years to enjoy.

On my last night in the E.W. there was no major trauma, but there was news of trauma that touched me. The novelist, teacher, and critic John Gardner had been killed riding his motorcycle to work. He had once read a story I sent him, responded kindly although I was unknown to him, and eventually published it in his magazine. I had never met him, but I was in his debt. Furthermore, I loved his writing, which should have gone on another twenty or thirty years. The accident was so typical of the ones whose victims we were seeing every night that I could picture all too vividly just what had happened. I kept seeing him roll into the E.W. *Dead on arrival,* the news report had said. I hoped there'd been no attempt to resuscitate him.

I went sadly through the motions of my work that last night. There was a man with a cut in the webbing between his fingers. I wanted to clean it and give him a Band-Aid, but Freddy insisted I put in a stitch. That meant a complex local anesthetization. I saw no reason for the stitch, but it was not up to me. I suspected Freddy of assigning it to me purely for practice. The man was by far the most irritating patient I had had. He virtually jumped off the stretcher at every mere cleaning gesture, and then I had to inject lidocaine in several places and put in the superfluous stitch. It was depressing, and I was glad when it was over.

After this, at two A.M., there was enough of a lull so that I could find some peace. I went to the chapel, which always provided a wonderful respite —a cave of emotional safety that I had come to many times. It was quiet, dark, pleasant, and empty, with a pretty pane of stained glass and the glow of both soft orange electric lights and candles. I sat for a long time, very grateful that the beeper did not go off. I took out a card I had bought earlier that day, a painting of a flight of geese low over a pond, all in soft dark blues and grays, and composed a little note to Gardner's widow. In those few peaceful minutes I brooded on the epidemic of trauma, and my sense of personal loss echoed back through my mind over the dizzying array of patients I had helped to take care of.

4

ANESTHESIOLOGY

The Technicians of Sleep

After the hectic three weeks of the busiest surgical emergency room around, I looked forward to the rest promised by a week of anesthesiology. This would have a normal schedule, starting at the reasonable hour of seven-thirty and ending at a remarkable three or four in the afternoon. I would have time to read and think, perhaps to digest some of my recent experiences.

At the same time I would have a chance to perform several procedures —especially blood-drawing, the starting of intravenous lines, and the much more challenging placement of an airway—to do so often and under sufficient supervision so that I would end by feeling confident of my ability to perform them. I would get to see a week's worth of surgery under quite benign nonemergency conditions, and from the other side of the sterile drape—that is, from the anesthesiologist's viewpoint, a relatively detached and philosophical perspective.

I would also, I knew, be treated to a dramatic personality contrast. If surgeons were hard-nosed, hard-driving, hail-fellow-well-met, locker-room types with a proud cult of toughness, anesthesiologists were intellectual and witty observers with an equally proud cult of detachment. It is they who are responsible for the patient's life from one moment to the next, and not the surgeon. The surgeon is by their lights only a mechanic. The gravest and most consistent risk of most surgery has to do with anesthesia, not with cutting and sewing, and the surgeons cannot make a move without their permission. Anesthesiologists are the chemists of human consciousness, the technological arbiters of pain, constantly walking the

74

line between life and death, and leading their patients along it. Under their watchful eyes, mists of oblivion course through the patient's blood and brain, and with one false move those same mists may obscure the mind forever.

The magic with which they control the mists keeps these physicians on the frontiers of physics and chemistry, as well as at the forefront of the neuroscience of consciousness and pain. Both these phenomena are far from understood, and anesthesiologists help to unravel them. General anesthetics, known since the introduction of ether in the 1840s and still central in all major surgery, have a thoroughly baffling mode of action. They have no common chemical structure or effect that can explain their alterations of pain and consciousness. They seem to act by dissolving mysteriously in the membrane of the nerve cells—more a physical than a chemical phenomenon. Consciousness, pain, the nature of cell membranes—these are heady subjects, whether one does research on them or uses them in clinical practice.

Yet anesthesiology was one of the few fields of medicine in which I never imagined myself a practitioner. Despite their view of things, anesthesiologists seemed to me to be subordinated to surgeons, who directed the central drama of the operating theater. It struck me that it must take exceptional strength of character not to *feel* subordinated in that situation, yet this was what most anesthesiologists achieved. (Some, including many women and foreigners not completely proficient in English, seemed to accept the surgeons' view of them as subordinate—little different, in fact, from the nurses and technicians who filled in for them on the easier cases.) Others, mainly ambitious men, were as haughty with the surgeons as the surgeons were with them. They viewed themselves as directors of the operating theater, with the surgeons as mere actors, requiring their subtler science to plan and guide the performance. Their detached sense of superiority was marvelous.

It was one of the more ambitious and aggressive exemplars of this latter category to whom I was assigned for the week. We were encouraged to fear him even by the surgical residents, many of whom prided themselves on their ability to terrorize medical students; one of the nicer ones, however, confided that Dr. Gill's bark was worse than his bite.

On Monday at seven Dr. Jonathan Gill met us in the anesthesia prep room, where a couple of patients had already been wheeled in anticipation of scheduled surgery. He was a short, energetic, bright-eyed, dark-haired man with heavy streaks of eyebrows, and he managed to look dapper even in surgical blues. He looked us over contemptuously and said,

"I don't suppose you know how to start I.V.'s." We looked at each other and advanced the claim that we did. "Well, you might as well get moving," he said. "When the patients are all prepped, find yourself an anesthesiologist and sit in on some surgery. We'll meet toward the end of the afternoon and discuss your assignments." He turned and began to strut away. Then he stopped and turned back. "If you have trouble, I'll be around."

As always in these situations, I grabbed a nurse and begged for help. She was busy but kind, showing us where to find the plastic bottles of I.V. fluid and where the I.V. starter sets and needles were kept. I had done this often enough in the E.W. to believe I knew how to do it. I approached the nearest patient—a curly-haired woman in her late fifties heading for simple thyroid surgery—loaded with the above supplies, plus blood collecting tubes, tape, alcohol wipes, iodine, and Band-Aids. Greeting her with my most practiced air of false confidence, I went to work. This one, and the two others I had time to start in the next half-hour or so, all went smoothly. Either this was beginner's luck or I now knew how to start an I.V., an essential medical-student skill. It was a small procedure, but not a trivial one. Through the bore of the needle would flow many of the anesthetics needed to make surgery possible; life-sustaining fluids to maintain water and electrolyte balance; antibiotics to control or ward off infection; and blood products, should an emergency arise that made them necessary. In some situations a patent I.V. line could make the difference between life and death. When there were no more patients, Terry and I looked at each other and went searching for anesthesia docs. I hooked up with Dr. Ramirez, whose English was poor but who obviously knew what he was doing. He first set up a patient who was having cataract surgery—a seventy-year-old man with mild coronary artery disease and no other potential complications. He anesthetized the man with a rubber mask, allowing me to do the "bagging"—pumping both anesthetic and life-maintaining oxygen by hand with a rubber bag attached to the mask. Although surrounded by skilled people who could take over if I failed, I felt a heavy weight of responsibility.

"You did intubation?" Dr. Ramirez asked. I realized he was questioning me about past experience and shook my head. "You seen it?"

"A few times up close."

"Today you watch," he said. It was more like an invitation than an order. "First, fill the chest." He pointed to the ambu bag in my hands. I squeezed it more vigorously than I had. "More," he said. When I had pumped to his satisfaction, he nodded, and took the mask off the patient's face. The patient was unconscious and in a profound and deliberate respiratory depression, but the natural compliance of the chest began to produce an exhalation. Dr. Ramirez took hold of the man's chin, stretched his throat, and opened his mouth in a smooth, quick motion using both hands. He reached out to a tray he had set up nearby, took a shiny metal intubation device, and unfolded it, which automatically lit a tiny lamp on the tip. He brought the lamp up to the man's mouth and said, "Look."

I looked into the man's mouth as he leaned out of my way. I had the thought that this man was exhaling the last breath he would have until the endotracheal tube was placed, and the placement was being delayed for my education. It was only a few seconds, though, and I knew that I ought not waste them while considering the ethical issues involved. I stared into the dark, pinkish cave of the man's inverted mouth, where his tongue was being pulled toward the ceiling by the pressure of the metal device in Dr. Ramirez's hand.

"You see the inverted V?" he asked me, obviously not the least bit tense about the time.

In the depth of the cavity, two straight pink membranes shone in the shape of an inverted V, exactly as we had learned in lectures and text-books. These were the vocal cords, the hallmark and frame of the vestibule of the airway. Behind them, seen within and around the V, was the black-ness of the trachea, that great clear tunnel to the lungs.

"Yes," I blurted out, only a second after the question. "Vocal cords. Beautiful." I could almost see them vibrate as the mixture of oxygen and anesthetic gas leaked past them out of the man's chest.

But Dr. Ramirez was already moving. "Watch them closely," he said. He now had in his right hand a piece of thick blue plastic tubing, pointed at one end and with a molded mouthpiece at the other. In his left hand he still held the metal tool, pressing the tongue out of the way and lighting up the passageway.

I kept my eyes on the shiny pink of the vocal cords, as the pointed end of the blue endotracheal tube slid past the teeth and tongue and soft palate and right into the triangle framed by the inverted V. At almost the same time, Dr. Ramirez had taken the ambu bag, now detached from the mask, and fixed it to the other end of the tube. He squeezed, and the man's chest rose again. My relief was physical.

I bagged again briefly while he set up the automatic respirator. The surgical nurses were gloving and gowning the surgeons, one of whom began preparing the patient's left eye for cataract removal. Meanwhile Dr. Ramirez took the patient's pulse and blood pressure, turned down the oxygen slightly, and injected a muscle relaxant intravenously. As I leaned over him he recorded notes in a tiny hand on everything he had done. His notes included the exact dosage and time to the nearest minute of every medication, as well as the route of administration, the stage of surgery or preparation for surgery, and the patient's response. The anesthesia sheet provided for a continuous record of vital signs, including respiration, heart rate, blood pressure, and temperature. This was the full medical and legal record, intensely scrutinized in court if the case should have an untoward outcome followed by legal challenge. Dr. Ramirez managed to keep it faithfully, while attending to the more immediate purposes of monitoring the patient and maintaining precisely the right level and combination of anesthetics.

As the patient stabilized, Dr. Ramirez began telling me about the functioning of the various lines and instruments under his scrutiny. Soon after that a nurse-anesthetist poked his head in through the door of the O.R. Dr. Ramirez looked back at him and nodded. He stood up and beckoned me away, and the nurse took over the controls, beginning his shift with the routine of taking vital signs, checking the instruments, and logging in with his update of the assessment.

"Routine?" he asked, as Dr. Ramirez hit the door.

"Completely. Mild angina." With a few further remarks about the anesthetic, he was gone.

I followed him into a second O.R. where events were neither routine nor pleasant, although there was certainly no emergency. Dr. Ramirez approached the situation with the same efficient aplomb. The patient was a young man with a malignant tumor of the upper jaw who was having drastic, devastating surgery on his face. As we walked in, about half of his upper face was being removed from the surgical field and placed on a table high above him, where it was almost at eye level for all of us standing around it. An experienced nurse looked pale and had her mouth and eyes wide open.

I was taken completely by surprise, having had no idea what the case was about until I walked through the door and confronted the grisly specimen as it was being deposited on the table. I felt faint for just a moment and looked slowly toward the field. The young man's head was mostly a bloody cavity, the remainder being partly covered by a drape, and it was impossible to think of it as a face. All I could think of was what a high price he was paying to get a chance at staying alive. Dr. Ramirez, talking to me, noticed that I was not paying attention to what he was doing, and I snapped out of it. He adjusted the instruments, took vital signs, recorded his findings, and, after ten or fifteen minutes, turned the situation back over to the nurse-anesthetist who had been there when we arrived.

We proceeded to a third O.R., where the woman whose I.V. I had started a few hours earlier was having her thyroid gland removed. The I.V. was still running, with the time in my handwriting and my initials scribbled on the tape holding the adapter to her arm. Dr. Ramirez used it to run some saline into her a little faster.

We proceeded this way through the lunch hour, going from O.R. to O.R., spending anywhere from fifteen to forty-five minutes in each one, without a break. Mainly we circulated among the three cases we had started with, and Dr. Ramirez did his best to keep me aware of the status of each patient, but with the complexities of the anesthetic combinations and his problems with English it was not easy to follow.

I was looking forward to watching the patients brought out of anesthesia, but shortly after two o'clock Dr. Gill stepped in and gestured me out of the O.R. Terry, who was already with him, and I followed him out of the surgical suite, changed, and met him at his office. He began asking brutal-sounding questions, then after a little suspense provided his own crisp, informative answers. He was fundamentally friendly and had a delightfully ironic sense of humor. I suspected that I might end up liking him. But at the moment the man with the torn face was very much on my mind.

Dr. Gill discharged us at about three-thirty, but not before letting us know that anesthesia would not be so relaxing as we had hoped. Each day we would be sent home with an assignment, and we had to know the material cold by the next morning. For the last day of the rotation, we would be expected to have memorized the indications, dosages, and routes of administration of thirty common emergency-room drugs. He pointed at the bright red emergency medicine cart that was by now familiar to me. "You shouldn't be hanging around emergency rooms and O.R.'s and even hospital corridors without knowing how to use the drugs that are in that cart." This seemed reasonable, but the thought of memorizing it all by Friday was another matter.

He knew this, and knew we needed to get started immediately. At the same time he gave us our assignment for the following day, which was to learn the pharmacology, indications, adverse effects, half-life, and precautions of one narcotic and one muscle relaxant. I drew morphine and Valium.

I had my work cut out for me. But on the way home I managed to sit by the river for a while, marveling at the fact that I was free before the end of the afternoon. The sun was shining brightly, the river was blue-gray and calm, and the horrors and indignities—as well as the heroic acts—of the Galen Memorial Hospital seemed for the moment very far away.

I arrived the next day almost as tired as I had been on surgery. After the children had gone to sleep—later and later, it seemed—I had taken out the pharmacology and emergency medicine books, and made index cards corresponding to thirty or so common emergency drugs. Fortunately the information I needed was readily available. I mastered the assignment on morphine and Valium, and planned to study the thirty cards throughout the week during any lulls.

It turned out that my success in starting I.V.'s the day before had been beginner's luck. Today the patients were not very pleasant, and their veins were positively uncooperative. I discovered several new ways to do it wrong. Some veins were tough and mobile and almost impossible to "nail." Some were frail and collapsed easily. Some were so thin that you put the needle through them and out the other side before you knew you were in the vein at all. And some had valves in odd places that the needle got hung up on, refusing to flow.

I was liberated from this frustrating assembly line by Dr. Ramirez, who asked me if I wanted to do an intubation. I jumped at the chance. Maybe I would have better luck with that procedure. He took me into an O.R. where a young woman, a slim pretty brunette, was awaiting surgery. She had a condition known as melanocytic hyperplasia, resulting in small pigmented lesions—brown spots—on many parts of her body. The surgery would remove them, for cosmetic effect as well as for the prevention of malignant transformation. She was extremely nervous. Fortunately hers was the one I.V. I had started completely smoothly that morning. She recognized me and we smiled at each other.

The surgeon, Dr. Ruskin, a tall, thin, graying man with a bright and cheerful air, tightened his gloves methodically with interlocking fingers while Dr. Ramirez placed the mask over Cindy's frightened face. He spoke to her with formulaic phrases but in soothing tones, and let the anesthetic pass into her lungs. Soon she was sleeping calmly, and Dr. Ramirez beckoned me over. As I sidled up next to him, he pulled the intubation tray into position where I could reach it easily. Dr. Ruskin, who was watching us, sized up the situation.

"I want you to do the intubation," he said to Dr. Ramirez. "This is a private patient. Service patients get service intubations, private patients get private intubations." He spoke matter-of-factly, even cheerfully, but decisively. There was no question of chain of authority here. All physicians concerned with a case had to be in agreement before a medical student could get involved. It was not up for any further discussion.

As for me, I was not thinking about the disappointment—it was only Tuesday, I would get to do others—but about the concept so clearly articulated by Dr. Ruskin. During my clinical experience, I would see evidence daily belying the frequent pronouncements about all patients getting the same treatment. But rarely would I hear the reality of hospital discrimination so clearly articulated by a senior physician. I admired Dr. Ruskin's frankness.

Dr. Ramirez monitored the patient's vital signs and adjusted the flow of gases. He suggested that I try to find another case where something more interesting might be happening. Dr. Ruskin was slowly excising the third pigmented lesion, and beginning to sew with what seemed to me the exceptional care of the good plastic surgeon. I went to look for something more interesting to do.

I bumped into Dr. Gill in the hallway, and he pulled me into an O.R. where they were doing not surgery but a special examination under general anesthesia. It was the sad case of a baby girl with paralyzed vocal cords, undergoing laryngoscopy for detailed visualization of the cords. Because she was so young there was no prospect of getting her to sit still for the procedure. Therefore she had to be exposed to the risks of general anesthesia even though it was not an operative procedure. I was not able to get near the baby's head, but a color television near the ceiling in a corner projected the field that the examining physicians were studying. It showed a child's version of the larynx I had seen so clearly during two intubations: pinkish cords—these with some red bumps on them—coming together to form an inverted V. They were pronounced by one of the examiners to be improving.

After this brief procedure I returned to Dr. Ruskin. The two nurses with him were doing a facial version of foot-tapping while he sewed one of the last few lesions. The anesthesia station had been taken over by a technician I didn't know, so I stood back and watched the surgery.

Dr. Ruskin was bragging pleasantly to no one in particular. "Do you realize that I chopped a whole cord of wood myself this weekend? Outside in the cool country air, bare from the waist up, swinging the double-bladed ax over and over again? And I wish I could show you my hands. I didn't even get blisters." He went on in this boyish vein, which I found somehow charming, while the two nurses threw deeply sardonic looks at each other.

Finally he finished sewing the last lesion site, pulled off his gloves and gown, and strode out of the O.R. The nurses burst forth with a series of negative comments, some of which, interestingly, concerned the slowness of the surgery. The woman had been under general anesthesia for two and a half hours. According to them another surgeon could have done the same work in fifteen minutes. This didn't seem likely to me, not if the cosmetic result were to be truly excellent, but if true, it was a devastating criticism of Dr. Ruskin, who would be exposing a patient to a grave and unnecessary extension of the anesthesia risk.

The technician and I turned the patient on her side and detached her from the respirator. I held *my* breath until she began breathing, then coughing, a healthy reaction to coming out of anesthesia. We wheeled her out of the O.R. and down the hall to the recovery room. I stayed with her until she came out of her deep sleep, coughing and teary-eyed, looked at me, became a bit calmer, and then closed her eyes again.

The baby girl who had had the laryngoscopy was in the recovery room. She was awake and staring around the room with terrified dark eyes. Slowly, with a predictable rhythm I knew well from home, her mouth formed a widening grimace, she took a deep breath, and she let loose with —nothing. *Of course, you idiot,* I said to myself after a long moment, *her vocal cords are paralyzed.* Deeply moved by this utterly soundless crying, I walked over to her stretcher and poked around until I found the pacifier I knew had to be there. I put it in her mouth, and after a few seconds her face softened as she began to suck. My ears had been filled with the silent wailing, and now I felt greatly relieved.

A tap on my shoulder brought me around to face Dr. Gill, whose crooked finger announced the day's moment of truth. Under the grilling in his office, I promptly listed nine of the ten actions of morphine I was supposed to have learned, and the tenth came to me after some stumbling. The next day's assignment was to draw a graph of intracranial pressure— the pressure inside the brain—according to changes in oxygen pressure, carbon dioxide pressure, and blood pressure in the systemic circulation. After some rather humorous pontificating by Dr. Gill, I was on my way home.

On the bus going home I found myself staring at people's veins. I assessed at least half the passengers with my I.V. needle in mind. Here was a young man with enormous, sturdy, stable veins, there an old woman with prominent veins that looked inviting but could be treacherous. For a long time I stared at the graceful blue veins on a pair of arms, wishing I could get my own hands on them. Finally I looked up and realized that the hands belonged to a beautiful woman whom I had completely failed to notice—except for her veins.

I could not get I.V.'s off my mind. I remembered a story told me by a man who had had an I.V. placed while he was in the hospital for evaluation of a colon problem. After the placement, it felt wrong. "Is it supposed to hurt?" he had asked the nurse.

"Well, every needle hurts a little," she had said, in a tone appropriate for an eight-year-old.

"No, I mean a lot."

"There, there. Just be patient a little while. It'll be O.K.," and she was gone. The pain became excruciating. The patient called a second nurse over to ask about it. She was more brusque and equally condescending. Finally the skin near the I.V. entry site began to become red and swollen, and the pain had reached the point where tearing the line out was no longer a conscious decision. Shortly thereafter the patient had his daily visit from his physician, who simply looked from the dangling apparatus to the arm, felt the swelling, and said that the I.V. had been improperly placed. His apology, the man said, mitigated the pain, but not the humiliation of having been ignored and condescended to. It was a story that pointed up impressively the truth that the patient is on the lowest rung of the hospital ladder of authority, with opinions that must be managed rather than considered. I did not want to be the cause of such pain.

The next morning, exhausted again—data for the graph of intracranial pressure proved to be more difficult to find than I had guessed—I was starting my first I.V. when an anesthesiologist I had not seen before volunteered to help me. He was in his mid-fifties, slightly plump, and had a Slavic-sounding name. His English was worse than Dr. Ramirez's, but he made it clear to me that he thought the way I had been taught to start I.V.'s—puncturing skin and vein with an 18-gauge needle—was a form of torture.

He demonstrated his method, which required the injection of a tiny bleb of lidocaine, a local anesthetic, next to the vein, with a very small needle. The larger I.V. needle was then introduced through the small anesthetized patch of skin over the vein. "It's more humane," he said, simply but emphatically.

I was an easy mark for that consideration, and I immediately resolved to use his method exclusively. I remembered an episode of "Ben Casey" in which a foreign physician (also with a Slavic accent) eliminates a patient's awful postoperative pain by placing a rolled-up towel under her neck. This was supposed to speak volumes about the hidden knowledge of physicians from foreign lands, more attuned to their patients' welfare and bearing centuries of folk knowledge worth more than its weight in morphine.

But when I began trying to use this new method, I suffered a further technical setback. The bleb of lidocaine presented a new obstacle to accurate puncture of the vein. The 18-gauge needle may have hurt less, but the whole procedure would have to be done somewhere else if the vein were missed. Still, I managed to start some lines by the new method, and the word "humane" echoed in my mind.

Then I had the general good luck to bump into Nina Hamadeh, a Lebanese physician whom I had once treated for a minor head injury in the Emergency Room. When she remembered who I was, she became my guardian angel. She was lighthearted, competent, friendly, and completely calm.

About the East European humane method of starting I.V.'s, she said with a wave of her hand, "Oh, well. You know, that way you just stick the patient twice. And I find the lidocaine makes it hard to get into the vein. So what's so humane about that? You should do what you feel comfortable with. Pick a method, practice it, and master it, whichever it is. After that you don't have to worry."

Within minutes of our meeting she took me into an O.R. and gave me my first intubation, making it seem like the easiest thing in the world. "Just make sure you visualize the cords. If you can see them clearly, you really can't miss." I pulled back the chin of the fiftyish, plump lady whom she had just put under, and pulled her tongue up and away with the intubation device. The cords rose up in the cavity like a monumental archway.

"Do you see the cords?" asked Dr. Hamadeh calmly.

"Yes!" I said, a bit too emphatically. She nodded and extended the tube toward me.

The clock was ticking on the oxygen in the patient's lungs. I took the blue tube in my hand, made a wish, and aimed for the upside-down V. The tube plunged in without a hitch, until the mouthpiece was at the patient's lips.

"Is it in?" I asked.

"It can't be anywhere else" was the serene answer, and we hooked the tube to the oxygen and secured it in place. But we listened to the chest just to be sure.

In this procedure I went from strength to strength, mostly under the eye and hand of Dr. Hamadeh. For the rest of the week I made an effort to follow her like a shadow. She was always friendly to me, always helpful, and—whatever I did—full of praise. She simply knew how to manage my ignorance into competence. By the end of the first day I had done three intubations, each as successful as the first. She also became the first anesthesiologist who seriously told me what was going on in the O.R. She showed me in detail what was written on the charts and even had me keep some of the records myself—always by far the best way to learn.

By mid-afternoon I felt so good that I was immune to Dr. Gill's barbs and amusingly humiliating interrogation. I still did not understand the multiple determinants of intracranial pressure, and I took up the challenge of the latest assignment with even less enthusiasm. It was to write the package insert (the information for physicians) for "the ideal inhalation anesthetic," one that had not yet been invented. I was tiring of Dr. Gill's games, and I knew that I would have to spend a lot of time with my flash cards memorizing the data on those thirty emergency room drugs. To top it off, that afternoon was the weekly meeting of the students with the course head. Contrary to expectations about the "piece of cake" anesthesia rotation, I had seen very little of my daughter and infant son.

Some time after midnight, having read two or three times through my index cards on the thirty emergency drugs, I was getting punch-drunk, and decided I had to liven things up a bit. I named my "ideal inhalation anesthetic" Jonathane, after Dr. Gill, whom I identified as the somewhat wacky inventor. I placed him at the "Gill Memorial Hospital," a play on the name of Galen, which was often called "Gale Memorial" or even "Gale Mem." I proceeded to give the drug its essential characteristics, an exercise that proved more enlightening than I had thought, since the continuing elusiveness of an ideal gas anesthetic was and is both scientifically and historically intriguing. Mine was volatile, effective at low doses, rapidly acting and rapidly decaying in action, safe at high doses, noncontaminating to the atmosphere of the O.R., and nonflammable. According to my account, however, the eccentric inventor had been too optimistic about this last feature. He had produced an explosion destroying a wing of the hospital and blowing himself into the next county. From my notes scrawled on a yellow pad I typed up the document.

Actually, the piece did a good job of fulfilling the assignment, and even the explosion alluded to ether, introduced in the 1840s, which *is* the ideal inhalation anesthetic except for the fact that it is explosively flammable. The Bovie, the electric tool used in every O.R. for cauterizing surgical wounds, could ignite any flammable gas. The challenge to research was to invent an equally good anesthetic gas that was nonflammable. In a sense,

Dr. Gill had reinvented ether in my account. I must say I loved it. If he did not think it was funny, so be it. It was worth the risk.

On Thursday, I pretty much stuck with the old, "inhumane" method for the I.V.'s, and did moderately well, although for one lady who announced her terror even as I approached, I decided to use lidocaine. One other patient, Annie DiMasio, was extremely nervous but tolerated the placement well. She was twenty-seven, very thin, and pleasant. I tried to talk with all the patients I dealt with as a matter of course, and although she was nervous she was easy to talk to. After some trivial conversation, I asked her what surgery she was in for.

"Augmentation mammoplasty," she said diffidently. I had not heard this particular surgical term before, but it was not difficult to figure out that what it meant was to give someone bigger breasts. I tried to be nonjudgmental as well as nonsmiling and to keep my eyes more or less off her chest.

"My doctor says I can go home today after the operation. That's right, isn't it?"

Questions like this always put me in a spot. I did not want to appear discouraging or even ignorant, but above all I had to avoid raising patients' expectations in situations where they might not be fulfilled. "If he said so, I'm sure it's true," I said. "As long as everything goes well."

Either Annie sensed my private judgment or she simply wanted to talk, to justify the operation to herself as she headed for the O.R. "My husband likes big-breasted women. It wasn't his idea that I do this, don't think that. It was mine. But he's always looking at them, you know? I'd like him to look at me like that. Dr. Ruskin says I shouldn't think it's gonna change my life. I don't, I guess. But I still want to do it."

As she looked into my eyes for a reaction, I felt myself softening. Her logic had something to recommend it, but the moisture in her pretty brown eyes spoke volumes. "I really have nothing," she said, and almost laughed. This seemed more or less like an invitation to look at her bony, boyish chest, which was easy to assess under the johnny. I smiled and pressed her hand. "I'm sure it'll work out really well," I said, pretty much believing it.

Dr. Ruskin's involvement seemed somehow logical. That charmingly egotistical braggart was going to improve on nature's handiwork and sculpt this young woman's existence into a new shape. There could hardly be a more vivid Pygmalion story. I resolved to try to see at least some of the procedure.

Thanks to Dr. Hamadeh, I now had the confidence to be more aggressive about intubations, and I soon had two more to my credit, one supervised by her. I was out in the hall looking for another opportunity when Dr. Ruskin swaggered by looking as if he were on his way to a dance. Since he was smiling, I grabbed the chance to ask him if I could watch.

"Watch, yes, scrub, no. And I want you to stand far back from the table. I do this as a super-sterile procedure."

In the O.R. I folded my arms and stood way back. This was a private patient if there ever was one. Ruskin's meticulousness was even more impressive here than it had been at yesterday's surgery on the pigmented lesions. Annie was now asleep, and he exposed her chest. He insisted on prepping the field entirely himself. He did not want even the most skilled nurse anywhere near it.

"There are two keys to this procedure," he said, clearly glad to have me for an audience. "Complete hemostasis, which I'll show you later. And complete asepsis." He painted her chest and belly at least three times with iodine. "It's a simple procedure, just a matter of introducing the silastic implant and sewing it in. The failures all result from infection and bleeding. All you need is a little collection of pus or a clot next to the implant, and you have a grotesque cosmetic result instead of the beautiful one you might have had. So I work slowly, obsessively, and alone."

The procedure took four hours. After the meticulous prepping, a slit was made at the lower margin of each breast for introduction of the implants, and a space cleared in the breast by teasing the subcutaneous tissue away from the chest wall. However, nearly two hours elapsed before the implants were brought forward, time spent entirely in the attainment of hemostasis—the stoppage of all bleeding, all oozing of blood, from every vessel that had been exposed in the mammary region, however small. Sponge in one hand, the Bovie in the other, Dr. Ruskin wiped and cauterized a seemingly endless stream of tiny vessels. The circulating surgical nurse and the nurse-anesthetist grew impatient. The circulator said, "Does this procedure usually take this long?"

Dr. Ruskin did not change his tone of voice or stop patiently cauterizing vessels. "Some people do it as an outpatient procedure, in an hour or so. Then when the patient comes back a few weeks later with hard lumps in her breasts or asymmetrical prostheses, they do it again. Some of them keep doing it until the patient gives up on ever having a really good result."

The nurse-anesthetist, a large but ordinarily deferential man, said, "There was some talk about her being discharged today."

This remark stopped Ruskin cold. He looked over the drape at the nurse-anesthetist. He spoke slowly. "She *is* being discharged today. That's what I promised her, and that's what I'm going to do." After this hiatus he returned to cauterizing.

The nurse-anesthetist changed his tone of voice to that of a respectful subordinate. "I thought it was pretty unusual for someone to be discharged after being under for this long."

"It is unusual," said Dr. Ruskin without changing his pace. "But I've done it before, and I'll do it this time. There's nothing wrong with it."

I decided that this might be one of those situations where I could use my protected status as a naive medical student to ease the tension. "How come she insisted on going home today?" I asked.

"She wanted to think of it as a minor procedure. She had friends who had it done as outpatients, in and out in an afternoon. So it was important for her not to have to stay overnight in the hospital."

I couldn't decide whether he was being exceptionally sensitive to the patient's rights and needs, or merely taking an unacceptable risk to make sure he didn't lose her to one of his assembly-line competitors. The nurse-anesthetist gave me a look behind his back that suggested skepticism about the safety of the decision as well as about the surgeon's motives.

Some, if not most, of the gravest risks of many operations arose from the use of general anesthesia. There are twelve thousand anesthesia-related deaths a year in the United States. That is one reason why anesthesiology has become a completely independent medical specialty, and why many surgical procedures are considered improper except in hospital settings where fully trained anesthesiologists are constantly on call. It is also the main reason that anesthesiology was the only specialty that prohibits residents from being on call for more than twenty-four consecutive hours. Sleeplessness may seem ominous in other specialties, but evidently a slip of the knife is not deemed so dangerous as a slip of the anesthetic dial.

Prolonging general anesthesia to do more meticulous surgery is one thing—although I still wondered whether Dr. Ruskin was simply slow. But sending a patient home after four hours of general anesthesia, when the anesthesia people think monitoring is necessary—that seemed to be a different category of judgment.

My attention was distracted from these abstract matters by Dr. Ruskin stepping away from the table. He asked the circulator to open the packages containing the breast prostheses. Using careful sterile technique, having gloved up but without touching the implants themselves, she broke the packages open and let the implants slide gently onto a sterile tray. They were soft globes of clear viscous liquid enclosed in a clear, seamless, rubbery plastic sheath. The light coming through them made them seem quite pretty, like tabletop modern sculpture done in plastic.

"Have you got one that's not sterile, that I could touch?" I asked rather timidly. It seemed important to me to have an idea of the consistency, since that would be a major determinant of the reactions not only of anyone who might be touching the breasts but of the patient.

"No, but if you come to my office I have one there I can show you."

He looked the prostheses over on the tray, and without picking them up, returned to the patient. Very slowly, he removed the lengths of gauze with which he had packed the right breast, and checked it again for the slightest sign of bleeding. Using the Bovie, he cauterized a few places again. Then he took one of the implants and set it very gently into the pocket he had prepared. After checking again around the prosthesis, he began suturing.

"Looks pretty good," he said cheerfully.

"It looks great," I said. I was really amazed. I had been wondering all along how the patient's husband, having lived with her for years in her old form, could possibly be fooled, when the artificiality of the thing would be so obvious. But here I was, watching the whole procedure, and as soon as the surgeon put the prosthesis in, her breast was prettier.

Dr. Ruskin said, "I'm not giving her all that much, you know. If they ask for a D cup size I send them to somebody else. I'm just changing her from an A minus to a B plus." He went on with his suturing, leaving a very fine incision line hidden precisely in the fold below the new breast. Then he repeated the entire procedure with the left breast and implant.

By the time he was finished I resolved to get off my high horse about cosmetic surgery and to stay off. Who was I, or any doctor, to be making speeches to people about how they should learn to appreciate the endowments nature gave them? Only they knew what it was like to live in their bodies. Of course, it would be wrong to add medical authority to illegitimate and oppressive cultural voices, especially if they were male voices directed at females. But it was equally wrong to pretend that cultural distinctions about these matters were not important. Finally, it should be up to the patient to decide how to use the technology of cosmetic surgery that might be available.

At this point Dr. Ridgely, whom I had not met but whom I knew to be the chief of anesthesiology, opened the door of the O.R. He was a very distinguished-looking sixty-year-old man with a sad pleasant face and professorial glasses. He looked at the clock and at Dr. Ruskin. "She can't be discharged today," he said very calmly.

Dr. Ruskin looked up from his work, which at this point consisted of sponging the two wounds clean. "I promised her she could go, and there's no reason why she can't."

"She's been under general for four hours. That's the reason. She can't be discharged today."

The door was closing on Ridgely when Ruskin made his slightly shrill answer, "We'll see about that."

After a decent interval, I thanked Dr. Ruskin for letting me stand in and indicated how impressed I was with the procedure. "I think I have to review my attitudes about cosmetic surgery," I confessed.

He nodded, evidently pleased. "Anytime," he said.

It was late in the afternoon, and I found Dr. Gill in his office in a chipper mood. I confidently handed him my version of the "package insert." He loved it—got a kick out of the play on his name and recognized that I had fulfilled the spirit of the assignment. I was relieved and pleased, and getting to like him more.

In the end, he didn't remember the thirty emergency drugs. I wasn't well prepared, although I had spent more time memorizing. You don't master an assignment like that in a few days. Yet I could certainly have produced data on fifteen or eighteen, which was a lot more than I could have done the week before. No doubt sooner or later I would have to know how to use those drugs, and this was a good start. But his forgetting was almost as much a disappointment as a relief.

The last day of the rotation went smoothly. I started five or six I.V.'s without a hitch. Mainly, I used the straightforward method, but bent the needle slightly as the East European doctor had recommended. His lidocaine method came in handy for two patients who seemed unusually sensitive to pain. I now felt adept at both techniques and could use them selectively. I got one more intubation, which I performed without a problem, for a total of six, a respectable number. I was thankful that I had run into Dr. Hamadeh.

In a single week I had made a step toward real proficiency in the placement of artificial endotracheal airways and the starting of intravenous lines. Adding the technique of "bagging" the patient—breathing for the patient with an ambu bag—I was firmly on the road to mastery of the critical "ABC's" of emergency care: Airway, Breathing, and Circulation. Alone in a well-stocked Emergency Room—which I certainly hoped I would not soon be—I might, just might be able to save someone's life.

5

WARD SURGERY

Crossing the Boundary

Shortly before 6:30 Monday morning, I appeared in the E.W. to find a dense crowd of white jackets, growing thicker by the minute. These were the people, mostly young men, with whom I would spend almost all my waking time for the next three weeks. They were in a state of high anticipation, milling and talking, white Styrofoam cups of coffee in hand. They were gathered for the most essential practical ritual in all of hospital medicine: morning walk-rounds.

For half of them, these rounds merely punctuated a thirty-six-hour shift. For the other half, coming back from at least a few hours' rest, it was the beginning of one. Transfer of critical information about events during the night was a prime purpose of walk-rounds, but there were others. In the anomic social world of the modern hospital, this is the one time when each patient is in the presence of virtually all the physicians responsible for his or her care, as well as of medical students and key representatives of the nursing staff. For the residents and students, it is the only time of the day when one can pay attention to every patient, in methodical succession, with colleagues whom one could ask for consultation or orders.

Since this was my first experience of ward medicine, it was also my first experience of hospital walk-rounds, except for the brief rounds we conducted on the few patients in the overnight ward. My experience here would, I knew, be completely different. I would have no independence—one of the great advantages of the Emergency Room—and I would be doing few procedures myself. I would have little to contribute, and I might well get in the way. Still, I would be exposed to the most serious and complex cases faced by general surgeons.

Marty Wentworth, the eccentric and deliberately—methodically—intimidating chief surgical resident, appeared, sucking at his coffee. He was a slightly overweight thirty-year-old man of medium height with a crewcut and a blond moustache. It was his job to teach and supervise the interns and junior residents. From his fresh look he was obviously one of those who had had the weekend off. "Let's do it!" he barked, and the team began marching upstairs to the main wards.

I understood little of what went on that morning, knowing nothing about the patients and little about the routine of the surgical ward. I stayed in the background with Margaret Steinberg, a fellow medical student I had been with in the E.R. We were jointly assigned to one intern on this team, Mark Rice, a short, friendly blond fellow who came from Oklahoma. We introduced ourselves to him and followed the fifteen or so rounders up to the ward. There were periodic stops to look at X-ray films, but the main activity was trooping into and then out of group and private patients' rooms.

Since I knew I would be hearing about these patients every day and helping to care for some of them, I tried to take notes, but it was hard to follow, and the residents, as always, communicated in slang and shorthand. Of a middle-aged man in liver failure, semistuporous and yellow from head to toe, Marty announced to the group in his room, "This is definitely a case for Resurrectene," which I soon figured out had to be a fantasy drug for hopeless cases. In the Surgical Emergency Care Unit—the S.I.C.U., pronounced "sick-you"—we saw an alcoholic with blackouts who had had surgery on his carotid arteries, which were thought to be supplying insufficient blood to his brain. (This was a controversial procedure then, and has now fallen into disfavor.) Harry, as they affectionately called him, was not doing well at all, having developed a systemic infection postoperatively, on top of his chronic liver and kidney problems. Marty shook his head and said, "He's ridin' the roller-coaster of polypharmacy"—a code phrase for too many drugs.

It seemed bizarre to me to be going into a patient's room with fifteen doctors and nurses first thing in the morning—many patients were roughly awakened by our appearance, and there were rumors that some residents woke patients by kicking the beds. But mine was not to reason why, and I followed faithfully and quietly, suppressing even the most seemingly pertinent questions about treatment and course of illness. I was, however, *asked* questions. As we stood over a hernia patient, Marty asked me to give the boundaries of Hesselbach's Triangle, which I vaguely remembered learning about in anatomy but which I certainly no longer knew.

"Know it by tomorrow," he said, in a not at all friendly voice. Rounds ended after ninety minutes or so as we crowded into the X-ray file room in the E.W., where new films on certain patients were displayed and discussed.

As soon as rounds were over, I had the dubious pleasure of scrubbing for the first time with Marty Wentworth. Despite having been in operating rooms frequently on Anesthesia, and scrubbing once or twice for the O.R. during Basic Clinical Skills, this was the first time it felt real. It was a cholecystectomy (a gallbladder removal), routine except for the patient's obesity. Mike Colucci, a new intern, was going to be doing the procedure under Marty's watchful eye, and Mike guided me through the scrubbing process. He was very cheerful and friendly but somewhat nervous. For now, I contented myself with trying to scrub the skin off my hands, twenty strokes on every part of the fingers and hand, then ten on the second round, then three. I had guilty visions of a devastating infection given the patient by one of my germs. I was a risk without benefit, a fifth wheel there for my own enlightenment.

I opened the door into the O.R. with my rear end, backing in with hands elevated, touching nothing. The patient, an unconscious, naked, formidably fat woman was stretched out on the table in the middle of the room, having her belly painted with brown antiseptic. A pert efficient-looking surgical scrub nurse named Sally called out, "What size glove?" "Eight," I guessed, aiming high in case I was wrong. She patiently held the gloves for me while I fumbled with them, trying desperately to follow the rules of sterile technique. It was her job to see that I didn't contaminate anything, including my own gloves and gown, and she watched me like an owl, ready to pounce on any misstep. Getting the gown on sterilely was not easy, but with her help I managed to stay clean. I kept my hands in the air (they were starting to hurt, since the blood was draining out of them) until I saw that Marty folded his hands over his chest, which seemed terribly wrong until I remembered that of course the arms and front of his gown were sterile, too. I did the same.

Marty and Mike draped the patient, and then we all approached the field, Marty and Sally on one side, Mike and I on the other. I still had my arms folded.

"Put your hands here," said Marty, slapping the area of drape over the patient's thigh. I did, feeling stupider than ever.

"You ready?" he said to Mike.

Mike nodded.

"O.K. then, let's do it." He ran his finger over the purple line he had drawn on the patient's abdomen, and Mike followed the line with his scalpel. Gobs of yellow and white fat appeared, tinged with red bleeders.

"Awesome," said Marty of the incision. They cauterized the bleeders with the Bovie, mostly oozers but also one tiny impressively pumping arteriole.

"Go ahead," Marty said impatiently, and Mike started to cut down into the fat. "This your first gall bag?"

"Yeah," said Mike. "I've done four appies, though."

"Well, these are harder. Just do what I tell you and you'll be all right."

"We've got a few lipids on board," Mike said, meaning the inches of fat he was slowly cutting through.

"That's the name of the game. Just keep on cutting."

Once they had set up a routine of cutting, sponging, and cauterizing, Marty felt free to start talking to me. He grilled me on the anatomy involved in this procedure, most of which I didn't know, not having had advance notice of what I would be in on. Then he launched into a shrill tirade.

"There are a lot of stereotypes about surgeons. All of them are true. Surgeons are narrow-minded . . . bigoted . . . stupid. We're very stupid, all we know is cut, cut, cut, tie, tie, tie. It's true; we really are stupid. We're nasty to our wives and kids. And we don't know any medicine. All the stereotypes are true. Oh yes. And we're male chauvinist pigs."

"Including the women?" I asked, taking a chance on humor.

"Even the women. Fortunately there are very few of those. We've managed to keep most of 'em out. And you know, none of 'em are any good. Watch what you're doin' there, Colucci, Jesus Christ." His voice was taking on a high-pitched, strained tone. "By the way, you were late this morning." I thought back. Yes, maybe six or seven minutes.

"Yeah," Mike said, "I'm sorry, I had to—"

Marty came down hard on him. "No excuses. We're not interested in excuses. We just want you to do your job. Goddamn it, how long are you gonna hang around in that fat?"

The tension in the room was now so thick you could taste it. Marty found some nasty remark to make about almost every move Mike made. In between he managed to keep up a running series of questions to me, most of which I couldn't answer, and to rib me about my ignorance and about medical students not being what they used to be—he was about six years out. By this time I was holding a large retractor—the main job of the medical student in any operation—pulling back as hard as I could to expose a decent field for Mike to work in. I was standing awkwardly and my back and arms were beginning to tire.

All this while rock music was playing rather loudly on a small radio on a shelf in the corner. From time to time Marty would hum and sway with the music, holding a scalpel in one hand and a clamp in the other. "What a great song," he said to Sally at one point. "Isn't that an awesome song? Nah, you probably don't like it. You probably like Barry Manilow."

Finally they were through the abdominal wall, and they found an inflamed gallbladder containing several stones. They let me feel it—the first time I had my hands inside an abdomen. Then I went back to holding the retractor. Marty began to grill me again, this time about arterial branches I had already demonstrated my ignorance of. Mike was now working on the most crucial steps of the operation, and the tension did not ease at all.

At last Mike said, "Marty, I think you'd better guide me through this a little more closely." He was working through a small incision, as Marty had insisted, and in deep fatty tissue. Marty just yelled at him some more, repeating like a chant the words, "No excuses, we don't want any excuses, we just want you to do your job." Mike kept going, and inadvertently cut the cystic artery.

Now, this was not really a total disaster. It was supposed to be cut a little later anyway, supplying as it did a gallbladder that would no longer be there. But it was supposed to be tied off in two places before it was cut, and then cut deliberately and intentionally, not by accident earlier in the procedure.

Marty was merciless. "Goddamn it, Colucci, are you trying to kill this patient? Get a goddamn clamp, goddamn it, and get a hold of the goddamn thing before she bleeds out on the goddamn table." Out of the well of flesh lined with deep fat a rhythmic jet of bright red blood was spurting and spraying. We all had spots of blood all over us—gloves, gowns, even my glasses. I knew that it would take several minutes for an artery this size to bleed enough to pose a problem, but nevertheless that small steady fountain of blood was an impressive sight. I was pulling on the retractor for all I was worth, and Mike was desperately trying to grab hold of the artery and clamp it. All the while Marty never stopped yelling. Soon Mike found and clamped the artery and the crisis was over.

I was ready to write off Marty. Teaching little, he had created relentless tension that had confused and insulted a valuable young doctor and resulted in a significant avoidable accident to a patient. It was not just bad teaching; it was bad medicine.

Later that day, when I was at trauma rounds for the first time—there were six or eight different kinds of rounds that we were supposed to attend weekly—I had the satisfaction of seeing Marty and Dr. Carter, two of my least favorite people, arguing bitterly over the issue of whether 5 percent albumin had any value as a rehydration fluid.

Marty was on his way out of high-powered academic medicine, scheduled to finish his six-year training program within a couple of months. He was contemptuous of academics and researchers, even if they were also surgeons, and at rounds attended by senior surgeons he showed his contempt quite openly.

Reading *Time* magazine and loudly flipping pages during the rounds, which were supposed to review all the serious trauma cases seen during the week, he contradicted Carter to say, "Five percent albumin has no value whatsoever as a rehydration fluid."

Carter, who after all ran the emergency trauma service and taught that it did, defended his practice and teaching, and Marty countered by citing chapter and verse from various studies, which supported his contention. It was the first inkling I had that Marty actually read something. The main effect of their argument was to embarrass both doctors in front of the senior surgeons, residents, interns, and students. It was obvious from the discussion that the issue was unsettled in the literature, and by taking inflexible positions in an arrogant, absolute way, both of them looked silly. Of course, that didn't stop either of them from continuing to articulate the same arrogant positions in situations where they were not open to challenge.

The next morning at rounds, Marty asked me again for the borders of Hesselbach's Triangle, and since I had learned them cold overnight, he left me alone for a while. There was a new patient whom they referred to as "the man without a face," and I thought it must be the man whose face I had seen removed because of the tumor. But it was another man, a disastrously mangled suicide attempt. He had drunk a lye-containing corrosive solution and suffered severe destructive burns of his face and mouth. His was the only room we never went into.

Margaret, who had been on during the night while I was off, talked to me about the gallbladder operation, which she had heard about from Mike. "He's so sensitive," she said, "and Marty knows exactly how to get to him." So at least I hadn't distorted the episode in my mind; even among surgeons there was a limit to what the chief could dish out and what the intern could take.

I scrubbed with David Milano, a darkly handsome senior resident a year or so behind Marty in the training program. There was no nonsense about him, and he was not exactly friendly, but he was much more pleasant to work around than Marty. He and Mark Rice were doing a herniorraphy (a straightforward repair of an indirect inguinal hernia) on a twenty-eight-year-old marathon runner. The patient's head was on the other side of the drape, but the body, except for the hernia, was just about perfect.

Milano guided Mark matter-of-factly through the procedure. Partly because the structures were close to the surface, but mostly because the patient was in such good physical shape, the anatomy was ideally exposed. Milano taught from it, clearly and comprehensibly, so that while Mark was learning the operative procedure, I was learning the anatomy.

I remembered an anatomy lesson in which the instructor had asked, "What is the most common surgically correctable congenital defect?" The right answer was "an unobliterated processus vaginalis," a mouthful of Latin that simply referred to the defect underlying a hernia. The processus vaginalis is the passage through which, embryonically, the testes descend from the abdomen. In most male infants it is obliterated after the descent. But in the minority in whom it isn't, a loop of bowel may descend through it, at any time during life—the most common sort of hernia. The trick is, few people think of a hernia as a congenital defect.

I was musing on this, and connecting it up with Milano's superb anatomy review, when the door opened and a figure in surgical greens appeared and then quickly left. I caught only a glimpse of Marty's back. Then I realized that the background rock music—much softer than it had been in Marty's O.R. the day before—had stopped.

After a moment or two during which he was using a finger to push aside some fascia in the wound, Milano looked up and said, "Hey, what happened to the radio?" I kept quiet. Sally, the scrub nurse, explained to him what had happened. His face contorted momentarily and he threw his head to the side. Then he looked back into the wound and began working again. "Damn," he said. "Well, he's the chief, so he has that prerogative."

I hesitated and then said facetiously, "Next year you'll be the chief, and you'll be able to do the same to someone else."

He looked hard at me. "Damn right I will," he said and went on with his work.

After the hernia surgery the same team and O.R. were scheduled for a patient at the opposite end of the spectrum of adult life and health—Kathleen Grady, a pleasantly plump woman in her early seventies with apparently localized cancer of the colon. Milano resected her colon—cut out a piece and joined the ends together—with the same matter-of-factness he had used on the hernia, but he was prouder of this one. He had had to consider a colostomy—bringing the cut end out to a hole in the abdominal wall—but this turned out to be unnecessary. He explored her abdomen carefully and found no evidence of tumor spread. And her colon was completely clean of feces, so that the chance of infection was minimal. It was a highly successful procedure that had a good chance of curing an otherwise deadly disease, and Milano and Rice were both delighted.

So was I. It felt good to have been a part of something so simple and so plainly effective. As for exposure, I was getting an ample share. I had had my hand deep inside the abdomen, feeling for tumor along with Milano and Rice. I had crossed the boundary that separates the body from the world, a boundary that is inviolate to all except those with the inclination to kill and those with the knowledge to heal—the two categories of people who hold power over human life and death.

Going back to the ward, I ran into Mike Colucci in the hall. It was the first time we had had a chance to talk since the obese gallbladder. He half-complained, half-apologized about the whole thing, which somewhat surprised me—after all, I was only a medical student—and seemed to want my opinion. I made my feelings known.

"Yeah," he said diffidently. "Marty does tend to get a bit short-tempered." I grew bolder, realizing that, medical student or no, he was looking to me for some kind of reassurance. "If anything went wrong there," I said as we parted, "I blame him."

Instead of lunch that day, I went to social service rounds, which seemed of obvious interest to an anthropologist. Although they were on the medical-student schedule, the residents had told me explicitly and repeatedly that I did not have to—should not—waste my time with them. This sort of discrepancy—a common one it turned out—showed not primarily a discordance between the views of senior physicians and residents as to what medical students should do. Instead, it tended to be a dichotomy between the *stated* ideals of a rotation and what it actually was meant to be. Medical students with the common sense or cynicism to take those ideals less seriously than I had an easier time of it. But I took the residents' advice as a sign of lack of interest in the social and psychological frame-work of illness and recovery, and asked Mark if I could go along with him.

Only interns—no experienced residents, which should have tipped me off—nurses, and social service personnel attended these rounds. They were, in fact, a waste of time, but only because they were done so poorly. The interns and nurses summarized briefly the medical and surgical aspects of each patient on the ward for the benefit of the social workers, but virtually no time (perhaps one to two minutes out of forty-five) was devoted to social or psychological remarks (to call them "discussion" would dignify them too much). The social workers said nothing except to ask for occasional clarification, thus forfeiting, it seemed to me, an opportunity to educate interns who badly needed a better grasp of things they knew about.

Mark Rice was almost insultingly perfunctory in his summary of his patients who might (because they would have to be placed in nursing homes, for example), require attention from the social service people. In a typical summary he mentioned that a patient was being moved to an adjacent building reserved for patients who pay. A social worker asked why. "That's because he's imminent. He's gonna meet his Maker pretty soon now, so they want him to have a little privacy. They did that before with another patient." His quick blue eyes reflected almost as much confusion as to why his superiors did certain things as contempt for these proceedings and a desire to be quit of them.

We had X-ray rounds daily at four o'clock. These were a rather pleasant interlude in which the small ward team sat around in the dark reviewing the day's films and discussing the patients. One of the residents brought Tootsie-Roll pops for everyone each day, and today he had remembered the medical students too. I was touched. I was trying to hang back in the dark, sucking on my lollipop, when Marty pointed out to me that there was a seat next to him up front—the worst possible spot. He gestured me into it.

Fortunately for me he was not in a bad mood. He grilled me on the films we saw, but not relentlessly. Discussing the hernia patient, he asked me why men had more hernias than women, and I told the standard story about the unobliterated processus vaginalis.

"That's an anatomical reason," he said. "Now I want a social reason."

"Because men do more lifting?" I ventured.

"Awesome." He looked around at the residents. "Wasn't that an awesome answer?" He looked back at me. "Right. Because men get out into the world and do something, while women sit at home eating cream puffs and listening to Barry Manilow. That doesn't tend to build up as much intraabdominal pressure. Right?"

I was beginning to get the idea that his contempt for Manilow was special. I decided to take a chance. "That depends," I ventured, "on whether Barry Manilow causes reverse peristalsis. That would give you some increase in intraabdominal pressure." He loved it, and when he burst out laughing everyone else did too. I hoped my problems with Marty were over.

At the end of X-ray rounds we were passing out of the closet of shadows, still sucking our lollipops. Of Harry, the drunk who was still hanging on in the S.I.C.U., Marty said "Don't give up the ship," and there was some discussion about which naval commander had uttered that immortal phrase.

Bob Andrews, a senior resident due to become chief when Marty left in a couple of months, gave me a sympathetic look. He was a tall, soft-spoken, gentle man who seemed to break every rule of the surgical stereotype: although certainly a team player, he was always slightly detached during the episodes of joking about patients. "This is about the highest level of culture you get with surgeons," he said directly to me. "John Paul Jones. My wife says surgeons are as multifaceted as plates." We laughed at that, and I remembered but did not repeat a remark I had heard about orthopedic surgeons from a woman who had switched from pediatrics to orthopedics: "Smarter than a stone, but not as smart as a tree."

According to the plan of rotation, I was on that night—my first night on the ward—with Milano and Rice. We were in the S.I.C.U. checking on Harry and the other patients there when a beeper sounded loudly. Milano picked up one of the two beepers on his belt. Rice said, "Yeah, it's the code beeper," and both of them started running.

They were in the stairwell before I realized I had better start following them, so I pounded up the stairs, too, three at a time. This was something I was not in shape for. Although I had been jogging almost daily before I began my rotations with the Emergency Room, I was now over a month away from that. Sleeplessness, lack of exercise, and poor diet were now my rule. The residents were years younger than me, and all seemed to be in excellent physical shape, maintaining their exercise programs religiously.

Sleep deprivation, bad hospital meals, and vending-machine junk food did not seem to faze them.

It was four flights in the end, and I was more than a flight behind them, but I surmised they had exited on the floor of our ward. I ran from the stairwell to the point where two long corridors crossed, looked in all possible directions, and saw a great crowd of uniforms bulging out of the room that I thought belonged to Mrs. Grady, the lady who had had a colonic resection to remove her cancer.

As usual in code—resuscitation—situations, I resolved to make myself useful if possible, see and learn as much as I could, but above all stay out of the way. Peering among the white coats, chest heaving and heart pounding, I saw that Milano was already administering the code, barking orders in a tense, methodical fashion. The EKG machine with the cardio-version paddles—for delivering a stimulatory shock to a heart in certain conditions of abnormal rhythm—was being rolled into place. Milano and Rice were intubating Mrs. Grady while one of the nurses kept up external heart massage in a sturdy rhythm. When they finished the intubation I caught a look at Mrs. Grady, and her face had an alive but vacant stare.

I asked one of the junior nurses what had happened. "Nobody knows," she said. "She was sitting up in bed, talking with her family, and she just keeled over." The code, like her operation earlier, was successful, but her breathing and heartbeat had stopped for some minutes, and both were maintained artificially for about thirty minutes more. It was not clear whether she had had a stroke—the CAT scan of her brain turned out to be uninformative—or was "only" suffering the consequences of oxygen deprivation secondary to a nearly fatal cardiac arrhythmia. In any case she was mentally inaccessible, a condition everyone hoped was temporary. Her family stood in a state of obvious distress in and outside of the waiting room, and I was glad I wasn't the one who had to talk with them.

It was exciting to be on the hospital floor in the evening. As it turned out I did not have a patient to admit and work up, but I spent some time talking in Spanish with a mildly obese woman who spoke little English. Her chart showed that she had come in with a severe right upper abdominal pain and a high level of serum amylase, both of which had resolved within a day or two of her admission. This was consistent with the diagnosis of a common bile duct obstructed by a gallstone that she then spontaneously passed. But since other, more ominous explanations were possible, she was being kept around for observation and testing. Mark Rice found me at her bedside and told me to set her up for a sigmoidoscopy—examination of the lower colon by introducing a light into the rectum. After performing this uninviting but mildly interesting task together, and finding nothing, we went down together for the ten o'clock meal.

This all-you-could-eat-free-of-charge supper was a time for brutal and funny postmortems and other second thoughts, and for mutual, merciless ribbing. Jack Carter had often said to the E.W. residents, "Don't be afraid to send a questionable patient to the O.R. just because they might make fun of you at the ten o'clock meal."

Tonight the surgical residents were joking contemptuously about the "mopes," their nickname for nonsurgical physicians. The name seemed to have originated from the acronym for medical out-patient service—outpatient services being regarded as the most contemptible of medical activities. It was their way of saying that nonsurgeons were best at taking care of patients who either a) weren't sick or b) couldn't be helped.

"When in doubt, whip it out," said Mark decisively.

"Yo," Milano shot back. "Whip that mother dog out through a smokin' hole."

Another term for nonsurgeons was "fleas." I was on my third piece of what passed for roast chicken when a large, bearded resident with a Norwegian-sounding name, whom I didn't know, pointed at me with his fork and said to Mark, "This one's probably a budding flea." Mark gave me a chance to answer for myself. I had sense enough not to say that I was interested in psychiatry. "I'm thinking about neurology," I said.

The Norwegian came out with a loud derisory snort. He grinned at me and looked around the large circular table. "Neurologists are the worst fleas in medicine!" he said.

"Worst fleas?" I asked, setting myself up.

"The last," he said, looking into my eyes, "to leave a dying body." This got a good laugh from everyone, including me.

"Well," I said weakly, "I'm still considering neurosurgery."

After trying to cheer myself up by wolfing down a large amount of bad food, I followed Mark upstairs and went on final evening rounds with him, listening to hearts and lungs, pressing on tender bellies, and helping him write his progress notes. There did not seem to be any immediately operable cases coming up from the Emergency Room, so we went to sleep.

After a marvelous five hours' rest, we began pre-rounding at six, so that the team wouldn't look too stupid under Marty's walk-rounds grilling. This time I followed Milano, and when we went in to see the Spanish woman, she awoke slowly, recognized me, and gave me a smile that was worth three hours' sleep. Rushing out of her room—pre-rounds were incredibly fast—I asked Milano what he thought about her. Having read her chart and thought about her case a bit, I figured I might learn something from discussing it with him. He turned to me and said, "A clear case of gok."

"Gok?"

"G.O.K. God Only Knows."

Later in the morning I scrubbed with Bob Andrews on another obese cholecystectomy, this one on a fifty-year-old man. The intern was also doing his first gallbladder removal. The structural parallels with the first day's episode of Marty "teaching" Mike were striking, but the tone, details, and outcome were completely different. Bob was a thoughtful, patient teacher, and the whole procedure was a pleasure to watch, not only for the smoothness of the surgery but for the excitement and effectiveness of the training.

By the time we got to the last rounds of the day—this time they were G.I., or gastrointestinal rounds—I was half-asleep and had to work not actually to nod off. But at one point I was stirred awake by the mention of Anthony Eden. Some of the senior surgeons were talking about his gallbladder—he had evidently had an interesting complication that had got a lot of press.

Across the room I noticed that Margaret Steinberg and Marty Wentworth were looking at each other, whispering, and shrugging their shoulders.

Margaret finally asked, "Who was Anthony Eden?"

A senior surgeon glared at her, at Marty, and at the other residents, many of whom were nodding in support of the question. "That takes my breath away," he said. "Doesn't any of you know who Anthony Eden was?"

After a long embarrassing silence, I broke my rule about keeping my mouth shut at rounds in order to say something about the British statesman who had been a key figure in World War II and the Suez Crisis. But the senior surgeons, much impressed with the ignorance of their residents, were still shaking their heads in disbelief. They had personally arranged the surgical residency so as to make it impossible for the residents to be aware of anything outside of surgery, and now they blamed them for ignorance.

Shortly after six—I had been counting the minutes—rounds were over, and Marty convened us to check on the completion of the day's tasks. "O.K.," he said finally and dryly. "Those who are off can go."

The following morning, after a long night's sleep, I scrubbed in on a surgery that gave me an unexpected insight into the constraints of surgical residencies. A fourteen-year-old boy was having an excision of a tumor of the right parotid gland, a salivary gland located near the articulation of the jaw. Marty Wentworth and David Milano were scrubbing in together. This surprised me, but it soon became apparent that the operation was unusual and neither was familiar with it.

They worked away cheerfully, more or less in tandem, evincing exceptional interest. Still, Marty found the time to discourse crudely on various subjects, notably the threat of nuclear war. He asked me if I belonged to Physicians for Social Responsibility (I did) and showed a mild positive surprise. Given his generally reactionary views, I was surprised at him as well. Then he said, "I know what I'm gonna do. I'm moving to Santa Fe, New Mexico."

"What's so special about that?" I asked.

"Well, aside from the fact that it's one of the world's most beautiful places to live—I mean it's really awesome—it's one of the few places the Russkies have got no damn reason to bomb. Where is that goddamn facial nerve, Milano?"

"You tell me," he answered. Both of them had their fingers inside the very messy-looking glob of yellow tissue that is the parotid gland.

Removing the parotid gland with its tumor is easy enough, but the trick is to do it without destroying or even nicking the facial nerve. The nerve, which controls most of the muscles of facial expression, plunges right through the mass of glandular tissue, and branches into five parts, all inside the gland. This pattern makes the procedure gravely risky.

After two hours, Wentworth and Milano still could not find the facial nerve and its branches. Finally Marty, as reluctantly as befitted a chief resident yelling for help, called for Frank Gardner, a senior staff surgeon. Gardner appeared, looked at the field, said they had been too timid, and within five minutes of more aggressive poking found the nerve and exposed it, quite a distance from where they had been looking. He was very nice about it, and Milano and Wentworth were both good sports.

Marty was only three months away from leaving his residency and entering private surgical practice. Yet he had seen only three of these (Milano only this one) and was obviously not at home with the procedure yet. It was a good argument for extended and intensive surgical residency. If it were shorter than six years, or if the hours were more reasonable, would Marty have seen even three? And if he hadn't, would he be adequately trained?

After the surgery I followed Marty and the others to Grand Rounds—perhaps the second most important ritual of hospital life. We entered at the bottom of a steeply pitched amphitheater to find a sea of white coats —students, interns, residents, nurses, and most important, gray-haired senior surgeons—staring down expectantly at the platform. This was the one time of the week when every person connected with the surgical service was supposed to be present. Junior residents, particularly interns, were expected to bring in a patient, stand in the military at-ease position beside the wheelchair, and summarize all pertinent aspects of the case in exactly sixty seconds. After the presentation, all present would spend up to thirty minutes analyzing the case. Mark Rice, I knew, was up today, and he was terrified.

The first case was a three-year-old boy with Wilms' tumor of the kidney, a curable childhood cancer that in this case had recurred more than once. Through a long series of complex operations—really heroic efforts—the boy's life had been saved.

The second case, wheeled in by Mark, was an eighty-six-year-old man. He gazed casually up at the room full of surgeons. "Good morning, friends!" he greeted them. Mark turned his wheelchair so that he faced toward the audience, and he added, after a beautifully timed pause, "I hope you're my friends." This got a big laugh.

Mark was trembling visibly, but he made the presentation in something like fifty-eight seconds. The man had had a mass in his left lower abdomen, some years after surgery for an infected diverticulum of the colon. After much confusion and analysis, the abdomen had been explored and the mass removed. Pathology analysis suggested it was a growth formed around the nidus of a tiny piece of talc, which could only have come from the glove of a surgeon (or medical student) at the earlier surgery. (Surgical gloves are coated in talc on the inside for ease of gloving. The importance of wiping them with a damp cloth before surgery had been mentioned but not emphasized. I resolved to clean my gloves with extreme care from then on.)

I was on that night, got little sleep, and stayed in the hospital until almost midnight the following night, because of an emergency involving a patient assigned to me. During a routine check she had complained of belly pain, and I had not been able to hear any bowel sounds through the stethoscope. Milano confirmed this. "Never let the sun rise on a silent bowel," he intoned with the cynical but real emphasis reserved for a clinical pearl. X-ray showed a twist in her small intestine that needed to be resolved that night. Luckily, I had the weekend off. Saturday was my daughter's fourth birthday, and on Sunday we spent a day in the country.

Monday morning I learned that the "yellow man," the patient with liver and kidney failure, had died. He was the man who had been pronounced a candidate for Resurrectene, and who was otherwise the butt of extensive joking. He had been "D.N.R."—Do Not Resuscitate—a status that caused some conflict with the nurses. One day the previous week Marty had asked Mark Rice, "Have you talked with the family?"

"Yes," said Mark, "I've talked to them. I didn't tell them about the code status, but I did tell them the situation is not good." This puzzled me. My understanding was that D.N.R. could not be assigned to a patient without family advice and consent. Perhaps that was why this case had angered the nurses? Nurses were sometimes more in favor of heroic measures than physicians, perhaps for religious reasons. In any event, the yellow man had stopped breathing some time on Sunday and had not been coded. It was the first death of a patient I had been involved with, and it was surrounded by ambiguity.

Later in the morning I was in the O.R. with a senior surgical resident who had been away the previous week at a scientific conference. He was a quiet, thoughtful, slow-moving man with wire-rimmed spectacles who had managed to get a Ph.D. in immunology as well as an M.D. by alternating research with clinical training. His particular animal research model for the problem of transplant rejection was the sheep, and Marty had broken everyone up at rounds one day by announcing that Chris was absent because he had to make a speech about sheep at a 4-H Club convention.

The senior resident was rather humorless and not too friendly. This might have been a welcome change from the usual brutal banter in the O.R., but he was so single-minded in his silent determination that I almost wished Marty were there to break the ice. We were operating on a young man who had pleural blebs—little pockets of air trapped in the lining of one of his lungs. The procedure, called pleurodesis, involved "taking down" the lung—collapsing it and teasing it away from the chest wall—and then scrubbing the chest wall like crazy so that when the lung was reinflated it would adhere to the countless minute wounds we had made with our scrubbing. It was a strange, crudely physical procedure in this realm of high technology; and when my turn came to scrub inside the chest—it was tiring enough so that we really had to take turns—I was exhilarated and frightened by what was certainly the starkest physical intimacy I had ever had with another human being.

After the surgery I ran into Margaret, and we rode up in the elevator with Marty. "What's new on the floor?" he asked. I said I hadn't been up there but I'd heard that Mrs. Grady had come back to the floor from the S.I.C.U. after her code with no change in her mental status. Marty shook his head disgustedly. I said, "Reminds me of the end of *One Flew Over the Cuckoo's Nest.* Remember that? When he comes back to the ward again, but without his brain?"

Marty was grim and firm. "Her family thinks she's responding to 'em. Her husband comes in and talks to her, tries to wake her up. He sees a reflex and thinks she's responding. You have to tell them. Really, you have to say to them, 'No, you're wrong. She's *not* responding.'" This wise if rough advice was about all the teaching we got on the subject of how to talk to the family of a patient who had suffered extensive and irreversible brain damage.

There were really two lessons here. First, contrary to the advice I had remembered from my preclinical years, there are times when it may be helpful to take away the patient's hope—or at least the patient's family's hope. Second, the physician must be firm and authoritative. This paralleled the early lesson from the neurologist who had lectured us on how to convince terminal patients that they are really going to die. Marty was a past master of that kind of firmness, and in fact most residents seemed to learn it in a hurry. The only trouble was that most physicians then felt it necessary to be firm in every situation, however precarious or ambiguous or trivial, whether or not it was necessary, and whether or not they were sure of what they were talking about.

At rounds that evening with the senior surgeons, resuscitation status was a principal topic. Marty had to defend his decision not to resuscitate the yellow man, since the nurses had complained through higher channels of authority on the service. He did so without difficulty (a chief resident is rarely seriously challenged by the senior staff), and made known his opinion that Mrs. Grady should also now be D.N.R., a status her family was probably not ready to learn about, much less accept.

Marty was the perfect picture of the tough-minded, dedicated, no-nonsense physician caught in a tangle of ethical, legal, economic, and bureaucratic red tape. He finally almost shouted in exasperation, "Today there are two meanings to D.N.R. One is 'comfort measures only.' That means kill 'em, get rid of 'em, like we wanted to do with that lady last week. The other is 'no heroic measures for resuscitation.' That means if they get a major infection, you treat it. Half the time we don't know which is which."

He was angered and frustrated by the trap of terminology, subtle distinctions he did not understand and that could easily drag him into a court of law and even perhaps end his career. But no one else there really understood either. The legal concept of D.N.R. was relatively new and constantly evolving. You couldn't look it up in a book and be safe, since your future would depend not on what was in the book but on what had been decided by a jury or judge that morning. These considerations were on the minds of the residents almost constantly.

After rounds the senior staff surgeons and "visits"—nonstaff physicians with hospital visiting privileges—went home, and the residents collected in a knot standing near the door. Mike Colucci brought the discussion down to earth by asking Marty's advice about the use of the Kanner tube. After the gallbladder incident, I was amazed that he would take a chance on setting himself up. But Marty was nice, apparently glad not to be talking ethics and law any more.

"Everyone goes through a phase where they think it's great. I went through a phase like that in my fifth year when I thought it was the greatest thing ever invented."

"But it works sometimes," Mike offered tentatively.

Marty's reply was exasperated but for him generous. "Everything works sometimes." He waved his hand dramatically toward the shelves of surgery books. "That's why half the stupid operations that have been invented keep getting done. That's why we have two-thirds of the medicines we've got. Everything works sometimes. That doesn't mean anything."

The next morning on rounds Marty was still in high form. It was the day Mark and Margaret were scheduled to be filmed for a television news program, and when we rounded through Mrs. Grady's room he said to Margaret, "This one would be a good one for T.V." She now lay on her side chewing her gums incessantly and staring in one direction, toward the ceiling. I could almost hear the narrator's voice: *The operation was a success, but the patient's brain died.* We trooped down to the S.I.C.U. and when we were rounding on Harry ("Hoppin' Harry", Marty called him, still "riding the roller-coaster of polypharmacy"), there was a discussion of which of two relatively advanced antibiotics would be best for him now, as his sepsis once again had escaped from control. Marty showed his contempt for this hairsplitting discussion by taking a quarter out of his pocket and flipping it. "Heads it's genta," he said, short for gentamycin. It was genta.

The first surgery was scheduled late that morning, so I spent some time talking with some of "my" patients. An elderly Armenian man with one arm whom I had met in the overnight ward was ready to go home after morning rounds. I had difficulty recognizing him; he literally looked like a different man. His hair was combed slick on his large round head, he was dressed casually but handsomely, and he was constantly smiling. With a little encouragement he began to talk about his first emigration from Armenia to Greece: "I couldn't find any love there. My family was back in Armenia. So I said, O.K., if I can't find love here, I'll go back there. That's O.K. by me."

We talked some more, mainly about health and diet. Nothing pleased me more than watching a patient go out the door, and after he left I read over his chart to review some aspects of his course of illness. One of my daily assessment notes from a few days earlier read: "Patient continues to improve. Lonely."

Another immigrant who was desperately out of place was not so lucky. His abdominal pain was confusing to everyone, and he described his condition in broken English. He was somehow slightly annoying and very charming both at the same time. " 'Scuse me, Doctor. I no know nothing. I estupid. You much esmarter than me. But I gotta tell you I no can eata this hospital food. I eata nothing. Lilla bit, I throw up. I needa go home. I go in the garden, take a tomato, take a grape. I eat. I take a lilla bit wine. But here no. Hospital food I no eat nothing. You senda me home, I eat."

He certainly wasn't eating, but there was no prospect of his going home in the immediate future. What he said didn't sound unreasonable to me, and I talked to Margaret about him. We decided to bring in some grapes for Mr. Scaglia, pending the approval of a resident or at least an intern. That approval was given, and I brought some grapes in the following day. They weren't from his garden, but they seemed to make him happy.

During visiting hours the next night I had some time to watch Mrs. Grady's family. I remembered what Marty had said, and I realized, perhaps for the first time, that I was a part of how they experienced her illness. I always introduced myself carefully as a medical student; especially given my age, I did not want any mistakes made about my stage of training. But, explanations and labels notwithstanding, patients and families often had trouble telling medical students from doctors, and medical students often had the chance to talk with them at leisure—more leisure, at least, than residents.

I watched from the hall as Mrs. Grady's three daughters tried to get some response from her. They were extremely touching, talking to her in a way that was patient and endearing. One, with a bleach-blond ponytail, jeans, and very high heels but a beaten, drawn, tired, working-class look, stared into her mother's face and eyes for at least thirty seconds while the eyes slowly and randomly opened and closed. "Mother," she said. "It's me, Laura, Mother. Can you hear me? We're all here, Mother. We're all here with you." She noticed me watching and stopped with an embarrassed smile.

A bit later a son arrived and asked me a few questions that seemed less naive than his sisters'. Then he went over to his mother and repeated the same patient phrases his sisters had been trying for an hour. He'd driven in from his home in the country, two and a half hours away, every night after work, to participate in this ritual. After his sisters left, he asked me some slightly more pointed questions about the prognosis, and I spoke gently but very discouragingly about her prospects for neurological recovery. I gestured toward the rosary pinned to her pillow and tapped it lightly, immediately wondering whether that was proper. "It's really out of our hands," I said. This was easy, but the words at least were true. I could only imagine the sorts of words Marty would have used, and I felt like a weakling. Still, I had told the truth. And I remembered again the advice that had seemed so wise to me: *It is not the job of the physician to take away the patient's hope.*

That night at the surgeons' table at the ten o'clock meal, the remarks were particularly brutal and funny. Sjogren, the big Norwegian, said that he was on "crispy critters" this month, which turned out to mean the pediatric burns clinic.

"Toasted toddlers," said Milano immediately in recognition. "Really cheerful."

"I like it," Sjogren said.

Milano began talking about a woman with severe carotid artery disease.

"Watch out," the Norwegian said. "She might shoot some cookies into her helmet." It took me a while to figure out that cookies were emboli and her helmet was her skull: a fragment might break loose from a plaque and go to her brain, causing a stroke.

Then Morgan, one of the interns, a very handsome dark-haired man with a boyish look and bright blue eyes, began bragging shamelessly about his previous night's date. At the same time a conversation was going on between Sjogren and Milano about a patient with a head injury whom they had treated for abdominal injuries. Morgan overheard them and interrupted himself to say, "She's been transferred to Flagg Seven." This was the floor where the neurosurgical intensive care unit, the N.I.C.U., was located. Transfer to the N.I.C.U. was often a dead-end trip.

Sjogren looked across the table and smiled through his brown beard. "Your girlfriend's been transferred there?" His confusion was deliberate, and Morgan flushed.

I took advantage of the lull: "Yeah. He fucked her brains out, and now she's on Flagg Seven." This got one of the biggest laughs of the evening at the table and secured me a place as a "regular guy." I supposed Morgan's embarrassment was only what he deserved for recounting his exploits so graphically.

Marty arrived and banged his tray down on the table, shaking his head in disgust. "I just had a long conversation with a family of a lung C.A., squamous cell. You know, those wonderful conversations you love to have where they find six different ways to tell you you have to be wrong about the prognosis, the diagnosis, something? Well, this was the family of the *wrong patient*. After about ten minutes she said, 'Wait a minute, Dr. Wentworth. We're the *Giulianis*. You know, the *Giulianis?*'"

Mack, tall and strong-looking with a soft, slightly nervous face, was right behind Marty. He set his tray down beside Marty's. "I can top that," he said. "Today I was operating on a breast lump. I open the breast up and it looks mean and ugly. Path confirms it's bad news. What am I supposed to do? Take the goddamn lump out or take the goddamn breast off? I didn't even know the patient." This would have been the woman I had admitted the night before for a breast biopsy in the morning. He hadn't asked me about her. I wondered if he had read my admission note in the chart, five pages of densely packed information.

"What did you do?" I asked, but he ignored me.

"I really feel for you, Mack," said Marty sincerely. "I mean there you are, operating on a breast lump in a woman you've never met." He wolfed down a few forkfuls of potato and gravy. "Colucci!" he yelled across the table. Colucci gave a start and almost dropped his fork. "How's Mr. Scaglia?"

Mr. Scaglia, the man we had got the grapes for, had had a hernia repair that morning. Colucci answered timidly, "He has a small scrotal hematoma," a collection of blood in his scrotum.

"He's lucky he still has a nut," said Marty decisively.

"Damn right!" said Mike, with a nervous smile and a comradely air.

Back on the ward, I admitted a patient with the classic symptoms and signs of gallstones. The straightforward workup took only about an hour and a half. Then I went to the nurses' lounge to get a cup of coffee, perhaps my twentieth of the day. Several residents were sitting around waiting for some unnamed inevitable crisis. I was beginning to worry about all this coffee—it was a definite risk for peptic ulcer disease, and a recent good study had linked it for the first time to cancer of the pancreas. I was sucking on the Styrofoam when Milano said, "You drink a little bit of coffee."

"Staff of life," I said.

"If you sign up now, I'll do your Whipple for you at today's prices." The Whipple procedure involved partial removal of the pancreas.

"Thanks," I said. "I'll get somebody else."

The next day at G.I. rounds, Marty and the residents presented three intestinal surgery cases done the previous week, two of which I had scrubbed on. Marty was typically arrogant and offhanded, but there was a consensus among the four senior surgeons that these operations had all been done incorrectly, with major errors about the procedure to follow, how far to carry it, how to complete stagewise or temporary repairs, and so on. Fortunately there had so far been no disasters in consequence of these errors. Marty laughed loudly. "Well, it looks like we're 0 for 3," he said.

In addition to rejecting the way the residents had handled the cases, the senior surgeons disagreed among themselves. Two of them had diametrically opposed views on the usefulness of stapling anastomoses—connections between two cut ends of a tubular organ. How arbitrary many of these decisions were, and how inappropriate the arrogance with which they were made and defended. Most surgeons conducted business in a context in which no such routine challenge was likely. Furthermore, this was no backwater; these were among the very best surgeons in the world.

I was off Thursday evening but then on all weekend. On Saturday night a few of us who were on watched the television news program that Mark and Margaret had been filming for all week. The remarks and laughter were brutal to the point of bitterness. It was not jealousy, but contempt: every patient was good-looking, basically well, and a clean-cut success. These neat cases represented perhaps 10 percent of those on the ward and even less of the residents' real time and work. It was ludicrous, and they resented it.

"They should have put Mrs. Grady on," Mack said. "She looks so nice, with her eyeballs stuck up in the corner of her eyes like that. Or the Man Without a Face. Or Hoppin' Harry, lying there so peaceful-like, staring at the ceiling—with Marty reading his progress notes as a voice-over."

Later I found Mark Rice at the bedside of an alcoholic woman in her fifties who was considered crazy and hypochondriacal. She was in the hospital for removal of a benign colonic polyp, but she was constantly complaining of pain from a stab wound she claimed to have received four weeks earlier. She had been carefully and repeatedly examined, and it was not likely that such a wound had occurred.

"Well, when am I going to start to get my appetite back?" she was asking Mark in an insistent whine.

Mark's reply was serious, reasoned, and physicianly. "You'll start to get your appetite back when you start to feel hungry." This seemed to satisfy her, and we both turned and walked out of the room, having great trouble keeping a straight face. When we got into the hall and out of earshot I said, "Did you just make that up?"

"Yeah," he said with a wonderful twinkle in his eye. "And you can quote me on it in your next book."

There was no time for me to find out how he had heard I had written a book, because we were beeped to the O.R. for a case of multiple trauma. A woman had attempted suicide by jumping off an overpass onto a major road just outside the hospital. She had fractured her pelvis on both sides, fractured her first three ribs, also on both sides, and had a pneumothorax —air in her chest causing a partial collapse of a lung. She was losing blood into her pelvis, an area large enough so that she could bleed to death without an external wound. Two of the residents were trying to explore the pelvis, to find the points of bleeding and stop it, while two others resolved her pneumothorax. The procedures took about half the night.

I later found out that she had been in the Emergency Room, accompanied by her mother, just before her attempt on her life. First she had presented with an obscure abdominal pain in the surgical emergency clinic, after a wait of several hours. When she was finally examined and no findings emerged, the surgeons also discovered she had a history of schizophrenia and got rid of her fast; but she then had to wait all over again before she could see the psychiatrists. (And this in the best-staffed and busiest psychiatric emergency clinic in the region.) While waiting, she broke away from her mother, ran out of the hospital, climbed the overpass, and jumped.

Monday morning, on walk-rounds, we all went into her room and collected in a semicircle some distance from her bed. She lay completely constrained, weak and helpless, in a lower body cast and in one arm and shoulder cast, with tubes in her nose and in her free arm. Her face was nonetheless distressingly alert.

Mark presented her to the group, and Marty asked him a few perfunctory questions. No one spoke to the patient, touched her, even met her eyes during the five minutes we spent in her room. Marty was making a move to gesture the group out when she began speaking. She was looking around at the white coats in abject fear and confusion. She said wanly, in a thick regional working-class accent, "Can I have something for the pain?"

Marty stopped and looked at her from where he stood about four feet from the bed. "You bet!" he barked. This was the single exchange that occurred between this patient and a physician during the daily period at bedside.

We passed Mrs. Grady's room but didn't bother going in. Marty waved his hand in her direction and said to the junior residents, "Nothing new?"

"Nothing new," Mark said. As usual we passed the room of the man without a face and rounded on him in the hallway. He was recovering, if you could call it that. There was nothing new with him either.

In the large ward room there were now six patients. One had the largest goiter any of the residents had ever seen, about the size of a grapefruit. It was the sort you see in certain very poor countries and otherwise only in textbooks. Milano asked her why she hadn't come in sooner, before it got so large. "I kept meaning to," she said matter-of-factly. "I never got around to it."

At the end of rounds we crowded into the X-ray file room to see an inside view of the goiter, which impressed the radiologists as much as it did the surgeons. "Is this lady for real?" one asked. "The only way I can figure it is she doesn't own a mirror. Here's our other prize-winner," he said, as he slapped another film onto the viewer. This one was an upper G.I. series—a visualization of the upper gut with barium—which showed an enormously distended common bile duct filled with many large stones.

Mack was standing next to me in the dark. We both gazed at the strange shadows. "Take a good look at those X-rays," he said. "You'll never see anything like either one of them again in your life." I remembered that the bile duct film had been discussed very briefly at X-ray rounds before, but no one had bothered to tell me what it showed, and I was grateful for the hint. But the films were memorable in more ways than Mack thought. Each was a tribute to one of the most conspicuous failures of modern medicine: noncompliance. These patients had been so reluctant to see a physician that they had allowed minor problems to reach grotesque, medical-curio proportions. What encounters with physicians in the past made these mature people with normal mental functions allow their illnesses to get so out of hand?

I had kept going to social service rounds, hoping for something worthwhile to happen, and the next day, something did. There was a fifteen-minute discussion of Mrs. Grady's family—their inability to accept the impossibility of doing anything to improve her mental status. One minute she had been sitting up in bed talking with them after completely successful surgery, and the next she was a "vegetable." According to the floor nurse, the family felt abandoned by the doctors and were taking out their frustrations on the nurses. They had been very upset by a doctor who told them, "She has beautiful gases." This was only medicalese for stable lung function, meaning she was doing well off the respirator; but they'd thought it was a facetious remark and were shocked and hurt.

Mark did not have much to contribute to this discussion, and he finally turned to me to help get him off the hook. I pointed out that I had told members of the family that her physical condition was steadily improving but there was no reason to believe that her mental condition would improve. I urged that this very religious family be seen by a priest. I had seen one occasionally on the floor, and I knew he was assigned to the hospital; but I had no idea how he came to see one patient or family rather than another. Evidently no one in the room—there were three social workers, five nurses, and an intern—had thought of this before, but they seemed to think it was a good idea.

That night I was on again. I admitted another patient for breast biopsy, wondering if she, before the procedure, would meet the surgeon who would make the intraoperative decision as to whether or not to remove her breast. I spent two hours examining and interviewing her, which was considered too long, but I couldn't get it down much below that and still have a manner that allowed me to live with myself.

I stopped in to see the woman who had attempted suicide, as I did at least a couple of times a day. She lay in her casts in the same position, tubes and all, always looking extremely alert and inexpressibly frightened.

"How're you doing?" I asked brightly.

She looked at me out of round dark eyes in her large, childish, chubby face. She always answered the same way in the same thick regional accent and the same flat intonation: "I'm in severe pain." Sometimes, as tonight, she also said, "My thoughts are racin'." She did not have delusional ideas, or hear messages, or see things that weren't there. She just had racing thoughts, about everything. And the few sentences she pronounced were uttered almost questioningly. More than once she apologized for what she had done, for "causin' all this trouble." I told her she did not owe anyone any apologies. I tried to see her as often as I could, but her demeanor was so poignant it became hard to bear.

Mark and I went down to the ten o'clock meal, but there wasn't to be one for us tonight. We were beeped from the cafeteria into the O.R. where two cases had come in from the Emergency Room. Marty was gowning up for an emergency abdominal exploration. An old man named Gilligan had been found unconscious on the floor of his apartment, where he had lain for an unknown length of time. When he was finally partially aroused he complained of abdominal pain. His bowel sounds were absent.

Mark was needed on the other case, so Marty and I were alone together on the Gilligan case. By the time I got my gloves on Marty had opened the abdomen. The stench was terrific and reminded me of an awful smell I had once encountered in Africa, when a buffalo had been butchered after three days of walking around with a bullet in its belly. Then I had had to sit down. Now it was hard to stay by the operating table.

Mr. Gilligan had had a complete infarct, or blockade, of his superior mesenteric artery, a major supplier of the intestines. As a result, a long section of his bowel was dead. At least two feet—normally a shiny pinkish or beige color—were black, with adjacent segments showing intermediate colors due to partial capillary refill from collateral vessels. When I got used to the stench and was steady on my feet, I began wondering how long this man had had to lie alone after the infarct in order to have this much rotten gut.

I was also apprehensive about working alone with Marty, but this was unnecessary. He was in a wonderful mood—in his element, in the middle of the night, with no big-shots breathing down his neck and no nurses swarming around like flies. He was his own man, in a world he completely controlled. He did what seemed to me a magnificent job sewing in a venous graft to replace the infarcted section of artery and, cursing all the way, cutting out a long section of bowel.

"This is awesome, awesome. I don't know how much to take out of this fucking thing. How much should I take out?" he asked almost cheerily.

"You're asking me?"

"This looks pretty good," he said, holding up a section of pinkish bowel. "Should I leave it in?"

"I guess so," I said. "It looks good to me, too."

Somehow, with all these matter-of-fact, obscenity-laden remarks making for the fine mood, Marty allowed regret for the patient to come through—which I had never seen him do before. As we worked through the night, I gradually realized that the patient didn't have a chance, and that Marty actually felt bad for him, a feeling mitigated, but not erased, by his pride in the work he was doing.

The next morning at rounds Mr. Gilligan seemed better, and I was ready to cheer, but those who knew were not optimistic. In the afternoon he deteriorated markedly, and Marty took him down to the O.R. for reexploration. He found a more extensive section of newly dead bowel, and this time there was no point in trying. The following morning, Thursday, he was no longer there, having died during the night.

Marty was not in a good mood. We passed the bed of a patient who suffered from intermittent claudication—pain in the legs due to compromise of the arterial supply. Marty's plan was to put in a bypass graft. Bob Andrews, the gentlest and most courtly of the residents, wanted to try angioplasty, a relatively new technique for widening the clogged vessel by introducing a catheter into the narrowed portion and opening up a balloon; his father, a vascular surgeon, had helped pioneer this technique, which was replacing some forms of bypass surgery as a safer, less invasive, less expensive, effective procedure. But Marty said no, without an explanation.

Another patient had a gangrenous middle toe on his right foot, scheduled for amputation that morning. The toe was various shades of green and black. Marty took hold of it between his thumb and middle finger and wiggled it a bit. He assigned Mack to do the operation with him. Then he went on, without washing his hands, to the next patient, a Jehovah's Witness with a hand-lettered sign—"No blood products"—hung over his bed.

Across the room my eye was caught by a young mother of two who had had a simple appendectomy and was now well and ready to go home. Her beauty was enhanced, as it is for most people, by sleep, and her long brown hair lay in charming disarray on her pillow. Her right leg, slender and gold-brown, was drawn up beyond the sheet on the bed.

Mack said to Milano, "Positive G.C.," gesturing at her.

"No kidding!" said Milano, and he and several other residents laughed softly. "Does she know?"

"I'm sure the nurses'll tell her."

G.C., I thought, *G.C. Oh, right. Gonococcus. Gonorrhea. Damn.* And I looked back at her, wistful as a moon-struck boy.

Finally we rounded on Mr. Leary, a middle-aged man with a rare condition known as Fabry's disease who had lately developed a cardiac arrhythmia. Marty, who for reasons I had not understood always gave him special attention, was obviously disturbed. When we were all out safely in the hall, he muttered, "We ain't never gonna be able to present this guy at Grand Rounds unless we get him fixed up." He was almost twitching. He took Milano aside by the arm and said, "I'm serious. You know, we gotta present this guy a week from today." And they went off talking in low tones.

After rounds, we all sat or stood by the nurses' station while Marty went over the patient list and the O.R. schedule, assigning cases to the residents. This was the usual routine. When he came to the femoral artery bypass case, Bob politely asked him again whether he would be willing to consider angioplasty. Marty reddened, his eyes wide and bulging, his mouth tight. He threw his clipboard across the whole length of the desk, knocking over a cup of coffee that soaked the papers and clattered noisily into a corner. Everyone stopped short and turned. Marty began yelling. "Who's the chief resident here? Are you the chief, or am I? Now what did I fucking say? Did I say it was gonna be a bypass? You bet I did. I said it was gonna be a bypass and it's gonna be a fucking bypass. You got it? Or you need me to say it again?"

In his most calm and courtly voice, Bob replied, "I got it, Marty."

"What do you make of that?" I asked Mack later.

"Oh, that's just Marty. Bob's all hot on angioplasty because his father helped invent it. But Marty's father and grandfather were both surgeons, so he's not too impressed."

I didn't see what this had to do with it, but I didn't think I would get much further, so I changed the subject. "I'm beginning to think this is a hereditary profession. Mark's father's a surgeon too. Yours?"

"My father's just a drunk," he said cheerfully.

"What does he do?"

"Oh, he's an English professor." Mack went on his way.

I lingered for a moment. On the bulletin board above the small puddle formed on the table by the coffee Marty had spilled, a new item was posted. It was an embossed announcement on heavy ivory-colored stock that read in fine black italic print:

JOHN ROBERT TAYLOR, M.D.
Announces the Opening of His Office
For the Practice Of
GENERAL SURGERY
at
658 Park Avenue
New York, New York 10010

Office hours   Telephone:
by appointment   555-6845

Well, I thought. The Holy Grail. It must have been a source of inspiration to the residents, to see such palpable evidence of success on the part of someone who was just recently one of their number. Marty would soon be heading for the same fertile ground, but it was hard to visualize him in private practice. I was beginning to appreciate the value of private practice: at least there, a man like Marty would be as much at the mercy of his patients as they would be at his. For all my support for socialized medicine, I did not like the idea of patients not choosing their physicians.

"Are you busy?" Mark was talking to me, and I snapped out of my reverie.

"What's up?"

"Would you mind taking the stitches out on that appendectomy?"

"My pleasure," I said, and meant it. It was not every day that a medical student got to spend a few minutes with an attractive young woman. Then I remembered she had just been told that she had gonorrhea. What sort of mood would she be in?

She was wide awake and sitting bolt upright with an untouched breakfast tray in her lap. She looked angry and hurt.

"Good news," I said. "I'm here to take the stitches out. I'm sorry to disturb you during breakfast."

"That's O.K. I'm in no mood to eat."

"Not feeling well?" I swung the tray away and sat down on the edge of the bed.

"I'm fine. I'm glad I'm gettin' the stitches out. I'm supposed to go home today." She paused and looked away, fingering her long brown hair. "And when I get home I'm gonna kill my husband." She looked back at me.

"Oh?"

"Yeah. Didn't you hear about that test I got? Everybody seems to know about it."

"I did hear something about it. It's not everybody. It's just the people who are directly involved in your care."

"Well, it seems like everybody. I don't know if I'm gonna kill him or not, but I'm sure gonna get rid of him."

I covered her carefully with the bedsheet before pulling up the johnny, so that only the bandage on the appendectomy wound was exposed. She had a smooth slim body, and her slightly buck teeth somehow seemed to add to her charm. "Is it really that bad?"

"I can't even believe it. He picks up a disease like that and brings it home to me."

I gently pulled the bandage away from the wound. "Let me know if I hurt you," I said, moving very slowly. "Do you really want this to bring an end to your marriage?"

"Shouldn't I? I just don't know if I should kill him or just kick him out."

"How old are your kids?" The stitches, over a pink wound that was healing nicely, made a ladder down the smooth skin of her belly. I painted the wound with Betadine. As slowly as possible, I opened the stitch removal kit and took the scissors and tweezers to the first stitch.

"The boys are eight and six."

"Have things been going well? It may hurt or itch a bit when I pull each stitch."

"Until this. It's O.K. It doesn't hurt."

"Is he a good father?"

She hesitated. "He's a terrific father."

"Is he a good husband?"

"He always was a good husband until now."

"Do you think he has someone else, something serious?" The stitches made a little pile on the blue paper from the stitch removal kit. There were only about six left, and I was trying to make the process last as long as possible. I went even slower.

"Oh, no, I know what it is. It's his night out with the boys." She seemed calmer. She took a deep breath and shook her head. "So what do you think I should do?"

There were only three stitches left, and I gave up the pretense and stopped. "It sounds to me like you have a basically good marriage. You said he's a terrific father. You love him?" She pouted a little, waited, and then nodded. "You know," I said, "I don't think he's the first married man who did something like this." She smiled and even grunted a laugh.

"I guess not."

"It doesn't mean you shouldn't talk to him about it. Even yell at him.

But it sounds to me like you don't want your marriage to stand or fall on this."

She was smiling and getting her color back. I took out the last three stitches. The wound looked beautiful. I cleaned it with antiseptic again and put on a new bandage.

"Are you married?" she said. I nodded. "Kids?" I told her about them. She looked into my face for a long time. "Thank you for talking to me. I feel much better," she said.

The job of stitch removal should have taken three minutes. I had been with her about fifteen. I didn't know whether she really would have left her husband, and I'd never know whether she would end up staying with him. But something told me that those extra twelve minutes were among the most important of my two months in surgery.

That morning I scrubbed with Bob and Mike on an obese cholecystec-tomy—a gallbladder removal on yet another rather fat lady. This was the same operation I had scrubbed in on with Mike on the first day, except now he was being supervised by Bob, who was a prince, instead of by Marty. Although it was only Mike's second "gall bag"—he had done other operations in between—and although he was still quite nervous, this one went as smoothly as tying shoelaces. Bob's patient guiding voice obviously calmed Mike, and Mike seemed a different person after fifteen or twenty minutes. My stay on the ward had been framed by these parallel proce-dures, elegantly demonstrating the worst and the best of surgical teaching.

In the evening at the nurse's station people were as usual milling and jostling each other in a buzz of activity. While I was turning through the card rack I noticed that Mr. Gilligan's card was still there. Mack was standing next to me stamping up some blood forms on another patient, and I pointed it out to him. In a smooth motion, without missing a beat, he grabbed it and flipped it into the wastebasket a couple of feet away.

"He doesn't need that anymore," he said, with something between a smirk and a smile. Both of us went on with what we had been doing, but after he went away I retrieved the card from the wastebasket and slipped it into my pocket.

Saturday, my last day, was uneventful and pleasant. I scrubbed with Bob again on a healthy patient with multiple small lipomas—fatty growths just under the skin that were being removed for preventive and cosmetic reasons. Mark was there, and because the surgery was so safe and the lipomas so numerous, all of us—even me—got to do some of the work. Bob offered to let Sally, the scrub nurse, try one, but she was afraid her supervisor might find out. She was much more experienced in the O.R. than I and more likely to do the job well, but the hospital's insurance would cover me and not her.

I did three whole excision procedures myself, from cutting the skin through teasing the tumor out to sewing the small wound. The cosmetic result was considered essential here, so we did a plastic surgery stitch with very fine thread that brought the skin edges together by running parallel to the surface and never breaking it. There had to be no wrinkles and no clots, and the edges had to be perfectly juxtaposed. It was not easy, and I was pleased to master it. "Hey, we'd better get Plastics down here to see this," Bob joked.

I said good-bye to Marty Wentworth while he was scrubbing for another operation that I would not be in on. "I hope you learned something," he said.

"Sure," I said, without a pause. "I learned that very often surgery is the most conservative option." This was one of his favorite formulaic phrases, frequently prefaced by, *"If there's one thing I want you to take away from this rotation . . ."* He nodded in his gruff version of solemn satisfaction. Evidently it had not occurred to him that I was making fun of him.

Up on the ward I walked around with a heightened sense of all that was going on around me. I noticed that the nurses had taped to the wall a poem typed on now yellowed and brittle paper:

PLEASE SEE MY NEED

Take time to hear my words
Please know that I'm still here
Outside I'm weak and sick and worn
Inside my heart knows fear

I have so much I want to say
There's much undone to do
I don't want a world of cold machines
I just want some time from you

You check for fever—you check for pulse
And then you're on your way

Oh please just sit and hold my hand
A few minutes—can't you stay?

Skip my bath. Don't change the sheets.
Use this time instead . . .
Let me share the fears I know.
Please, sit here by my bed.

Inside I beg, but I can't ask
Your time is yours to give
So many need your help and care
So many—who will live

I've used up all the life I have
I now await the day
So God, I pray you'll see my need
Please send someone who will stay

It was unattributed. I remembered the poem I had copied down in the microbiology lab over a year earlier, in which patients with syphilis were grotesquely ridiculed, and decided to copy this one down as well. It was the only time in my two months of surgery when I would encounter such sentiments, even in an aside or an allusion, and it had taken me three weeks to notice it.

The medical students could leave in the middle of the afternoon, and it looked sunny and inviting through the hospital window. I stopped to say good-bye to a resident.

"Come back for your fourth-year surgery elective," he said.

I shook my head. "No," I said. "I'm doing my fourth-year surgery elective in Santa Fe, New Mexico." This was where Marty was going into private practice.

He was speechless until he got the joke. A restrained smile played around his eyes and mouth. "That would be awesome," he said finally. "Awesome."

6

NEUROSURGERY AND NEUROLOGY

Lesions of the Soul

"Scientific Detail Overwhelms Regard for Human Needs at Medical Schools," proclaimed a *New York Times* headline during my last week on surgery. The article reported the first comprehensive review of medical education by the Association of American Medical Colleges in fifty years. A blue-ribbon committee of medical educators and administrators had conducted the study. "Specialization and the rapid rate of advancement of knowledge and technology," their report was quoted as saying, "may tend to pre-empt the attention of both teachers and students from the central purpose of medicine, which is to heal the sick and relieve suffering. . . . The relief of suffering requires that physicians have an exquisite regard for human needs," which must be "taught largely by example." The study took three years and cost a million dollars.

Around this time I also happened to see the first episode of "St. Elsewhere," a new television series billed as a true-to-life doctor show. The situations were certainly more realistic than those I had seen on "Ben Casey" and "Dr. Kildare," the doctor shows of my childhood. The young physicians seemed appropriately stressed, and the language had a realistic salty flavor, although nothing approaching the harsh vulgarity of real house-officer talk. But what was completely unrealistic was that the television doctors cared profoundly about their patients, not just as cases but as people. In the main plot, the hero was losing a teenage patient to a fancier hospital; heartbroken because of his affection for her, he slept in her room. In the subplot, a psychiatric resident had literally lost a depressed patient, who was wandering somewhere in the hospital. All her thoughts centered on the welfare of this patient, whom she seemed to view as something like a sister.

These motives were laughable. The main thought of a resident in the first situation would have been, *Damn, that was a great case, I could have used it on rounds,* or more likely, *One less to worry about; easiest turf this week.* As for the subplot, the psychiatrist's main thought would have been the proverbial and ubiquitous, *My ass is grass.* And of course, both cases were way too "clean" to be real.

But despite my growing cynicism, I was looking forward to my time coming up on neurosurgery and neurology. One of my main interests in medicine was in brain malfunction. I might well decide to go into neurology, or even—although this was unlikely because of the long, hard course of training—neurosurgery. Neurosurgeons were known as the most civilized and cultivated of surgeons. They were even said to care about such matters as the problem of mind. Though Sjogren had called neurologists the worst fleas in medicine, I also remembered the words of my neurologist-clinical preceptor during my first year in medical school: "If you want to be a *fixer,* don't go into neurology; but if you want to be a *healer,* it may be the field for you."

In my first encounter with neurosurgery, I was ushered into an O.R. where one of the world's most famous brain surgeons was operating on a thirty-one-year-old man. The great man of course took no notice of us. I was watching the procedure with a visiting neurosurgeon from Japan, who in broken English told me about the patient. I glanced quickly over the record. The patient was an attorney, a partner in a major law firm who had been disturbed by worsening headaches that had finally begun to wake him up from sleep. (I remembered a clinical pearl: *Headaches that wake the patient are almost always sinister.*) Various medical treatments over the course of a year or so had been unsuccessful, and recently he had begun to have seizures. Finally a CAT scan of the head had shown a shift in the midline of the brain—ominously indicative of a space-occupying process going on on one side of the line.

The Japanese surgeon showed me the CAT scan, hanging, back-lit, on a viewing box on the wall. I could just make out the shift in the midline. It seemed to me there were no other abnormalities on the scan, an impression confirmed both by the radiologist's report in the chart and a shrug of the Japanese surgeon's shoulders. Nevertheless the patient, Gerald Edwards was his name, was presumed to have a tumor; the clinical picture, combined with the midline shift, were said to be unmistakable.

I turned back to the center of the brightly lit white room. Dr. Brennan had reflected—turned back—the brain's protective covering called the dura mater, Latin for "hard mother." The right side of the brain was exposed in all its corrugated glory, holding a substantial part of Gerald Edwards's soul. Dr. Brennan held a suction device in his right hand and activated the vacuum with his foot. I knew from my neuroanatomy courses, and also from some work I had done on rat brains, that the consistency of brain tissue is gelatinous; one can stick one's finger through it with little resistance. There was therefore no need for a scalpel, only the suction device. Dr. Brennan leaned forward and began to destroy the right frontal lobe.

I knew from the chart that the patient was right-handed, which meant that the left side of his brain would almost certainly be dominant for language. Nevertheless the right frontal lobe played some role in certain higher mental functions. I looked at the CAT scan again, and saw as little as before. When I turned back there was already a substantial hole, rapidly widening. With the help of the Japanese surgeon and the scrub nurse, Dr. Brennan now prepared two samples in test tubes for the pathologists, and sent them out, but he went on sucking without waiting to hear the results.

I was amazed. I knew that what I was watching had to be legitimate, but I couldn't get used to the idea of such destruction. This wasn't a colon, it was a brain. And why couldn't I see any tumor on the CAT scan? Was this man losing a major part of his brain on the basis of a clinical hunch?

There was a crackling and then a voice, probably female, on a loudspeaker. "First two samples normal." These had been subjected to frozen section examination by an expert neuropathologist. Dr. Brennan paused briefly and cocked his large head as he listened, thick gray curls showing at the edge of his blue paper cap, but then went right back to vacuuming brain tissue. As I listened to the sucking noise of the vacuum, I remembered an old joke about neurosurgery: *"Slurp!* There goes the eighth grade. *Slurp!* There goes the seventh grade. . . ."

The cavity had widened from about two to four centimeters, and I looked at the Japanese surgeon for reassurance. He seemed perfectly calm. Two more samples were now sent out, again without an interruption in the procedure. At some points the achievement of hemostasis was a challenge, but for the most part there was only the slow, patient sucking away of brain tissue, which fled in little pinkish gobs through the long plastic tube.

"Sample three normal," said the scratchy voice on the loudspeaker. "Sample four normal." This time Dr. Brennan did not look up. I could hardly believe my eyes and ears. He was calmly sucking away a brilliant young man's frontal lobe and not even flinching when the path samples showed normality.

A fifth sample was normal as well. By this time a large proportion of the right front half of the lawyer's brain had been removed, and an enormous gaping hole remained behind. Finally the loudspeaker said, "Sixth sample, mild anaplasia." More samples went down and more brain was removed. Mild anaplasia was nonspecific and not terribly impressive. "Here it is," said the scratchy voice at last. "Seventh sample, low grade astrocytoma." Now Dr. Brennan paused for what seemed a long time. I almost thought I could hear a soft sigh of relief.

Probably not. I had underestimated his judgment. As the surgery and sampling went on, there proved to be a large and highly malignant astrocytoma, a tumor that certainly would have killed the young man in the very near future if it had not been substantially debulked. It might eventually kill him anyway. An enormous amount of the right hemisphere had been removed, and it remained to be seen what the cost in mental function of this lengthened life would be. But the tumor that Brennan had seen in his mind's eye—the one that couldn't be seen on the CAT scan—was large and malignant and dangerous. It was comforting that in this age of supertechnology a great surgeon could still fly more or less by the seat of his clinical pants.

Rounds with the neurosurgical residents began at six in the morning, half an hour earlier than with the general surgeons, perhaps because their surgery took longer. The senior resident was Peter Byron, a reserved and somewhat gruff, short man with blond hair that kept falling in front of his glasses. Rumor had said he was nice, though, and he confirmed this by the way he talked with his patients.

He did something in the first minutes that immediately endeared him to me. On six A.M. walk-rounds, instead of flipping the lights on in each room and parading in with the troops to a dazed, half-asleep, psychologically stunned patient—as Marty Wentworth and the general surgeons had done—Peter carried a flashlight pointed up at the ceiling. He entered the darkened rooms holding the flashlight and spoke to the sleeping patients in more or less gentle tones. There were only three residents in the group, and the other two, whose first day on the service it was, looked puzzled. But by the second day all three of them carried flashlights, the two junior residents following Peter's lead. The group looked like a little chorus of Christmas carolers, holding their flashlights toward the ceiling like candles, gliding from bed to bed and room to room.

Here a young woman was asked about her facial pain; there a middle-aged woman about her seizures; and still farther on an elderly man with a stroke was asked to name some common objects: "Necktie . . . that's a necktie. Watch. I just told you, watch. Oh, you mean the glass of the watch . . . yes, that's a . . . crystal. Crystal." Sometimes it would take a prompt, like "cr . . ." Although it seemed to me a pretty archaic form, a failure on "crystal" would generally be considered to be evidence of a mild anomia —an inability to name things, which could in some cases be traceable to a specified lesion of the brain. In the N.I.C.U., the neurosurgical intensive care unit, the lawyer Gerald Edwards lay in a stuporous condition, which was not an ominous sign at this stage. Dr. Brennan would be in to see him later, but for now Peter Byron pronounced him stable. I looked at his vital signs and they looked good to me too.

I scrubbed with another staff neurosurgeon, putting in a shunt—basically a drainpipe—in a baby with hydrocephalus, or "water on the brain." The internal cavities of the brain, called the ventricles, are normally fluid-filled, like an underground river system. They produce half a liter of fluid, much more than their total volume, every day, and if the exit channels for the used-up fluid are blocked, the fluid collects and places intolerable pressure on the brain. Proper placement of a shunt would allow this nine-month-old girl to grow normally and to live a normal life. It was good to be in on an operation that was almost guaranteed to result in a true medical miracle. As I looked at the anesthetized child with her shaved, slightly misshapen head, I wanted to foretell for her a world of future happiness. I began to think that being a brain surgeon might be worth seven brutally difficult years.

Later I admitted a patient in her mid-fifties who had been experiencing headaches and dizziness for just over a year. I was in the medical student's usual sink-or-swim situation. Told nothing about the case, I was expected to interview and examine her and then to form hypotheses about her problem and suggestions for treatment. Essentially I was supposed to pretend to be knowledgeable and wise, or else why was the patient wasting her time with me? Yet I was also supposed to refrain from answering questions I was not qualified to deal with, which might mean the most important issues on the patient's mind.

I had by now done dozens of admissions, and I was certainly becoming adept at the mechanics of interviewing and examining, as well as the social side of the situation, but the basic embarrassment of pretending to be something I was not, accurate introductions notwithstanding, was still painful. Yet I knew it was not a waste of time. Almost always the medical student's admission "note" in the chart—four to ten pages of densely packed information—is the most thorough part of a patient's record, and interns, residents, staff physicians, and nurses sometimes read it carefully. From time to time a medical student will notice—"pick up on"—something in the history or physical that everyone else has missed, and very occasionally this can make the difference between success or failure in treatment, even life or death.

Also, the medical student almost always spends more time with the patient than anyone else. What psychiatrists call the "therapeutic alliance"—a doctor-patient relationship tending to promote understanding of the illness and compliance with the treatment—is sometimes greatest with the medical student. And not infrequently, the medical student is in a uniquely good position to give comfort.

Letitia Simpson's left-sided headache over the back of her head, combined with dizziness, had worsened over the course of the past year. She sometimes experienced a "dazzling" in either eye, followed by pain in the opposite brow. She heard an occasional knocking in her left ear before the headaches began. And she was always tired. "I feel as if something is taking me away," she said. She had had migraines with fainting spells as a child, but these had stopped many years earlier.

A thin woman with curly red hair and large glasses on a pleasant lined face, she seemed extremely nervous and tired. She was scheduled for an angiogram—an X-ray of the brain after injection of dye into certain blood vessels—in the morning. She knew that the result of this test might lead to brain surgery, and she was terrified. She had spent the past few days agitated, depressed, and crying.

My physical examination of her, which embarrassed her only slightly, was not very informative. It is often said that 85 percent of the information needed to make a diagnosis is in the history, with most of the rest coming from tests. This dictum had always made me wonder why so little emphasis in my medical training was placed on how to talk to patients, and I suspected that this was because so few doctors knew.

There was not to be any great "medical student pick-up" with Letitia Simpson. All I knew about her problem was that she was suspected of having an abnormality of blood-vessel structure in the brain. Migraine, which in her case might not be related, was part of a vast spectrum of disorders of brain blood vessels resulting in almost every symptom the human brain can produce, from pain and dizziness to stumbling and visions. I reassured her about her surgeon, who was superb, and about the hospital in general. This seemed to make her feel better, or perhaps it was only that I spent time with her.

With Marcia Rosen, whom I met the next night, comfort was not so easy. This dark-haired, dark-eyed thirty-year-old had evidently been pretty before some obvious damage had distorted a part of her face. She was one of many patients on the neurosurgical service who had waged an extended and losing battle with pain. In her case it was excruciating facial pain, due to an unknown abnormality of the nerve supplying sensation in the face. She had had several of the most current and specific surgical procedures. These had damaged sensation on the left side of her face, and left her eye constantly red and tearing, her eyelid drooping, and her facial muscle tone somehow terribly wrong. None of the procedures had mitigated the pain.

In a state of constant fury against her surgeons, toward me she was defensive and contemptuous and yet somehow dependent and even conspiratorial. She had come to physicians with a terrible, frightful pain, and they had resolved nothing, only inflicted further great irreparable damage. She had wanted to become an actress and now they had destroyed her face. She was hurt and lonely and frightened. The pain and her resentment of her doctors had become her life. She wanted to know which side I was on, and I couldn't tell her, since I didn't know myself.

Certainly I could not reflexively support the profession. I had once heard a lecture by a neurosurgeon who after a whole career of operating for intractable pain, had concluded that this was a futile enterprise. He reached this conclusion only after he had reviewed and tried every known procedure at every level of the spinal cord and brain that attempted to separate the person from the pain. Soon afterward he had given up neurosurgery for a new career in preventive medicine and public health. A number of patients on the ward suffered pain that could not be explained, or pain combined with depression, or pain that seemed to violate physiological principles, or pain in a limb that was no longer there. No one suspected them of faking. Often there was nothing that could be done for them, yet sometimes a previously untried medicine—something unexpected, perhaps, like an antidepressant drug—or a surgical procedure interrupting a part of the presumed "pain pathway" eliminated their pain completely, and that utterly changed their lives.

Marcia was now scheduled for a procedure in which two holes would be drilled in her skull, preparatory to a leucotomy procedure, a very minor successor to the old frontal lobotomy. She had no idea whether this would help her, and neither did I. She was obviously trying it out of desperation,

and wanted to have my support, if not for the surgery at least for her
hatred of her doctors. I could not give her either; and, since the operation
would be done in two stages, with the brain part postponed, I would not
even be around to see the result.

Two days later I stood in on surgery on Letitia Simpson's cerebellum,
a major brain center for the coordination of movement. The angiogram
had been positive, showing an A.V.M., or arteriovenous malformation, in
the blood vessels supplying the cerebellum. This could account for many
or most of her symptoms; it was a congenital malformation, and the appropriate treatment was removal. Because of the approach to the cerebellum
needed, she had been anesthetized in the sitting position, and her skull
was bolted to a big metal frame erected around her. Most of her curly
carrot-colored hair was shaved off, and the weight of her head at least was
suspended from the bolts. The neurosurgeon was helpful throughout the
procedure, telling me about each step of the penetration of her brain. The
A.V.M., when exposed at last, looked like a giant blood spot on an egg yolk,
and it was rather relieving to see it go. I was confident that this would all
do her good, but I had never, even in the O.R., seen a human being in such
a grotesque position, and it made me unreasonably sad.

By the end of the week Gerald Edwards, the young lawyer who had had
a great chunk of his brain removed along with his tumor, was sufficiently
recovered to be visited and interviewed. As usual, I was given no guidance
as to how to go about talking with someone in his situation, but I was
interested enough in the effects of brain damage to have read a good deal
about them, and I overcame my timidity fairly readily.

When I entered his room, he was sitting up in bed, talking on the
telephone. I said I could come back later, but he was ready to end his
conversation. He was a man of medium build with a small dark moustache
and pale skin. He was friendly and invited me to sit down. He lit a ciga-
rette. I told him that I was a medical student and that the purpose of my
visit was to educate myself about his tumor and about what he had lost as
a result of the surgery. If I could help by communicating anything to his
doctors, I certainly would. In any case I would write a note in his chart
summarizing what I had learned.

He was apprehensive but insightful and engaging. He articulated methodically the subtle and not-so-subtle changes in his behavior and ability,
carefully distinguishing problems he had had before the surgery, because
of the tumor, from those that appeared afterward. As soon as he started

speaking my greatest fears for him—having watched Dr. Brennan remove so much of his brain—were alleviated. He was intact, *compos mentis,* amusing, already trying to work. Perhaps the theory that much of the brain is merely redundant tissue was correct?

He said that his major problem was with memory. Last night he had told a friend the same two jokes twice in one conversation. After being gently informed of this by his friend, he still could not remember having told the jokes the first time. In the months when the tumor was taking over his brain, he had experienced such forgetfulness, but on prompting had always been able to straighten things out.

He had also confused two friends with each other, telling both of them to come on the same day. " 'No one else will be here,' I told them. I told both of them that. Somehow I thought they were one person." This did not seem to bother him as much as I would have expected, and then I remembered that right-hemisphere damage was often associated with a lack of concern about many aspects of the illness and its deficits. People suffering acutely from paralysis of the right side of the body, indicating *left*-sided brain damage, were often extremely upset by their movement deficit, while those with the corresponding loss on the left side of the body, indicating right-sided brain damage, often shrugged their shoulders in eerie unconcern.

"I tried to shave twice this morning," he said. "When four or five people come around in a morning, I can't keep them apart in terms of what they said. I really need to have only one activity going on." He could not tolerate interruptions: they made him feel dizzy and completely lose his train of thought. "When that happens, I become frustrated and angry. I may start getting despondent." In such a mood of despondency he had had one seizure.

He was keeping notes about everything now, and small pieces of paper were strewn around the night table, the bed, even the window sill. He had made two phone calls to one of his office partners, trying to use the pieces of paper. I told him it reminded me of what doctors and medical students do—writing scores of notes on index cards and then stuffing them into a shirt pocket; what we called the "ectopic brain," an analogy to ectopic tissue, which is tissue found in a part of the body where it doesn't belong.

I knew that this was an apposite but optimistic analogy. Brain-damaged patients make good use of slips of paper, and they use them to bring back some portion of the effectiveness they have lost. Medical students may suffer temporary brain damage from lack of sleep—and I was to experience remarkable evidence of that—but we used our "ectopic brains" to extend our memories beyond what was otherwise humanly possible. Gerald Edwards was still recovering. He would probably get some of his memory and organizational skills back, but I was not hopeful about his ability to go on practicing law. Still, he was alive, and his devastating headaches were gone. Most important, and most amazingly, he was still Gerald Edwards.

This survival of identity is far from being the rule in brain afflictions. The following week I started on neurology, in another branch of Galen, half-way across town. From the brutal surgical and neurosurgical schedule of every other night on call, I now switched to every fourth night, and I was looking forward to that. But I did not yet know how hopeless the patients would seem.

The first, presented at Grand Rounds on the first day, was a forty-year-old mother who seemed to me, for all intents and purposes, to have lost her soul. I was not sure what I meant by that; no one is, I suppose, who is not religious. She was, now at least, a short, overweight woman of indeterminate middle age with a vacant stare out of gray eyes, a pasty complexion, and a bloated face. She was presented by the residents to Professor Lippmann, one of the best neurologists in America. The patient's mother was present, and she helped to clarify the history appearing in the record.

Edie's dementia had begun with an onset of insidious changes in her personality at the age of thirty-seven. She had become agitated and inexplicably hostile to those closest to her. She had also lost her personal habits of exceptional neatness and cleanliness. Although it eventually became apparent that she had a relentlessly progressive disease of the brain, these early episodes created an extraordinary psychological and moral quandary for her husband and three children. As her deterioration progressed her hostility fortunately waned, and she became abnormally placid. She lost her memory for both recent and distant events. Finally, in the last few months, she had begun to lose her continence, at least of urine. Any one of these changes would have represented a devastating change in Edie's personality, raising the question of whether she was still the same person; all of them taken together were tantamount to destruction, in any meaningful sense, of who she was.

"Would you believe it, I feel great," was her answer to Professor Lippmann's first question, and then after a pause, "My legs are gone." (There was no evidence of anything wrong with her legs.) She obeyed commands to rise, walk, and lift her arm, but was not able to close her eyes on command, although she could mimic this movement. Her reflexes had an abnormally persistent quality instead of waning with repeated elicitation, and she automatically grasped Professor Lippmann's finger when he used it to stroke her palm, even after agreeing to hold back. This lack of inhibition in certain reflexes is characteristic of deterioration of the frontal lobes of the brain.

All medical students memorize more than once a list of the treatable causes of dementia to ensure that complacency will not lead to the wrongful consignment of a human being to a fraction of human life. Edie had been carefully evaluated, and all treatable causes of dementia ruled out. She had led an exemplary life, had never used drugs or abused alcohol or cigarettes, and had never been seriously ill. The only finding in her elaborate evaluation was a widening of the grooves in her cerebral cortex, indicative of brain atrophy. This finding, together with the nature and course of her illness, was consistent with, although it could not prove, a diagnosis of early-onset Alzheimer's disease. "Healthy body, shattered mind," was the classic designation for this tragic condition. Other possible diagnoses were other slowly progressive dementias of unknown cause.

That was about the extent of the illumination of the case. I was fascinated; here was evidence of how the brain worked, seen in its deterioration, and some of the evidence, such as that suggesting frontal lobe atrophy, was specific and of the sort that could eventually help to build a theory of mind. But I felt the discomfort of the involuntary voyeur who guiltily enjoys what he is seeing. Had Edie's mother, and her other relatives, really given up hope, and were they just doing this as an act of generosity to medical science? Or was there still some shred of hope present, leading them to expect, against all advice, that these deliberations might actually lead Edie out of the empty labyrinth? If the former were the case, then everything we had done that morning was justifiable; if the latter, then it had all been inexcusably immoral. Or were some of us, like me, kidding *ourselves* about the outcome? This would tend to blur all such moral distinctions.

What happened the next morning did not require so subtle an analysis. Rounds in neurology began at the civilized hour of seven-thirty, and by eight o'clock we were at Edie Matthews's bedside. Nathan Stearns, the chief resident, a tall, heavy-set, cynical Englishman with a limp from childhood, looked around the room to make certain that only staff members were present, smiled his cynical smile, and began making fun of Edie to her face. He asked her a series of completely unnecessary questions, and she repeated in a nervous automatic way the last few words or a key phrase from each question, a problem known as echolalia—meaningless repetition of what the patient has heard.

Nathan limped closer to her, put his face up to hers, and said, "Echolalia! Echolalia!"

She furrowed her brow, smiled nervously, and repeated, slurring the word a bit, "Echolalia."

This probably would have gone on, but a resident stuck his head in the door and said very rapidly, "If anybody wants to see a big pontine infarct, page me and I'll show her to you." He began to close the door, but opened it again, checked to make sure that the patient was one who was *non compos mentis,* and said, "But do it soon, before she dies."

Nathan laughed and shook his head. "O.K.," he said, "let's see the rest of the players."

The rest of the players were not a cheering lot: two mildly demented old ladies with recent strokes, whom one of the junior residents referred to as "bookends"; several epileptics whose seizures had become intractable, including one young woman who was having repeated brain operations for them; two patients with Parkinson's disease who were in the hospital for frightening "drug holidays"—a controversial procedure in which patients were taken off L-dopa for a time, which some neurologists thought made the drug more effective when the patient was put back on it; a sixty-six-year-old man with suspected neurosyphilis, the late final stage of untreated syphilis; two young men in vegetative conditions with terminal brain illnesses; and a thirty-five-year-old woman with a severe crippling exacerbation of multiple sclerosis.

Of all these patients the only ones with diseases considered generally and clearly treatable were the epileptics and the Parkinsonian patients. But they were there because treatment was failing, and I was to learn that the "miracle drug" for Parkinson's disease, L-dopa, was at best a partial or temporary miracle in the midst of a relentlessly progressive disorder. I repeated to myself the healer-not-fixer adage of my first-year clinical preceptor, and I knew that the patients here needed whatever the neurologists could do for them. But I was beginning to doubt that such a steeply uphill fight was really for me, however interested I might be in the brain.

As the days went by I also began to understand more fully the bitterness and cynicism that some of the residents in this field exhibited. It was brutally difficult to face these patients day after day, to see the extremity of their need, to know that they needed you to do whatever you could, and yet to be able to do so pathetically little for most of them. I thought constantly *Research, research;* but research was not going to help the men and women on that ward that month, only their successors years or decades in the future. Many of them were willing subjects for studies of new treatments, but I knew enough about the studies and about the complexities of the nervous system in general, to know that this kind of clinical research had a low yield. The work that struck me as promising was more fundamental: the chemistry of neurotransmitters, the biophysics of membranes, the genetic machinery of the nerve cell, the radiation physics of brain imaging. As for the kind of research that interested me most—the effects of brain damage on the mind—that was so abstract in intent that its relevance to the suffering of these patients was highly questionable.

The attending physician for the month, an Australian named Bradley Gerard, conducted rounds later in the week. He consistently mispronounced the names of patients, including one who had personally corrected him and another who represented one of the families that had endowed the hospital. One of the patients whose name he pronounced two different ways had been on the ward for two full weeks.

Roger DeMay, a Parkinson's victim, was one of his private patients. He had had the disease for twenty years, and his hospital record was a history of treatment and advances in it. He had had a thalamotomy, a brain operation, fifteen years earlier, performed by a famous surgeon who pioneered it as a treatment for Parkinson's. And he had been one of the earliest recipients of L-dopa, which made him also one of its most long-standing veterans.

Therein lay the problem. L-dopa at best arrested the further deterioration that was an inevitable part of the natural history of untreated Parkinsonism. More often it did less than that, allowing deterioration to leak through over a period of years, requiring increases of medication dosage to the limits of what was tolerable. One strategy for dealing with this situation was to take the patient off L-dopa for a week under careful supervision in the hospital. Like many treatments, this one was based on sound theory—that the dosage required after the "holiday" should be lower—but its effectiveness was controversial.

It was also painful to watch. In fact, it was exactly like watching the L-dopa miracle in reverse. Mr. DeMay, a sixty-two-year-old man with thinning white hair, began to experience a slowing of his movements and a difficulty in initiating movement (classic bradykinesia) immediately, and this worsened steadily. From one day to the next his face became more stony, exhibiting the characteristic masklike quality, devoid of expression, associated with Parkinsonism. The disorder had little effect on the mind, so what we were watching was an alert mind becoming gradually trapped in a rigid musculature, a cage made up of his own face and body. As might be expected, he began to seem dejected, although what proportion of this was due to the abnormality of expression, what to the direct effect of withdrawal of a brain-altering drug, and what to a normal reaction to gradual paralysis, was impossible to say.

Dr. Gerard, when we were out of the patient's hearing, said, "This guy is the perfect example of a crazy Parkie. He actually secretes pills away around the house in case his doctor tells his wife to take his medicine away. He's just like an alcoholic. He's addicted to L-dopa." Unlike the alcoholic, of course, he had desperately needed the L-dopa long before he ever encountered it. Mercifully for all of us, he was put back on his pills, with slowly increasing dosage, two days later, and he began to demonstrate the original L-dopa miracle—in the positive direction—almost immediately.

On my second night on call we admitted a tragically stricken woman named Annie Mae Dillon, a pretty, black young mother who had suffered a ruptured aneurysm—a distended and weakened portion of an artery— in her brain, two days after giving birth to a normal, healthy baby. She had a stiff neck and a headache of extreme severity, and her CAT scan showed blood in the grooves of her brain. The treatment was to administer drugs to keep the brain from swelling, in order to decrease the pressure and the damage, and to keep her in a room by herself in near darkness lying absolutely still, without disturbances. The major danger was a "re-bleed," bleeding again from the same or another aneurysm.

I had got myself assigned to a resident named Steve Scoble, who not only exuded confidence in his knowledge and ability (being maddeningly handsome may have helped build his confidence) but was also the nicest of the residents by far. This choice was to prove even better than I had guessed. He turned out to be one of the most humane and decent house officers I met during my clinical years, and I never saw his judgment or competence questioned by anyone.

"This is serious," he said about Annie Mae. "This lady, as Dr. Gerard would say, is at death's door."

We also admitted a strange young man with a long-standing psychiatric illness who was now coming in for a thorough neurological evaluation. His name was Billy Tirell, and he had been knocked around for years with a variety of psychiatric diagnoses. When he dropped out of college, or more precisely, faded out, he had been viewed as depressed but even then he had had auditory hallucinations in the form of singing voices. His mother, who still took care of him, was a psychotic in remission who had had her own first breakdown shortly after his birth, and his father was a violent alcoholic who died while Billy was a child. During his childhood he was a good student but socially maladjusted—clingy and inclined to tantrums in early childhood, and wetting the bed until age nine. He was sexually abused by an uncle, and he had developed a number of strong idiosyncratic religious beliefs, among which—not surprisingly—was the belief that sex is dirty.

Billy had been treated at various times with virtually every type of drug in the psychiatric pharmacopoeia, and he had been on very high doses of the antipsychotic Stelazine for years. He had also had extensive psychotherapy. But his episodes of abnormal behavior were worsening. Lately they had taken on a more physically expressive quality, and he would repeatedly lick and stroke his mother, sometimes angrily. Because the episodes were discrete and consisted of stereotyped behavior, Billy's psychotherapist suggested that he have an EEG—an electroencephalogram, or brain-wave test. The EEG showed a pattern possibly consistent with an atypical form of epilepsy, although it could also be the typical abnormality of the schizophrenic patient.

When Billy became floridly psychotic despite the enormous dose of sixty milligrams of Stelazine daily, it was deemed useful to pursue the possibility that he did not have schizophrenia after all, but rather an exotic and identifiable brain disorder. Or perhaps the two superimposed on one another. He came to our unit for this evaluation, because of its reputation for analysis and treatment of subtle neurological disorders that might masquerade as psychiatric disorders. This interest put the unit on the frontier of knowledge and research in neuropsychiatry, since discoveries there might conceivably trace, using the most advanced techniques of brain evaluation, the neurological basis of psychiatric disorders.

Steve and I were keenly interested in such possibilities, and Steve immediately began alluding, only half ironically, to the possibility that Billy would help us to discover "the key to schizophrenia in the brain." From the viewpoint of Billy's best interest this goal of ours was probably unseemly. But it was our responsibility to see that he got a thorough neurological evaluation, and our excitement ensured that he would get exceptionally careful attention. For now, however, there was only the sad spectacle of a thin, pale, tense, wide-eyed twenty-five-year-old man, already losing his hair, frightened as a child saying good-bye to his mother in a terribly foreign place. He said little afterward, but the fact that he remained so tense when on so high a dose of a major tranquilizer was impressive. When he did speak, he said only, "What are you trying to do to me?" My patient explanations did not satisfy him.

After the physical examination it was necessary to subject him to the procedure of lumbar puncture—L.P.—to withdraw a sample of the fluid bathing his brain and spinal cord—the C.S.F., or cerebro-spinal fluid. The sample would be screened for a variety of possible abnormalities, including infectious organisms, and would give other clues to the state of his brain. Mastering the L.P. was one of the main goals for the medical student in the neurology rotation, and so far I had bungled two and then done one properly. There was a famous and oft-repeated rule of clinical teaching in medicine, "See one, do one, teach one." This rather chilling summary of the transfer of medical technique seemed laughable in its abruptness, and the residents often answered it with what they called The Galen Rule of Teaching: "See one, screw one, do one."

In any case, I was feeling lucky. With Steve looking over my shoulder I introduced the long thick needle into Billy's lower back between two vertebrae; pushed; and felt the pop of the dura mater as the needle entered the fluid-filled cavity below the end of the spinal cord. I hoped I had not injured any of the numerous nerve roots suspended in the fluid. Steve handed me the long glass column used for measuring pressure. I attached it to the needle, and released the fluid into the column. It rose clear and smoothly in the glass, with no sign of turgidity or blood tinge, but it kept rising to the abnormal pressure of two hundred ten. Steve and I looked at each other. It could have been a reflection of Billy's state of psychological tension, but it could also have signified one of a variety of neurological abnormalities. I collected some of the C.S.F. in two tubes to send down for laboratory analysis.

The previous day I had talked with an attending physician, about fifty years old, who had won an L.P. contest in his fourth year of medical school. He and his roommate, both of whom were going into neurology, had been tied with ninety-eight each on graduation day, but he had gone back to the ward after the ceremony and picked up two more. As I explained to Billy that he would have to lie flat for at least several hours to prevent a possibly severe L.P. headache, I decided that, for this month at least, I would be satisfied with ten.

After admitting Billy, around midnight, Steve and I peeked into Annie Mae Dillon's room again. As he opened the door to her room a crack, Steve turned to me and said, "What are we gonna do if she re-bleeds? We're gonna shit. We can't do anything. She'd just die right here waiting for the neurosurgeon. There's no neurosurgeon in the house at this hour." So her life might be lost because she had picked a branch of Galen where there wasn't always a neurosurgeon in the house. She lay still in the dark with a single little night-light—like my daughter's to keep away the demons—burning in a corner, no brighter than a candle. We stood at the door quietly, making sure not to wake her. She was breathing normally. The hush seemed almost sacred, and I suppose both of us were doing something that had a good deal in common with prayer.

Rounds the next morning were cynical and funny as usual. Outside Annie Mae Dillon's room—she had remained stable through the night—one of the residents began presenting her. A noisy cart rolled by in the hall where the group of us were standing, and the resident stopped presenting. Nathan Stearns followed the cart slowly with his eyes. "Is that the new alarm clock for the patients," he asked laconically in his most understated British voice, "or is it just Morning Symphony?" He turned back to face the resident, Barry Gerhardt, as the cart went out of earshot.

Barry continued. "Any questions about Dillon?" he asked, as if he had just given an entire presentation drowned out by the cart. This broke us up for a moment, but we soon composed ourselves enough to listen to his real presentation, which was still ominous.

We also rounded outside the rooms of the two young men who were functioning at a brain-stem level. One was in a coma with intractable seizures after sustaining a fever of 108° Fahrenheit. He was a married homosexual with an unexplained illness, and his code status was D.N.R. Nurses entered his room with only the strictest sterile precautions, gowned and gloved almost as if for surgery. I asked Steve what his story was, but he said only, "He's on the way out, I hope. Going to that great I.C.U. in the sky."

The other was a forty-four-year-old near the end of a four-year battle with the same type of tumor that I had seen removed—or at least partly removed—from the brain of Gerald Edwards, the young lawyer with the slips of paper. It was a malignant tumor of the white matter of the right frontal lobe, and it had recurred after an early successful treatment. Now it had spread throughout both hemispheres of the brain. He had seizures, almost constant infections and fevers, and, recently, gastrointestinal bleeding. He was not expected to survive much longer, but he was not D.N.R., a situation that disturbed the residents greatly. They discussed it extensively. His wife still insisted that everything be done for him, but his mother was said to be "getting close to the 'suffered enough' stage." The residents particularly resented the procrastination of the attending physician who, they thought, lacked the courage to put appropriate pressure on the family.

Steve, a second-year resident who was relatively new in neurology, lowered his voice. "Let me ask a question just between us. If this guy gets a code, is it a slow code?"

Barry, the third year, said, "This is a medical student's code."

Nathan nodded. "Nobody has to know," he said.

Steve smiled and said finally, "It's between us and God."

When, a few nights later, I admitted another man who was also suspected of having the same type of tumor, I was beginning to think there was some sort of epidemic. Francis Giannetti was a sixty-eight-year-old man with a kind face and a balding head of gray hair. He seemed exceptionally fit for his age, and his body was tanned and muscular under his blue wool robe. As he lay in the bed he seemed relaxed, although worried and sad, and he immediately put me at ease.

He had been perfectly well until three months earlier, when he experienced a pain in his right hip while jogging. This had progressed to a weakness, and then a dragging, of his right foot, a weakness in his right arm, and finally to a series of changes in mental status that he described variously as "a high" and as depression. There was no headache, dizziness, or nausea; but "a temporary high would come and slow me down, just like I had an extra drink." He began to have problems in following conversations, and trouble in directing the ten employees of his wholesale paper company. A spasm in his right calf and a tremor in his right hand finally brought him to the doctor, who referred him to a neurologist, who admitted him to the hospital.

When I examined his mental status systematically, getting beyond my immediate spontaneous affection for him, I realized that there were a number of problems. He was not only depressed and slow-moving, but hesitant in speaking, with frequent pauses to find the right word. He had a slight naming problem with rare or unusual words, and his tiny handwriting was shaky, with many errors. He had difficulty counting back from one hundred by sevens—a classic test for attention deficit in adults—and he had a small problem copying simple drawn figures.

I had become fairly adept at performing the obsessively detailed and orderly examination of the nervous system, and the findings in Mr. Giannetti's case were dramatic and consistent with all he had said. The weakness in his right arm was worst proximally—near the shoulder. There was some wasting of his biceps muscle. He had trouble flexing his right hip and foot and had decreased vibration sense—a subtle test for sensory deficit—

on the right side. The picture was a bit confusing because he had some old orthopedic problems that had nothing to do with his new neurological deficits: low back pain, arthritis in the fingers of his right hand, and a slightly bent-necked posture. But on the whole the picture was consistent with the possibility of a space-occupying process in the left, dominant hemisphere of the cerebral cortex—the hemisphere that controlled both the functions of language and the use of the right side of the body.

I did not like to picture Mr. Giannetti following the path taken by the man in a coma down the hall. I began hoping, unreasonably, that he would turn out to have some highly curable problem. I also began to be protective of him in small ways. I resented it when Steve came into his room at two-thirty in the morning, having just then finished his other work, and woke him up to examine him, without bothering to read my six-page admission note summarizing the history and physical. I knew that Steve had to examine him himself, at least minimally, but it seemed to me that he could have stopped in earlier, and that he could have profited from reading my note first.

Afterward, while Mr. Giannetti was having predictable difficulty getting back to sleep, Steve and I sat at the nurses' station and, after reading my evaluation, he scrawled a brief admission note of his own. Before signing it, he looked up, disgusted with himself. "What a shitty note," he said. "'Agree with medical student note,'" he quoted from his entry. "Jesus! How bad can I get?" Nevertheless, I took this as a compliment. This had never happened to me before, and it was a heady feeling—but two hours later the light was still on in Mr. Giannetti's room.

Once a week we had neuroradiology rounds with a good-natured, funny man named Monty Weisberg. We would sit in a dark room arranged like a small classroom, munching doughnuts, gulping coffee, and rubbing elbows with the top professors in neurology and neurosurgery while Dr. Weisberg flipped one CAT scan, skull X-ray, or angiogram after another on to the projection platform that threw them up on the screen. On a bulletin board was the lead copy from an ad in a doctors' magazine: *The only way to learn neurosurgery is to open people's skulls and practice.* See one, do one, teach one, I thought.

Dr. Weisberg was a short muscular man around forty, with a mop of dark hair and thick dark-rimmed glasses. "Let's take the haiku approach to history," he announced, trying to head off any long-winded patient presentations by the residents, who were supposed to give a thirty-second clinical précis for each film. Of the first CAT scan he said, "This is definitely a case of reduced tread life," meaning generalized mild brain atrophy.

"Are you sure this patient is not an orthopedist, maybe one who's a bit past it? You know the one about the best two years of an orthopedist's life? . . . The sixth grade?

"Next!" he shouted, putting up a skull film. "This chassis is completely kosher from bow to stern." And of a patient who had had an epidural blood clot—on the outside of the outer covering of the brain—successfully drained by the surgeons, he said, "Well, you know the neurosurgeon's motto: *You can't lose them all.*"

At around eleven we went upstairs and in the elevator Steve's beeper whistled its insistent message. Steve leaned over, craning down to get his ear close to it. *"Call . . . extension . . . four eight two six . . ."* said a mechanical voice. This was the neurology floor, so Steve didn't bother picking up the elevator phone but shot out when the doors opened. By the time I got to the nurses' station he had already talked to them. "Edie Matthews is seizing," he said. We ran down to her room and one of the nurses was preparing a syringe with the antiepileptic Dilantin, knowing that he would order it. Edie lay in the bed shaking, her usually soft body in tight spasm, her absent expression now contorted and glazed. She had been discharged from the hospital and was preparing to go home when the first seizure began. The injection Steve gave her ended the seizure, but only temporarily, and a few hours later she began seizing intractably and did not respond to the usual treatments for forty minutes, a life-threatening circumstance known as *status epilepticus.* She survived the episode, but she would have to remain in the hospital for some time.

Several days later, Mr. Giannetti had his scheduled CAT scan, and the news was not good. It confirmed the surmises made from the clinical data, that he had a characteristically destructive and irreversible cancer high on the convexity of the right frontal lobe, and it carried the gravest possible prognosis. I followed Dr. Gerard into Mr. Giannetti's room to hear how he would convey this information.

It was mid-afternoon, and the television was on in the darkened room. Dr. Gerard walked up to the bedside and talked over the soap-opera patter. "The CAT scan results are in," he said matter-of-factly but almost gently. "It's just as we thought. Probably a glioblastoma multiforme. It's not good news, but it's no different from what we expected."

"Does that mean it's malignant?" Mr. Giannetti asked.

"That's basically what it means, yes. Although it can't be said with absolute certainty without a biopsy." He turned to me and said, "Maybe you can stay here and explain to Mr. Giannetti a little bit more about the findings."

I nodded, since I had no choice. Then to Mr. Giannetti he said, "I have to go to clinic. I'll be back later and we can talk about it some more."

He was gone, and I began to explain more fully about the CAT scan and its implications. I couldn't hear myself very well, and I said, "Do you mind if we turn off the T.V.?" He picked up the remote control device and turned off the sound. To turn off the picture required a jarring and noisy flipping through all the channels; it was as if it were designed to make it difficult to turn it off, and he didn't try. Slowly he began to concentrate on talking with me, and his eyes drifted nervously back to the set only occasionally. It was clear that the medical details were not what he most wanted. He had already consciously accepted the fact that he was lost, and what he seemed to need was some time to work that fact into the deepest recesses of his soul. "I was so healthy," he said with a sad smile. "I was just getting into shape, jogging. I thought it was just a muscle cramp from jogging."

I sat down and listened to him. He began to talk freely, not about his illness but about his life. He had built his paper business from a one-man part-time operation into a busy firm with ten full-time employees, by working single-mindedly for thirty-nine years. "But without my wife I couldn't have done a thing," he said. "She was my right arm. Nowadays, I know, it's not supposed to be that way, they're supposed to do their own thing. But in those days we were different, and we were proud."

He had three grown children who meant more to him than anything, and he especially wanted to talk about them. A son and one daughter were married, with children of their own, but unlike many grandfathers he seemed to want to dwell more on his own children than on theirs. A second daughter was a painter, now on a fellowship in Italy, and he spoke glowingly about her success. His voice and face were full of love.

He was meditating aloud, almost as if there were no one in the room. But if no one were there he would not have allowed himself to speak. I said as little as possible. I heard no regrets, no recriminations, no analysis, not even sorrow really—only *This is what I did, and it was good.* There may have been the slightest tone of *It was good, wasn't it?* and I was glad to supply the affirmation. I felt greatly privileged by the opportunity to witness his accounting of his life, and I remembered the advice of the Jesuit priest who had become a psychiatrist: *The dying are courageous. They will help you to help them.*

Billy Tirell, the schizophrenic with the possible seizure disorder, was gradually weaned from his powerful tranquilizers and put on antiseizure medications—particularly a relatively new one, carbamazapine, which was believed to have antipsychotic as well as antiepileptic actions. As he came off Stelazine, he became increasingly alert but remained floridly psychotic. Instead of talking occasionally through a druglike stupor, he spoke frequently and rapidly, but the subjects were the same: the policemen who were trying to find him, their connection with the ballplayers whose names he kept on long lists, the religious persecution he had suffered because he had his own religion and refused to join any of the established ones. And he always had a suspicious or frightened look in his eyes.

After a week in the hospital, Billy wandered into the room of Roger DeMay, the Parkinsonian patient on drug holiday. Billy looked rather strange, and this strangeness was no doubt exaggerated for Mr. DeMay by the fact that he was trapped in his cage of unresponsive muscle, and couldn't flee or even call for help. Billy frightened him terribly, merely by standing at the foot of his bed. When a nurse—unfortunately, the most disaffected and insensitive one on the floor—took his arm and tried to urge him out of the room, he struck her. She called security and had him placed in four-point restraint. Or so her own account went the following day, at joint rounds with the head nurse—a man named Ira Feld—other members of the nursing staff, Steve Scoble, who was the resident concerned, and me.

What the nurse did not say was that ever since Billy had arrived she had insisted that he was dangerous and that the neurology service was not an appropriate place for him to be; this made everyone tense and defensive. Protestations by Steve and me that his record showed not a single instance of violence in the five years of his illness—regardless of which drugs he was or was not on—and the obvious fact that he was a pathologically shy and inward person, undesirous of contact, much less conflict, had fallen on deaf ears. The head nurse, an ambitious man who had good relations with the hospital nursing hierarchy, saw a need to protect his staff and an opportunity to exercise control over the residents. He was unresponsive to arguments about the purposes of Billy's evaluation or even about the general function of the unit in caring for patients with illnesses on the borderline between neurology and psychiatry. He was firm in his belief that his nurses should not have to be exposed to the risk of dealing with a psychotic patient. They were not psychiatric nurses, and they did not have the training or the facilities to deal with such patients. If the residents wanted him on the floor they would have to allow the nurses to keep him in restraint.

As we left the meeting I said to Steve through clenched teeth, "I can't think of anyone worse than that woman to have been put in charge of Billy last night."

"That's not the point right now," he said curtly and, I realized, properly. "The point is we have to deal with this situation."

We went to see Billy and found him completely docile in his bed, with big leather straps pinning his wrists and ankles to the metal framework of the bed. "Dr. Scoble," he said, whining like a little boy, "Dr. Scoble. I love you, Dr. Scoble. Please. Please let me out of this purgatory."

"I can't let you out right now, Billy," said Steve.

"Please, Dr. Scoble. Please."

"Not right now."

He was to stay in restraint for some days. I asked if he couldn't be transferred to the psychiatric floor and be in more experienced hands while continuing his neurological evaluation. The answer to this was that he was poor, and his insurance would cover the stay on the neurological service but not an admission to psychiatry. If he were to go to a psychiatric hospital it would be a state hospital, and there he would certainly not get the neurological evaluation he needed.

I was supposed to write a progress note on Billy every day, and so I had to record these unfortunate new developments. I wrote a long and detailed note summarizing the situation, particularly the evidence that Billy was not dangerous and concluding that the nursing staff was not really prepared to deal with a patient like Billy. Although I was careful to use the same words the head nurse had used, I meant them, of course, differently. And it was the first and only time during medical school that I signed the letters "Ph.D." after my name.

Later the head nurse said, "I read your note," which in itself surprised me. "I don't quite agree with the wording of your interpretation." I hadn't expected him to, but I found him pleasantly open to communication, and this may have got the whole thing settled, and Billy out of restraint, a little sooner.

The neuroradiology conference that week was as funny as ever, with Monty Weisberg—who was not just a stand-up comic but also a crackerjack neuroradiologist on the frontier of brain imaging—keeping us in stitches as usual. Professor Lippmann, I noticed, rarely laughed, but he also never commented negatively on Dr. Weisberg's routine, and occasionally I thought I saw a smile play across his solemn face. One CAT scan showed an ominous pattern of multiple defects in the core of the cerebral hemispheres, thought to be due to many tiny infarcts, or blockages of the arterial supply.

"This is what I like to call the Clearasil syndrome," said Dr. Weisberg, "blackheads all over the basal ganglia." A medical student on the neurosurgery service made the mistake of saying that he thought a patient might have a reduced amplitude of the cremaster reflex. This was a normal retraction of the scrotum after light stroking of the inner thigh. It was considered unreliable and rarely signified anything. "Here we have it," said Dr. Weisberg derisively. "The cremaster reflex, with Bo Derek."

"William H. Tirell," he next announced abruptly, and, my heart beating fast, I stumbled into a sketch of Billy's history, physical, and hospital course. He moved the CAT scan around until the image came into focus and orientation on the screen. "This, in the words of the great philosopher," said Dr. Weisberg, "is *gornisht mit gornisht,*" Yiddish for "nothing with nothing." He mentioned a few subtleties of the scan that might be of interest if they were more strikingly abnormal—slightly larger grooves and ventricles on the left, suggesting a subtle relative atrophy, and allowing the right brain to nudge the midline over just a bit. But this did not add up to anything that he would dignify with the label "abnormal" and certainly nothing that would merit a diagnosis.

Together with Nathan Stearns and another resident, I visited the man with the "Clearasil syndrome." We found him in a comfortable lounge in a private wing, sitting alone in his wheelchair, the late afternoon sun streaming in through the window. He had become demented as a result of numerous small strokes and had what was known as a fluent aphasia— a loss primarily of speech comprehension combined with a tendency to produce a "fluent" stream of contentless, slurred speech, with a paucity of nouns and an absence of intent or meaning. He had been an English professor, and the destruction of his ability to find words for his thoughts —he was groping for them more or less constantly—seemed a particularly painful punishment. Because of this, and because he had become demented through an extremely common disease process, I identified with him more strongly than with some of the other patients. I left him, hoping that, whatever else might happen to me, I would not outlive my brain.

On morning rounds we saw the young woman with the severe exacerbation of multiple sclerosis. "I'm definitely better," she said very cheerfully. "I mean, forget the Olympics, right? But I can lift this leg, which I couldn't do at all before." She pointed to her left leg, and demonstrated, with a smile. She was scheduled for a trial of cyclophosphamide, an experimental drug thought to reduce the severity and length of exacerbations of M.S. I had asked Nathan if he would take me to see her, ribbing him about the lack of bedside teaching. He told me to go and see her myself first, but since I was not assigned to her case, I thought it would be an intrusion. At least if he were with me, the visit might have some use to her. Today after we left her room I asked him about cyclophosphamide.

He laughed cynically. "Let me tell you something," he said. "Hospitalization for M.S. is not about cyclophosphamide or oligoclonal banding or any other cute experiments. It's about teaching the patients how to go to the toilet when they've lost control of their bladder. It's about making sure they can still breathe. That's what they ought to be teaching you, not all this garbage about cyclophosphamide. You people are not learning how to take care of patients."

That morning Mr. Giannetti was in a confused but moderately good mood. He was going to be discharged without treatment for the immediate future. Since his tumor was in the left, dominant hemisphere, he was not a candidate for the sort of radical surgery I had seen done on Gerald Edwards, the lawyer—it would leave him in a condition worse than that of Edie Matthews. He would eventually get chemotherapy, but at present the cost-benefit analysis of instituting it was not favorable. It would not alter the course of the tumor's growth very much during the next few months, and it would destroy the quality of his life. He had to leave the hospital empty-handed, except for what was essentially a death sentence, but he knew that he had a few good months, and he was determined to make the most of them.

The two men in coma continued in their ambiguous and tenuous state of life; they helped to show me the extent to which the modern physician is concerned with the judicious promotion of death rather than life. Michael Jones, at the end of his fight with cancer, was not D.N.R., but increasingly difficult resuscitations performed with increasing reluctance would soon end his life. His wife and mother visited him every evening, and I sometimes saw his wife kiss his face with inexpressible tenderness.

Ralph McLaughlin, the younger, homosexual man, was D.N.R., but the meaning of this status was a constant source of contention between Steve and the nurses. The controversy involved the suctioning of fluid out of his mouth and throat. The nurses interpreted his code status as consistent with frequent suctioning, while Steve wanted all suctioning discontinued. It was clear from talking with his family that they—especially his wife— had given up on him and grieved, so the nurses' position was puzzling. Late one evening, Steve talked to the wife.

"I just don't want him to die by choking," she said.

"I know," Steve said gently. "But unfortunately that's the most likely way that he's going to die." She agreed to reduce the suctioning to once a day. This did not result in any change in his condition, but it did increase the chance that he would die.

Edie Matthews was stable after her episode of status epilepticus, but she seemed to have fallen into a primitive mood of resignation. She chewed gum constantly and looked at the wall with a vacant stare. Perhaps she could realize that she had been about to go home—an idea that surely still had meaning for her—when she was robbed of that chance by the unexpected electrical storm in her brain. Her code status was D.N.R. and she would probably soon die, most likely in the midst of a continuous seizure. Her husband and a daughter came to visit her occasionally, trying to suppress the amazed, embarrassed looks on their faces. I saw the daughter, a rather typical teenager, with a dark mop of hair and an adolescent slouch, standing outside the room one afternoon after saying good-bye, looking at the person who was once her mother, measuring, I imagined, an incalculable loss.

But the most poignant visitor was Edie's mother, a plump, tired, poor woman with dyed dark hair and heavy black shoes. Since the new seizures, she had become more of a fixture than a visitor, remaining with Edie almost constantly. She had got permission to set up a cot beside the bed, and she slept on it every night, like a mother with a child on the pediatric ward. She slept poorly. More than once I had seen her in the middle of the day, sitting beside the bed, leaning over the railing, asleep on her folded arms, while Edie lay on her side, chewing gum and gazing into her mother's sleeping face. At the end of her life Edie's relationship with her mother was very like what it must have been at the beginning.

Billy Tirell stayed on the ward for almost a month. He remained calm and was gradually released from restraint; his psychotic ramblings subsided finally on a combination of antipsychotic and antiepileptic medications. His EEG, which had to be repeated, showed evidence of abnormalities less subtle than those on his CAT scan, but nevertheless equivalent to what many schizophrenics show who have no identifiable neurological abnormality. No one could say definitively whether his neurological findings were a relatively minor coincident problem in a schizophrenic, whether they were the consequence of years of treatment with powerful brain-active drugs, or whether they might in fact be neurological clues to the basis of his psychiatric disease. After discharge he would continue to live in a severely impaired, heavily medicated state, in fear of his next episode of florid psychosis.

On the last night I was on, Steve and I admitted an extremely pretty young woman with shoulder-length dark hair and large brown eyes who had recently begun practicing law. She was having her second prolonged episode—several weeks this time—of mysterious tingling in her arms, combined with weakness in her fingers. The first time she had been admitted to the hospital she had had every appropriate test, and she had been negative for all of them except for the new one, on spinal fluid proteins, called oligoclonal banding. Even without that, the appearance of the symptoms she described for the second time, after several months of remission, was highly characteristic of multiple sclerosis.

But the diagnosis was not definite, and in fact could never be definite without autopsy studies. The definition emerged clinically as the number of recurrences mounted, all following the same pattern, with other explanations ruled out. So it would be Steve's job to tell her that she probably had one of the most dreaded diseases that can strike a young adult, and yet that he could not be sure. Furthermore, if she had it, she could have decades of relative health with occasional recurrences, or a rapid downhill course lasting a few months, or anything in between. He did not try to tell her much on the first night, but she knew quite a bit from her first hospitalization, and the dread in her face was painful to see.

Later we talked with her parents, a sophisticated, well-dressed couple from another city, who had flown in immediately when they heard about their daughter's hospitalization. We sat around the table in a little conference room with no windows but two glass walls looking out on the ward. The father, an emotionally controlled businessman, was palpably afraid. Steve gave a little lecture about the possibilities and the tests, but he let them know the highly likely outcome, as well as the fact that there was no real treatment. He drew a chart on a pad with the differential diagnosis, and drew diagrams showing the tests that would be used to help produce a conclusion. The drawings were on an attractive pink advertising pad with the name of a new oral contraceptive blazoned across the top, and under the name, in large letters, "Reliable. Predictable. Boring."

One of the last things I did on the rotation was to sit down and talk with Nathan Stearns, who turned out to be more interesting and impressive than I had at first realized. He was completing his sixth year of residency —not his fourth, as was the case for most chief residents in neurology. He had done three full years of internal medicine before deciding to do neurology. He had thus paid an exceptional price for his forthcoming certification, and since he was coming out of one of the best programs of its kind in the nation, he could expect to begin a lucrative career as a clinician.

Instead, he was quitting clinical work to go into laboratory research on the brain, research of exactly the sort I thought most necessary to bring neurology out of its therapeutic dark age. In this work he would forfeit most of the income he might have had and be looked upon as a kook by most of his relatives and friends. If he was cynical about the patients on the ward, it was not because he had no compassion for them, but because the enterprise of clinical neurology in its current form disgusted him. In his brutal joking routine over Edie Matthews's bed, he had not meant to make fun of her but of Professor Lippmann's Grand Rounds the previous day, of him and all the professors who expounded so eruditely on patients for whom they could do nothing. Having finished a lengthy and dehumanizing apprenticeship, Nathan was going to apprentice himself yet again, this time to a leading brain scientist, try to contribute something that would enable the neurology professors and residents of the future to give patients like Edie Matthews something more than an academic spotlight.

When I discovered the decent, even noble man under the cynical mask, I decided to ask him the question that had been on my mind since my last conversation with Mr. Giannetti, the question that had disturbed me, really, since my first year in medical school, when another neurologist had given the class his unsettling disquisition on how to be authoritative with terminal patients. How do you tell a person he or she is going to die? Nathan's answer was starkly different.

"It doesn't matter what you say, really. I mean, you have to get the facts across, and you do that straight out, but that isn't the point. It's what you do after that. It doesn't matter what words you use. What matters is that you put your ass in the chair, and keep it there. Not near the edge of the chair. Way back in the chair. You don't look at your watch. You don't think about the other thousand things you have to do. You just sit there and stay there and listen and say a few words. Mainly you listen. But the most important thing is that you stay." This wise advice corresponded, thank goodness, with what I had done with Mr. Giannetti more or less by instinct.

Nathan was one of the few house officers I met who struck me as fitting one common stereotype: the sensitive young physician who had been hurt so consistently that he had become a hard cynic. This was a common hypothesis about the cynicism of residents, but in my experience most of them had arrived at their outlooks without ever going through the presumed stage of vulnerability. Nathan had, I believed; and he was sufficiently self-aware to have decided that he no longer belonged in clinical medicine. In this awareness he was superior to the others, although of course he was not my idea of a doctor. But—to pay him a compliment that could not be paid to many of his colleagues—he was not his own idea of a doctor either.

7

PSYCHIATRY

The Mind-Body Problem

I had been looking forward for years to my rotation in psychiatry, in the Sullivan Psychiatric Institute associated with Galen. In a sense it was the beginning of what I had gone to medical school *for*.

As an anthropologist I had studied "human nature," a phrase I had, after much reluctance, become willing to use. The principle "Nothing human is alien to me" had been embraced by many philosophers. As an anthropologist sleeping in the sand in a grass hut in the Kalahari Desert, or sitting around the fire all night talking and singing and laughing with people in one of the most primitive of all human groups, I had lived that principle. I went to medical school partly because I wanted to live it at the bedside as well.

I thought I had come to understand something about the nature of the human organism—its evolution, variety, constitution, and function. In medical school I hoped to study what happened when that organism broke down. I would see with a penetration that only clinicians earn, the flaws left in it by eons of evolution. I would see it in extremes of fear and pain, in the grip of disability, and on the brink or under the threat of death. To these exquisitely privileged encounters I would bring my knowledge and experience of human biology and behavior in familiar and exotic settings, and of the available facts and theories of why we are who we are. And I would have the one great opportunity I had previously lacked—that of using my knowledge to intervene, precisely and professionally, I hoped— to prevent and alleviate human suffering.

Because my previous work and interests had been in the realm of human behavior—its development in childhood, its cross-cultural variety, its evolution, its biological bases—psychiatry seemed the ideal medical specialty for me. It was a field I had followed closely for years before beginning medical school, and I felt I could make a contribution to it. By previous training I was a so-called expert on some aspects of human behavior, and by inclination I was interested in all the psychological and social dimensions of illness. I wanted to know more about human behavior than anyone else in the world, and central to that goal was an understanding of how human behavior breaks down.

I knew that psychiatry was divided. During the 1950s and 1960s, after a long uphill struggle, psychoanalysis and other approaches influenced by Freud came to dominate the field. But proven new drug therapies—for schizophrenia, mania, depression, anxiety, and other disorders—were generating enough excitement so that the best young minds in the field were now mastering the chemical equations of psychopharmacology, just as they had once mastered the intellectual labyrinth of psychoanalysis.

The Freudian old guard continued to insist, it seemed to me rightly, that it still had a piece of the truth. It felt threatened (and was) by everyone from journalists to insurance companies, including patients and medical students who held up the example of drug treatments as having greater scientific validity: they had a sound physiological basis, a common ground with treatments in the rest of medicine, and above all rigorous studies proving their efficacy, according to definable if limited criteria, beyond reasonable doubt. It seemed certain that basic and clinical research would continue to improve these treatments and would generate new ones from one year to the next.

Psychoanalysis and depth psychologies in general proceeded on a completely different footing. Their common ground with the rest of medicine was mainly in history-taking and categorizing procedures. They appealed to other physicians in being an intricate extension of traditional "bedside manner" (one of the wellsprings of Freud's "talking cure"); yet they formed a difficult-to-master, hermetically sealed intellectual framework that had some of the elegance of a logico-deductive scientific system. Incidentally and not unimportantly, they had a broad base of support among nonmedical intellectuals, for whom their symbolic and exegetic potential was paramount.

But their treatments had no proven efficacy. They *seemed* as if they should work. Delving as they did into the mysteries of the soul, they showed respect for the dignity of the mentally ill and the complexity of their problems. This seemed to contrast favorably with the "Throw a drug at it and see if it sticks" sort of approach, which was psychopharmacology at its worst. But study after study had failed to show any positive impact on the patients, and psychoanalysts were beginning to fall back on the old defensive claim that what they did for their patients was not amenable to research. This claim did not satisfy anyone else.

In their teaching and writing, in the inner sanctums of their discipline, they still relied heavily on the writings of Freud and other near sacred texts. While these exercises were certainly scholarly, they had nothing to do with research in the modern medical-science sense, and they gave the field the appearance of a cult. This appearance was reinforced by the fact that they had a ritualized and difficult initiation, psychoanalysis itself. And the pedigree of analyst and analysand was considered crucial: "She was analyzed by So-and-so, who was analyzed by Freud." This, like the biblical begats, signified inherited authority.

There is no place in medical science for such enshrinement of the ancients, and it served to reinforce my skepticism. Yet I knew from my own life, and from my work on child development in an African culture, that psychoanalytic concepts and theory had a seat-of-the-pants validity. The unconscious, repression, projection, infantile sexuality, the dream symbols—these and many other ideas that had passed into common parlance—were the first and still the best specialized, nonreligious language for thinking and talking about the human soul. I had no thought of becoming a psychoanalyst, and I had rigorous personal standards for research on behavior and the mind. But there was a baby in the psychoanalytic bath water, and I was reluctant to join the legion of brain chemists who were willing to dump it out the window. So my mind, like the Sullivan Institute, and like the field of psychiatry itself, was divided.

Katherine Ballard, our preceptor for the rotation, was a psychoanalyst in her early forties; she was a thin, tall, slightly asthenic blond who wore her hair in a 1950s permanent coif. Six of us met in her office, which was furnished with large soft chairs and of course a couch, which I avoided sitting on—because, I told myself, it didn't look comfortable. The room was expensively wood-paneled and had a small blackboard in one corner. It looked nothing like any hospital or clinic treatment room I had ever seen, and here Dr. Ballard took care of her patients.

The schedule she handed out called for us to attend a substantial number of conferences and seminars each week; to be in on the intake interviews of at least two prospective patients in the outpatient service; to visit various inpatient wards, including the children's ward and the mental hospital of a nearby state prison; to take night call once a week; to observe electric shock therapy; and to spend the rest of our time on an inpatient ward to which we had been assigned. There we would come to know and follow closely patients who were hospitalized for mental illnesses. One such patient would be assigned to us as a primary responsibility—under full supervision—and we would present the details of that patient's illness and treatment at a conference at the end of the rotation.

There could not be an opportunity to sit in on sessions of psychoanalysis, since this form of treatment required exceptional privacy and hinged on the special trust established between patient and doctor. But Dr. Ballard would conduct a series of seminars on it, with a substantial amount of reading. For almost the first time since entering medical school, I was reminded of graduate education. One of her special interests was in patients with the "borderline" syndrome, a difficult-to-define but generally-agreed-upon category that was worse than ordinary neurosis but not as bad as psychosis. She described one patient who had had a stable adaptation to an anxiety-ridden life but who had "decompensated"—fallen apart psychologically—on the couch that some of us were sitting on. Free association had led to a frankly psychotic flight of ideas, and the patient, who had never before had such an experience, had been returned to her usual tense level of neurotic adaptation only with difficulty over a period of weeks.

This case served to illustrate several things. First, mental illnesses were serious, and seemingly stable patients could "turn sour" or "dribble off the court," just like medical and surgical patients. Second, if lying on the couch and freely associating could precipitate a psychotic episode, then obviously psychoanalysis was doing *something*. Every powerful therapy in medicine had the potential for major harm. Demonstrating that the "talking cure" could cause a drastic decompensation showed that it was dangerous, which appealed to our medical-student sense of clinical drama and our desire for the sense of life-and-death responsibility. The supreme rule was "First do no harm"; but in reality having the power to do harm was a source of excitement never far below the surface of a physician's adaptation.

Finally, the case seemed to show that there were seriously ill patients who could be helped by psychoanalysis. Schizophrenia, in which Freud and his disciples had dabbled, had provided both useful and misleading insights into the workings of the unconscious mind. But it had been taken away by the brain chemists, who had proved that they could treat it.

Psychoanalysts—after a long rearguard action that was harmful to many patients—had conceded that their methods were inappropriate for schizophrenics and had given up almost all claim to cure or markedly help it. A similar outcome seemed to be in the offing with the more severe forms of depression, although there it was likely that psychodynamic approaches would continue to play a role.

But for the borderline syndrome there was no drug treatment, not even one that showed promise. The patients were usually well and stable, and were amenable to the formation of a relationship with a therapist. Indeed, they were almost too amenable. They were known more for the tenacity of their dependency on their therapists—threatening suicide every August, when their therapists left them for vacation, for example—than for any other feature of their behavior. So they also appealed to the physician's sense of importance and of the ineffable mystery of the doctor-patient relationship. It was not surprising that the psychoanalysts wrote scores of papers on the syndrome.

Before dismissing us, Dr. Ballard called for a volunteer to prepare a presentation on the elements of the psychoanalytic theory of defense mechanisms. Since I knew this well and would have to volunteer for something or other soon, I took it on. With that we were sent out on the wards.

By request I had been assigned to a unit that was aggressively pharmacological, the opposite of Dr. Ballard's approach in every way. On the Sullivan's Burdick unit were patients who were severely ill—schizophrenics, manic-depressives, and profoundly depressed patients—but who had a chance to get better and be discharged within a matter of weeks to months. Their recovery would be mostly on the basis of proven drug therapies; and since Burdick was on the frontier of research in psychopharmacology, there would be no dalliance with unproven psychological methods. Which was not to say that the psychological and social dimensions would be ignored; merely that they would be invoked in the most pragmatic way possible, as supports for biochemical recovery and without elaborate theories or talking cures.

Burdick was set up and furnished for the most part like a rather posh dormitory, with pleasant small rooms for individual patients and common rooms—a kitchen and dining room, a lounge, and a game room—for socializing. Most of the rooms could be locked from the inside, but not so that they couldn't be opened from outside with a key. The nurses' station, in the center of the unit, had glass walls looking out on the hall, a Dutch door that usually had its top half open for dispensing pills, and a conference room with blackboards. Across the hall from the station were two isolation rooms that could not be locked from the inside; they were all-white and were furnished only with mattresses.

The blackboard in the conference room listed the names of each patient, the date of admission, the type of payment—usually insurance—and the date on which the money would run out. Patients were targeted for discharge by that date. This did not necessarily mean that they were considered sufficiently recovered to leave by then. They might have to be discharged to a state mental hospital for the remainder of their treatment. It also did not mean that treatment on Burdick would automatically expand to fit the time allotted to it. But it did mean that if something useful were to be done, it had better be done in that time frame.

The day began on Burdick with sit-down rounds at eight o'clock, and so I was sleeping later, and arriving in better condition, than I had in months. All psychiatric residents, social workers, and nursing staff were present. I soon discovered that nurses were more sophisticated, had greater responsibility, and participated more fully with physicians in decision-making here than in any other medical setting I had seen. All patients on the ward, a total of twenty or twenty-five, were reviewed in detail, particularly with respect to progress during the last day and night or over the weekend. I had been professionally involved in research using behavior observation, and the nurses' progress records on patients seemed to me remarkable.

Decisions were made each morning about medication adjustments and level of privileges: "no sharps or flames"; "on grounds with chaperoned groups"; and the like. Patients with suicidal ideas or a history of suicide attempts were assigned to be checked on every fifteen or even every five minutes, and patients with a history of hypersexual behavior had their allowable social contacts reviewed. Blood tests for certain drugs, whose efficacy depended on the maintenance of a carefully defined blood level —like lithium, for manic-depressive illness, or carbamazepine for epilepsy with psychiatric features—were reported on. Expectable side effects of the drugs were carefully described and treated by dosage adjustment or with additional medication. And decisions for discharge were made.

After this conference, usually around mid-morning, we made walk-rounds. These were limited to three days a week to minimize disruptions in the patients' privacy. Six or seven of us had to walk into the patients' rooms, and anyone new, like me, had to be introduced. Patients had to stand or sit answering questions about delicate aspects of their mental and emotional state. As usual I was torn between the desire to learn and the realization that I was invading their privacy while offering very little in return.

The patient I was to follow closely was Howard Cullen. Howard was a large, overweight, friendly young man who had been referred from another hospital for evaluation and treatment of a major psychotic disorder that he had had since adolescence. He had an identical twin brother who was in prison for committing homicide during a psychotic episode of his own. He said that his father was "a saint," but that "my mother is a witch, sick, emotionally ill." He also said that he had been abused as a child: "My mother would just scream and hit us." Throughout his childhood he had frequently tortured animals, and he had wet the bed until age nine.

The twins' two illnesses were intimately woven together. During their high school years he and his brother began using drugs together, including alcohol, marijuana, LSD, mescaline, amphetamine, and opium. When they were eighteen years old, his brother was hospitalized in his first psychotic episode, and six months later Howard had a similar experience. At that time he believed that he was an Indian chief who had come back to lead an uprising against the white man. The following year he had an episode in which he believed he was a prophet, in fact, several prophets: Jesus, Buddha, and Krishna in succession. He had numerous hospitalizations, usually for several months at a time, and when he and his brother were out of the hospital at the same time they experienced shared delusions. But, despite the common features of their illnesses, he insisted they had very different personalities.

Howard also believed that he was "psyonic"—a word he had coined to denote "having an infinite number of personalities. I become people that I'm with," he said. "I take on different personalities." He had multiple religions, all of which he spoke of with respect. But lately he had begun to experience a loss of faith. He had episodes that he called anxiety attacks, and during these he had hallucinations. Lucifer and Mary Magdalene came to him; they were against him because of his loss of faith. He had begun to sympathize with the devil, and devoted a chapter of a book he was writing to telling people to be kind to him. It wasn't the devil's fault, he said, that God had created him to fall from grace.

During what he called his "anxiety attacks" he liked to put ice packs on his head. "Freezing my brain is the only thing that helps." He had found that when he hallucinated his best tactic was to stare at the hallucination until it went away. This worked for all of them except for a light of variable brightness that glowed all the time.

"Do you see it now?" I asked.

"Sure. It's right there." He pointed abruptly into the air between us. "It's always there."

He also had depressions—which he said were easy to deal with compared to the anxiety attacks—and delusions of grandeur: "I want to be a brain surgeon," he said. He had never completed high school and had an IQ in the normal range but with below-average attention span and memory. "I want to discover an enzyme to cure mental illness." I consciously tried not to look skeptical; but he soon said, "I'm gonna do it!" with simple and confident emphasis.

His illness was complicated by two separate and critical factors. First, he used and abused street drugs chronically whenever he was out of the hospital. This, I knew, greatly reduced his chance of ever getting well. It was not mere irresponsibility; he thought the illicit drugs he took were helping him. They were a way of dealing with his symptoms on his own, to supplement the always-imperfect effects of prescription drugs. His inability to stop taking them was a matter of will power in one sense, but in another was only a manifestation of his illness. And two years earlier it had led to an overdose, which had led to a breathing stoppage and some time spent on a respirator. This in turn had led to seizures—probably due to brain damage.

The second problem was that in his early twenties he had developed ulcerative colitis. He had had to have his colon removed and his small intestine brought out through an opening in his abdominal wall—an ileostomy. Three months before coming to the hospital this time he had tried to slice off the ileostomy with a knife. "The hallucination told me to," was his very clear explanation. "There were demons who told me I'd never be happy."

However, what actually precipitated this latest hospital admission was that he had gone to a small city some distance from his home and begun aggressively preaching the gospel in the park. Since his method of preaching involved some sexual references as well as intrusive behavior and a variety of bizarre ideas, he was detained by the police, who readily uncovered his psychiatric history.

When I talked with him, for hours, he seemed to be in an upbeat mood and thinking clearly, even about his hallucinations. "I'm not afraid of nothin' any more," he said. He was forthcoming and warm, and seemed to want to be helpful to me, as well as to be helped. There were times when I thought he might be putting me on. But there was no doubt, either from his interview or from his record of hospitalizations, that he had a very serious mental illness.

I was basically satisfied with the history I had taken. Although it was not my job to decide on a diagnosis, it seemed to me that Howard was what was called an acute or remitting schizophrenic. That is, he had episodes of being relatively well between his psychotic breaks, and they did not seem to get closer together or worse with time. Although there were some "affective features" in his illness, such as intermittent depression, these came later and did not seem prominent enough to change the diagnosis of schizophrenia, which Howard had carried throughout his adult life.

John Brandt thought differently. He was director of the Burdick unit and the hospital's *enfant terrible* of psychopharmacology. He did fundamental research on the effects of lithium on nerve-cell membranes and was also on the frontier of clinical research in the biochemical treatment of psychosis. He was a tall, lean, austerely handsome man in his early forties, with a ready smile and laugh and horn-rimmed glasses that he had to keep pushing back onto his nose. He was on Burdick or in his lab at least twelve hours a day. His residents and patients loved him. His practice was what he called "medical psychiatry," and his attitude toward psychoanalysis was one of absolute contempt.

"My father was a surgeon," he said, "and I practice psychiatry the way he practiced surgery. Sure I talk to my patients, and what we have to say to each other is important to the treatment—just as it was in my father's surgical practice. There's teaching, there's being nice to them, there's finding out all you can about their illness, sometimes there's even friendship. But talking to them is not the treatment. Medicine is the treatment."

His bedside manner *was* wonderful. He had a natural knack for putting some of the most seriously ill patients at their ease. He made them calm, joked with them, gentled them into an affable mood in which they could talk about their crazy thoughts without quite so much agitation.

With the residents who were on his side he was a superb teacher and adviser. But to his colleagues on the other side of the fence he gave no quarter. At meetings, rounds, and conferences, through shared patients, and through the residents (who had to have training in psychoanalytic psychotherapy as well as in drug treatments), he constantly made his opinion known: *Depth psychologies have no proven role in the explanation of mental illness; psychotherapy has no proven role in the care of the mentally ill.* He was never diplomatic about it. "Show me the evidence," he would say with a derisory smile. "Just show me any kind of evidence." He had become quite isolated and was disliked and feared by the old guard of psychoanalysts, who were still very much in charge of the hospital.

He told the story of a patient he had met years earlier when he first came to Sullivan. The patient was severely depressed and was under the care of a psychoanalyst. As time went by the patient became more depressed, and John urged his doctor to administer antidepressant drugs, which had then been in use for more than a decade. The therapist insisted that the patient be allowed to "work through" the depression without artificial interference. This, he felt, was an essential psychodynamic process that would prevent future depressions. The patient became completely withdrawn, immobile, and physically ill, an illness that was not properly assessed by the psychoanalyst or anyone else. Finally John went to the head of the hospital, who pronounced the situation a disgrace and took the patient away from the psychoanalyst. Treatment with antidepressant drugs broke the depression in a matter of weeks in the way that had since become universal practice, at which point the patient became psychologically accessible to psychotherapy.

But not everything in the realm of drug treatment had produced such a consensus. In addition to the great chasm that stood between the medical psychiatrists like John Brandt and the psychoanalysts, there was a secondary rift within psychopharmacology itself, and patients like Howard Cullen were poised at the brink of it. The brain chemists had wrested schizophrenia away from the analysts. But they were now squabbling among themselves about just what sort of patient *was* schizophrenic. English psychiatrists had, for at least a generation, used the diagnosis much more restrictively than Americans had. They preferred to call most remitting forms of psychosis manic-depressive illness, also known as bipolar affective disorder.

The distinction was by no means academic. The treatment of choice for schizophrenia was the so-called major tranquilizers, like Thorazine, Stelazine, and Haldol. But they had proved to do both more and less than tranquilize. All effective antischizophrenic drugs had in common the action of blockading the neurotransmitter dopamine, and there was considerable evidence that this was the action responsible for their remarkable clinical effect. Their introduction in the 1950s caused a drastic reduction in mental-hospital populations. They brought many psychotic patients into close enough touch with reality so that they could be safely returned to the community. Thousands of studies had since followed this fruitful lead linking schizophrenia at least indirectly to dopamine.

But, like most powerful treatments, the antischizophrenic drugs had powerful adverse effects. There were such immediate side effects as restlessness or spasms of the lips and tongue. These were transient and could usually be corrected by dosage adjustment, change of drug within the broad category, or addition of a second drug to control them. Much more serious were the so-called "tardive dyskinesias"—literally, late-appearing movement abnormalities. Resembling some aspects of Huntington's disease and other disorders of movement, they ranged from the merely annoying to the incapacitating. They occurred in as many as 5 percent of patients treated for several years with antischizophrenic drugs, and eventually, perhaps, many more. And in a large proportion of these patients, they were permanent. Clearly then, if there were another effective treatment, every patient should have that option.

Lithium might be such a treatment, provided that the patient had the diagnosis of manic-depressive illness. In England many patients were so diagnosed who in the United States would have been called remitting schizophrenics and maintained on antischizophrenic drugs, with their attendant risk of late-appearing movement disorders. That was why it was no trivial matter what the patient was called.

John Brandt, along with a growing faction of other medical psychiatrists, thought that vast numbers of American schizophrenics had been misdiagnosed. His therapeutic strategy did not hinge on the sophistry of diagnostic labels. He simply thought that any person with a remitting psychosis deserved to fail a lithium trial before being exposed to the risks of long-term treatment with antischizophrenic drugs. Lithium was not without its problems. It had the very rare side effect of a potentially fatal abnormality of blood cell formation, and its therapeutic effect in general depended on the maintenance of a blood level within a narrow range. Less would be ineffective, more would be toxic. This led to the major expense and inconvenience of a hospitalization for at least several weeks in order to establish the therapeutic blood level for a given patient and the doses needed to maintain it. These drawbacks had made American psychiatrists slow to adopt lithium. But it had, by the end of the 1970s, become accepted as the treatment of choice for manic-depressive illness. It had proved to reduce recurrences. Now the question was, who had schizophrenia and who had M.D.I.?

About Howard Cullen, John Brandt had no doubts. Cullen had a number of substantial periods of being well, he had depressions, and he had swings into elevated mood, including hypersexuality, during some of his psychotic breaks. These were features of manic-depressive illness, and his years of "schizophrenia" notwithstanding, he was a candidate for a lithium trial.

Following the protocol that was usual at Burdick, he was started on Haldol, a rapidly acting antischizophrenic. This was to be tapered off as the lithium level was built up. If his psychotic symptoms resolved after several weeks of therapeutic blood levels of lithium, he would stay on it permanently—with regular checks of vulnerable blood cells. He might never again have to be exposed to drugs with the risk of a permanent and crippling movement disorder. And the lithium should be at least as effective in preventing future psychotic breaks.

On my first night on call I was assigned to work with Ralph Bassler, a second-year resident. He was a plump, reserved young man with heavy glasses who was definite about his diagnostic competence but a bit uneasy having me around. I sat with him during the admission of new patients and was allowed to ask questions of the patients.

The first was a boyish-looking man—bright, sensitive, with a creamy complexion and lively, moist, anguished blue eyes in a troubled face. Paul had been referred to the Sullivan after his sixth arrest for exposing himself, this latest time in front of a police station. He was facing jail. Leaning forward tensely on his chair, he began to tell his story, and he convinced me that he was concerned more about getting help than about staying out of jail. A person had to be pretty troubled, I thought, before exposing himself in front of a police station.

He described a lifelong history of cross-dressing—dressing up like a woman—beginning at the age of seven and increasing until he was in college. Once, when his mother surprised him doing this, and said, "Wait till I tell your father," Paul had stayed out all night. He had frequently set fires and hurt animals as a child. (These, together with bed-wetting, were said to predict adult sociopathy—the virtual absence of a conscience—but this did not seem to apply to Paul.) He had also been labeled "hyperactive" and had done poorly in school. His mother had been depressed, and his father had beaten him; there were no incidents of sexual abuse. He was the third of five brothers, and his parents had made it clear to him that they had wanted a girl.

As a teenager he was often suicidal and reckless. He drank, smoked marijuana, and took LSD, and continued to do poorly in school. His cross-dressing began to involve masturbation to orgasm. In college though, for some reason, "I went through a complete change. I became a different person." He continued in cross-dressing, and it even became worse, but he felt happy and able to concentrate on his work, getting straight A's in physics at the university. This had lasted for about a year, when the exhibitionism started.

Despite all this, he developed romantic and sexual relationships with women, but during sex with them he had fantasies about exposing himself.

He was now in a relationship with a young woman who knew about his problem, yet loved him and wanted to help him. He knew that her patience would not last forever.

He had been in psychotherapy for three years and had committed himself to another hospital once, without a change in his compulsive cross-dressing or exhibitionism. I did not see a great likelihood that his stay at Sullivan would produce a different result, but at least it would keep him out of jail for a while. His fears of homosexual approaches and attacks in jail were probably realistic but were also extremely complex. At the end of the interview he was looking at me with an intense, frank appeal for help, from one human being to another, and I felt sad and guilty that we had so little to offer him.

Later that night we admitted Sharon Beattie, a twenty-year-old suffering from depression and paranoia. Her earnest, intelligent, well-to-do parents had been through this with her once before, and now they had driven two hundred miles to bring Sharon to Sullivan. Her father was a likable businessman who somehow managed to talk too much while maintaining the impression of distinguished reserve. Perhaps this was his way of fraying around the edges. In the lobby across from the admission desk he stopped to talk gently with a little girl who was copying a painting, just as his own daughter was signing her commitment papers. Somehow this misplaced attention endeared him to me instead of alienating me; but then I had a soft spot for fathers of daughters.

In the hospital where they had first taken her earlier in the day she had been put in restraints in a bare room, with only a cot and without sheets or a pillow case. Reporting this, her father said, "We were more upset by it than she was." Here her mother finally objected. "No," she said, "I think Sharie was pretty upset."

Sharie sat with us now in her hospital room, tense, tearful, agitated, and frightened. She had first become depressed about four years earlier. For about a year, she had been isolated and withdrawn, without energy or ambition. Then she had got better and attended an art institute for a year, after which a steady decline had begun. She had swings of motivation and energy, but her mood was never good. Eight months ago she had been put on a standard antidepressant drug, and after several months had developed sleep disturbances, confusion, and paranoia. The dosage was increased and she worsened. A test, sometimes useful with depressed patients, that measured the level in the blood of the stress hormone cortisol after an attempt to suppress it artificially, showed an extremely high level. Sharie's cortisol production was intense enough to overshoot drug suppression by a large margin. This could be interpreted to mean that she was under severe stress internally, whatever face she presented to the world.

But that night she did not need a blood test to prove that she was under stress. Her face expressed anguish, confusion, and shame, and she answered questions woodenly. Her parents, especially her father, did most of the talking.

My naive diagnosis was one of agitated or anxious depression, but Ralph Bassler was completely confident that Sharie was a manic-depressive currently in a "dysphoric mania." This meant that she was at the high point of the energy cycle and having paranoid psychotic thoughts; her mood, far from being euphoric, was full of anxiety and pain. Ralph's interpretation puzzled me, but I accepted it, knowing I had a lot to learn—even in psychiatry, where I thought my basic intuitions were good.

It seemed a subtle distinction but it had diametrically opposite implications for treatment. In his view, she had been depressed for a long time when overtreatment with the antidepressant Imipramine had caused her to cycle into a dysphoric, or bad-mood, mania. Pending consultation with Dr. Brandt, Ralph placed her on Thorazine, an antischizophrenic drug, to control her paranoia for the immediate future; and on lithium, which would be gradually built up to a point at which the Thorazine could be discontinued. Unlike the exhibitionist, Sharie could expect a marked improvement in her condition—conceivably, if Ralph was right, even a cure —during the course of her stay at Sullivan.

Shortly after this, we were called to the scene of a fight between two patients in one of the parking lots. Ralph was the only D.O.C.—Doctor On Call—on the hospital grounds, and so was responsible for everything. He had a walkie-talkie instead of a beeper and got the message from a rasping voice at the switchboard. Fortunately the patients, teenage boys who had been out for ice cream with a nurse-chaperoned group, had not done each other serious damage. They stopped almost as soon as we began to pull them apart.

Half an hour later we were getting ready for bed when the rasping voice came over the walkie-talkie again. This time Ralph really moved, and I had to jump and run to keep up with him, crossing the hospital grounds in the moonlit night. A young woman on one of the short-term psychotic wards had climbed up to the caged light bulb in her room, broken it, and used one of the fragments to cut her wrists. Since she had been on five-minute checks she had had only a few minutes to bleed; but she needed restraint, and we had to hold her down and stop the bleeding at the same time. She certainly needed stitches, and I thought I might have the chance to use the skills I had mastered in the surgical emergency clinic. I was a lot closer to my time of sewing wounds than Ralph was to his, and I felt ready to step in and take over. But protocol was for all such cases to be sent by ambulance to Galen itself; and, after settling her down with a good dose of talk and Haldol, we sent her over.

Early the following week I got my opportunity to see E.C.T.—electro-convulsive therapy, commonly known as shock therapy. This was the treatment that cost Thomas Eagleton his vice-presidential nomination in 1972 as running mate to George McGovern. The mere fact that Senator Eagleton had once, long before the nomination, had three shock treatments for a depression, was enough to disqualify him in the eyes of many Americans. More recently, E.C.T. had been banned in Berkeley, California, by a vote of the city council, an extraordinary interference by local government in approved and long-standing medical practice. To the average intelligent person, it seemed to be a form of medieval torture masquerading as therapy, imposed on patients too deranged, depressed, and helpless to defend themselves.

The reality was quite different. I already knew from my reading of much recent research that E.C.T. was of proven value in the treatment of severe depression and of possible value in some other mental illnesses. In many instances of depression it had proved itself the only treatment that helped, and in breaking those depressions it had changed countless lives for the better. It had the significant side effect of causing disturbances of memory, but these were almost always minor, and I knew no effective treatments were without risk or cost to the patient. It always puzzled me that some of the same people who considered death from anesthesia complications an acceptable risk for some forms of cosmetic surgery considered memory disturbance an unacceptable risk for the breaking of an incapacitating depression.

E.C.T. was administered at Sullivan's medical clinic, a small well-lit room with a comfortable examining table at its center. The psychiatrist in charge was Herbert Reid, a pleasant, balding man in his mid-fifties, and he was accompanied by a fully trained and certified anesthesiologist. At the side of the room was a machine that could both record the EEG, or natural brain waves, and deliver electricity to the brain. The procedure was for the patient to be anesthetized with a short-acting barbiturate and then briefly paralyzed with a drug that prevented muscle contractions.

Electrodes attached to one side of the head would induce an electrical storm resembling an epileptic convulsion, except that it would be limited to one half of the brain and would not be transmitted to the muscles. Ideally, at least, it was a convulsion of brain circuits only.

Before I knew it the first patient was wheeled in, and I was helping her settle in on the table. She was a woman about fifty years old, whom I only knew as Alice, and every time I had seen her on the ward she had been profoundly depressed and lethargic. She spent all day in her room staring at the walls, occasionally trying her hand at a simple word puzzle. She had had all the standard biochemical antidepressant therapies, and years of psychotherapy as well. Nothing had helped. She was now about to have her third E.C.T. session.

Alice took off her glasses and lay, apprehensive and still, on the table. The electrodes were placed on her head. A blood pressure cuff was put on her arm to monitor her circulation. A needle was introduced into a vein in the crook of her elbow, and through it a general anesthetic with a short course of action was infused. In a few moments she was asleep and unresponsive to mild pain. The muscle-paralyzing drug was introduced. It was one that worked on the same principle as curare, the poison widely used by South American Indians for bringing down prey. Within a few more moments paralysis was achieved and a shock was delivered to the right side of her brain.

That was it. It was over. There was no convulsion in the muscular sense, because of the curarizing drug, yet there was no awareness of being paralyzed—which would have been a terrifying sensation—because of the general anesthetic. As I stood there trying to figure out what had actually happened, Alice's paralysis was already wearing off. It would take as much as an hour or so to come completely out of the anesthetic, so we turned her on her side to prevent suffocation in case she should vomit, always a risk with a general anesthetic. She was wheeled into a curtained bay in an adjoining room where a nurse would watch her, and the table and apparatus were prepared for the next patient.

Dr. Reid tore the long sheet of paper out of the electroencephalograph. "See that?" he said, surmising that I was bewildered. There was a long squiggle at the beginning that looked to me as if it could be a normal EEG tracing. This changed somewhat at the arrow he had used to designate the anesthetic injection point. Then, after a second, larger arrow, was a dense spiking wave that was highly distinctive. This, I realized, was the convulsion.

"That's it?" I asked, incredulous.

"That's it," he said, smiling.

Three other patients received the treatment within the next hour. None, as far as I could tell, had any discomfort other than the effect of the general anesthetic. All four were drowsy for at least an hour, and I waited for them to become alert so that I could talk with them. One was a physician, and he was especially helpful. He articulated in professional terms what the others said in plain language. This treatment was valuable. It was helping him to recover a normal mental life. It was not fun, but it was neither dangerous nor damaging in any significant way.

Compared to the devastating invasions of body and brain I had seen in surgery, or even compared to the risks of some psychiatrically potent drugs, this much-maligned shock treatment was mild. To complain bitterly about the loss of a few days of memories would be like pointing to the scar on your chest after open heart surgery, and saying "Look at the mess those bastards made of me!" If intractable depression was like a living death—and I thought it was—then electro-convulsive therapy, when it worked, was lifesaving.

When I gave my talk on psychoanalytic defense mechanisms and the nature of psychotherapy, Dr. Ballard seemed quite pleased. I put the list on the blackboard, and as I went over the items one by one—repression, projection, sublimation, denial, ritualized undoing, and so on—I convinced myself again that these concepts had to have validity. In the decades since Freud had introduced them, they had become part of almost every educated person's model of the mind. They could not have had such plain and easy validity in everyday life without being somehow true. Yet, I knew, this did not make them a valid theory of mental illness or a basis for its treatment. It was a point vividly illustrated by one of our sessions in child psychiatry.

The physician who led these, Suzanne Hager, was a charming young woman fresh out of her residency who was now being trained in child psychiatry in a psychoanalytic mode. I had done research on behavior development, which she had not, and I had children of my own, which she did not, so I was slightly inclined to feel superior. And I believed, both from my research and from my experience, that there was some truth to the Freudian model of child development. I even brought to the seminars some telling illustrations from my own children's lives—for example, the time my daughter came home from nursery school having decided that she wanted to have a penis. But I also insisted on the common sense dimension of such anecdotes—for example, my daughter's eventual (and typical) explanation that she needed the penis so that she could "pee standing up." As Freud himself was supposed to have said, sometimes a cigar is only a cigar.

The papers we read and discussed were very hard to credit. One recent one that Dr. Hager put great stock in was a theoretical paper arguing that it was possible for children to be depressed—evidently a great point of contention in her field, owing to an elaborate early theory that had made this seem impossible. Another paper, which she held up as an example of research in child psychoanalysis, had no data of any kind. The bibliography referred only to other theoretical papers, about half of which were by Freud. It was as if William Osler's aphorisms were to have been made the center of modern medical writing, with "research" papers consisting of individual case histories and theoretical musings taking off from those aphorisms in moderately original directions, using the case as an illustration.

After a couple of these rather dismal seminars, when Dr. Hager had begun to be embarrassed by even the gentlest of my questions, I was relieved to learn that we would at last have a case. A nurse brought a ten-year-old named Ricky from the children's ward, and Dr. Hager interviewed him while we sat behind a one-way viewing window. All we had been told about him was that he had been hyperactive for several years and that this hospitalization had been precipitated by a misguided suicide attempt in which he had swallowed a large number of vitamin pills. Although this seemed amusing, it was not; he thought they were dangerous, and his next attempt could conceivably be with anything.

Ricky was a very beautiful dark-haired, light-complexioned boy who seemed quite tense, but in a positive way, as if he might be just full of life. Dr. Hager and he built some block structures together on the floor while she drew him, in a sensitive, nonthreatening way, into a conversation about his mother and father. Nothing very impressive was revealed. The parents, it could perhaps be surmised, were somewhat distant and conventional, but in this seemed no different from many middle-class parents. But his tension began to reveal itself—mainly through gestures and expressions—as composed partly of anger. They sat at a table together and she encouraged him to draw. His drawing showed a house with a steeply peaked roof and a family beside it such as many another child might have drawn.

As we watched them through the one-way window, the nurse who had brought Ricky over, and who was sitting beside us, whispered a running commentary. When he had first arrived at Sullivan he had been "ricochet-ing off the walls." He had been put on a stimulant related to amphetamine, which has the paradoxical effect of settling down hyperactive children. He had gradually adjusted to life on the children's ward. This morning through an oversight the early-morning dose of his stimulant had been skipped. He had got it after breakfast, just before coming over, but it had not yet had time to take effect. Consequently, according to the nurse's interpretation, he was more or less bouncing off the walls again.

Dr. Hager was apparently not aware of this, and nowhere in her session with Ricky or in her half an hour of discussion with us afterward did she allude to his diagnosis or treatment on the dimension of hyperactivity. She talked extensively about his anger against his parents and attributed his tension and jittery demeanor to repressed rage. The house with the peaked roof was a phallic symbol, evidence of his paramount conflict with his father.

None of us had the heart to tell her what the nurse had told us, so we went along with her interpretation for the sake of the discussion. Perhaps there was truth in it. The nurse's analysis certainly seemed simplistic. But on the other hand, how could Dr. Hager's possibly be right if it omitted those considerations entirely? Was hyperactivity the fundamental prob-lem, successfully treated by the drug—except for this morning? Or was the basic problem really repressed anger, masked but not erased by the drug, reemerging because of a complex interplay between falling drug levels and sensitive conversation about Ricky's parents? These were questions to which I had no answers. But the basic error of analyzing this patient either without knowing about, or without considering the drug treatment, hung in the air.

Morning rounds continued to be an awkward experience, but one filled for me with the excitement of learning. Sharon Beattie, the young woman Ralph and I had admitted with "dysphoric mania," had improved some-what over the first ten days, despite not yet having a therapeutic lithium level. She still described herself as depressed but said that she was "ninety-three or ninety-four percent free of paranoia." She was allowed to go off grounds with her family, who came on weekends. She'd been keeping a journal, and she was making beautiful drawings of trees and seascapes, which she put up on the walls of her room. She wanted very much to go home. "The occasional textbook case of bipolar illness," said one of the residents after we left her room one morning. The plan was to get her lithium into the therapeutic range, taper her antischizophrenic drug, and send her out looking "like a rose."

I'd spent at least an hour each day with Howard Cullen, the "prophet," who had also improved more or less steadily. He was suffering anxiety attacks and so had to "freeze" his brain with ice packs, and he made many inappropriate comments, frequently of a sexual nature. But he was mostly free of frankly psychotic thoughts. After a few days he said, "I realized I'm not telepathic." This realization apparently did not sadden him, as I had romantically thought it might. Except for occasional visits from the devil, which were treated with transient increases in Haldol, his only remaining hallucination was the always-present light in the air.

It was a real problem getting his drugs into the therapeutic range because of his ileostomy, and John Brandt speculated that he might never before have had a therapeutic level of *anything*. He threatened to sign a three-day notice, as was his essential right, to enable him to leave the hospital unless commitment papers could be signed within three days—unlikely in his case—or he changed his mind. But with my help—I had the closest relationship with him—he was talked out of it. He began occasionally to play the harmonica, which he did very well and with great feeling. He offered to play for me, and I was very moved. Occasionally he was seen dancing alone in his room.

Alice Blake, whose E.C.T. I had been in on, got steadily better with continued shock treatments. She did not become what anyone would call lively, but her profound depression lifted. She became more talkative, developed relationships with other patients, and even smiled from time to time. She seemed better to everyone, including, at last, even herself. I was completely won over to the idea of a role for this form of therapy.

Every other patient was unique in half a dozen ways, and as far as I could see there were no textbook cases. There was a beautiful tall Korean girl with enormous eyes and long dark hair who usually wore a silk smock with bold blue-and-white stripes. She stood, swaying slightly, saying incessantly in the most plaintive voice, "Please let me go home. Please let me go home. Please let me go home." There was a white-haired black woman who was intractably depressed. To add insult to injury, she lost her apartment while she was at Sullivan. She had no money and wanted to work but could not find a job. Her daughter refused to take her in, and her insurance, along with her time at Sullivan, was about to run out. "I'm very sad, that's all," she said one morning tearily. "It's very sad when a person has worked . . . honestly . . . when a person has always worked and has no place to go."

There was a depressed alcoholic in his mid-fifties who went home on weekends and, despite his wife's best efforts, managed to drink furtively. This made his depressive illness almost impossible to treat. There was a young homosexual with a probable diagnosis of schizophrenia who had wildly extravagant paranoid delusions, involving major figures of the American and Canadian governments being in cahoots with certain doctors at the hospital. And there was an angry, vulgar teenaged girl who had some combination of manic-depressive illness, hyperactivity, and atypical epilepsy. Her mania took the primary form of rebellious hypersexuality. She told her parents she planned to become a prostitute. She wrote and sent explicit sexual poetry to male patients, and she had been found in the arms of more than one of them. The constant come-on look in her eyes made me extremely uncomfortable.

Hypersexuality was a daily theme on the Burdick ward. Manic and near manic episodes were characterized by euphoria, recklessness, and (usually minor) defiance of authority. Many of the patients, even if not manic, were desperately in need of human warmth, and this was especially true when they were beginning to feel well. The ward was a milieu designed to facilitate reentry into normal life. Consequently there were limits to the limits that could be set. Improving patients had to be steadily graduated in responsibility before they could hope to be discharged, and this inevitably meant that every day some patients would be abusing some privileges.

For example, Chrissy Lewis, a thirty-two-year-old Midwesterner who had been hospitalized for mania eleven times but was now coming out of a depression, was found in bed with Bob Vance, a charming, quite manic married man who claimed he was planning to leave his wife. Chrissy was weepy and confused. Her sleep was troubled, and she was placed on five-minute checks to prevent sexual infractions. Yet Chrissy and Bob were found kissing several times during the next few days, despite the restrictions on both of them. After one of these episodes he called his wife to tell her he wanted a divorce, and then was found in tears. At this time he had Chrissy's underpants in his pocket. Bob was also discovered to have been sleeping with another patient off the ward on the hospital grounds. He said of her, "She's the reason I'm doing well here," but he was forbidden contact with both women.

These patients could not be physically restrained or locked in their rooms. They were adults who had to learn to adjust to real life, but their illnesses made them a bit like children. More precisely, they were like rather wild teenagers. They had learning to do, not just chemical imbalances to redress. These encounters were psychiatrically risky at best, and a pregnancy would have been an unmitigated disaster. Yet the balance of risk and benefit in treatment seemed, on reflection, not fundamentally different from what it was in other branches of medicine.

In general I was interested in the role of the chaplaincy in hospitals, and I came to believe it could be greatly expanded. This was ironic for an atheist, but logical for a professional anthropologist. There is no society known to social science in which spirituality does not have a role to play in healing. Most of the patients I met were at least believers, if not religious. If there were any truth at all to the presumed effects of mind on body, then spiritual counsel almost had to be good for them.

But for psychiatric patients it seemed to me to have a very particular role to play. Their suffering was in some sense primarily spiritual. Many were preoccupied with obsessive or even delusional thoughts about God, such as Howard Cullen's prophesying and meetings with Mary Magdalene and the devil. Although I had been religious as a teenager and could sympathize with all sorts of beliefs, I was now so skeptical that my sympathy seemed hollow. I thought that some patients could profit from talking with someone who at least took seriously the existence of an incorporeal realm, and who could discuss it in terms that would transcend my level of psychologizing.

I went to see the director of the chaplaincy, who happened to be a rabbi. He was very nice, although puzzled by my visit. He certainly agreed that an expanded role for the chaplaincy would be a nice idea, but he had nothing to suggest regarding special communication with patients like the ones I described. His view of them was more or less interchangeable with those of chaplains in nonpsychiatric hospitals. I also interviewed a monk who had come on the ward; I hoped that in his dedication to a spiritual life he would have a special perspective on his manic-depressive illness or on the spiritual life because of his illness. Perhaps he even had visions? He never knew what I was driving at. His manic episodes were entirely conventional—goofing off behind a pile of dirty linen all day when he was supposed to be working at the monastery laundry or shouting angrily at the abbot that he was thinking of renouncing his vows.

Some days later I came on the ward in the afternoon, after a seminar on law and psychiatry, and found a chaplain intern talking in the lounge with a group of patients. It was the first time I had seen such a discussion, and I was intrigued and delighted. Cynthia Warner, the black woman with no place to go, talked quietly about her little revivalist church and the central support it had provided in her life. Howard Cullen then held forth about his dream in which the devil had come to him, while she looked skeptical. The teenager who wanted to be a prostitute said that she did not believe in anything.

The chaplain intern—an earnest-looking Southerner who kept brushing his straw-colored hair out of his eyes—did not engage them at all. None of the threads led anywhere. Several times, he made the point that the best path is the religion you were raised with, whatever that might be. Thus he could approve of Cynthia's religious life, although it was quite different from his, and certainly not anything so original as Howard's. His assumption seemed to be—and this was confirmed by a cheerful, dull little conversation he and I had afterward—that beliefs the patient held or arrived at independently were part of the illness. He could not of course seem to be proselytizing for his own religion, which was Methodism, but he had been trained to discourage lively originality like Howard's. He refused to treat it as a legitimately held belief system, even for the sake of a conversation that might help to orient Howard to a more widely shared reality. Obviously, if a chaplain could draw out patients on the spiritual aspects of their mental disturbances, it would not happen here.

One of the high points of the rotation was my day at Riverville, the state prison, which included a large psychiatric unit for the housing and treatment of the criminally insane. Because of my relationship to Howard Cullen, I had got permission to meet and interview his twin brother Frank, who had been incarcerated at Riverville several years earlier, after his psychotic homicide. But first there was a tour, followed by a three-hour session observing recommitment proceedings.

The tour was chilling. There were hundreds of inmates—all male—many of whom had committed acts of violence in deranged mental states, others who had suffered breakdowns while in prison—schizophrenics, manic-depressives, alcoholics, drug addicts, and epileptics whose particular form of that illness could take a dangerous explosive turn. Many were big, powerful-looking men who seemed to be repressing tremendous energy; others, rather sadder, had illnesses that made them withdrawn, incompetent, or moribund. Virtually all were on powerful psychoactive drugs. As we entered each ward or section immense doors and gates locked behind us, and each time I felt for a moment almost as imprisoned as they. They walked in circles in the courtyard, sat on benches staring into space, rocked and walked snapping their fingers, watched television, talked or played games together. I looked for a face that would remind me of Howard Cullen's, but there weren't any—or rather there were too many.

The wards were dingy and coldly designed, with institutional paint and old hard furniture. The rooms were small and ugly, and the isolation rooms were pathetic, frightening structures consisting of nothing but tile—except for the occasional padded cell. On each unit was a shabby little nurses' station where the men's medication was kept, along with the hospital records describing their illnesses and progress.

I had been spoiled at Sullivan, one of the best and most well-endowed of all psychiatric hospitals. Here such diagnostic subtleties as schizophrenia versus manic-depressive illness, psychosis versus epilepsy with psychiatric symptoms, continual monitoring of blood levels, and so on were given short shrift. Each man got enough Haldol or Thorazine to keep a lid on him, and that was about it. I sat with a psychiatric resident as he interviewed a series of violent men for a scheduled review of their medications. He was as patient and thoughtful as he had time to be in only a few minutes. But if he had been that patient and thoughtful with the residents of the Burdick, he would have been thrown out of the program.

Only a decade earlier the psychiatric wards at Riverville had been the subject of a popular television news program, and their resulting infamy had awakened the state legislature. Sweeping improvements had been made, and what I was seeing was the relatively happy result of all those improvements. I shuddered to think what it must have been like before. As it was it seemed to me a necessary, adequate and relatively humane form of control, but it certainly was not good medicine.

Still, I greatly admired the professionals who worked there. They took constant risks, worked under dismal and threatening conditions, and were looked down upon by their colleagues in other fields of mental health who did not have their sort of courage. Not only the psychiatrists, but even more so the psychologists and social workers on the wards seemed to me extraordinary people. Some were women. All had chosen to spend their lives among severely disturbed and dangerous criminals, in the hope—against all odds—of doing something to help them. It was not their fault that society did not take seriously the treatment of the criminally insane.

One of the facts uncovered by the television news people was that it had been possible for a man to be committed for life without ever having his case reviewed. This virtual life imprisonment without parole occurred after what might have been a small infraction. The mental hospital at Riverville was not supposed to provide shortened, easy sentences for criminals who would otherwise have long, harsh prison terms; but neither was it designed to provide cruel and unusual punishment to criminals who happened to be crazy.

So one of the results of the changes had been frequent recommitment hearings. Under the old system the patient-prisoner had to initiate a hearing, and many did not have the wit or resources to do this. Now each man had an automatic recommitment hearing annually. The premise was that he could walk out the door unless the state could show that he was a clear and continuing danger to others. In other words it had to be proved that he deserved commitment, as if for the first time.

Fortunately for the state, and typically for the patients as well, this was not difficult. A judge came to Riverville one day a week and, in a conference room on a hospital ward, held court on the men whose year was up. Usually there was a court-appointed lawyer for the patients. The state provided evidence from hospital records and from testimony by the hospital staff that the patient required continuing commitment. When I watched, the first three patients, who appeared genuinely hopeful of release, were quickly processed according to this formula. "Well," said the very young lawyer as he closed his folder smiling, "I'm through for the day." The fourth man had a lawyer of his own, who tried halfheartedly to secure the patient's release to the cushier hospital setting he had come from. But during his last stay there he had thrown a number of chairs around and then thrown a mental health worker across the room. He was recommitted to Riverville.

The last case was a celebrated one. Two years earlier, the patient had gone out on a busy street with a sharpened screwdriver and attacked a number of drivers and pedestrians. Now his obviously well-to-do parents were present in the makeshift court with a lawyer they had brought in from halfway across the country. The lawyer styled himself as an expert on abnormalities of copper metabolism. He argued that either an excess or deficit of copper could cause violent emotional disturbances. The evidence he cited weakly supported the possibility of brain damage from copper excess. There was no evidence on the other side, but it seemed logical to him that it could work both ways. The final link in his syllogism was that the patient had allegedly drunk very large amounts of milk as a small child which, he believed, could reduce the availability of copper to the body and brain.

The lawyer did not push this theory too assiduously. He seemed to realize it would not sway the judge, but he "just wanted to get it into the record, by way of information, for the future." This was a caricature of the biochemical approach to mental illness, which the lawyer knew was in the ascendancy but obviously little understood. The parents seemed anxious and satisfied. The patient, like the others, seemed hopeful of securing his release. Like the others, he was recommitted.

I walked across the courtyard to another ward to keep my appointment with Frank Cullen. Two sets of bars closed behind me. As I came on the ward, a meeting was in progress. Mike Berger, a pale, bearded psychologist I had met earlier, stood in front of a group that turned out to be all the men on the ward—about thirty of them—making a few announcements. His ability to manage this group was extraordinary. A fat, sweet-looking boy in his early twenties was shaking so violently that his chair was making a racket.

"Stop that, Roy," said Berger. The boy stopped. Two men crowded together in a corner jostled each other, and one gave the other an elbow. Berger called their names sharply, and they stopped. Other men threw good-natured taunts at him, which he ignored. The tension was thick, but his command was total.

After the meeting he took me into his office, where he had to interview a new inmate before giving me a chance to see Frank Cullen. In the middle of the interview he suddenly became very uneasy, though the patient's demeanor had not changed. He began questioning him about having picked up a rock at a certain bus stop in a neighboring town and threatened people waiting for the bus. After sending the man out, he told me that he had recognized him from the bus stop incident, for he had been one of the people standing in line and had reported the man to the police. This constituted a personal connection from outside the prison, and it meant that there would be grave and predictable risks entailed in having the man on his ward. It was only a matter of time before the patient recognized *him*. Berger transferred him immediately.

When Frank Cullen came in, we interviewed him together. He was stunningly like and yet different from his brother. He had the same features in a thinner, less friendly face, and wore a small moustache instead of an unruly beard. His body was lean and muscular in contrast to Howard's teddy-bear softness. He spoke more harshly—defensively, I thought —and was much less forthcoming. He explained that he had killed a man he was rooming with while having a delusion that the man was involved in a plot against him. The devil had come and told him to do the killing, which he had done with a knife. He volunteered, as Howard had done, that the two of them had shared the same delusions and also that they were very different people. That was certainly true. Did they prove that schizophrenia was genetic, or that much of the human spirit was independent of the genes? They had grown up with shared genes and largely shared experience, but they seemed to have the same illness coursing through different personalities. One of them, a warm bear of a man, had danced in public and preached the gospel of a unified, sexy world religion, while the other, tough and hard, in an otherwise similar delusional state had destroyed a human life.

My presentation of Howard's case to the faculty and staff went smoothly. Howard had been getting better. He played the harmonica, began going out with groups, cooked the hall dinner one night, and reported that he felt "great." He stayed free of hallucinations except for the light, and one day he told me that even the light was gone. It was known that his hospitalization was his first real lithium trial, and it was considered likely that all drug treatments he had had since the ileostomy had not been adequately absorbed. Now he had had a completely successful hospitalization in the most professional hands, and he was, at least for now, quite well. When I said good-bye to him he played the harmonica for me for the last time, and we shook hands. He thanked me warmly and told me that he thought I would make a very good psychiatrist.

But I knew that his continued health would depend on a delicately poised balance of factors. Would he comply with his medication regimen as an outpatient? Would he appear regularly for tests of his lithium level? Would he stay clear of street drugs—those archenemies of stability in psychosis? The answers to these questions would depend on how favorable his home environment was, and on the sophistication of his psychiatrist. She would have to do much more than just dispense drugs. I remembered a clinical pearl: *The main role for psychotherapy in psychosis is to get the patient to keep taking the drugs.* She would have a harder job with Howard than anyone at Sullivan had had, and I silently wished her wisdom, warmth, a sense of humor, and luck.

Sharon Beattie continued to draw her trees and seascapes, but her hospital course was complex. She cycled out of her dysphoric mania into a depression with some paranoid ideas. She was treated with an antidepressant, but her depression lifted too soon for the drug to explain the change. However, this improvement was transient. She became depressed again and stayed in her room for days. She had been hoping desperately to go home for Christmas, but this did not now seem likely.

Cynthia Warner finally found a place to go. Some relatives of hers who worked with the Salvation Army were going to take her in. This placement put a smile on her face and greatly improved her psychiatric prognosis. Alice Blake, who had been getting the E.C.T., also continued to improve. She emerged from her room regularly, socialized, and went out with other patients. Her memory disturbance was minimal and so far limited to an inability to remember events on the mornings on which she had treatments. Chrissy Lewis was discharged without in the end becoming pregnant, as was Marisa, who had stopped talking about becoming a prostitute and was discharged to a residential school for problem girls.

On my last night on call, a middle-aged psychiatrist presented himself as a patient. Shortly after his arrival the resident I was working with was called away to an emergency, and I was left alone with him for the rest of the intake interview. It was remarkable and touching the way he was able to treat me as his doctor. Unlike most patients, he knew exactly how little I knew. He took it upon himself to teach me about his illness and how to assess it, and he did this subtly, without a trace of arrogance or resentment. If I asked a question obliquely, his answer would pose it again in a more apt form, even while clarifying the point. And he was able to do this without what I could have called intellectualization or denial. He was in anguish throughout the interview and did not attempt to conceal it.

He had been suffering from manic-depressive illness for ten years, had had an intermittent drinking problem, and had made at least one major suicide attempt. His father had suffered from chronic depression, but his two brothers and two grown children were free of psychiatric problems. His own depressions, of which this was one, usually allowed him to keep working, and he was proud of his effectiveness as a physician. But at home he was isolative and miserable. Taking a lot of Valium, he was still able to sleep only three to four hours a night. A few weeks earlier, he had separated from his wife of almost thirty years. And he knew that he was at risk of a major depressive episode.

In one respect he did not act like a patient. He was friendly with the director of the Sullivan Institute, and he had arranged to check himself in under a special agreement. He would board on one of the wards at night, but from seven A.M. to seven P.M. he would be free to continue with his usual activities, mainly his psychiatric practice. It seemed to me strange for a suicidally depressed man to be conducting a full psychiatric practice during the day and yet be under surveillance on a psychiatric ward at night. But who was I to argue with the institute's director?

When the resident came back, I summarized the case in the patient's presence. The resident asked a few more questions and then signed the patient in. After we had checked the patient into his room on the ward and were writing our progress notes, he told me that he objected strongly to the patient's special arrangement. "V.I.P. treatment in medicine is always a mistake. But it's especially a mistake in psychiatry. He's a patient, but he's not. We're not really in charge of him. It's a betwixt-and-between arrangement that's a setup for a disaster." He noted in the chart his disagreement with the arrangement in terms as strong as the politics of the situation would allow.

Some weeks later I ran into him at Galen. He himself was keeping an appointment for an evaluation of a heart problem.

"Remember what I told you about V.I.P. treatment? That psychiatrist tried to kill himself. He missed by an inch with the Seconal this time. While he was at his office. While he was under his V.I.P. arrangement. Remember what I told you. You can be a doctor or a friend of a doctor. But when you're a patient, you have to be a patient." And, with a smile, he went off to see his cardiologist.

8

PEDIATRICS

Suffer the Children

After Psychiatry I had two weeks off for the Christmas holiday, a luxurious and restful time for thought. My book, which had been published a few months earlier, was being well received. I was trying to answer the correspondence and other expressions of interest it was generating. But it was difficult to switch back and forth from being a know-nothing medical student to being a wise authority.

A strange, ironic conflict of this kind occurred when I went to a high-level Washington conference on mental health research. I was invited as an anthropologist, because of my book. Although I had been to many conferences, I had never been to one with so many important people.

The conference was convened by the director of the National Institute of Mental Health in association with a famous actress and her husband, a well-known businessman, active private supporters of mental health research. Seated around the table were some of the most highly regarded brain scientists in the world, and they reported their recent discoveries—some of which had already been acknowledged with major prizes—with clarity and elegance. Foundation executives and science journalists from leading newspapers and periodicals were there as observers.

At the conference dinner on Saturday evening I chatted and then danced with a famous advice columnist, who had a well-deserved influence in national mental health circles. (When the N.I.M.H. director wanted to disseminate new information on the recognition and treatment of alcoholism, he called her, she mentioned it in her column, and he had forty thousand requests for his pamphlet in one week.) I shook hands with a famous newspaper publisher, I joked with scientists I had revered from a distance, I exchanged anecdotes with a former presidential aide, and I interrupted a conversation between a senator and an attractive young psychologist to ask the young woman to dance.

This was heady wine for a superannuated medical student. Only a few days earlier, I had been on the lowest rung of the ladder of the mental health hierarchy, following orders slavishly and begging for crumbs of knowledge from psychiatric residents—themselves still wet behind the ears. Now I was called upon to comment on the anthropological view of human nature and what it had to offer mental health research. I gave a formal talk about one of my research interests—cross-cultural universals of early psychological development, in relation to brain development. I also offered occasional comments when it seemed appropriate to introduce some fact or concept from anthropology or evolutionary biology.

But the greatest difference from every other academic conference I had been to was that now I had had a tiny bit of clinical experience. I had crossed the line from ideas to practice. I was among those at the table who had faced the mentally ill and tried desperately to think of something to do for them. I had been interested in mental illness for years, but now it had faces: Billy Tirell, Howard Cullen and his brother Frank, Sharon Beattie, Alice Blake. The pace of research on mental illness, the need for funds, the impending breakthroughs—these were things I now took personally and more seriously than ever.

The most exciting moment of the meeting for me came when a non-M.D. brain scientist connected with Galen Memorial described a patient whose case he had heard about, a sixteen-year-old boy with an unexplained progressive movement disorder lacking the classic features of any known syndrome. The scientist displayed the boy's CAT scan, which showed a probable defect in the brain in the caudate nucleus. The boy had been scheduled for a controversial type of brain surgery, and no one at the meeting could quite figure out why.

I knew the patient. I had seen and examined him, together with his neurologists and neurosurgeon, and had listened to their debates about his condition. I did not have a convincing explanation for the surgery he was getting, but at least I could provide first-hand knowledge of the details of the case and of the arguments on both sides. And above all, I could insist that the boy was not just a CAT scan or a case study but a patient—a suffering, frightened, increasingly desperate boy.

I had sympathy for the physicians who had seen him and who knew how badly he needed help. I understood the flaws in the logic that led to the choice of surgery; but I also knew that the surgery was not very risky. I had seen the boy stagger around his hospital room and struggle to form a few incomprehensible words. I spoke in defense of his doctors. They may have been guilty of imprecise science, but they were on the front line, eye to eye with the boy. And at the moment when I stepped in between this patient and the scientists at a conference table in Washington, I became more of a doctor myself.

I also shared in violating two of the "four laws of medicine": If you don't know what to do, don't do anything; and, Never call a surgeon. In defending what was done, even halfheartedly, I had shared the responsibility—almost as if I had been holding the knife.

After the meeting my wife, children, and I went on a real vacation, on a warm stretch of Florida beach. This gave me some time to catch up on sleep, to get to know my family again, and to think about the whirlwind I had temporarily emerged from.

I was ready to decide that I could not become a surgeon. For someone my age, with a young family, the training was too long and the every-other-night call schedule was too arduous. I would miss seeing my children grow up, almost as if I had been away for many years. With so many sleepless nights, it was possible my health would break down. I remembered the health questionnaire we had filled out in Basic Clinical Skills which had shown I was markedly more at risk than my fellow students. How would I stand up against them in a brutal five or seven years of surgical residency? More important, perhaps, was the psychological brutality of the surgeons—their cultural narrowness, their locker-room vulgarity, their unparalleled and often unjustified arrogance. I had been cautioned not to stereotype them, and of course there were exceptions. But the mode, not the exceptions, created the surgical "culture." The stereotype fit my experience. I would not want to spend much time among them.

It had seemed an idle fantasy, yet it was difficult to relinquish. Of all the doing that had attracted me to medicine, the surgeons' was the most impressive, not because it necessarily worked better, but because it was so drastic an intervention. The rush of excitement as the trauma victims were wheeled in, the split-second timing, the forced, abrupt, life-and-death decisions, the drama of the operating theater, the reverential obedience of the nurses, and the constant crossing of the boundary of another person's body—these had an appeal that was rare or nonexistent in other fields of medicine. When I was most honest, I also had to face the fact that the sheer masculinity of the surgical profession attracted me. Even the few women in it had joined the cult of machismo. I did not like to admit that I was not man enough to flash a scalpel blade with the best of them, but finally, my chance at their imaginary clash of blades was undermined by a real clash of values.

Anesthesiology was never a possibility. Its role was so specialized that it did not seem like a part of real medicine. Its practitioners were not treating the sick, only preparing and managing them so that someone else could treat them. The idea that I might spend my life in the O.R. but *behind* the drape, forever a spectator and subordinate in the surgical drama, was untenable.

I did not rule out neurology, and it fascinated me more than ever. I respected its practitioners as wonderfully literate, usually sensitive, medically sophisticated intellectuals. At their scientific best, they were discovering both the functioning of the nerve cell and the organization of the mind. At their clinical best, they were also physically and spiritually comforting patients with devastating illnesses. But what were they doing for those patients? The fact that this question was in many of their own minds almost as much as it was in mine had turned some of them bitter and cynical. I feared a similar outcome for myself.

Psychiatry, despite its theoretical chaos and its position as a neglected stepchild of medicine, still remained the most likely possibility for me. There and perhaps there only, all my previous work and thought would have important, transferable value. I felt disaffected with the baroque explanations of psychoanalysis, especially since it seemed impossible to show that it did anything for the patients. Psychoanalytic patients, for their part, were not always clearly ill. They sought and, at its best, got, a professionally guided form of extended self-examination. Philosophically, I was sure that it had to be of value. If the unexamined life is not worth living, then the psychoanalyzed life might well take on some new validity. Some of the patients might never get better; they might go on musing about the same cluster of life problems for ten years or more. Yet who was to say that psychotherapy was not an essential part of their adaptation, without which they would be much worse off? If diabetics had to remain on special diets and insulin for a lifetime, without ever getting better— usually, in fact, getting worse—then why couldn't borderlines and other nonpsychotics stay in psychotherapy for a lifetime, dependent on constant treatment, but stable and relatively well?

Medical, or biological, psychiatry was ever more appealing to me. It was real medicine based on real science. The illnesses were dramatic and devastating to the patients. They were sometimes life-threatening, and were soul-threatening—threatening to the essence and value of life—in all cases. Unlike patients in other branches of medicine, except for the one illness the patients were usually well. Their pain struck me as worse than almost any physical pain I had seen, and there was no anesthetic or analgesic to shoot at it like a magic bullet. They were often young adults who, if helped, could sometimes lead normal and highly productive lives.

Research in biological psychiatry—on neurotransmitters and their receptors, on nerve cell membranes, on brain imaging, on the efficacy and side effects of new drugs—paralleled research in neurology, and was as exciting and as rigorous as anything in medicine. And best of all, the patients usually got better and often got well. I decided that of the clinical fields I had experienced so far, a career in medical psychiatry would probably be right for me.

While on vacation my wife and I both became patients. This gave me an unpleasant but needed glimpse of medicine from the other side of the pain. My wife picked up a virus from one of the children. She had a cough, runny nose, and sore throat, and she lay in bed one evening with a low-grade fever. As the night went on her temperature rose and she became increasingly uncomfortable. She could not sleep at all. She wanted to know when the fever would start to "fry" her brain. I fed her aspirin and tried to reassure her, but when she went over 104° by mouth, at two o'clock in the morning, her anxiety infected me. I decided to stop trying to be a medical hero at her expense, and we went to a nearby hospital emergency room.

It was not empty, but there did not seem to be any serious cases in the entrance or waiting room. I expected to move right along from the clerk at the admissions desk to a physician. I soon realized—as I should have, from my own emergency room service—that no such speed was likely. The clerk heard our story, looked my wife over from behind the desk, and occupied us for a while with insurance forms. No medical drama here. Then he asked us to sit and wait.

My reaction was strangely mixed. I stewed for a little while in resentment. My wife was burning with fever, exhausted from sleeplessness, and had a painful and constricted throat with a hacking cough. We hadn't come down here on a whim. She needed to see a doctor. I was a third-year medical student with a few months at least of clinical experience, and I had decided she was sick enough to see a doctor right away. Who was this clerk with no medical training to tell us to wait? On the other hand I also felt somehow reassured. The "know-nothing" clerk, if he had sat behind that desk for any length of time, knew how to assess the urgency of cases. *He* had to decide who should be sent back immediately. My wife did not strike him as being in that category. With my arm around her, feeling sympathy for her pain and fear, I mentally crossed the line back to the impersonal, health-professional side—just for a moment—and realized I agreed with him.

She turned out to have a throat culture positive for strep, but in the sense meant by house officers on call, she was not "sick." That is, she was not in any sort of urgent danger. On the way out I asked the clerk how he had arrived at his decision. He shrugged his shoulders. "A fever that's high enough to be dangerous usually makes a person delirious or something. They don't come in and sit and answer questions and fill out forms."

"Of course," I said, smacking my forehead with the heel of my hand. I walked out shaking my head, laughing at myself, and going through the catechism: How is a high fever dangerous? It can cause damage to the nervous system. How do you know that it's getting that high? The nervous system tells you by putting out some unexpected behavior, like delirium. What if the brain seems to be working normally? Then the risk is not yet very great.

My mother had lost her hearing in an extremely high fever as a child, and so I may be particularly sensitized to that sort of risk. Also, I would not be proud if I had been completely cool-headed in assessing my wife. But I had to laugh at myself. After years of training I had been taught a lesson in medical common sense by a desk clerk who couldn't have passed any of the academic gantlets I had run through. After I got over my resentment and embarrassment, I was grateful for the lesson.

My own minor illness was a very bad toothache. This is a pain that can quickly go beyond the level of annoyance or distraction. After a night of throwing aspirin at it, I went to the dentist, a pleasant young man who had only recently moved to Florida. I needed immediate root canal work, and he was able to go ahead and do it. Under lidocaine anesthesia the pain went away, and he dug away at the roots with a special excavating tool. The goal was to destroy the nerve roots by smashing them up and digging them out of the canals. This would leave a dead but perfectly serviceable —and painless—tooth. I went out feeling cheerful and pain free until the anesthetic wore off. The original pain came back with a vengeance. It was now Saturday night. My chances of seeing a dentist anywhere in the

Southeastern United States were nil. My calls to the dentist who had done the work eventually produced a phone number of a dentist who was covering for him, which eventually produced a phone number of a dentist who was covering for *him*. This phone number, after a delay of some hours, produced a telephoned prescription for an analgesic with codeine. It did little, but it took the edge off the pain enough to get me through the next thirty-six hours.

The nice young man reopened the canals on Monday morning and discovered that I had an unusual anatomic variant, an extra, fourth, rootlet he had not cleaned out. I could have begun musing on which Caribbean dental school he had escaped from before coming to Florida to prey on senior citizens, but instead I sympathized with him as a fellow soldier on the front line. He was doing the best he could.

My inability to find a dentist on Saturday night reminded me of a story told by one of my medical school professors. Before becoming an anatomist he had been a general practitioner in a rural Dutch community during the war. At three o'clock one morning he heard shouting below his window.

"What's the matter down there?" he had asked, half asleep.

"I had a tooth pulled today. Now my mouth is bleeding terribly," said a difficult-to-understand male voice.

"Why don't you see your dentist?"

"You can't wake a dentist up at three o'clock in the morning!"

Dentists and doctors might both be front-line soldiers in daylight, but at night the dentists left the field to the M.D.'s.

I was to spend the month of January in outpatient pediatrics at Galen. This was a relatively nonstressful way of fulfilling my third-year pediatrics requirement, although I thought I might then go on to do more later. In fact I had not yet ruled out pediatrics as a specialty for myself. I had done research on the growth and development of infants and children in Africa and the U.S. for more than ten years before I entered medical school. I was intensely interested in children as far back as I could remember, and when I had two children of my own; they rekindled my fascination with all things relating to human development. They had also reminded me of the sheer joy of being with children, and given me a practical reason to become well versed in the diseases and accidents of childhood.

My schedule involved a peripatetic sampling of a variety of basic and specialized clinics. Each week I was to spend several mornings in the pediatric outpatient service; several afternoons and one night in the pediatric emergency clinic; and the rest of the time in specialized clinics of my choice. I chose pediatric neurology, pediatric endocrinology, which included disorders of growth and development, and pediatric psychiatry.

On the first day, as soon as I showed up in the emergency room, the resident said, "Great! A warm body!" and sent me in to see a sick child who had not yet been seen by anyone. This went on all day. I had gone six weeks without touching a patient—in psychiatry and on vacation—and months since being in the charged situation of an emergency room. I had not seen children as patients for months longer than that, since Basic Clinical Skills. So I was more than a little apprehensive.

But by the end of the afternoon I had realized that I was more or less competent, and more surprisingly, I had confidence. This setting was most like the surgical emergency clinic—an experience that now seemed an age ago and had not been extensive at that. Yet the feeling, the facility, returned—the feeling of knowing *something* the patient needs to know; of being able to help.

My first patient was a plump ten-year-old boy with an exquisite tenderness midway on the outer edge of his left foot. He had only been running and playing and had had no blow or fall. Yet I knew immediately that he had to have a fracture; it was an improbable place for a sprain or muscle injury. The tenderness was extreme, and he could not bear any weight on it. He was just obese enough so that the deceleration of his body against the foot in running might actually splinter bone. The X-ray showed a type of injury known as a Jones fracture—an evulsion or pressure-induced fracture—of the fifth metatarsal bone.

My second patient was a baby boy who had been crying all night. He and his parents were miserable in the pathetic, special way that I knew from similar episodes with my own children. His right ear was red and raw from his pulling on it. I was not adept enough to really see the eardrums of a tiny screaming baby, but I knew his problem was a middle-ear infection.

The third was an eight-year-old girl who had fallen about seven feet—landing on her feet—and had pain in her right ankle. I examined the range of motion and the tenderness of the ankle and concluded that it was a sprain, in spite of the distance of the fall. X-ray confirmed my diagnosis.

And the fourth was a boy in his late teens who had been hit in the nose with a hockey stick and had a nasty-looking cut just at the bridge. I cleaned and examined the cut, and concluded that there was no need for stitches.

Steri-strips, little pieces of clear sterile adhesive, would hold the edges together nicely.

The attending physician supervising the residents did not agree with me. She thought it should be stitched. But because of the boy's age, he would end up being stitched in my old hangout, minor surgery. So she called the resident on duty there, and Mark Reid showed up. I had not seen him since I had left Marty Wentworth's surgical service, and he was quite friendly. His assessment confirmed mine, and Dr. Hingham accepted it: Steri-strips.

These were all minor problems with minor solutions. To an experienced physician they were fairly easy, but I was not an experienced physician. Still, I was right over and over again. I was surprised and proud, and my luck held up throughout the afternoon and evening.

One of the great responsibilities of the pediatrician is the management of parents' anxiety. I did that naturally and well, since I was one, as few if any of the residents and young physicians were. I remembered a clinical pearl: When your assessment has shown that the child is not sick, you still have to treat the parent's anxiety.

The following morning I attended a clinic in pediatric neurology and saw a patient for whom there was no parental anxiety because there were no parents. He was a twenty-four-year-old "boy" brought to the clinic by an attendant from the state residential school for the severely disturbed and mentally retarded, for a regularly scheduled appointment with his neurologist. The original diagnosis in the chart, "childhood schizophrenia," had been made at a time when this diagnosis had been popular and was considered meaningful—the time when, as a high school student, I had been working with similar children. His diagnosis was more properly something like autism combined with broad-spectrum retardation. Oddly, he had always been exceptionally good at arithmetic calculations. At the age of seventeen he had begun to assault people. Nevertheless, his mother continued to keep him at home with her for another five years until she was finally forced to give him up to the state school. He had lived there for two years.

Petey was a well-formed, slow-moving, small but slightly overweight boyish man with restless brown eyes. He had difficulty initiating movements. His neurologist, Dr. Silverman, wanted to show me Petey's calculating ability, and I encouraged this. There were always conflicts for me between the need to learn and the injunction to protect the patient from unnecessary indignities, but in this case it seemed all right from Petey's viewpoint to get him to show off the one thing he could really do well.

So Dr. Silverman gave him a three-digit number which he easily and quickly squared in his head. On the second and third numbers, however —all were of comparable difficulty—he was wrong, and he knew it without being told. He looked frustrated. On the fourth number he thought for five or ten seconds, mumbling to himself. Then he looked up, jumped out of the chair, and attacked Dr. Silverman.

Amid Petey's flying fists, three of us—the attendant from the state school, Dr. Silverman, and I—managed to get him under control and pinned down on the couch. There, held down gently by the attendant, he began to talk to himself aloud, with an edge of anger, referring to himself in the second or third person: "He's a big man now. Petey's not a baby. O.K. Time out. You're not a baby. Take it easy. Yes. O.K. You're a big man now. Take it easy." This touching discourse had obviously been absorbed from all the stock phrases used by his mother and his caretakers in the past. At length he settled down and had his examination. No changes were seen since his last visit six months before, so no changes were made in his medication. As I saw him and the attendant to the door, Petey was as calm as he had been when he came in. The attendant, a strong young man, was trembling. He said, "This was my first time taking a patient out by myself."

"You did well," I said, and thought, all of us are learning.

While Dr. Silverman dictated a note on the consultation, I noticed a cartoon on his wall. The four panels showed a classroom with pupils becoming increasingly unruly. In the first a pupil observed, "Mrs. Weed is coming unglued." The second and third showed the hapless teacher in increasing stages of distraction, with descriptions of her deterioration from the point of view of the students. And the fourth panel said, "So they're putting me on medication to slow me down."

It was comforting to see this evidence of Dr. Silverman's awareness of the complexity of childhood hyperactivity—not to mention his sense of humor. As I thought back on my African experience, I remembered children with a broad spectrum of activity levels, from sluggish to intensely active. But since they were not in school, they never came into a situation where sitting still and focusing attention for hours at a time was crucial to success. Running around in the bush and going rather quickly from one activity to another was almost always appropriate. It was the historical novelty of schooling, imposed on the natural range of variation in human children, that created the "disease" of hyperactivity.

Still, schooling was a *necessary* historical novelty, and few if any parents in our society would be willing to forgo their children's success in it on the basis of some anthropological theory. In a sense, hyperactivity is only a sociological conundrum, and there is a danger—certainly realized in some unfortunate cases—of medicating a child to solve a problem that is really the teacher's. Does the child need a stimulant to dampen hyperactivity? Does the teacher need a tranquilizer or a change of job? Or should the solution be social—a reduction in class size, say, or new pedagogic methods? For the most extreme cases, the suggestion of drug treatment after other approaches had failed was usually an act of compassion.

Two of the patients who came that morning after Petey left challenged my conception of such issues. Both were girls. I knew that learning disabilities, including activity and attention problems, were at least four times more common in boys than in girls, and could manifest themselves differently in the two sexes. Other than global mental retardation or emotional disturbance such as Petey's, they could be of two broad types. First, a child could have a specific defect in an activity such as reading (dyslexia) or arithmetic (dyscalculia). In a very few cases these disabilities were proved to be associated with developmental defects of the brain. For most, controversy raged over whether the defect was in the "hard wiring" or in some unfortunate series of experiences. Second, a child could have difficulty that cut across many domains of ability. This might or might not be associated with hyperactivity.

The pediatric neurologist's strategy was to give a battery of tests. Dr. Silverman's, which I sat in on, took most of a day. It included a standard intelligence test, the Wechsler Intelligence Scale for Children (W.I.S.C.), as well as many more specialized tests. Some exposed difficulties in reading, some in arithmetic, and some quite specifically in attention. If specific learning disabilities were detected, one could invoke special tutoring, altered expectations, and other strategies for remediation or circumvention, depending on how "hard wired" (really a euphemism for "how difficult to remediate") the problem was judged to be. But if the problem was one of attention deficit and/or hyperactivity, then treatment with a class of stimulant drugs resembling amphetamine could sometimes change the child's behavior dramatically.

Cindy, thirteen, was brought in by anxious middle-class parents who insisted that she had no attention problem except when dealing with subjects that did not interest her. This seemed to me a valid challenge until Dr. Silverman patiently explained that by definition, "Attention deficit is a lack of capacity to pay attention to something that doesn't turn you on." It suddenly occurred to me that I might have it. I certainly varied widely in my ability to pay attention in medical school lectures, depending on how interested I was in the subject. But of course, I wouldn't have got this far unless I had managed to attend to a great number of things I didn't care for much. Cindy was much more restricted. She could pay attention to almost anything about horses. But could this get her through school and through a modern American life? Of course Dr. Silverman could have recommended that she plan her future around horses, but this obvious solution did not appeal to her or to her parents. She got a trial of Ritalin, the standard therapy, and an instruction to come back in two weeks.

The second girl was an extremely charming and pretty ten-year-old with a much subtler attention deficit. A year earlier she had been failing in school, and her attention problem had shown up on the test battery. Ritalin had greatly improved her concentration and her school performance. At the beginning, after it had begun to succeed, she had had a two-week trial with a placebo, and her parents and teacher all agreed that her problem had reemerged during the trial. Reinstituting the drug eliminated the problem again. She was back for her first six-month reevaluation. Now she would have another such "off-trial," to be repeated every six months until the problem might be (as it often was) outgrown.

I entertained doubts about these children. They were not obviously "bouncing off the walls." They had subtle problems that many people, including many experts, would interpret in psychological terms. But the drugs in use for this purpose had been shown to be effective, though the long-term gains were more controversial. There did not seem to be any highly undesirable side effects. And Dr. Silverman at least was using them in a responsible way, testing them regularly for continued effectiveness and using them only in children who showed themselves on the test battery to have a particular problem with attention. Still, I wondered whether it would really be so terrible if Cindy were somehow to try to make a life for herself with horses.

Working in the general clinic of the pediatric outpatient service was another experience that made me feel like a doctor. I worked under the supervision of Dr. Haley, a short, friendly, good-looking man about forty years old. He generously trusted me with his panel of patients and, while keeping tabs on my every move, somehow managed to treat me like an equal. We worked side by side, plowing through the folders set up by the nurse each morning. I worked in an office examining room adjacent to his.

I pulled out a folder, studied the case, called the patient and parent in, interviewed them, examined the child, and then, after forming an assessment, presented the case to Dr. Haley, who asked me a few questions and examined the patient himself. He signed any necessary prescriptions, but I dictated the evaluation note, sitting alone in the office he had assigned to me, pressing switches on the dictaphone, and gazing out at the vastness of Galen Memorial, feeling professional.

The panel of patients was Dr. Haley's own, so that the clinic was like a private pediatric practice. Babies, children, teenagers, and young adults came with minor aches and injuries, for routine check-ups, for permission to participate in certain school activities, for prescription refills, or just to reassure their parents they were healthy and normal. ("Diagnosis: Concerned Parent" was a common conclusion after a telephone call, leading to a clinic visit that was otherwise quite unnecessary.) My skill at interpreting parents' concerns was once again at a premium, and I felt almost like a practicing pediatrician.

I also learned a lot about myself. A two-year-old black girl in a frilly pink dress was brought in by her mother because of an itching rash and a cut on her lip. Dermatology was not one of my strong points, and what little I knew was virtually nontransferable to black skin. It looked like eczema to me, but I knew I would have to wait for Dr. Haley to "eyeball" it. I was conscious of, and embarrassed by, my ignorance about black skin, which made it seem a barrier.

Worse, when I turned to the lip cut—it was shallow, but had produced some swelling—I found myself thinking about child abuse. We had been trained to consider the possibility that any injury could be nonaccidental, and there were certain patterns that were highly characteristic. But this was a very unlikely possibility, and it occurred to me that I might not even have thought of it except for the fact that the patient was black. Dr. Haley, knowing the family, discounted the suggestion, and I began to wonder whether objectivity was possible. I remembered discussing affirmative action in medical school admissions with a conservative preclinical professor. He refused to credit my argument that black patients needed at least some black doctors—that white doctors could not be expected to perform with precisely equivalent understanding, responsiveness, and compassion. He was wrong. And I was not immune myself from the tendency to form racial categories.

Confirming something like the converse of my argument, I found myself dallying for a few extra seconds between patients in order to gaze at a patient in the waiting room. She was about fifteen, tall for her age, blue-

eyed, with flowing shoulder-length blond hair and a perfectly propor-
tioned face. Her body was, in conventional terms, perfect, and her complexion was a smooth cream color infused with healthy pink. For the
moment at least, I could not remember ever seeing a more beautiful
woman, and I longed desperately for the luck to have her (and her mother)
in my examining room. All that day, I could not get her out of my mind.

Another teenager, who came in by herself, was a stately, stylish, eighteen-year-old black woman who looked as if she could be in her mid-
twenties. She needed a refill of her medication for menstrual cramps. A
few questions led to the information that she had menses like clockwork
every two weeks, lasting five to seven days. I checked her chart again,
which contained no mention of this pattern, although she told me she had
had it since beginning to menstruate at age twelve. Her gynecologist,
whom she had last seen a year before, had made nothing of it, she said.
Around that time she had had a work-up for dizziness, including a glucose
tolerance test, but puzzlingly without a work-up for anemia. She had had
sex occasionally but had never been pregnant.

Dr. Haley agreed with my assessment that she needed a better gynecological evaluation, as well as a complete blood count and a measure of
ferritin, the iron-binding protein. I felt proud of this clinical "pick-up" and
better about my "racism." In fact, it occurred to me that if I had had the
same set of problems with the blonde, I might have been too nonplussed
to figure out which questions to ask—a sort of bigotry in reverse. The
possibility of an inverse relation between emotion and effectiveness has
general implications in medical practice and training that I was at that
time only beginning to think about.

At the end of the day, just before leaving the hospital, I was chatting
with a woman physician who was an expert on severe burns in childhood.
I was trying to explain to her indulgent ear something about my strange
career development when she got a call from radiology. She invited me
to go along saying "There might be something interesting," and we continued talking on the way to the X-ray file room. In the darkened room,
the radiologist pulled out an envelope from the film rack. "It's that nine-
month-old burn case," he said. "You know which one I mean?" He took
four films out of the envelope and slapped them up on the viewers, which
glowed white in the darkness behind the shadowy film. Images of almost
every bone in the tiny body were lit up on one or another film on the
screen.

"Why all those X-rays for a burn?" I asked.

"I didn't like the pattern of the burn," she said.

The radiologist's finger began pounding on the images. "Here," he said flatly. "Here. Here. Here."

The baby had two rib fractures, two upper arm fractures, and an upper leg fracture, all healed or partially healed and therefore not new. None of them showed in the medical record, for the simple reason that the mother had not brought the child in to have them treated. This was a classic pattern of nonaccidental injury. The burn that had tipped the doctor off had had too regular a border around the body, as if the baby had been held down in a searing hot bath. Accidental burns produced more thrashing and turning, with more random distributions of skin damage.

This one had occurred, the hospital was told, when the baby had been left alone by the mother with her boyfriend. But the X-rays showed that the fractures had occurred at unknown times throughout her short life. The baby would now have to be legally protected from her mother. This physician's considered alertness—much more than her expertise in burn treatment—had probably saved the baby's life.

Another night in the emergency room brought further lessons. I examined a ten-year-old boy who had fallen a distance of seven feet and landed on his head on a concrete schoolyard. He had not lost consciousness, but he had an ugly blue lump at least two inches high protruding from his forehead near his hairline. As a father, I saw this as the ultimate fall, short of a life-threatening disaster. I assumed he would need a skull X-ray, at least, but I was quite wrong. The attending physician, Dr. Kellner, gave me a lesson about the appropriate threshold for ordering skull films— including the inevitable Xerox copy of a paper on it. One would have to X-ray hundreds of lumps as big as this one before finding a small fracture. And then what would be done differently? The parents, who seemed reliable, were instructed to bring him back if he experienced nausea or vomiting—a sign of undue pressure on the brain—or if he became drowsy or delirious. They were to wake him up from sleep every two hours during the night, to make certain he was arousable. And they were to treat the ugly lump with standard symptomatic measures.

Dr. Kellner, a chubby, brilliant man who fancied himself a cynic but with children became a delightful, hopeful clown, also gave me a lesson about fever control. A three-year-old with a few days of cough and medium-grade fever was brought in, by a mother concerned about how to keep the fever down. He recommended children's Tylenol or the equivalent—not aspirin, because of the risk (in childhood) of precipitating the serious rare condition Reye's syndrome.

He also said, "Fill up a bathtub with tepid water—not cold, just slightly cool to the touch. Put on a bathing suit, and get into the bath with the kid. Don't drown him. Just gently immerse him and keep pouring water over him until it brings the fever down. And watch him for delirium. If he starts doing weird things, talking strange, anything like that, it means his brainiac's acting a bit funny. Then you bring him in and we fix him up." *Brainiac* was Kellner's cute slang for brain. He was a father himself, and the image of him, an overweight teddy bear with curly dark hair and heavy glasses, sitting in his bathtub in a bathing suit soothing a feverish toddler, was both believable and marvelous.

Later we saw a nine-year-old boy who was asthmatic. He was in distress, and his difficulty in breathing was frightening. The mother, rightly concerned, was afraid to keep him at home, and I didn't blame her. But after we settled him down and drugs cleared his airway, Dr. Kellner did send him home again. Still later, I would learn, they presented themselves at another hospital, and the boy was admitted. "It's a judgment call," Dr. Kellner said. "I didn't think he deserved admission. They either thought differently about the same picture, or they saw a different picture as the night wore on. We can't admit every asthmatic who wheezes. The vast majority of them are fine within a few hours of taking over a hospital bed. We're supposed to be cutting costs. Or so they tell me."

A few hours after discharging this boy, Dr. Kellner was arguing with an intermittent psychotic, well known in the Emergency Room, who was the father of two sons with congenital heart disease. The man was intense, almost hysterical, in his demand to have one of the boys admitted. He threatened to sue. "And that's the least I'm gonna do." But Dr. Kellner was, as they say, "a wall." He did not see justification for an admission. This boy, too, ended up in another hospital before the night was over.

As I was pulling up his hospital record on the computer in the waiting area, I did a double take. The mayor—*the Mayor*—was parading alone through the double doors, sitting down at the triage nurse's desk, and rolling up his sleeve. Before I knew it a nurse was taking his blood pressure as if it were the most ordinary thing in the world. I later found out that it was. The mayor had a heart problem, and when he had symptoms, which was not infrequently, he presented himself in the Emergency Room for a check-up. I knew that medical care was not democratic. But this image of this middle-aged politician with a face familiar to me from countless newspaper photos being ordered around and taken care of like any other patient in the emergency room, although without the wait, somehow made me feel proud.

The pediatric neurology clinic did not usually concern itself with such subtle problems as learning disabilities. One Thursday afternoon I helped to examine and take care of a grim parade of nervous-system disasters. These children made the adult patients on the neurology service seem almost hopeful. Not only were they equally without recourse, but they were *children,* and at least the younger ones had not a glimmer of understanding of what was happening to them. Some with hereditary disorders had been ill from the time of birth. Others had been struck by an infectious syndrome, a tumor, or something from that maddening neurological category—a well-defined syndrome without the slightest suggestion of a cause.

Parents brought these children in, full of the same hopes that parents of normal children have—hopes they slowly realize will never be fulfilled. Between them and their children there was a poignant distortion of the mutual hope and trust that is universal in normal families; and yet, there was also courage and love. One handsome eighteen-year-old boy with rapidly progressive multiple sclerosis could barely walk, but he sat in the waiting room wearing a bright new purple jogging suit and Nike shoes—it was the way he always dressed for physical therapy—with his mother, and they joked together.

At the child neurology conference at the end of the afternoon we saw a two-and-a-half-month-old baby girl who was dying of a rare enzyme deficiency. The disease, which began at birth, had to do with inadequacy in the energy-producing mechanism within the cells of the body. She was pretty, but pale and weak, with a pathetically feeble cry. She wore a frilly pink dress and had a pink ribbon in her thin, light brown hair. Her soft brown eyes had an almost mature sad look. Her parents doted on her as any parents might on a perfectly normal baby, except for their profound, accepting sadness. This baby's older sister had died a year earlier with the same symptoms, the same relentless genetic disease. This second time around her parents—who had received genetic counseling advising them of the high risk of having another baby with the same disease—had not only to grieve, but to grieve guiltily. As they hovered over the baby's bed after the presentation was over, they made a tableau that was tragic and pathetic at once. Camus felt that the death of children proved the nonexistence of God. What would he have said about children like this, who died so slowly and so terribly?

At the other end of the spectrum of pediatric patients were young women suffering from anorexia nervosa. This was, literally, self-starvation, basically a psychiatric disorder with broad implications for physiological health. Starvation, whether for external or internal reasons, had such consequences as cessation of menses, osteoporosis, thyroid abnormalities, liver abnormalities, cardiac arrhythmias, and kidney failure. Mortality from this organic deterioration was estimated to be as high as 10 percent, in addition to a 2 to 5 percent risk of suicide. And the disorder, although affecting less than 1 percent of women, typically beginning in the teenage years, appeared to be rapidly increasing in frequency. Because of its onset in adolescence, patients with anorexia often remained in the care of the special unit in the pediatrics division, despite being well into young adulthood.

The first patient I met with this disorder proved to be in some ways typical. Nancy Turner was twenty-nine years old, but appeared much younger. With her large brown eyes and delicate face she would have been pretty if she had not been so incredibly thin: she was five foot four and weighed only eighty-eight pounds. She was not dissatisfied with her weight but felt that she could stand to lose another pound or two. She had not menstruated for years. She occasionally went on dates, and enjoyed dancing, but never allowed relationships with men to become serious. She lived with her parents, and she described verbal struggles with them that were those one would expect to hear about from a girl in her mid-teens. She was still consciously dieting in an attempt to lose weight, and if she lost a few more pounds she would have to be hospitalized to save her life.

Renee Salter was somewhat different but also quite typical. She was a pale, bony premedical student. She came to the unit under pressure from her parents and the administration of her college, who had recognized that she had a potentially life-threatening eating disorder and had suspended her from school to force her to get help. A few years earlier she had been an aspiring ballerina, but her body had been not quite right. Her hips were too large, and she had been slightly overweight, a fact pointed out to her incessantly by her teachers and fellow ballet students.

In the end she had failed to change her body enough and had given up ballet and put it behind her. She was now devoting herself to study leading to entry into medical school. But hers was devotion with a vengeance. She was not a very good student, but she did absolutely nothing but study,

depriving herself of all pleasure and social interaction. She had no relationships of any kind with men. She lived with her parents, avoiding arguments as well as she could. And she dieted and dieted and dieted. She was
way below the weight she had once tried unsuccessfully to reach. Her hips
were still large, but every fat deposit was gone. She claimed to have no
further interest in dance, but I noticed that she was wearing running shoes
with laces that carried the logo of the New York City Ballet.

"How do you feel about your weight right now?" I asked her.

"Not too bad. I'd just like to lose maybe one more pound." Judging from
the way she looked, her physical examination might lead to a hospitalization that same day.

Nancy and Renee typified different expressions of personality in anorexia nervosa. Nancy was somewhat flamboyant and histrionic, apparently
evincing avid interest in men. Renee was ambitious, ascetic, and severe.
Both kept men at arm's length, had profoundly distorted body images,
and had succeeded in keeping, by certain criteria, essentially prepubescent forms. Neither had normal menses. Both lived at home in
intense dependent relationships with their parents, psychologically
similar to those of young teenagers. And neither, it seemed, wanted
to grow up.

Both, like most anorexics, felt superior in certain ways to everyone
around them. They had achieved control over their bodies, rejecting the
most fundamental imperative of life—eating to stay alive—ostensibly in
order to conform to an extreme aesthetic ideal. The injunction "mind over
body" was their most vivid reality. The culture around them insisted upon
thinness, and they would show that they could measure up better than
anyone—including, of course, their doctors. Sadly, they were similar and
typical in one other way too: neither, in statistical terms, was very likely
to get well.

My work in the Emergency Room continued to be gratifying, but the
place where I felt most like a real doctor was still the outpatient clinic.
There I saw many worried mothers whose children had colds and belly-
aches and rashes, and who went out with some kind of reassurance that
all was well—a diagnostic label, a nostrum, a prescription, and above all
the sense that they had been seen by the doctor, an event that took the
edge off their fear. They had walked through the door of Galen Memorial
Hospital, knowing that many people never reemerged from it. In this
place of death and suffering, of organ and limb removal, of radiation and

poisons, of treatments more drastic and painful than some diseases, their children had been seen and allowed to go out unharmed. This could only mean that they were fundamentally well, and that the little ache or pain or distortion that had brought them there would not stand in the way of their children's lives or cast a shadow over them but be suppressed and pass and be forgotten.

Once, a few years earlier, I had been doubled over with belly pain, vomiting frequently over a period of hours. For some reason, ever since childhood, nausea had been for me the most frightening sensation. On this occasion, after putting up with it "stoically"—driving my wife half-crazy —for most of a day, I finally let her call the Emergency Room of the university clinic. The resident said, "Yes, that's the flu that's going around this season. It causes nausea and vomiting. It lasts for a few days." When my wife transmitted those few words I felt such an immediate and immense sense of relief that I knew that I needed no further assistance—no visit, no drugs, no special information. Just time and patience. I was no longer afraid. A transfer of the simplest information had healing power.

Many children were brought in without any aches or pains, just to be certified normal: babies having regularly scheduled visits, with or without immunization, or school children with forms to be filled out. These sorts of preventive medicine programs, although they rank low on the scale of medical prestige and receive meager rewards, are among the most critical functions performed by doctors. Such screenings frequently turn up problems that have gone unnoticed by parents. Babies are found to have inverted or everted feet, umbilical hernias, or a wide variety of other correctable defects. An eighteen-month-old girl came in for a scheduled well-baby visit and was found to have labial fusion—the lips of her vagina were stuck together. This common minor problem, which could become serious, was readily treated with an estrogen-containing cream.

Occasionally the phrase "F.L.K." would be dropped in a discussion. These initials, I was told, stood for "Funny Looking Kid" and meant that the child might deviate from the normal shape of face and body in a less than obvious way that could suggest a diagnosis of mental retardation or another form of congenital defect.

But the clinic was most often an opportunity for reassurance or "great pick-ups." These were the potentially serious problems that could be completely prevented by a sharp-eyed resident or medical student. One pretty ten-year-old came in with a bad belly pain that she had had for twenty-four hours. I examined her and found the tenderness to be clearly localized to a point in the right lower quadrant of her abdomen. Bending her right knee to her chest made it worse. Although I had never seen a child with appendicitis before, I knew that this was it. Dr. Haley confirmed my assessment, and I called the surgeons: she was operated on within hours, and while she waited—as much for my own sake as hers—I kept going in to see her.

The same day, the exquisitely beautiful teenager whom I had been unable to forget returned to the clinic, and this time she and her mother did end up in my examining room. She was still suffering from headaches. I could not remember ever being made so uncomfortable by a routine examination. She seemed already accustomed to the privileges and burdens of great beauty. Still, it would not do her any good to have a doctor who lost his marbles in her presence. Yet I was disoriented by her beauty, and even touching her seemed a violation of something sacred. Routinely putting my hand inside her blouse to get the stethoscope into place, so that I could listen to her heart and lungs—even with her mother looking benignly over my shoulder—seemed like the most outrageous act of sexual exploitation. Fortunately, I could call in Dr. Haley. He seemed either unaffected by her, was used to it, or was a much better dissembler than I; in any case his presence was a relief to me. His lack of concern about her headaches, given his general professional detachment, was reassuring.

In the pediatric endocrinology clinic I learned about the complexities of biochemical balance in diabetes and thyroid disease, as well as a wide spectrum of disorders of growth and sexual development. It also introduced me to a man who would become one of my great medical heroes. He was Johann Ringler, a man in his early fifties who had emigrated from Germany as a child. He came from a family of physicians, and its traditions seemed to stream through his veins. He used to describe his father's rural medical practice in reverential tones, full of the excitement of old-fashioned clinical practice: "My father used to be able to diagnose diseases by their odor." He and his two brothers had all become physicians, and he at least was following, psychologically, in his father's footsteps. Although he was perfectly comfortable with the most advanced technologies—technetium scans of the thyroid, radioactive implants, growth hormone manufactured through recombinant D.N.A.—and although he himself was active in laboratory research, he was the most sensitive clinician I had ever met.

The children and the teenagers loved him. He was a large, warm, expansive man with a resonant friendly voice. He spoke in charmingly accented

English, and he knew the concerns of the kids—he had three teenagers of his own. In matters pertaining to sex—for example, a boy whose genitalia were feared to be too small—he would say to the youngster, "Do I let Mom stay, or do I kick her the hell out of here?" What the kid wanted, went.

With the teenage diabetics, an especially recalcitrant group, he was scarcely less than a conjurer. Their disorder involved a derangement of the body's most fundamental metabolic activity—the conversion of nutrients to energy. The deficiency of insulin meant that an ordinary diet would be poisonous, leading eventually to blindness, kidney damage, and other problems. Before insulin replacement, these children would have been destined to die by young adulthood. With insulin, and with proper dietary discretion, they could now live long lives. Except for their diets and their insulin dependency, they were perfectly normal, appealing youngsters in every way. Since they looked so healthy, it was hard to remember that their lives could be destroyed by failure to keep to their insulin and dietary regimens.

But who ever heard of a teenager with dietary discretion? These were like all others—hanging out at McDonald's, hovering by the school Coke machine. There were "good" diabetics among them and "bad" ones, those who kept to their diets and those who didn't. Fortunately, it was no longer necessary to rely on a spot check of blood sugar, easily arranged to look good by a crafty kid. A relatively new test, hemoglobin A_{1c}, summarized the recent history of blood glucose levels, but could not be rapidly adjusted by twenty-four hours' worth of being good.

Dr. Ringler would put his arm around the diabetics—all of them, good and bad alike—make them look him in the face and convince them that he wanted them to live. To the good ones, he would try to burn into their souls the correctness and importance of what they were doing. To the bad ones, he was tolerant and warm, chastising like a father and trying to bring out the best in them. "I am not saying that you have to give up everything. I want you to eat the food you like. I am talking about starting with the smallest, simplest things. I am talking about, when you come to the end of the hot dog, you throw away the last inch or two of the roll. That's all."

Even when it seemed hopeless, he made his cajoling speeches. Diabetes made a mess of the body's elegant balancing act, and theoretically could be completely corrected by manipulating that same biochemistry. In practice—or as Dr. Ringler would say, "pr-r-r-raxis"—correction depended not only on balancing the equations with the right inputs (insulin, glucose, and so on) but on such intangibles as discipline, self-image, social class, rebelliousness, peer pressure, habits, and television. These things could really throw a wrench in all the doctor's lovely balanced equations. Dr. Ringler was that rare physician in modern medicine who could manipulate the equations with the best of them, yet never falter in his understanding of the complex human forces among which the equations had to rest.

Through his clinic, too, came a long parade of children with problems of growth and development. They were too short (usually boys) or too tall (almost always girls), too thin or too fat, developing breasts or pubic hair too early or too late. These were not trivial problems. Sometimes they signified a major hormonal derangement that had to be corrected, sometimes not. But invariably they placed these boys and girls out of step with their peer culture, more unforgiving of deviation at adolescence than at any other time of life. Virtually every teenager, however attractive and normal, experiences embarrassment about his or her looks at some point during this rough epoch. In a culture such as ours, in which the quintessential social act is comparing oneself to someone else, teenagers with their metamorphosing bodies are constantly looking at themselves and at each other, worrying about little or nothing. These kids looked too, but actually *had* something to worry about. Dr. Ringler would sit facing them after the history and physical, and hold his pen between their two faces. "If this pen would be a magic wand . . . what one thing would you like to have changed?" And then he would add, "Or would you rather keep that a secret?" And I knew that he wished desperately that his pen really were a magic wand.

Sometimes the children were on the margins of the normal range. One boy, Dennis Jenkins, was a beautiful, dark-haired, sharp-eyed twelve-year-old who did spectacularly well in school but could not go out for sports because he was too small. I interviewed him and his parents, and I weighed, measured, and examined him. He had practically no fat in his skinfold. I remembered a clinical pearl: *If you can't pinch an inch, the treatment for short stature is meat and potatoes.* I compared his hand-and-wrist X-ray with the large photographs in the book that provided the standards and calculated his bone age. It was eleven, younger than his chronological age, indicating that he still had a great deal of growing to do.

My diagnosis, of short stature secondary to insufficient caloric intake, was confirmed by Dr. Ringler. I knew that there had been recent research apparently showing that in short stature within the normal range, without a deficiency of growth hormone, artificially administered growth hormone could increase height in growing children. This opened a Pandora's box of possibilities for intervention. When new technologies of production made growth hormone cheap enough, what was to prevent any mother or father from demanding it for a child—even a child of normal or greater than normal height?

Some doctors would surely accede to those demands, but I did not need to worry about Dr. Ringler. He came in, reviewed, and confirmed my assessment, put his arm around thin, handsome, little Dennis Jenkins, and in his warmest, friendliest voice tried to cast a spell that would turn the skinny boy into a hearty eater.

He also knew when to hold back. He did not put his arm around Margaret Dunbar, for example. Maggie was a tiny, awkward fourteen-year-old girl with dark hair and freckles, a slightly misshapen body and a winning smile. She had Turner's syndrome, a relatively rare chromosomal abnormality—one instead of two female sex chromosomes—that left her with a series of physical defects that included short stature, rudimentary gonads, heart defects (in Maggie's case minor) and a wide neck and chest. She came in with her voluptuously attractive twenty-three-year-old sister, a professional nurse who could interpret for her as well as be her ally; although not large, she must have weighed nearly twice as much as Maggie. She was not vulgar but clearly sexual, with bright blue eyes, slightly curly, shoulder-length blond hair, tight black jeans, and a soft wool sweater pulled over large breasts.

Maggie had been followed since infancy by Dr. Ringler, so there was no need for an extensive interview or examination. The issues were clear. Maggie had not entered puberty, and under natural conditions she would not. Dr. Ringler could offer her puberty—a course of estrogens would bring it about—and, although she could never have children, she would have all the wonderful transformations that most of her classmates had had several years earlier. She did not want to drop much farther behind them. The drawback was that the estrogens would stop her growth. And Maggie wanted to keep growing and to reach the "magic" height of five feet—an unlikely goal for her, since she was only four feet six. She could not expect to grow more than a few inches in any case, but the estrogens would stop her growth completely. The growth plates near the ends of the body's long bones would continue to generate new length as long as they were not exposed to too much estrogen. Estrogen is part of the body's design for shifting the investment of energy from growth into reproduction at the time of puberty. (In fact, in exceptionally tall girls, estrogens can be used to slow or stop further growth.)

It was remarkable to watch this charming young person try to decide between a couple of inches of further growth and an almost immediate transformation into a woman. Her sympathetic sister was supportive, loving, careful to explain everything, and yet equally careful not to direct her. Maggie looked thoughtful for many minutes and finally chose puberty.

9

OBSTETRICS

The Anatomical Volcano

Delivering babies is one of the great privileges accorded medical students and one of the things most cherished in memory even by doctors who do not go on in obstetrics. As with so much in medicine, I marveled that I would within a couple of weeks be so transformed by new learning as to be able to perform this miracle more or less safely. As for childbirth itself, it seemed almost surreal. Women who had once had some difficulty accommodating an erect male organ without discomfort would stretch to accommodate the relatively gigantic head of a birthing baby. Remarkably, almost all of them would survive. Here was one of the rare situations in which the events were urgent and dangerous yet the outcome usually positive. Mothers left the hospital not merely relieved that they had not died but exhilarated, exulting, their arms full of new life.

The doctors on the obstetrical staff were the usual mix of marvelous, terrible, and ordinary people. Dr. Suskauer, the head of the course, was a dour but unthreatening man with large lips and a pointed nose who had been an engineer before becoming a doctor. He was devoted to the development of ever-more-advanced technology for the continuous monitoring of fetal health during pregnancy and labor. Tom Raleigh, a second-year resident, was a sweet man who was wonderful to me but who was under great stress and advised me immediately not to go into obstetrics. He looked enough like me for patients to confuse us. Frank Caggiola, the chief resident, seemed like an Italian street kid—a skinny, handsome, charming hood. He smoked constantly, often sitting somehow curled up in a small hard chair, wound as if ready to strike. He frequently brushed his long black hair out of his face, made funny, cynical remarks, and laughed loudly.

Patients came in through the double doors from the corridor by the elevators, walking with a husband or friend or wheeled in a chair or bed sent up from the Emergency Room. If they were close enough to being in real labor to pass the gantlet of clerks and nurses, they would go to one of the labor rooms off the main corridor, get undressed, and get settled in bed. These rooms had a relaxed atmosphere. One of them had a poster on the wall behind the bed showing a brown-and-white puppy with floppy ears—of nondescript breed—sitting, stuck and forlorn-looking, in a wooden salad bowl. The legend read: "Almost anything in life is easier to get into than out of." There they would spend as many hours as it took to get to the second stage of labor—the delivery of the baby. At this point, with full or nearly full dilatation of the cervix, they would go to the delivery room, a specially equipped operating room that could handle anything from a perfectly normal delivery to an emergency hysterectomy to save the mother and/or the baby.

Central in every sense to the labor floor was the board. This was a big blackboard just opposite the receiving desk and nurses' station, covering a large expanse of hallway wall. The board was constantly changing and constantly watched. It charted up-to-the-minute developments in the course of labor for the two to ten women on the floor. I learned that even I could (and should) make changes in the data for any patient I was dealing with, and this made me feel like an integral part of the team.

I knew something about labor, having done research in reproductive biology and, more to the point, having gone through two labors with my wife. I had the sense on that floor, as I had nowhere else in medicine, of attending a relatively benign and positive but still very powerful and frightening natural process. It could be influenced, of course, but only just so much, especially in these days of widespread natural childbirth. It was relentless and intractable, like a squall or an earthquake inside a woman's body, and it was basically going to run its course no matter what we did. We could slow it down a bit in some cases and speed it up in others, but we couldn't decide to put it off, say, until next month—and neither could the patient.

This inexorability was refreshing. Inexorability in medicine is generally of the worst kind with the most dismal outcome. But here the outcome was almost always positive, even if there were grave obstacles to be overcome. Here, for once, I could exult in the inability of physicians in all their arrogance to get control of a natural process. Not surprisingly many obstetricians lost interest in normal birth and switched to subspecialties such as high-risk birth or infertility or gynecological cancer. The resulting vacuum was filled by labor nurses—knowledgeable, resilient people who functioned almost as midwives, guiding women through all of labor except for the actual delivery, when the obstetrician took over.

My belief was (and is) that obstetrics and gynecology should ultimately be taken over by women (a belief not shared by most patients), and so it seemed good to me that obstetricians (still mainly male) were not around for most of the labors. I felt as if, in a sense, it was really none of their business, as long as the labor was normal. It was in some ways more a spiritual or psychological experience than a medical one. The labor floor was like the temple of a fertility cult. Antechambers were filled with women in the throes of rhythmic pain, predictable and aimed at a great end that many of them had decided upon and planned for with husbands or boyfriends. These men were usually in the chambers with them, going through something themselves that would probably change their lives. Something crucial was taking place in each of these romantic bonds. Families were being born, or extended. And most important, all were witnesses, communally and not unceremoniously, to the onset of a human life.

We attended them, puttering and incanting, with our instruments and rituals alleged to ward off evil. We put our special stethoscopes on the great swollen bellies and listened for the tiny rapid ticka-ticka-ticka of the baby's heart in the midst of the whoosh of uterine blood. Then we smiled and said calming things. We turned the wheel of the little pregnancy calculator—I kept mine in my shirt pocket—that predicted the estimated date of confinement from the starting date of the last menstrual period. This plastic wheel, a drug-company gift, was like a calendraic mandala with which we could see the future and foretell it for the mothers: a normal birth at the right time or a premature and unpredictable one. Either way it gave the comfort of knowledge. At the last stage of labor, with the pains becoming great, the rituals of regulated breathing would begin. *Breathe slowly and shallowly at the onset of the contraction; now, as it intensifies, blow-blow-blow-blow it away.* At a critical moment, the woman was rolled out of her room, the antechamber, and her moving bed would swing open the double doors into the delivery suite. In the delivery room—as it were the *sanctum sanctorum*—she would be transferred to a platform, like an altar, on which, often in anguishing pain, she would spew forth this chaotic and unpredictable presence, this new living and breathing creature.

From beginning to end she was attended by the labor nurses, the priestesses of the cult. Each was assigned, for her twelve-hour shift, to only one patient, and when she took a break for a meal or a cup of coffee it was brief and there was somebody covering for her. Her job was to stay by the laboring woman's bedside and to perform the human magic that gives courage and hope, that not only makes pain bearable but actually reduces it. This magic was in thousands of words, gestures, instructions, admonitions—sometimes tender, sometimes harsh and inflexible—and touches of the hand. Women in labor are going through something as standard as it is overwhelming, and yet they behave very distinctively. Something comes out in them—something individual—one sign among many that indicates who they are. Labor nurses, like other magicians, read the people they are dealing with; their magic is uniquely designed to work on one woman, badly in need of help, at a critical juncture of her life.

The board was the ever changing message of the oracle, the Sibyl's leaves, the writing on the wall. The shift changed at eight o'clock, but we were expected at ten to eight, at which time all the nurses (and all the residents and students) from both shifts converged before the board. There the departing priestesses, with much waving of hands and many incantations, transferred the secret knowledge—as well as the laboring bodies—of the patients, to the others who were just coming on.

I reviewed in my mind the things I had learned about childbirth. I had a vivid memory of an anatomy lecture in the first year of medical school: a bullet-headed man with a southern drawl—an obstetric surgeon—had given us a tirade against home birth. One would have thought he imagined that untrained midwives were about to take over every birth in the state. He described the varying shapes of the female pelvis and their favorable or unfavorable relationships to labor. He did not mention it, but I knew that the cephalopelvic "crunch" of difficult, painful childbirth was a legacy of imperfect human evolution. Apes had it easy. But when humans began to walk upright, the pelvis had had to become adapted for weight-bearing. This made it short and stocky and tough (like the unlovable obstetrician-lecturer) and unsuitable for the birthing of a baby. Meanwhile the same baby was evolving a larger head to accommodate a larger brain. Hence an evolutionary squeeze.

Still, most babies got out through the birth canal, thanks to the aptly named "forces of labor." Intense and painful contraction of the muscular wall of the uterus, combined with voluntary and involuntary increases in intraabdominal pressure ("bearing down"), pressed on the baby, shoving his or her head out through the birth canal. The head acted more or less like a battering ram, stretching the cervix open and over itself (a common metaphor was that of pulling on a turtleneck sweater) and then distending and forcing itself out through the narrow vagina. I couldn't help thinking of the lecturer's head as the ideal battering ram, wishing that every baby could borrow it—but just for the process of birth. I remembered, too, how distorted the shape of my daughter's head had been after my wife's twenty-two hours of labor. It was perfectly normal, but I had convinced myself that something horrible had happened, seeing the alteration of shape that was the product of the typical forces of labor.

Throughout this process the baby, any baby, was going through a surprisingly systematic series of postural changes. Although it was not invariable, the process had a mnemonic that worked like a charm: Every Damn Fool In Egypt Eats Eggs—Engagement, Descent, Flexion, Internal Rotation, External Rotation, Extension, Expulsion. Often the head had to be encouraged out by the doctor trying to hook his fingers under the chin from outside (the eyes would normally be facing down). After the delivery of the head, the shoulders had to be delivered—first the upper, usually the right, then the lower. After that the body would typically, though not invariably, be easily expelled.

During my first week, there were two twin deliveries. The very first delivery I observed on the floor was the birth of twins to a Vietnamese woman with a left lower leg prosthesis. Watching the twins emerge brought back to me all the fears I had experienced with my wife's two deliveries. How could such an enormous creature emerge through such a small channel? How could evolution—or for that matter, God—have produced such an imperfect system? How could the baby's head and body survive such compression? Mrs. Ngo was unperturbed by the questions that I found so distressing. She had a capable labor nurse, though it was difficult to work magic without a common language, and no one had come in with her as a go-between or to give her emotional support. Yet she proceeded calmly through the birth of the twins with only a few whimpers. I could only speculate on the source of her aplomb, and I invented for her a tragic and violent personal history in her native country, a history that made giving birth to twins seem easy by comparison.

The other pair of twins was born to an Israeli woman who had previously been infertile for several years. Treated with clomiphene, which promotes ovulation, she had first had a stillborn child and then her current twin pregnancy. Multiple birth is always a risk with clomiphene treatment, and infertile couples were often visited with an unexpected (and not always welcome) bonus. Since multiple births are risky, sometimes producing defective infants, this is one of the many situations in medicine where the physician is caught between a rock and a hard place. But these twins, a boy first and then a girl, were perfect. The double occurrence of a double blessing, a chance embarrassment of riches, had thus initiated me into the technology and pragmatics of human beginnings.

For several days I did not try to do any deliveries but only to watch them, putting my hands on occasionally when invited by the obstetrician. I spent a lot of time with laboring women, learning a little about the immensely variable course of labor and also a good deal about the technology of monitoring fetal welfare. Most of all, perhaps, I learned some of the right things to say and when to say them as well as when to shut up. My prior experience with this—supporting my wife during her two deliveries —had taught me that no *formula* for psychological preparation or support meant anything in the event, although in general terms preparation and support were of great value. During labor itself (as well as delivery) what mattered most was to pay attention to the patient. She would tell you when and how you could help, if at all.

I also had the chance to scrub with and hold retractors for surgeons doing Caesarean sections. This was reminiscent of the more exciting aspects of surgery, but had the outcome of two healthy young people—one brand new and one, as it were, slightly used—that made it much more appealing than general surgery. Furthermore, it was often an emergency: voices rasping over the loudspeaker, a crowd of nurses and residents rolling a bed down the hall, residents doing an abbreviated emergency scrub, and an anesthesiologist, having given up on getting a spinal anesthetic in place, getting ready to "crash" a young woman and her baby into the dangerous condition of general anesthesia. The adrenaline ran high, and records were constantly being sought and set for minimum time from the initial skin incision to the emergence of the baby—not just for competition's sake, but because the integrity of the baby's brain could depend on keeping that time short.

But the most exciting, the most eagerly anticipated, activity on this service was the opportunity to do normal deliveries. My own first delivery was of a Chinese woman who spoke no English but who, unlike the Vietnamese woman, had another woman, a relative, with her. She had been recruited through a clinic in the Chinese section of town where the personnel were familiar with Chinese language and culture. Debbie Walters, the labor nurse who was guiding me, knew a few words in Chinese and I began learning them. But the labor progressed so quickly that second stage—the delivery of the baby—began within an hour of the mother's arrival at the hospital.

After that the only useful Chinese word I had—and I used it a lot—was the word for "Push." The precipitous delivery occurred in the bed before the obstetrician arrived and there was no time to go down to the delivery room. With the help of Tom Raleigh, the second-year resident, Debbie and I slid the patient down to the foot of the bed. This was to give the baby room to be born, and avert the risk of its being crushed against the bed. The trick was not to drop the baby. By the time the head emerged my rubber gloves were covered with amniotic fluid and blood, and so of course was the baby. It seemed impossible to catch and hold the baby without dropping it, but I somehow managed. I handed it off to Debbie as soon as I could—I was too nervous to notice what sex it was—took the large scissorslike clamps and clamped the cord in two places, and then with the surgical scissors cut between them, attending to the unnerving yet decisive feel of flesh severing in the blades.

"It's a girl," Debbie said. She held her up so the mother could see her, and the other woman repeated the message in Chinese.

Raleigh, who was watching me like a hawk, was speaking in a soothing tone of voice but still giving very firm orders. I was holding the clamp attached to the cord leading into the vagina. "Check the tension in the cord. Don't yank on it. Just pull it gently. When it's ready to give it'll give, and the placenta will come. Sponge the perineum and let's see what the tear looks like. Good. It's just a second degree. Very good for a precip. I'll let you sew it. Not too much blood either. Pull on the cord gently again. Gently. Not ready yet. Don't force it, there's no hurry."

I stole a glance at the baby; unbelievably, she was fine—lying on her back under the warming lights, staring around with big dark eyes, and trying to get her hand into her mouth. Her fine, straight, black hair was wet, and her healthy yellow skin was partly flushed with red.

I pulled on the cord again and the placenta began to give. Soon the membranes appeared, shiny, wet, gray-black, and balloonlike, in the vestibule of the vagina. "Push," I said again in Chinese; she pushed, and the placenta was delivered. Raleigh and I checked it—intact, with two arteries and one vein in the cord. (A nonintact placenta could mean a dangerous retention of part of it, which could cause a hemorrhage; a cord with abnormal vessels could indicate a fetal abnormality.)

The easy and pleasant part was over. Sewing the tear, or in other cases the cut made to prevent the tear or in some of the worst cases, both was all that remained. This was a part of childbirth I never quite got used to.

According to the "natural childbirth" philosophy, tears in the mother's flesh should be preventable without a surgical cut, or episiotomy. Even during my wife's own childbirth classes I had doubted this, and now I learned for sure that even hours of massage to soften the vulnerable tissues, following months of preparation through exercise and relaxation, could not reduce the risk of a tear to anything near zero.

Therefore, tears had to be accepted as part of the reality of childbirth, and deliberate cuts were often a reasonable way to prevent them from getting out of hand. This seemed to me an ultimate insult to women, and the whole business of injecting and cutting and sewing in the petals of the flower of female sexuality—especially at a moment that should have been and often was one of the times of greatest triumph in a woman's life—was almost physically painful to me. It underscored as much as anything the obstetrician's saying that "Childbirth may be physiological—'normal'—for the species, but it's damn near pathological for the individual." I sat on a stool with my back aching, with my paper shoe covers steeped in amniotic fluid and blood, leaning forward toward the wound, digging one stitch after another into the intimate, swollen flesh.

Afterward, I was pulling my gown off and stuffing it and the gloves into the trash bin. I turned to Tom. "If there was a God," I said, "She would have figured out a better way to bring people into the world." He smiled tolerantly, having probably heard this one more than once before.

By the middle of the next week I was becoming comfortable with the process of labor and delivery, had made friends with all the nurses and most of the doctors, and was more help than hindrance in the labor and delivery rooms. The nurses on the floor seemed pleasantly surprised at a medical student who was not arrogant, who was interested in normal labor, who was willing to spend time with laboring women, and who—strangest of all—was plainly respectful of labor nurses. Moreover, on the labor floor I always showed a, for me, uncharacteristic enthusiasm.

My second delivery was of a frightened sixteen-year-old girl with an amputated right foot. The man with her had a different name from hers, and his attention was divided, since by an extraordinary coincidence he had a sister in labor at the same time in the next room. His girlfriend, whose name was Brenda, finally delivered into my hands a healthy baby girl, but not without a grotesque tear of her vagina and the supporting musculature, extending almost to her rectum. This was the worst tear I had seen and I must have looked miserable as I helped the attending doctor sew parts of it. I was thinking that Brenda had had very good reason to be scared.

"Don't worry about the tear," Dr. Stevens, the attending, said cheerfully in spite of my hangdog look. "That's how you learn." I hoped that Brenda had been sufficiently dazed to have missed that remark.

Delivery of the other baby—that of her boyfriend's sister—was textbook perfect. There was only the slightest tear of the skin and there was no bleeding. Dr. Stevens thought I should sew it, Tom Raleigh thought not. Dr. Stevens, an easy-going man in his fifties, was a good teacher, intellectually or at least academically outclassed by the top staff members of the obstetrics department, but very nice to be around and learn from. He talked to me extensively about hospital-by-hospital differences in procedures and about arbitrary idiosyncrasies of some of them: in one place a technique like forceps or a drug like magnesium sulfate was used extensively, and in another rarely. Local traditions were obviously important, and the data were evidently not conclusive enough to urge very much uniformity.

One morning as I was leaving the house I took down from the shelf an old copy of a book with three plays by Lorca. I had always wanted to read them, and this was a thin paperback that would slip easily into the pocket of my down jacket. I had time enough to read only a few pages a day, on the bus, after studying my obstetrics manual. Yet this was just enough to keep me in touch with the world of literature and thought. It gave me a sense of transcendence above and out of the frequently grim world of guts and blood. There was blood and guts in the plays, too, but they seemed purposeful, with the false but marvelous order of aesthetic imposition.

One of the plays was *Yerma*, the tragedy of a young married woman who cannot become pregnant. In the traditional culture of Spain in which the play is set, that circumstance dooms her. So the theme playing, like an occasional faint chord, as an eerie accompaniment to my service in obstetrics, was that of a tragic, intractable, and hopeless longing for a baby.

One of the dividends of working in obstetrics is of course the newborn babies—the exhilaration of their appearance and (usual) normality, and the reaction to them, the great helpless break-face grins of the mothers, almost irrespective of what they had just been through; the new fathers mooning at their wives and sons and daughters, as if stunned with uncomprehending admiration for the acts of courage and wild patience they had witnessed.

Keeping the baby from hitting the floor is of course the first priority. The next, before clamping and cutting the cord, is suctioning the mouth and nose, to precipitate the first breath and shorten the time without oxygen. This must be done with the baby below the level of the placenta, so as to encourage the last bit of blood in the cord to flow down a gravity-gradient into the almost independent little body. Then the cord could be clamped; the scissorslike clamps were dangling from the sterile drape on the mother's legs, with a pair of scissors stuck in a finger hole of one of the clamps.

When the baby was free, however, I had to stay with the mother. I now had one patient instead of two, and as I handed the baby off to a nurse or resident, I felt robbed of the chance to follow the new life. Of course, I kept my mind on the mother and on the job of taking care of her in the wake of what was in several senses almost always a trauma—the broad silly grin notwithstanding. But from time to time my attention would drift to the little creature baking under the lights, breathing unevenly but steadily, moving slightly, all ribs and mouth and blotchy red-and-pink- or red-and-brown-and-purple skin.

Whenever somebody else delivered the baby—something I let happen as infrequently as I could—I was permitted to stay with the baby. Although strictly speaking a baby with any sort of difficulty belonged to pediatrics from the moment the cord was cut, it was possible for me to switch roles and be the pediatrician-medical-student instead of the obstetrician-medical-student for a little while. I listened to the pounding of the tiny heart at such a furious rate—twice that of my own, which at such times was usually crashing loudly enough to count readily. I watched the chest and belly rise and fall, sucking at the air for life. I counted the toes and fingers, and checked the ears and facial features and genitals for obvious abnormalities. I tested the mobility of the joints and the patency of the anus and examined the skin for consistent changes that might indicate oxygen loss or some toxic reaction. I waited —and that patience was often the hardest and most important part—for all the things that I had mentally certified as normal to remain, monotonously, minute after safe minute, normal.

Throughout all this I had the sense of starting a new human being down the path of a healthy life, along with fleeting images of the baby as an adult. And of course I had a little of that moony, dazed feeling so evident on the fathers' faces: *A new life. My goodness. How beautiful.*

In these examinations I sensed also an intellectual continuity with some of the work I had done with African infants. Although in Africa I had never quite been present at a birth, I had sometimes been called right afterward, and on one occasion had seen the delivery of the placenta. The cultural ideal of the !Kung San, hunter-gatherers of the Kalahari, relating to child-birth was for a woman to go out by herself and come back with a baby. This stark contrast to the pattern in many other primitive societies and in ours appeared to be related to an ideal of physical courage, and to the belief that any failure of courage could make the delivery a disaster.

In Africa I would try to visit and examine each infant within the first ten days of life. I did a meticulous neurological assessment of them in order to detect any major differences from American newborns (there were none) and followed them as they grew. So when I came to the point of examining babies in the obstetrics unit at Galen, I already felt comfortable with the procedures. Their remarkable tininess didn't alarm me.

Nevertheless the purpose of the examination at Galen was of course not research, and my orientation was more pragmatic, and meticulous in a different way. I learned Apgar scoring from the nurses—a procedure de-veloped by Virginia Apgar for rapid assessment of the newborn—and mastered it accurately within a few days. Babies got two points each for heart rate (over one hundred), respirations (regular or crying), skin color (no blue areas), muscle tone (active motion), and reflex irritability (vigor-ous crying). With one or two points off for less ideal status in each area, a baby could seemingly fall quite easily below the normal threshold of seven, but in fact this did not happen often. Scores were given at one and five minutes, and improvements were usual. I compared notes with the nurses ("I took one off for color and one for tone") and soon came out consistently well.

When a baby was in trouble a pediatric resident would appear. My favorite was Dr. Russell, a fat, intelligent businesslike man in his late twenties who strode into the delivery room carrying his tools in a long metal box like a T.V. repairman. He was kind to me—pediatricians are the nicest people in medicine—and taught me a great deal. One baby we looked at together was four weeks premature, the product of a long, pharmacologically stimulated labor of a sixteen-year-old mother who suf-fered from pregnancy-induced hypertension (a dangerous condition for both mother and baby). Remarkably, the boy was fine. He got two points off for color (he was extensively blue) and one off for muscle tone and respiration at one minute, but by five minutes his Apgar had gone from six to nine. Soon he was in the nursery being gazed at longingly through the glass by his grandmother, a thin nervous woman somewhat younger than I.

Others were not so lucky. Babies were born below the margins of survivability (two pounds or so, or around twenty-six weeks) and essentially allowed to die quietly. The government had then recently decreed that something had to be done to keep all premature infants alive (an interfering policy, since struck down by the Supreme Court) but Galen doctors and nurses responded to this foolish rule by wrapping the fetus in a blanket and otherwise letting it alone. Even older, more viable premature infants placed in intensive care would cost anywhere from $50,000 to over $400,000 to keep alive, the cost increasing and the chance of survival decreasing with younger and smaller infants. In a finite health care budget, these dollars would be translated into illness and death of other patients, somewhere. I read an estimate that to keep a baby alive in an African hospital, for example, cost about $800. And I learned later that outside the hospital a million infant deaths a year could be prevented in Africa, each at a tiny fraction of that. Furthermore, one didn't have to go to Africa to find a way to translate dollars saved in the neonatal intensive care ward into effectively multiplied savings of life.

Nevertheless it was difficult to watch these tiny infants die. I remember one with sealed eyes and translucent skin that I wheeled up to the nursery. I was supposed to keep it warm and check its heart rate and respirations every once in a while, but only for the purpose of notifying the resident of its death. This happened after about forty minutes, and Dr. Russell and I told the father and grandmother who were waiting in the hall. (They and the mother had already been told that the baby would not live.) They were grief-stricken and relieved both at the same time—two completely appropriate reactions.

On my last day in obstetrics, I was determined to get my hands on as many babies as possible. I showed up early, which was no easy feat that day, for snow had drifted waist high in front of our house, the sidewalk and street were covered with two feet or so of clean white snow, parked cars were buried, and none were moving on the street. I dug out a pair of galoshes and began trudging through the drifts. After walking a few blocks I found a taxi on one of the larger streets; the city was dead, and I felt rather proud as I strode out of the elevator on to the labor floor. Everything was business-as-usual. Every nurse, every clerk, every resident seemed to be in place and on schedule. It was as if no one on the labor floor was aware that the rest of this large city had whined, groaned, and ground to a halt.

I attended rounds at the board—ten minutes to eight as usual—and began making my way around to the labor rooms, meeting the patients and their partners and emphasizing to the labor nurses, most of whom were now friends of mine, how much I wanted to get more deliveries. This sort of comical eagerness was considered quite acceptable for a medical student, even a superannuated one like me.

A nurse made a change at the board, and I realized I had missed a patient. Georgia Davis was fully dilated and pushing. An explicit rule of the labor floor said that medical students did not walk in on women in that stage of labor. You were to get to know them and their families long before that, preferably on their arrival early in first stage labor. Furthermore, I could tell from the name of the obstetrician that this patient was a middle-class paying customer, and an unwritten rule of the labor floor—as on every other floor of the hospital—was that middle-class paying patients had more right not to be touched by medical students than service patients did. I asked the nurse about her, and she was not encouraging. So I pretty much gave up on the idea of going in to her until Frank Caggiola, the superb chief resident who looked and talked like a street kid, insisted that I not pass up the chance.

I walked in to find a slender tall black woman in the middle of a contraction and about to roll off the bed. Nan, the labor nurse—who by her own description had "a bad attitude" toward medical students, meaning a low tolerance for their arrogance—was urgently trying to keep the patient on the bed and calm her, saying "Easy now, push, push." She obviously needed help but glared daggers at me anyway, since I had broken one of the cardinal rules. But the husband, a large handsome man, stood by the bed, slow to respond, and I was able to move in on his side and help Nan reposition the patient. As the contraction, a long one, ended, the patient's face and body relaxed. I felt awkward about having broken into the personal space of the labor bed so unceremoniously in order to help when help was needed. But I smiled and was friendly and held Georgia's hand, helping Nan to talk her through several more contractions, and then it was time to move out to the delivery room.

Out in the hall there were many hands on the bed, and Nan was able to get me out of earshot of the couple. She was properly angry. "Don't you ever, ever walk in on a pushy lady like that. ("Pushy" was labor floor slang for the last stage, in which a woman is asked to bear down actively.) You walk in at the right time, and no matter when it is or what is going on, you introduce yourself, you say that you are a medical student, and you ask for permission, *ask for permission* to attend the labor." Nan knew I didn't really need a repetition of all the rules of the labor floor, and she ignored my profuse apologies and *mea culpas* which began as soon as her tirade did, but she had every right to go on with it. I was clearly very wrong; but I considered it a sort of compliment that she was willing to spend her breath telling me how wrong I had been.

We ran down the hall behind the bed, and as soon as we began setting up in the delivery room it became clear that she was going to forgive me. Georgia Davis and her husband were warming to my presence, and not merely tolerating it. Not everyone considers birth a private event. In many cultures it is the center of a gathering, and the laboring woman feels the strength in numbers. In Georgia Davis's gathering I was initially an intruder but in the crushing immediacy of the second stage of labor I could be not only useful but also encouraging, and she and her husband welcomed me slowly, for a short, important time, into the circle of their lives. I delivered the baby with ease, under the usual supervision, and with no complications of any kind.

By the time the Davises and their daughter were resting in the recovery room it was mid-morning, and the board showed that Mrs. Hong, one of the women I *had* managed to meet earlier, was at nine centimeters. A woman could stay at nine for a long time, but she was a multipara—she had had two children before—and she had got to nine centimeters in only four hours. I appeared tentatively at the door of her room. Linda Costello, her labor nurse, finally turned, saw me, and with only the slightest movement of her head beckoned me in. She was known as a very tough nurse, but she and I got along well.

Mrs. Hong's companion was a charming, rather giggly niece who translated for her between Chinese and English. Mrs. Hong was supposed to have been delivered by a midwife, but the midwife was delayed by the snowstorm. I had come just in time. The labor was progressing fast enough so that anything scrawled on the board would be out of date as soon as it got there. We never had time to get out of the labor room. Tom Raleigh and Dr. Willson, the attending, came in to watch and help, but this delivery, like the previous one, was basically mine. I delivered a girl, easily, there in the bed in the labor room; there was a slight hitch, literally, with the uppermost shoulder, which caught for a moment behind the pubic symphysis. (This would be recorded as "mild anterior shoulder dystocia.") Dr. Willson reminded me of the risk of a delivery of this kind in bed: you solve anterior shoulder dystocia by pulling the baby down toward the floor (thus the positioning of the patient on the delivery table almost hanging over the edge, so that the baby can be pulled downward). In an emergency, he said, get the mother out to the end of the bed.

After these two deliveries, and the attendant surgical repairs, it was early afternoon. The board showed very little other activity. I visited two other patients who were both in early labor.

Leora Marshall was a young black woman with a gold leaf-shaped pin in one of her nostrils (and gold earrings to match) that emphasized the pleasant shape of her face. Her partner, James, was a handsome, athletic young man sitting, as if to spring, on the edge of his seat. I had not met him before, since he was out when I came in to see Leora in the morning, and I had been running around like crazy ever since. I was about to introduce myself when he preempted me by saying, in place of the usual greeting (and while pointing at Leora's belly), "A boy." He said this with a great, friendly grin.

"How can you be so sure?" I asked him. Leora looked on, smiling benignly but abstractedly, not as if she were in pain, but as if she had more important things on her mind.

"Whether it's a boy or a girl," he said, "it's gonna be a pro football player. So it better be a boy."

Tom Raleigh came in and suggested that James step outside. He wanted to check Leora's cervix, one of the very few such checks—each one held a risk of infection—she would get in this part of labor. Tom threw me some gloves and I opened the package carefully and put them on. Leora blushed. I could feel an opening that took a bit more than the tip of my index finger. "One centimeter," I said. Tom examined her. "One and a half," he said. "Okay," he went on, speaking to her. "Everything's going fine." He was a gentle, decent man, extremely harried by this residency.

I knew that I could not survive the regimen Tom lived under—not survive, that is, and still function well, as he did. I was on twelve hours and then off twelve—except for a few extra hours a week of lectures. He was on twelve on labor and delivery and then dictating or doing paperwork or making follow-up rounds for at least four hours a day beyond that. Somehow he still found time and energy to teach me—to lecture to me, to demonstrate, to give me a chance to practice. He went off again. He did not seem as thick-skinned as some of the others, and I worried for him.

The other patient in early labor was Cindy Granger, a nineteen-year-old who was a patient of Dr. Suskauer, the director of my obstetrics course. I was reluctant to get involved with a patient of his, but on the other hand I wanted the chance to work with him directly. He was a very tense but obviously intelligent man who had helped pioneer the use of sophisticated fetal monitoring techniques in modern labor suites. Unlike most doctors, any obstetrician, however important or famous, can be dragged into the hospital at any hour of any day to dance to the tune of a not quite newborn baby. I wanted to see Dr. Suskauer on the firing line.

Cindy, a sensitive young woman with a very low tolerance for pain, had come all the way from her hometown, where they no doubt delivered babies, for only one reason: she wanted an epidural anesthetic—lidocaine or a similar substance is injected into the sac around the spinal cord, eliminating sensation from the top of the abdomen down, without putting the patient to sleep. Epidurals are risky because if the anesthetic creeps up higher than it is supposed to, breathing can be impaired or stopped. This risk can be managed only in a hospital with a certain level of certified competence in anesthesiology.

Since arriving early that morning in the snowstorm, Cindy had wanted her promised epidural. But it was not so simple. As Dr. Suskauer had no doubt told her from the beginning, the epidural could not be administered until she was five centimeters dilated, since otherwise it might slow labor to a stop. Her labor had by now taken more than eight hours, and she was not yet up to five. Most of those hours had been painful and frightening for her, perhaps worsened by her false expectation that labor would be fully conscious but free of pain.

This poignant expectation was in a sense the logical outcome of the two tendencies that predominate in a woman's mind as she anticipates childbirth. One of these, ancient, ubiquitous, and permanent, is the desire to minimize pain. The other, more variable and more determined by culture, is the desire to have the experience, not to miss (or at least not to *have* missed) anything. Our primitive ancestors frequently had little choice in the matter, so they sometimes made a great point of the experience.

Among, the !Kung San, I knew, women conceptualized childbirth as an almost ritual trial of physical courage. Except for the first child or two, a woman was ideally supposed to manage the delivery alone and to face the ordeal and pain with a serene, solitary calm. In the modern history of obstetrics, European and American women went to an opposite extreme, and the ideal in the 1950s was to be put to sleep early in labor and to wake up and greet the baby some hours after completion of the delivery. But during the past decade women and obstetricians both have come to realize the value of fully conscious childbirth. Natural childbirth became an ideology, one with good medical reasons for it, to be sure, but going beyond them. And like most ideologies, it ended by coercing at least some people.

I had plenty of time to muse on these matters that afternoon, since both Leora Marshall and Cindy Granger were progressing so slowly. Leora's pro football player was not much moved by the mother's sluggish, fairly mild contractions, and it was clearly going to be a long struggle. As for Cindy, when she reached five centimeters and active phase labor—the phase in which dilation of the cervix increases steadily at at least two centimeters per hour—she got her longed-for epidural, which she had waited for with intense, aggrieved impatience. Her husband, a bright-eyed stocky young man, waited with her, with a mixture of excited antici-pation and dull fear. But her labor slowed immediately. She was not feeling the pain of the contractions, but they dropped from every three or four minutes to every six and the pressure gauge measured them as less intense. She was tired and needed sleep, which was finally possible. Nan, who was now covering her, was stroking her brow gently, saying formulaic phrases as if in a lullaby. Dr. Suskauer and I watched at a distance from the bed, and I gave him a look that said, "What happens now?"

He was uncomfortable, regretful, and modest in his assessment. "Well, there's nothing to do now but wait. Sometimes an epidural slows the contractions. Anyway, she needs some sleep."

Cindy slept for hours. I had a chance to get a meal and to read about epidurals and their problems. Outside the hospital the city was quiet and unmoving under the blanket of snow. It was really remarkable how on the labor floor every nurse, resident, and physician had managed to get in past the storm, uncomplaining, to meet the inevitable deliveries.

When Cindy was awakened by her contractions, she was shocked once again by the pain. She wanted another epidural and this time Dr. Suskauer decided labor had to be allowed to make some progress before there was additional anesthetic. She could and did get the standard analgesics, but these were far from enough for her. The anguish on her young face was reflected in her husband's. Both were tense and bathed in sweat. She had had the worst kind of psychological preparation, the false expectation of a complete avoidance of pain. Nan and I stayed with her and talked her through the contractions, giving her breathing instructions, breathing with her, repeating all the stock comforting phrases. Her husband tried to conceal his discomfort and behaved bravely and helpfully, but there was little that could lessen the pain for her.

Leora Marshall's sluggish labor was meanwhile also progressing slowly.

She was being monitored for fetal distress, and Tom Raleigh was checking in on her regularly. I saw her frequently, taking breaks from Cindy Granger. Her earrings had been removed—all jewelry must be removed going into surgery or delivery—but it had been considered the better part of valor to leave the leaf-shaped gold pin in place in her left nostril, an exotic elegant touch rare among laboring women.

She too was tired. By 7:30 P.M. she had been in the hospital for ten hours and in labor for fourteen. She was not in any great distress, but she was only at five centimeters and she still had a long way to go. I had not seen Tom Raleigh for a while. In all likelihood he had gone to check on one or two women who were laboring off the floor in the high-risk delivery suite —one was battling kidney failure, the other a heart defect. I checked Leora's monitor strip, which on one line recorded the strength of the contractions, as well as their timing, while tracing the baby's heartbeat on another. The fetal monitor required inserting a wire through the amniotic sac and hooking it right into the baby's scalp. It sounds barbaric and is rejected by some women insisting on totally natural childbirth, but the insult to the baby's scalp seemed minor compared to everything else that was going on. In any event it was a good way to follow the health and safety of the baby.

I was no expert at reading monitor strips, but even I could see that the normal depression of the baby's heart rate during contractions was continuing too long—it stayed down for too many seconds after the contractions were over. These decelerations "late decels" as they were called, were considered a dependable early sign of developing fetal distress. I went running around looking for Tom, or at least for the new primary nurse, Colleen, and when I found her I learned she had already come to the same conclusion and was also looking for Tom. He appeared shortly thereafter, harried as usual, but responding patiently and gently. He checked the strip and nodded agreement with us, but favored watchful waiting. To be sure, he consulted Dr. Caggiola, who agreed, brushing his long black hair back out of his eyes.

I went to the nurses' station to call my wife, and told her that there was no chance I would be off at eight o'clock. I was involved with the Granger delivery and neither should nor wanted to get out of it. We talked for a while about the two cases—both of us had an interest in them because of our two deliveries, by midwives, through emphatically natural childbirth. Cindy Granger seemed to have got as much trouble from interventions as she had got help. But the Marshall baby's life might literally be hanging by a thread—the monitor wire. And we had refused to have a monitor. We talked for fifteen or twenty minutes during what I supposed was a completely relaxed lull in both the labors.

When I came out of the doctors' lounge and locker room, the hallway around the board was strangely quiet, and the nurses' station almost empty of people. A nurse I didn't know—a float or a temporary—walked by and I asked her, "Where are all the doctors around here?"

She looked puzzled, and then looked toward the board. "I don't know. I guess they're all on that C-section."

"What C-section?" I asked nervously, glancing over to the board.

"*D-3,*" it read, for Delivery Room 3. "*MARSHALL/C/S.*"

"Oh Jesus," I said out loud to myself. "Will you wake up?" My feet started me down the corridor. Near the double doors leading to the delivery suite, James paced nervously, eyeing the *Do Not Enter* sign. Just as I was about to hit the doors a nurse emerged from them—smiling broadly. "Don't worry," she said, and it took me a second to realize she was not talking to me. "She's fine," she went on to James. "You have a beautiful baby boy." Almost as excited for them as I was peeved at my own absence, I rushed past James's relieved look and down the corridor to the sink, and scrubbed quickly after pulling on a mask.

In D-3 Leora Marshall was unconscious and intubated, her gold pin still in place in her nostril. On the other side of the curtain separating her head from her body, Tom Raleigh was sewing her uterus, which protruded through a gaping wound in her abdomen. I came to the anesthesiologist. "I hate to crash these young pregnant women," he said, meaning to put them under and intubate them on an emergency basis. Nobody likes to do that to someone who is not sick. But she was all right now; it would now be clear sailing. Under the warming lights on the little table in the corner, there was, as billed, a beautiful baby boy.

After that good lesson on how fast things can happen—how fast, for example, a "watchful waiting pose" can turn into a crash and a C-section —I stuck close by Cindy Granger throughout the rest of the evening. I knew I would not be needed in an emergency—my usefulness was greatest in the long hours in the labor room—and in a crisis I could basically only follow orders and try not to get in the way. But since this labor was going beyond the end of my last shift on obstetrics, it would be my last delivery for a while. It would be my ninth in all, but my seventh with my hands as the main ones delivering. I thought it should be lucky. I called my wife periodically, telling her I would be delayed further, as that Saturday night went by. I thus got a taste of what a career in obstetrics would be like, and she got to be an obstetrics widow for an evening.

Cindy's slow, painful, steady labor went on until almost midnight. Finally she was dilated enough so that we could take her to the delivery suite.

Dr. Suskauer, getting increasingly restive, not for himself but for Cindy, worked beside me on the delivery but let me do most of the hands-on work. Cindy had been laboring with a *big* baby boy. The head delivered easily, but then there was shoulder dystocia, and after the shoulders were delivered with difficulty, body dystocia, which was quite unusual. Her pleasant young husband—he had given the baby the stocky body that lodged temporarily in the canal—stood up at her head, sure himself, and reassuring her, that with the baby born and shown to them (I was now clamping and tying the cord) things were going smoothly. He and Cindy grinned.

Things did not go smoothly. The placenta should have delivered within a few minutes. After forty-five minutes of massaging, gentle traction, and other standard tactics, we had not gotten it out. Throughout this time Cindy was still in pain, pain she had every right by now to believe she should be free of. Dr. Suskauer was getting distressed. He was not in trouble, but he needed more than me for help. Help came in the form of Dr. Caggiola, who helped him do a D & C—dilatation and curettage— while I and an attending physician watched.

Blood poured out of Cindy in a way I had never seen in a delivery. It was staunched after an hour, with an estimated blood loss of two liters— something like a third of her total blood volume. She was soon given two units of whole blood in the recovery room. Dr. Suskauer, with a sheepish grin, apologized. He was still nervous. "It doesn't always work the way it's supposed to," he said. Frank and I walked out into the corridor in step with each other and pulled down our masks. He had that cute, cynical street-kid look on his dark face as he brushed his hair away. "If a thought ever crossed your mind about home birth," he said ironically, in his broadest working-man's accent, "I hope this takes care of it."

We passed the recovery room where Cindy was resting now with her baby, the fresh blood flowing reassuringly into her. Although I was never a fan of home birth, my fidelity to the idea of minimizing interventions *was* becoming seriously challenged. I began to reconsider my wife's two deliveries and the fates of our two children. Had we taken irresponsible chances in the name of some kind of childbirth ideology? On the other hand, an argument could be made, in a case as dramatic as Cindy's, that many of her problems came precisely *from* interventions. Perhaps, with proper psychological preparation and childbirth education, she could have done with fewer medicines and had a more normal birth. First she had insisted on having the epidural which slowed the labor, and eventually she had been in greater pain than ever; then the labor had had to be speeded up with Pitocin. What natural forces might have been at work in her were obscured and interfered with by a number of unnatural ones.

I was confused. This was my last official delivery on the rotation, and it had certainly been informative, but not exactly what I could call lucky.

10

GYNECOLOGY

The Machinery of Creation

The day I began gynecology was Monday, February 14: Valentine's Day. Throughout the country lovers were sending flowers and candy and poems and letters and gauche plaints and greeting cards, all serving to set in motion the living machinery of creation. For two of the most exhilarating weeks of my life I had helped to manage the products of that machinery—the nine months' output called, without irony, a delivery. If any manufacturer consistently made deliveries so painful, dangerous, and messy, it would be drummed out of the ranks of business. Nevertheless, through the combined forces of nature and medical magic, the goods generally arrived in something like usable condition.

Now I would encounter derangements in the machinery—failure to work at all, success at an inopportune time, and a variety of infectious and neoplastic—cancerous—diseases. I had been concerned, unnecessarily, about the effects on my sexual-response system of helping babies tear their way through the center of female sexuality—and then sewing it up again. Now I was to deal daily with all possible disorders of the nonpregnant female reproductive organs. No baby, no dramatically positive force of life, would draw my attention away from the illnesses. Would the experience make me unromantic—even unsexual?

The first house officer I met was Wendy Feinberg, a second-year resident about thirty years old, with a tired, sensuous face and large, soupy brown eyes. "It's got to be good luck that I'm starting out today," I said.

"Why?" she asked, exhausted but open and curious.

"Isn't Saint Valentine the patron saint of gynecology?" She was so tired that it took her a few moments to get it. Laughing generously, she acknowledged, "I guess he must be," and after that we were friends.

Only later did I learn that Wendy was the mother of a little baby with Down's syndrome. She was not bearing up very smoothly under the rigors of the residency, and she worried lest she be unable to finish the program. She seemed so tired and so worried about her future that I sometimes wanted to take her protectively in my arms.

Wendy was fresh from the same experience I had seen so many women go through in obstetrics. But *her* magnificent cataclysm had ended with the sort of outcome that all those other women dreaded. She had given her abnormal baby a beautiful name—Justin—and she spoke of him always with tenderness and love. She doted on his gestures and became eloquent, in her Brooklynese cadences, about his typical routines. But in addition she was enduring stages of awkward grief for the loss of all the hopes and dreams that go with having a normal baby.

We did surgery every morning and admitted patients for elective surgery every afternoon. There were clinics for family planning, infertility, Pap smear, culposcopy (examination of the cervix after a positive smear), and venereal disease. And there were the inevitable calls to the Emergency Room to determine whether a woman was in labor, to rule out the life-threatening emergency of a ruptured ectopic pregnancy, or to carry out the legally mandated examination of an emotionally devastated rape victim. I was supposed to be on every third night, but Wendy and the other residents frequently sent me home early.

My first patient was Laura Wallace, by her own description a chubby, talkative young woman with a charming, bubbly disposition and very curly hair. (She told me later she was part black, which one couldn't tell from looking at her.) She had suffered from years of infertility and had had her right ovary and fallopian tube removed because of intractable adhesions, places where the internal organs were in effect stuck together. In the normal abdomen or pelvis the organs are coated with slippery membranes that allow them to slide over each other freely. But sometimes— for example, after prior surgery—flaws in the covering membranes allow sticking points to emerge, and instead of sliding freely the pelvic viscera may become grotesquely twisted on each other and on themselves. These adhesions can easily and literally put a crimp in the fallopian tube that would prevent it from carrying out its delicate mission: to turn deftly, to harvest an egg just after its release from the follicle (a tiny fluid-filled bleb on the surface of the ovary), and to pass the egg gently down its length to come to rest in the uterus, or womb.

Laura's remaining ovary and tube were evidently not working well enough, and she was in the hospital for what was called a conservative laparotomy—a piercing of the side in order to save. I was reminded of the folk song in which Queen Jane, after a long labor, sings, "Please cut my side open, and save my baby." But what Laura's surgeons would attempt to save was her last chance at natural fertility. Theoretically, at least, they would open her abdomen and assess the adhesions and other abnormalities (if any) affecting the ovary and tube. Any kinks would be unraveled and any adhesions would be "lysed"—dissolved with a combination of teasing apart and saline irrigation. But, as she seemed to realize, this was only in theory. In practice the damage might be discovered to be so great that the ovary or tube could not be saved.

I was touched by Laura's story. She related in her bubbly way that she was adopted, and that she had three adopted siblings. She loved her adoptive parents and said she could not understand adopted people who searched for their biological parents or felt that the adoptive status was somehow second class. With these attitudes, of course, she was more than willing—happy, in fact—to adopt. But first, just one last time.

The following morning I was to scrub in on her surgery. But before that I had a chance to observe in another operating room. I had not been in an O.R., except for the very different, special experience of deliveries, for four months. The strict O.R. protocol—the sights and smells, the rules of sterility, the hierarchical ritual—brought me up short again. I stood on a high stool and watched a resident do a hysterectomy on a woman with a fibroid uterus. For some reason my attention became drawn to the prodigious hair on the resident's neck and shoulders under the blue surgical shirt. Here was one naked ape—more or less naked, anyway—taking away the reproductive capacity of another. It was for her own benefit, of course, to prevent pain, illness, death. But as he lifted the chopped, rough, misshapen womb out of her belly, I could not help thinking what a strange evolutionary circumstance this was.

I went to the O.R. where Laura Wallace was to have her laparotomy, but it was still occupied by a team doing a double mastectomy on a young woman with breast cancer. This was to me the most frightening operative disfigurement. It seemed more a castration than a hysterectomy did, and the thought of it never failed to chill me. A friend of mine had been killed by breast cancer the year before—a fine young poet and sensitive intellectual with an exquisite, ethereal beauty. She left a husband, two small sons, and many friends. Two successive mastectomies had promised and failed to save her. As this unknown patient was wheeled out of the O.R., I silently wished her—with more than the usual medical-student concern—all luck.

The room was cleaned and prepped for Laura Wallace. I now scrubbed and gowned for my first nonobstetrical surgery since October, and the thought of "getting my hands in" was dramatic and exhilarating. Stocky, nervous Joel Schwartzman, who held the peculiarly named position of Infertility Fellow, had also gowned and gloved, and was pacing impatiently in the O.R. He made small talk with the nurses. The senior surgeon, Professor Roth, was absent but eagerly anticipated. The patient was ready and waiting in the hall.

The words "tuboplasty" and "fimbrioplasty" were dropped. It took me a few seconds, but I worked out the Latin. These referred, respectively, to the procedures for fixing the tube and fixing the fringe on the tube, either or both of which might turn out to be necessary.

The acronym "I.V.F." was also mentioned: *in vitro* fertilization, the most dramatic and closely watched new procedure in gynecology. A few years earlier the first "test-tube baby" had been born to a woman in England. One of her eggs, removed from her body, had been fertilized by her husband's sperm, "in glass," and later reimplanted in her uterus. Laura Wallace was evidently considered a candidate for I.V.F., but there was as yet no I.V.F. in this or any hospital in the city—primarily for economic reasons. Professor Roth himself was a leading advocate of the method.

By the time he finally appeared in the O.R., Laura had been anesthetized and prepped. She lay with her head behind the curtain in the hands of the anesthesiologist. Her light brown belly was shaved and painted with Betadine. Dr. Roth's presence—handsome, white-haired, lean, impatient, strong—electrified the room. He was already a distinguished infertility surgeon, and the additional achievement (realized a year later) of becoming the founder and director of the only I.V.F. program in the city was soon to make him famous. Infertile couples were among the most intense, desperate, and devoted of patients.

Under Roth's careful eye, Schwartzman's pudgy fingers drew the knife, followed by beads of blood, across the brown antiseptic-painted belly. Without much difficulty, in spite of Laura's mild obesity, they moved through the multilayered barrier of her abdominal wall, and her pelvic organs were exposed. Roth's own hands were now the active ones, and I squeezed in next to him, pulling on a retractor to keep the wound open, trying to ignore the fatigue in my hand, and trying also, somehow, to stay out of the way. Roth checked the sites on her right side from which he had removed one ovary and tube several months before, and then he shifted the retractor and the viscera to expose the ones on the left.

Here he began to shake his head. He poked around in the same spots over and over again, tugged at the membranes, turned the ovary and tube over, stared, and shook his head some more. The adhesions were thick and numerous. Joel Schwartzman shook his head too. "You'll have to use a blasting cap to get that ovary out of there," he said. It took me a while to realize what he meant was not to remove it but to bring it into position from which an egg could be harvested for I.V.F.

Roth now had a decision to make. He could try to save the badly deformed tube and its fringe by manipulating them, changing their positions, and lysing the adhesions. Or he could decide that the maximum effort had to be put into giving her the best chance at *in vitro.* Fooling with the tube and fringe and then leaving them there, with the ovary in its original position, would certainly reduce the chance of a successful harvest of an egg. Was her chance at natural conception large enough to justify that risk? Was the prospect of I.V.F. close enough to warrant giving *it* so much weight? Laura had left the judgment to him, and he decided to remove the tube at once.

I thought again of Lorca's *Yerma.* Yerma's desire for a baby wells up from the most private, most authentic recesses of her being. The play moves powerfully forward on that motive alone. The same power moved the real-life drama of patients I met who came for help with infertility. In a society where many people avoided parenthood, an era in which birth prevention was a high priority, the plight of infertile couples was ironically no less poignant than ever and potentially no less tragic. There are few things sadder than the unfulfilled longing for a child.

Later the day of Laura Wallace's surgery, I did the admission workup on yet another patient scheduled for an elective fimbrioplasty. I was now beginning to think a lot about adhesions. How often were they the cause of infertility? Were they usually caused by natural disease processes, such as endometriosis? Or was surgery the dominant cause? And if the latter, what was the trade-off in fertility surgery? Might it not leave behind more adhesions than it lysed?

Late in the afternoon a staff obstetrician gave a talk on postoperative complications. I asked her whether adhesions were common. Amazingly, she didn't know. She had done hundreds or even thousands of surgical procedures and had almost certainly caused some adhesions. She had faced the problem of lysing adhesions as well as the problem of avoiding them. She carried the responsibility of teaching medical students about postoperative complications. Yet neither curiosity nor a sense of responsibility had led her to learn how frequently these dangerous anatomical abnormalities follow in the ordinary course of abdominal and pelvic surgery. And she was not alone—a major three-part article in the *New England Journal of Medicine* reviewing all that was known about modern abdominal surgery was also silent on the question of adhesions.

The next morning the new patient had her fimbrioplasty, and I once again scrubbed in on it. She had a much less difficult problem than Laura's, and its surgical resolution appeared to be completely successful. Coming back from that operation I happened to be passing Laura's room where Joel Schwartzman was beginning to have a talk with her. I walked in carefully, greeting her with a "How are you?"

"Not so good," she said, very glumly. The bubbles were completely gone. "They had to take out the tube."

I was prepared to hear disappointment but not this funereal tone. Ostensibly, only the day before her surgery, she had been prepared for anything. Joel answered her questions flatly but generously. However, he failed to give her the key piece of information: that the tube had been taken out *to increase the chance of I.V.F.* When I explained this to her, my comment jarred him into making a strongly supportive statement on the same subject.

Later that day her hematocrit began to drop, and it kept dropping, which ominously suggested internal bleeding. We gave her two units of blood and, fortunately, equally inexplicably, her crit spontaneously stopped dropping.

Several days later a visitor was in Laura's room for about an hour. I surmised from various sorts of circumstantial evidence that it must be Joan Kaufman, the social worker. Thank goodness, I thought; finally someone to look out for the person inside the embattled body.

When she emerged from the room I asked her for her theory about Laura's case. She had obviously been very attentive. It turned out that Laura's serene words about adoption were somewhat superficial. Her family had the same problems most have—neither more nor less—but, she confided to Joan, she blamed the adoptions. Occasionally her father had reminded her of her origins in an argument, and this cut her deeply. Joan was right to guess that for her adoptive parenthood seemed a distant possibility at best.

On the day of her discharge I saw Laura in the hall again, and we talked. In contrast to the usual effect of renewing one's appeal by getting dressed again, patients generally seemed less attractive to me with their clothes on. They became ordinary. Of course, they looked better when they got better, but if they had not been very ill, or if they were in for elective surgery, there was an almost unearthly beauty in the presence they made lying in the bed in the hospital gown. They were in a special, sacred frame, and their relative helplessness seemed to draw me close to them. It made them seem larger, more important, and more appealing than they perhaps really were.

In any case Laura was happy and bubbling again. She now understood her reproductive circumstances very accurately. She was still hoping against hope that she would succeed in *in vitro* fertilization. Dr. Roth's surgery gave her this hope, even as it took away her remaining fallopian tube. But the chances of success were not great, and at this point the hospital had not yet even approved the program. She was also putting in adoption papers. She could become a mother as her own mother had, and this seemed to satisfy her, too.

These encounters occurred against the background of a few lines of *Yerma* every day, as I read in its extraordinary poetry that story of a woman doomed by her intense and unattainable wish for children. During the same period two friends of mine were approaching the ends of their pregnancies. One had pregnancy-induced hypertension, a potentially dangerous condition for both mother and baby that appeared to be under control. The other, the wife of a very close friend, who was having a perfectly normal pregnancy, was following my recommendation that she go to the nurse-midwives who had delivered both of my children. I believed in midwifery under safe conditions, which in this case meant on a hospital obstetrical floor with an obstetric surgeon on duty down the hall. My friends were so far delighted with the choice, which gave them more personal attention than they could have had with an obstetrician and a chance to focus on the psychological aspects of pregnancy and childbirth.

Also in the background was the illness of one of my favorite uncles, now eighty-four years old. Shortly after beginning the gynecological rotation I'd heard that after another heart attack he was in the intensive-care unit of a hospital near his Florida home, battling congestive heart failure. Worse, he was delirious. It was a well-known I.C.U. syndrome, probably due to stress and impaired blood supply to the brain combined with drug toxicity. It was highly unlikely that his delirium would persist if and when his major cardiac symptoms resolved. But his paranoid ramblings were extremely upsetting to his wife, my aunt, whom I talked to several times from the hospital. I played doctor as well as I could, and tried to be reassuring, but the situation was frightening. My uncle was not getting any younger.

I was fond of Uncle Dave for many reasons: his natural charm, his love of children, his pride in his World War I record, his irascible right-wing view of the world, which was the opposite of mine. But I was especially fond of him because he had been the only person who was worried when I told him that I was planning to go to medical school. Everyone else had been excited by the prospect, had intoned "Never too old" and other similar homilies, and in general had talked as if they had the courage of my convictions. Unfortunately they could not go through it for me. They could not anticipate or experience the difficulty, the exhaustion, the humiliations, the disappointments, the pain.

Uncle Dave for some reason could. Perhaps it was his war experience, or the fact that he had grandchildren my age, or just his pragmatism. He had come to town for an American Legion convention—he was an active leader in it, as well as in the Veterans of Foreign Wars and the Jewish War Veterans. My wife, daughter, and I had decided to try to show him a good time for the afternoon, which was not difficult, since he was relaxed and easy to please. We were high in the air looking out through the glass windows on the top floor of the tallest building in town when I sprang my plans on him. I knew he revered doctors—on general principles, as a Jewish uncle, and because he had been a medic for a time during the war. I thought he would be delighted.

Instead, he looked at my little daughter, at me, and, through the great expanse of glass, over the city. I imagined that he was reviewing three generations of his own descendants, two world wars, two long happy marriages, the loss of an infant son, and a continuous series of struggles to make a business work. "I don't know, Mel," he finally said, in his rasping, warm voice. "A father, in your thirties. A family man." He looked at the baby again and shook his head slowly. "It's a tough thing, medical training. They don't fool around there. They can hurt you. Do you really think you can do it? Now?"

He seemed to be saying, *You are a mature man. Don't put yourself in position to be treated like a boy.* This conversation came back to me frequently as I made my difficult progress through the next few years. And when I heard that he was ill, I felt a special twinge of regret, and made sure to follow his progress every day. Fortunately, his heart began to work again. His delirium ended, and he went home from the hospital a little the worse for wear but as lucidly irascible as before.

One morning I was waiting for the bus, standing in a crowd of commuters near a busy intersection. I was sipping a cup of coffee and chewing on a doughnut half-hidden in a brown paper bag. *Yerma* was in the pocket of my down jacket—I would read just a few lines on the bus, since I was rationing it. The sun was shining. Suddenly a gaunt, drawn, haunted-looking man grabbed the doughnut and coffee out of my hands, and silently walked away. I knew there was a halfway house nearby, and I had sometimes seen a group of what might have been mental patients jogging by while I was at the bus stop. The man could easily have been a sometime resident of the halfway house, but perhaps he was only a local drunk. He seemed to carry a message about vulnerability, even with respect to the ill, that I ought to be taking seriously.

Earlier that week a youngish woman with relatively advanced cervical cancer had been admitted and scheduled for a radical hysterectomy. She was well known to the hospital staff; she had had extensive prior treatment before the radical "hyst" became the procedure of last resort. The doctors and nurses knew her by her first name, Emily, and they took a view toward her that was some combination of tolerance, compassion, and ridicule. She was thin and dry looking, with sunken eyes, alternately pale and yellowed skin, and dark hair no more than a few millimeters long—it hadn't grown much since the chemotherapy had knocked it out. She was one of the patients who, sadly, knew the hospital environment and the system so well that she'd been given an almost free run of it. She wheeled herself around in her chair, poked her nose in more or less where she wanted to, gave orders to doctors and nurses, and whined—usually but not always good-naturedly.

A few days after reacquainting herself with the personnel on the ward and the floor, Emily happened to wheel herself up to the nurses' station just when Frank Caggiola was making time with Joan Kaufman, ambling up behind her, swaggering in his lanky frame and brushing his black hair out of his eyes. Joan was writing her final assessment note on Laura Wallace.

Emily and Frank seemed to have a special relationship, and when she spoke to him it was with a proud and almost girlish sense of entitlement. Despite his frequent jokes at her expense behind her back, Frank had been rather good to her, and he had encouraged her to like him, even though he could not really like her. As soon as she saw him, she said, "Dr. Caggiola, I really need to ask you if—"

"Not now, Emily," said Frank without missing a beat. He continued up to Joan from behind, put his hands on her shoulders, and then slipped his arms around her. "How are you, you sexy thing?" He leaned around and kissed her. Emily watched, her concentration-camp-victim's head bent slightly toward the couple embracing a few feet in front of her wheelchair.

I was ordered to scrub in on Emily's hysterectomy the following day. A senior gynecological surgeon was involved, as were Frank and another, junior, resident. For the first couple of hours it was interesting, but the operation went on for eight and a half: they removed her uterus, cervix, supporting ligaments, ovaries, and tubes on both sides; then they did the nodal dissection, which was the tricky part. Her cancer had metastasized to the lymph nodes, and all of them in the abdomen had to be removed. This procedure posed a grave risk of injury to the great blood vessels of the abdomen, the nerves, the ureters draining the kidneys, and other delicate and vital structures. Her surgeons seemed to be enjoying themselves thoroughly; but I found the exercise both depressing and boring, and though I wished Emily luck, I waited eagerly for it to be over.

Afternoons that were not filled up with either surgery or admissions were available for attendance at the family planning clinic. This was an opportunity to see birth control (or the lack of it) in action. Gone was the feminist rhetoric about the exploitative aspect of focusing only on women; way in the background were certain niceties of detail regarding the statistical efficacy of one or another method. This was the front line, and the challenge was to get some kind of birth control in place that might help to stem the tide of unwanted babies—not for the sake of society but for the sake of the patients. A steady stream of young women came through the clinic, some married, many not, all sexually active and all wanting, with our blessing, to avert the natural consequences of their romantic acts.

Once, those consequences would have been inevitable and expectable. Now they were considered largely preventable, detaching forever the rough or tender acts of sex from the appearance of a baby, from the ultimate transition to parenthood. I plunged my gloved fingers into the sex of one young, healthy, vigorous woman after another, feeling for normal anatomy, pressing on the belly to feel for the uterus and ovaries, and finally examining the breasts. It seemed to me on those afternoons that nothing that had ever happened in the history of our species had social consequences so profound as the invention of effective contraception. Relations between the sexes, whatever their strange vicissitudes, were permanently changed.

Another consequence as well as cause of this change was the deliberate termination of pregnancy. I had an opportunity not only to see therapeutic abortions but to help perform them, and to "examine the products of conception." This was a euphemism for poking around among the fetal parts that had been sucked through the extractor into a jar. It was important to be sure they were all there, that nothing had been left behind—an error that could cause a life-threatening hemorrhage in the woman. Occasionally a saline injection would be used to precipitate expulsion of the fetus without scraping the uterus. In these cases I could examine the tiny creatures fully formed, and not dismembered, in the palm of my hand. On several occasions I deliberately took the extractor in hand myself, not just to learn how to do the procedure but to assume responsibility.

None of these experiences changed my basic outlook on abortion, which was that it was a necessary evil. Although in practical terms I could see that the law could not become involved in ruling on such subtle distinctions, I felt somewhat contemptuous of women I knew—especially educated women—who had had four or more abortions. If they had long-term partners, I felt contemptuous of the partners too. At some point, it seemed to me, forgivable error becomes unforgivable irresponsibility. Abortion was a tragic choice: a woman's right, when her back was to the wall, but not an acceptable form of contraception.

But of course, in a case like Tracy Whiting's, I found little place for moralizing. She was sixteen years old, a pretty girl with straight brown hair, a broad open young face, and a well-proportioned body. She was presenting with the dangerous situation of an incomplete abortion, begun but not finished at a local abortion clinic. She had a strange sort of teenage stoicism combined with confusion, awkwardness, and fear. She was entirely alone. Where was her boyfriend? In school. Her mother and father? She didn't want them to know. Her *father?* I kept thinking stupidly to myself. She didn't want her *father* to know?

Talking with her calmed her, I think, even before she got her anesthetic. But one of my most vivid and indelible images of that month was the sight of her smooth young legs split apart and slung in the stirrups, with a nonchalant resident poking deeply into the pink gash between them, sucking whatever was left of the new small life out of her body.

Later that day I lined up a priest for Teresa Graziano. When I met this young woman, she was wearing a rather provocative red nightgown instead of the hospital johnny, and a gold cross on a chain around her neck. The fullness of her body was conventionally perfect, except that in her lower belly there was an unexplained mass about the size of her fist that had been visualized on an X-ray study. She was very cheerful during the admission work-up, and I later realized that she had not been told the story that I had been told, namely that she had an excellent chance of having a malignancy on an ovary. This was a deadly cancer and it seemed somehow unfair to encourage her cheerfulness, which to me meant that she could not have understood the odds. These odds were discussed and understood by the residents. It was not my place to tell her, but I got hold of the hospital priest when I saw him passing in the hall. I told him that she was going to have surgery and that the news following it might be very bad. He knew who she was but had not known that she might be in that kind of danger. We shook hands in a new alliance.

We continued to have lectures almost every day at seven, some of which were about obstetric topics. One of the best was Dr. Suskauer's challenge to us to describe what we would do if we came upon a woman who was in labor on the subway. There were five of us on the rotation, and we all volunteered various ideas from what we had learned during our time delivering babies at Galen.

All were wrong. Nothing we mentioned was worth doing in that setting, he said, and the best thing to do was to "maintain a watchful waiting posture," meaning: keep your hands to yourself and your mouth shut and let mother nature do the work. In only one case would an intervention in that setting be sensible—a feet-first birth with the toes pointing up. The baby's head and neck were likely to be severely compromised after the delivery of the body. Dr. Suskauer drew a stick-figure on the blackboard, with the feet up, and then drew a cross at the head. "The mnemonic is, 'Dead men lie with their feet pointing up.'" It was unforgettable. The thing to do was to get hold of the legs and turn the baby. This could be a challenge, but was worth a try, to avoid strangulation. Other than this, though, the right answer was, *hands off.* I found this remarkable. Here we had learned so much about how to intervene, and it turned out that in a setting far from the hospital the right thing to do with all this knowledge was nothing. Suddenly and for the first time I understood how primitive people like the San, whom I had lived with, could get away with no obstetric technology. Dr. Suskauer, the engineer, the high priest of technology, was filing a brief to prove that childbirth, with all its problems, basically, finally, works.

Coming back from the family planning clinic one day, I ran into Dr. Roth in the elevator. I felt emboldened to engage him in a conversation. He had just returned from a meeting with the Galen Board of Trustees, at which he had once again been denied permission to start his program in I.V.F. He seemed hopeful about the eventual approval of the program, but he had little sympathy for the arguments in favor of delay. Was the procedure cost effective? Was it reliable enough to justify once again raising the hopes of a population of patients whose hopes had been falsely raised so many times? Would there be an ethical storm that would cost the hospital and the patients more than the procedure was worth? All such questions lost their legitimacy for him when he looked into the eyes of an infertile woman who wanted nothing more than to have a baby.

One such woman was Ellen Segal, a very tall, overweight woman with dark hair on her upper lip and irregular uterine bleeding—all signs associated with Stein-Leventhal syndrome. But the most important sign of the syndrome was the numerous cysts found on her ovaries when she had her appendix removed three years before. At around the same time she and her husband—he was a psychiatrist and she a psychiatric nurse—had begun to try to have a baby. They had now been unsuccessful for three years.

I attended the laparoscopy—an attempt to visualize her internal organs through a one-centimeter hole in her abdomen with a fiber-optics tube. I had seen marvelous spectacles in the abdomen through such tubes, but this time there was nothing to see. Even the trocar—the pointed metal guide inserted before the tube is threaded in—came up against rock-hard adhesions. The fallopian tubes and ovaries could not even be visualized. Dr. Roth and Dr. Schwartzman withdrew the trocar, having determined that there was nothing they could do.

Just before leaving the gynecology floor for good, and distracted by the many things I had to do before going, I went into her room—too abruptly, as it turned out. Schwartzman or Roth or both had already been there: she and her husband had their arms around each other, and she was crying.

II

PATHOLOGY

The Aspect of Death

On the subway on my way to Galen on my first morning in pathology I found myself in the comical but painful position of having an intense and then desperate urge to defecate. I knew what it felt like to want to go to the toilet badly, but this was off the scale. It was a feeling I had only experienced a few times before, and one that had always been associated with explosive diarrhea. I had felt something like this in Africa during a bout with amoebic dysentery—like a stick of dynamite going off, every twenty minutes or so, inside your rectum.

The comical part was the juxtaposition with my just-completed rotation in obstetrics. Innumerable times, following the example of the nurses, I had said to women in labor, "Bear down as if you were going to the bathroom." Ignorantly, but having to say *something*, I had told many women that labor would feel like "you're making the biggest poop of your life." And then I would usually think, *As if a man could know what labor feels like*. Well, now I was getting my comeuppance. If a man telling a woman what she would feel in labor was some sort of misdemeanor, then this punishment fit the crime like a glove.

And there was no escaping. All I could do was wait for the train to get to the hospital stop. But instead, it stalled in the station before that. Now all I could do was stand there, hoping for the train to move. I focused all my mental energy on what little I remembered of the functional anatomy of the rectum and tried not to look too desperate. I was in steadily increasing pain. It seemed now like a metaphor not only for childbirth but for all pain and illness. My body was alien and rebellious, a hateful thing that I wished I could get rid of. I was prepared to bargain with forces I didn't ordinarily believe in, in order to get free of the discomfort. And no matter how bad it got, I couldn't forget how ridiculous I was. I felt as if I had stood there forever.

When the doors opened briefly, a voice in the back of my mind shouted *This is your chance!* and I shoved several other passengers aside to get out. The doors closed again but the train didn't move. There was no bathroom in the station, and aboveground the neighborhood was one of unused warehouses. There was no help for me except at the hospital. I began to run, hoping that running would suppress the awful urgency—or at least take my mind off it. It did help a little. I tore across the bridge, over the river, toward Galen Memorial. All the while, I expected the train to pass me by, which would make me feel even more of an idiot.

I made it to the hospital way ahead of the train, with the urgency of my "labor" increasing precipitously the closer I got to the toilet. I was reminded of the *couvade,* that marvelous custom of certain South American Indian tribes, whereby a man would go through his own "labor" in parallel with his wife's. After days of conscientious, even drug-induced constipation, timed to coincide with his wife's last days of pregnancy, he would go out to the bush alone as she went into labor. There, while she had the baby, he would have the biggest defecation of his life—a simulation of labor. He would come back, report that *his* "baby" had been stillborn, and proceed to join his wife and "the other baby." With this preparation, it was believed, a man could truly take up the role and function of father.

Perhaps in my case it was the role and function of doctor—or, specifically, obstetrician—in which I was being spiritually certified. Perhaps I was paying my dues to all those women whose deliveries I had unceremoniously attended, an absurd male giving pat advice and formulaic instructions. And to my wife, who in her twenty-two-hour first labor had hurled curses at me I hadn't known she knew—not because I had done anything wrong but because I was the only one in the labor room whom she felt comfortable excoriating. I was getting a tiny taste—tiny—of the trial of women in labor, and I didn't like it a bit. The pain, the desperation, the humiliation, the helplessness—all seemed in retrospect good for me. But at the time a toilet seemed the only corner of paradise I'd ask for.

I made it; and it *was* diarrhea. I was left with stomach discomfort, a burning sensation in my anus, a grateful feeling of having got past something awful, and the sense that it would be back again soon. I resolved not to get far from a bathroom at any time during the next few hours.

The residents in pathology were a mix of career pathologists and rotators from medicine, neurology, and other disciplines. Most were not thrilled with the assignment. Because of my interests I was to be allowed to concentrate in neuropathology, although I would also be exposed to general path. The head of the service was a woman, Dr. Mattingley, an extremely correct and rather brilliant clinician and basic scientist. She exemplified the ideal of enthusiastic objectivity and disinterested medical sleuthing that was familiar to me from television and movie pathologists. As I shook hands with her, our first moment of greeting, her beeper sang out, and I followed her long hurried strides down to the path lab next to the neurosurgical O.R.

The lab was bright white and full of cheerful bustle. A super-cooled microtome was cutting frozen thin sections of tissue that was the unmistakable beige color of brain. Dr. Brennan was mentioned as the surgeon, and I knew that my guess about the tissue must be right. In my first encounter with neurosurgery I had stood behind Dr. Brennan himself, watching him destroy a large section of a young man's brain, and I had listened to the pathology reports at last confirming his clinical judgment. Now I was in the room where those samples had been studied. As in that first case, the judgment of Dr. Mattingley would determine whether the patient's brain would be partly removed and, possibly, whether the patient would live or die.

Dr. Mattingley, a senior resident, and I sat down at the conference microscope where the three of us could look at the same specimen and discuss it. It was ideal for teaching, though there was little time for that here. Dr. Mattingley put the first frozen section on the microscope stage. I tried to study it as she moved it around and focused. It looked to me like a smear of what could have been normal brain tissue—there were normal-looking nerve cells and supporting cells. But I was used to examining brain tissue in chunks that preserved the architecture, the elegant anatomy of the circuitry of thought. What I was now seeing was the product of suction, which destroyed all that elegance, and it took an experienced eye even to orient to it, much less to tell normal from abnormal.

I heard Dr. Mattingley's slightly lilting voice as my eyes swam in the frozen soup of pink and purple cells. "Nothing of interest here," she said of the first sample. We waited a few minutes while she chatted with the resident, and the microtome went on slicing tissue. She was handed the second slide and she adjusted it on the stage. "Well, here's something for sure," she said, "this is nice." The borders of the cells were less well defined. The nuclei were deeply colored, peculiar in shape, and eccentric. The whole sample of cells was less structured and less well differentiated. I could not have identified the abnormalities myself, but they were apparent once they were pointed out to me. It was a high grade astrocytoma —a very deadly tumor.

After the microscopic examination I got up to look at what was left of the tissue on the microtome. There was nothing much to see. But on the folded towel—it was a pretty, deep blue—in which the specimen had come up from the O.R., there was a tag with a woman's name and a birth date twenty-two years earlier.

Corpses, of course, are an integral part of medicine. This seems obvious, but to judge from the doctor shows on television, one would think they were only rarely encountered. Even pathologists doing autopsies spare the audience at home any actual specter of death, signifying the corpse's presence by looking significantly down—and out of the frame. But in real-life medicine one must be, if not comfortable with corpses, at least their easy and unruffled familiar. A psychiatrist interested in medical education once said to me, "What are we to think of a profession that takes its neophytes, on the first day, and shoves them into a room full of stinking corpses?"

What indeed, except that this gesture is not incidental. The gruesome stories about dissecting-room banter were certainly consonant with my experience. For instance, at the next table to mine in the dissecting lab, the students named their cadaver "Shop." This was so that when the end of the afternoon came, they could ritualistically, invariably, and hilariously say, "Well, it's time to close up Shop." The process of psychological hardening of medical students as deliberately pursued in the dissecting room seemed to work according to expectations. Perhaps it even worked too well. In this as in other medical school experiences most of the students seemed to embrace it. If they were really *going through* something, their trial was usually not evident to me. And any comments I made about my feelings—about, for example, the impossibility of really keeping every little piece of a body together, as required by both decency and law; or about the metastatic cancer of the pancreas we found throughout the belly of our cadaver, which was of an old woman—were met with incomprehension or with impatient, politely veiled scorn.

My dissecting partner proudly proclaimed that he had managed to get through college with only a single course outside of the sciences, a course in group encounters which he believed had changed his life. "Thirty-three courses in physics and math!" he announced more than once. He loved the process of scraping fascia away from muscle, while I just wanted to get through that and see the real anatomy. The parts of the course I found most helpful were the prosections—dissections done by the expert instructor for a small group of students. These revealed the anatomy exquisitely, bypassing the tedium. Once one of the preceptors said to me, "You really don't like to get your hands in there." I didn't think this was true, but there were certainly some things on an elderly woman's body that I was rather reluctant to cut. Her genitals, for instance. Her face. Her breasts. Her hands. As for the pure scut work, if my partner was eager to spend obsessive hours scraping fascia, I was happy to let him handle most of it. I learned the anatomy well enough. But in back of my mind there were always those murmuring questions about the person whose body this had been.

In the autopsy room, such cadaverous anonymity as was expected in the dissecting room was neither possible nor desirable. My first autopsy conference had taken place in the dark basement of Galen on a rainy Saturday morning at eight o'clock, long before this pathology rotation. The instructor was Dr. Craig, the formidable chief of pathology, a bull of a man with a gruff voice and impatient manner who was still somehow likable. In a little conference room mostly filled with a hexagonal chrome table we pulled on our latex gloves, tried to ignore the dense smell of formaldehyde, sat at the table, and waited. On the chrome trays in the center of the table were most of the internal organs of a single human body.

Dr. Craig began to present the case. It was that of a twenty-one-year-old Italian male admitted to Galen for his *forty-third* hospital admission. The diagnosis, of long standing, was beta thalassemia. This was a fancy word for what my aunt, the doctor's wife, had once called Cooley's anemia. It resulted from a genetic defect in the structure of hemoglobin, the oxygen-carrying molecule of blood, and meant that the patient was condemned to constant anemia, weakness, and difficulty in breathing.

The patient had first been admitted to the hospital at fifteen months of age with an enlarged liver and spleen. This was the result of impaired blood formation in the bone marrow; the liver and spleen were trying to take over this vital function. The baby had already been identified as listless, and a routine blood work-up showed severe anemia. Because he was Italian, as well as because of his age, he was suspected of having a genetic disorder of hemoglobin structure, and examination of his parents' blood revealed that both were heterozygotes, or carriers. Each had one copy of the bad gene and both had passed it on to him. Their mild abnormalities thus became his devastating one.

His spleen enlargement had worsened steadily. At eighteen months it was two inches below the rib cage, and at twenty-two months about four inches. During this period he had had many blood transfusions. As a child he was found to have pigmented gallstones, a byproduct of his illness and its treatment.

Psychologically, his situation was almost as much a disaster as it was medically. He was abandoned by his parents and cared for by his grandparents. His brother, who was free of the disease, had hanged himself. The patient had had to be transfused continually throughout his life; the hospital became his second home. Treated with narcotics for bone pain, he became addicted to them. Beginning in his teens, he had lived on his own. He was arrested on drug charges but was actually rejected by correctional institutions because of his medical problems. Nobody wanted him; he could not even get into jail. The presumed cause of his death, which occurred at age twenty-one, was a drug overdose.

We collectively pored over his vital organs, which sat neatly on the metal trays. All of them were dark and mottled, both under the microscope and by the naked eye. All were shot through with iron, deposited from the damaged red blood cells resulting from his disease and from his innumerable tranfusions. His discolored, disembodied, ruined vital organs bespoke a life that had fallen apart—that had indeed been defined by the process of falling apart from its ill-starred beginning. We saw projected, enlarged versions of the microscope slides that had been made from some of these organs, and they too showed the iron that had insinuated itself into every corner of his body. It was for me a first and most impressive demonstration of the power and the sadness, the retrospective logic and the admitted medical failure, the grotesque, fascinating, dark illumination of the autopsy.

The last time I'd been in that room was during my first rotation in surgery. I was sitting by the same metal table with the other students when Dr. Craig appeared carrying a very large piece of flesh on a metal tray. He slid the tray over so that it landed squarely in front of me, an uncertainly wobbling jelled mass.

"Describe it," he said.

I sat there staring down at it, dumbfounded. With my stretched-rubber-gloved hands I began turning it over. It weighed somewhere between five and ten pounds, was mostly fat, with a hard area in the middle, and was partly covered with yellow skin. Suddenly my face brightened. Sensing that I was about to come out with an answer, Dr. Craig said, "I didn't say guess what it is. I said describe it."

"It's a large piece of—"

"Large?"

I started again. "It's a twenty by twenty-five centimeter piece of fatty tissue, about half of which is covered with yellow skin. There is a hard grayish-yellow growth—"

"Growth?"

"—*region* in the center with extensions coming out of it toward the periphery. On the skin surface there is one area that, although very distorted, looks as if it could be a nipple."

He nodded approval. It was in fact an enormous breast that had been removed from an obese woman that same morning. And it had an enormous carcinoma in its center, spreading its tentacles grotesquely in every direction. This was the crab, cancer, its hard invasive body taking over in all directions, displacing normal tissue, destroying it, threatening form, health, life. Somewhere in the hospital a woman was lying in bed, breathing with difficulty in a grossly fat body, peering down at her single remaining breast, hoping against hope that this disfigurement had saved her life.

Now I was back in the same suite of autopsy rooms, not as a tentative visiting student testing the strength of his stomach, but in a framework of more or less total commitment. At any given time there were three or four corpses lying on the tables in attitudes of awkward repose. Pathology residents were hard at work on them, incising, stripping, sawing, removing organs and replacing them, studying the labyrinths of the newly inert body for the clues that could lead to the cause of death. I was assigned to the neuropathology residents, so that my main exposure was to the removal, fixation, slicing, and systematic study of the brain.

But I also was able to observe the whole autopsy process, and this gave me—just as it was supposed to—a new understanding of disease. To enable us to place the postmortem data in a fully meaningful context, we were responsible for summarizing the series of events leading up to death. This meant studying the "patient's" chart, doing the autopsy, and then writing up a story that had some sort of coherence. The process was like an ironic obverse of the usual patient discharge summary, which related in similar detail the events of the illness leading up to recovery. The logic of the autopsy report was similar. And the central ritual encounter was not with a live patient's body but with the lifeless remains it consisted of after death.

My first autopsy and brain removal was on a forty-seven-year-old mathematician. He had had one kidney removed in childhood because of a congenital defect and had begun to go into gradually worsening renal failure in his mid-twenties. For twenty years he had battled salt and water retention, high blood pressure, labored breathing—an involuntary attempt to correct the acid in his blood—and nausea and vomiting. Through all this he had somehow been able to keep on with his research, writing, and teaching. Finally his heart had begun to fail from pumping so long against such a high pressure gradient, and at last the acid imbalance had begun to affect his brain.

Now he lay plump and waxy on the table, his skin a peculiar yellow from, in effect, backed-up urine—as well, of course, as from the change of death. His neck had been propped and extended on wooden blocks. His scalp was reflected—stretched down—over his face, so that his features were outlined eerily through a thick inverted layer of hair and skin. A neuropathology resident was taking an electric saw to his skull. It was essential to wield the saw gingerly, so as not to lacerate the delicate brain.

It was also essential, as if in a very crude version of plastic surgery, to preserve the cosmetic integrity of the body, on the assumption that it might be placed on view. This was especially difficult with thin-haired or bald men. The United States had (and has) a very low rate of autopsies as compared with other Western nations. So pathologists and other physicians who consider it their duty to determine precisely the cause of death feel embattled. In the recently dead lie some of the secrets of future preventions, future cures. Every effort has to be made to avoid the slightest disfigurement that might further alienate patients' families from the process of postmortem examination.

The whine of the saw did spare the brain, and it was quickly exposed. The skull was deftly cut and removed, and special long curved scissors were used to separate the gel-like brain from the body. Every blood vessel, every nerve that served to maintain communication between the brain and the body, had to be severed carefully, or they would tear the brain apart when removal was attempted. The brain itself had to be held carefully in place, with the fingers and hand poised under and around it to keep it from tumbling to the floor. The word "deliver" was used for the moment of removal, and it did feel almost as delicate as the birthing of a baby.

I delivered the soft brain from the skull, cupping my hands around it as respectfully as if it *had* been a baby. It was soft enough so that it felt as if it could almost dissolve and slide through my fingers. I carried it slowly and carefully to the scale, weighed it, and transferred it to the formalin bath. I slipped it into that foul, noxious solution, fifteen hundred sixty-eight grams of tissue that had, a few days earlier, been alive with hopes, fears, denials, dreams, plans, and equations.

The previous weekend, one of the two pregnant friends who were about to deliver had given birth. It was Barbara's and Stan's second child, a boy, and all had gone exceptionally well. When we visited her she was in the pink of new maternal health, holding the baby on one arm, brushing her black hair away from her small, pretty face, smiling as if smiles might go out of style. The delivery had been easy, she felt fine, and the baby was perfect. She had entered the cataclysm of birth and come out the other side, whole, well, and having put forth a brand-new life. In Barbara's case, the sense of having come through was complete. There was only the slightest swelling in her feet and ankles to suggest that anything might be wrong. Although this was a social visit, I did press the skin of her instep, and my finger left a little pit, or depression, for just a second after I pulled it back. But the midwife was not worried, and I concentrated on enjoying the glow of new life that came from the mother and her baby.

I remembered vividly the dinner conversation in which Barbara and Stan asked me what I thought about the midwives we had gone to. I had tried to be cautious. I had tried to distinguish between what I might say as a doctor (or medical student) and what I might say as a father.

For ten or fifteen years the midwifery movement had been steadily growing throughout the United States. "Birthing rooms" or "birthing centers" grew up, replacing the labor room and the delivery room with a single room furnished like a bedroom in a home. Delivery in a birthing room, on the obstetrical floor of a hospital, just down the hall from an obstetrical surgery suite, was a solution that seemed to combine the best of both worlds.

In any case that was the choice my wife and I had made for the deliveries of both of our own children. We'd had two different nurse-midwives —nurse-practitioners specializing in midwifery—and both had seemed superb to us. They worked under the direct supervision of a team of obstetricians, and the obstetrician even saw us occasionally. But the midwives took care of us. The time available for discussion during the pregnancies, especially the first, did a great deal to allay our anxiety. They educated us about nutrition, exercise, fetal development, and the process of childbirth.

The deliveries—one difficult and long, one relatively easy and short—were well-managed and were something like peak experiences (in drastically different ways of course) for my wife and myself. They were completely drug free and essentially free of technology, choices that the midwives had understood and encouraged. The formation of our family and, later, its extension, took place in indelible moments of not merely normal but exquisitely heightened awareness. And if we had needed it, the midwives were backed up by trained obstetrical surgeons.

So when we recommended to Barbara and Stan that they go to the nurse-midwives, it was with a personal sense of the rightness of the choice. Yet I was conscious of the fact that I could no longer, in a situation like this, give advice that was merely personal.

On Sunday afternoon, the day after the delivery, Barbara "spiked a temp." It was not high—101.2°—but any fever more than twenty-four hours after a delivery was considered cause for suspicion. The midwife visited Barbara but did not see a need for antibiotics. This judgment was soon to become a grave source of contention. Monday morning, after a relatively calm night, the fever began to climb steadily. Neither Tylenol nor ice packs touched it. By the time intravenous antibiotics were started—or to be more precise, by the time they went into action—the fever was 105.6°, Barbara was delirious, and her life was in serious danger.

This course of events was reconstructed for me on the telephone that afternoon in the anguished voice of Barbara's husband. For a man like Stan, even anguish was controlled, and there was no hint of the maudlin or melodramatic. But I was close enough to him to hear, or perhaps to feel, that in the orderly house of his mind the timbers trembled.

The phone was near the microscopes in the neuropathology lab upstairs, and when I answered it I was still in a strange reverie. I did not have to move to reach it, and my eyes were swimming in the beautiful blues and purples and pinks with which a dead brain had been infused. I could almost forget that what I was looking at was the devastation left by a stroke, a blood-choked cavity surrounded by millions of dead nerve cells. Stan's unsettling confidences tore this vision away from my eyes, and a few minutes later I was asking permission to leave the lab early so that I could meet him at the hospital where Barbara lay in her fever. Soon I was with him, going over the details again and again.

It was clear that there was little I could do. The hospital's infectious-disease expert was deeply involved in the case, as were two obstetricians. I was not going to second-guess these people or offer any suggestions. I was going to try to interpret their reasoning for my friend. As a student of arcane languages, Stan knew better than I how very treacherous translation could be, but he figured that his chances of understanding what these experts really meant were significantly better with me around. This seemed reasonable. If there was one thing I had learned so far in medical school, it was a good working knowledge of the language of physicians.

The antibiotics were in place, streaming from the I.V. bag into Barbara's vein. Her temperature began to fall. The delirium had passed. And the baby was not sick at all. Barbara looked very pale, weak, and incredibly exhausted. And she also looked mistrustful, though confident of her life.

In the meantime, I felt responsible. I knew already that my lay status was gone forever, that medical knowledge, however rudimentary, would always force me to do more than stand by. But this was different. The crisis seemed in part the result of my recommendation. *I* had suggested that they go to the nurse-midwives, and a suggestion from me was now a suggestion from a medically trained person. It carried legal as well as moral responsibility.

In the ensuing days I went to the path lab and the autopsy room daily, although there was no mistaking that my attention was divided. A ninety-one-year-old boxer who had died of lung cancer had a brain that seemed to explain his declining mental function. He apparently had suffered from *dementia pugilistica,* the so-called "punch-drunk" state, a mysterious form of senility that appears many years after having had one's head pummeled repeatedly by powerful fists. On a more mundane level, a sixty-seven-year-old woman who had survived a quadruple bypass had died of a stroke.

A man in his forties who had had a revolutionary treatment for a leaking vessel in his brain—the implantation of a balloon that was blown up at the end of a catheter, first inserted through an artery in the groin—had died with the balloon in place. His physician, a famous French radiologist who was visiting Galen Memorial, came down to look at the brain. There in a slab on a metal tray the balloon sat among folds of brain tissue, having failed to fulfill its mission.

The doctor, a gray-haired man in surgical greens with a philosophical smile, was one of a new generation of interventional radiologists—radiologists who in effect operated on their patients' problems, through blood vessel catheters, rather than merely making images of them. They threatened to take away some major categories of patients from the surgeons, and this man was a pioneer in the method. He had come to Galen to teach it. But now all he could do was to gaze down on his handiwork, studying it with the detachment and technical curiosity it deserved—as a fascinating failure.

And of course there were also the daily rushed trips down to the O.R. to provide an urgently needed tumor type and staging. Study them as I might, I found the categories bewildering, and I knew that this was the sort of facility that came only with years of looking. Still, it was nice to have a small sense of urgency in a realm filled with the calm, timeless certainties of the dead.

After a few days of having her fever under control, Barbara developed a pain in her chest and difficulty breathing. I walked out in the middle of a morning brain-cutting session to return Stan's phone call and was soon, once again, at his side in the obstetric recovery ward. The differential diagnosis was between pneumonia and pulmonary embolism (these were clots or other debris that had lodged in the blood vessels of the lungs, having traveled there from other parts of the body). Neither disorder was pleasant and either could be life-threatening. I looked at her X-rays with her doctors, and unfortunately the classic signs that might discriminate between the two were not present. I accompanied her and Stan down to radiology for a ventilation-perfusion scan, often an ideal way of ruling in or out a pulmonary embolism. Unfortunately Barbara's scan left the issue still unresolved.

She either had a pulmonary embolism complicated by infection or a pneumonia of so far unknown cause. Embolism was thought to be quite common in the postpartum period, and recent studies had suggested that it might be underdiagnosed. The same autopsies I was watching and participating in showed that up to 60 percent of people dying from all causes had pulmonary embolisms, the vast majority of which were undetected during life.

It is generally thought that lung circulation serves in part as an adaptive mechanism, a filter to catch clots as they pour back to the heart in the returning venous blood. Blood from all parts of the body returns to the right side of the heart, which then pumps the blood to the lungs. Clots traveling this course will lodge in the lung circulation; were it not for this filter, they would enter the body's circulation on the left side of the heart, from which they would be pumped to all parts of the body with the oxygenated blood and lodge, most notably, in the kidneys and the brain, causing devastating functional losses. In the lungs, if the clots are small, they are relatively harmless, often producing no symptoms or signs. Even larger ones usually allow complete recovery. But a 10 percent mortality rate makes them events that command respect. Barbara's, if she had one, would probably have come from the blood vessels draining the uterus. Changes in the circulatory dynamics induced by pregnancy, as well as hormonal influences, favored such clotting. If there were an infection as well, the chances of a clot were greatly increased.

If Barbara's problem was pneumonia primarily, her condition was still dangerous. Ideally, the causative organism should be positively identified. If, as was likely, it was bacterial, then a specific antibiotic would be instituted. However, it would take time for the sputum and blood cultures to produce an identification. In the meantime, Barbara was transferred to the medical intensive care unit—the M.I.C.U.—where a broad-spectrum intravenous antibiotic was administered, where anticoagulant therapy was instituted to prevent further clotting, and where she could be very carefully watched.

Stan and I stayed in the waiting room of the M.I.C.U. for hours on end. He remained calm and dignified, but he was in a state of terror. Fortunately he had confidence in the infectious-disease expert, but he was furious at the midwife and the obstetrics staff. He stayed in the hospital much longer than I did, but even he had to leave to take care of their daughter, whom he naturally did not want to alarm. My wife and I helped with that, and late one evening when he came by to pick her up, he sat in our little living room and poured his understandably troubled heart out. There was a sob in his voice and the blood drained from his face. "I know she's going to die," he said slowly and deliberately. "I just know she's going to die." I had been with him through most of the conversations he had had with all of Barbara's doctors. Although I had not gone into the M.I.C.U. myself, I had talked to him extensively each time he visited her. I knew the details of the case on an hour-to-hour basis. I did not think she was going to die, and neither did anyone else who had so far been concerned with her case.

But Stan's words changed my feelings about the case. It was partly because I was his friend—he would not have said such a thing to any of her doctors. But he communicated his fear to me—not just the idea of his fear, but the fearful feeling itself. *Why not?* I thought. This seems like a classic childbed fever—the sort of thing women once died from routinely. Or, if it's an embolism complicated by infection, that too could take her life. None of the doctors could figure out what was wrong with her. Why should I trust them any more than Stan did?

That communication from Stan ended my complacency. I felt that I had to do more, something, anything reasonable. My position and resources were of course very limited. But I knew that Dr. Mattingley, head of the neuropath lab, was married to the foremost authority on lung diseases in the region. I spoke to her first thing the following morning, with Stan's terrible utterance still ringing in my ears.

"I heard about that case," she said. "He's been asked to become involved in it. Of course, he is very busy. But I will speak to him."

That afternoon he was at Barbara's bedside, a distinguished white-haired Englishman who was very concerned, very calm, and very much in charge: he essentially took over the case. Everyone was relieved. For example, the young pulmonary experts at the hospital had been urging Stan to allow Barbara to have an angiogram. This diagnostic procedure, designed to give a definitive answer to the question of embolism versus pneumonia, carried about a half percent mortality—one in two hundred. Stan's mood was such that he felt sure that Barbara would be in that small percentage. My own advice was that the gain in information would not be valuable enough. This was the opinion arrived at by Dr. Mattingley's husband, who was not inclined to shoot from the hip with dazzling new technology. And this was only one example. His reassuring effect on all of us, particularly Stan, was remarkable.

Two mornings a week and once in the afternoon we had brain-cutting conferences, at which formalin-fixed brains were laid out in slabs and examined by a group of neuropathologists. This was one of the few events I experienced in medicine that had the thoughtfulness of a graduate seminar. There was no great rush, and making an impression was not a principal aim of life for the people around the table. If it had been, they would not have become pathologists.

One I noticed in particular was Dr. Ericsson, chief of neuropathology at a big hospital in another city. He had a somewhat sad demeanor at these autopsy conferences. In one case, I remember, his voice noticeably slowed as he asked a few questions of the residents and students, trying to elicit a diagnosis of the cause of death. They could not give an answer, and so he pointed out how, in a section of the brain stem, the canal passing between two ventricles, or fluid-filled cavities, in the center of the brain was severely constricted. A drug overdose had caused swelling of the brain, which had tightened the brain stem canal, further compromising the outflow of fluid and exacerbating the condition. A vicious cycle had been set up, with a cascade of swelling that steadily worsened until death was inevitable. If, at an early stage, the patient—a young man—had been taken to the hospital, his life might well have been saved. He explained the neurological mechanisms, the neuropathology findings, and the probable physiological pathway to death, as well as any teacher I had known. But in his voice there was an unmistakable sorrow on behalf of this anonymous young man. Most physicians had no use for dead drug addicts; in a situation like this, with an interesting mechanism of death, they might be curious, but they would not be sympathetic. "Great case" would be about as emotional a comment as they would make. Dr. Ericsson used the word "tragic" twice. It stunned me the first time, and the second time I could hardly believe my ears. *"A tragic case."* It was the only time I heard that simple, descriptive word—that manifestation of sympathy, of elemental compassion—during the entire course of my medical education.

Barbara steadily improved. Whether Sylvia Hendry's antibiotic wizardry, or Dr. Mattingley's husband, or luck, or providence, or her own power of healing was the critical ingredient, neither I nor anyone else would ever know. It was never established whether or not she had in fact had an embolism, but the treatment she had responded to included a presumption of pneumonia. Either way, infection was likely. Stan's fear was now, understandably, turning to anger, and there was talk of a lawsuit. There was the possibility—memory for such a thing was treacherous—that at some point during the phase of active labor the midwife—the same who had delivered our baby—had examined Barbara's vagina with an ungloved hand, *while Barbara was on the toilet.* There was definite evidence that a certain amount of delay had been permitted between the appearance of the fever and the institution of antibiotics. This delay was considered by some to be within the bounds of acceptable practice, and by others to be beyond them.

My reaction was complicated. It seemed possible to me that Barbara had simply been unlucky. She had experienced the sort of life-threatening condition that had characterized the childbed experience of countless millions of women throughout history. Of those millions many had died. But in the United States in the 1980s this outcome was virtually unheard of. The possibility of an error seemed real, and I felt a heavy burden of responsibility for my recommendation and referral. I shared Stan's anger, but I knew that a major suit—and it was not clear that there were grounds for one—could deal a heavy blow to midwifery in our area, whether the suit was won or lost.

As time went by, the anger seemed to cool, and the suit never materialized. Fortunately, our friendship, which I valued very highly, did not suffer, and, most important of all, mother and baby, in the words of the wonderful cliché, continued to do very well indeed.

In the latter part of the month, then, I was able to concentrate on the dead and on what they could teach me about the living and the dying. On late Tuesday afternoons there was a brain-cutting conference that drew the greatest luminaries of Galen neurology and neuropathology—among the greatest in the world—as well as junior professors, residents, and medical students. Each of us was handed a photocopy of a case history, covering in rigorous detail the events from the onset of illness to the immediate causes of death. These documents were masterpieces of cryptic style, since they had to provide all the information that was available about the patient, yet without hinting at the final diagnosis. The final diagnosis was synonymous with the anatomical diagnosis—the one arrived at through autopsy, the one that would be revealed at the end of the afternoon.

These cases were never straightforward, so those of us who were ignorant had the pleasure of watching the great and the near great also squirm a little. The trick, as with any puzzle, was to provide a case description that resisted successful analysis, yet, when the answer was revealed, made you strike your forehead and say, "Damn it! Of course!" Frequently the cases were well-known disorders with atypical presentations—the sort of symptom picture or course of illness that the textbooks more or less ruled out for the disease in question. Others were simply "zebras."

"Zebra" is one of those wonderful medical nicknames that instantly evoke both a complex idea and a joke. Of some inexperienced physicians, and especially of medical students, it might be said, "He heard hoofbeats outside his window, so naturally he assumed it was a zebra." This covered the frequent habit of jumping to the diagnosis of a rare, "textbook" condition, when the symptoms could be accounted for by a vastly more likely everyday diagnosis. "Zebras," then, were very rare diseases.

It was a funny thing about zebras, though. They often illuminated basic principles of medicine and physiology that were lost in the wash of ordinary, inelegant ailments. They certainly could be fun—essential fun for those more experienced than I who were bored with the everyday disorders.

And then there was the justification given in a wonderful letter to the

New England Journal of Medicine. The doctor writing in said that he and his young son had gone to the state fair. There, in a crowd, they heard hoofbeats, and as the crowd parted a zebra appeared. From this, the writer said, he derived three lessons. First, there are zebras. Second, sometimes when you hear hoofbeats, it's a zebra. Third, if he had not at some time previously learned what a zebra looked like, he would not have known what it was when he saw it.

So the neurologists struggled marvelously with their zebras. Then, dramatically, the formalin-soaked veil of cloth would be removed from the brain slices, and everyone would huddle around the table in a knot. Microscope slides were projected on the screen, and the "pathognomonic"— identifying—signs of a rare, or, more embarrassing, a common disorder— the distribution of a certain brightly colored stain, or the tell-tale shape of a tiny body enclosing a virus—would manifest themselves to us in the darkness.

On Thursday nights the residents and students stayed late to pore over an unknown in a more relaxed atmosphere. These were pleasant and friendly times, with very little showmanship and a great deal of learning. The unknowns—a set of slides of a given pathological brain—were difficult. As I adjusted my microscope again and again, studying the arcanely deranged patterns of brain cells, stained and counterstained so beautifully, I wished that I could see more, know more, learn more; but in any case I was grateful to be there.

Toward the end of the rotation I had the opportunity to make several visits to a famous pathology laboratory—affiliated with Galen—in the state school for the mentally retarded. I wended my way among the low sad buildings, full of people with calm and vacant faces, some of whom were always about on the grounds. I thought about the horrible errors in their brains, tantamount to errors in the substance of their souls. Then I would enter the farthest building, sit down at the microscope, and gaze at exquisitely thin slices of the brains of some of their predecessors, trying to learn just what had gone wrong.

I was supposed to do a little independent study and make a presentation to the group of physicians and residents. The case I chose was not one of retardation—these were too discouraging—but a rare, relatively subtle and fascinating disorder—a zebra—known as Kallmann's syndrome. This was a familial disorder consisting of low levels of sex hormones in the male, combined with an inability to smell. The inability to smell was well understood to result from a congenital absence of the olfactory bulbs—small paired structures in the forward part of the base of the brain. The brain of our patient with Kallmann's syndrome showed no trace of the olfactory bulbs whatever.

But the low levels of gonadal hormones were something else again. These were difficult to explain, and I pored over a stack of papers in the files of the friendly professor in charge of the lab, trying to figure out what was known. Several key papers were in French, and I had to work to make out what they were saying. A senior French neuropathologist had thought that the explanation lay in the absence of some very tiny groups of cells embedded deep within the hypothalamus—a major structure at the base of the brain. But one of his disciples, in an almost painfully respectful paper, had destroyed his hypothesis, meticulously measuring, delineating, even constructing large wooden models of the supposedly absent little nuclei that were in fact present in three brains of Kallmann's syndrome patients. My patient's brain had them as well, so this lead went nowhere. There were no other clues, and after some days at the microscope, my eyes straining to see more, I decided that I would not discover the cause of Kallmann's syndrome. It had eluded my elders and betters, and it would have to stay in the wings of clinical brain science, awaiting someone more meticulous or imaginative than I.

12

MEDICINE I

A Failure of the Heart

As with any major department at Galen, the chief of service in the department of medicine was world renowned and ruled his domain with an iron hand. Harold Greenspan, a plump middle-aged man of medium height, was the author of a textbook of cardiology, the co-author of a textbook of medicine, and the supervisor of a suite of laboratories with dozens of junior members and postdoctoral fellows—all this in addition to running one of the largest medical services in the nation. He had legal as well as moral responsibility for hundreds of patients a month and dozens of scientific publications a year, not to mention the teaching of many medical students and residents.

Shortly before I started medicine on his service, his career had come under a cloud. A young researcher in one of his laboratories—himself an apparent star—had faked a series of experiments. Dr. Greenspan not only had missed this, but had run interference for the miscreant. It was one of the most publicized of a number of episodes in which men like Dr. Greenspan—caricatures of the overextended, high-pressure medical administrator—had found themselves drawn into a vortex of sordid revelations that undermined their own reputations and the reputation of medical science itself.

Each case was considered on its merits, and the supervisor in each was more or less implicated or vindicated—usually some of both—in a tacky examination of his relationship with the underling. One had failed to read the proofs of a book chapter he had written, wherein his minions had allowed lengthy passages to be quoted from other authors without citation

—in effect, accidental plagiarism. Another had supervised a person who painted black patches on white mice to fake a crucial experiment about the suppression of skin transplant rejection. Another had signed a number of published papers reporting data on heart function in dogs that had simply never been collected.

The discussion always focused—to some extent properly—on the details. No one ever said, "Hey, these guys are too overextended. This isn't business—it's medical science and patient care. You can't get that big and still be the man on the ethical spot, the man who signs the paper guaranteeing the patient's safety or the publication reporting a new discovery." No one questioned the system that enabled and encouraged these men to take on duties that they could not conceivably discharge.

In the case of Dr. Greenspan, the very week in which I started on his service saw a flurry of news reports about his own sticky situation. His picture appeared in a leading journal, sitting behind his big desk with his hands palms up in the air, shrugging his shoulders, his face a comical study in innocent protest. The caption, amazingly, quoted him as saying, "*I got a bum rap.*" Not even a Pulitzer-prize-winning cartoonist could have drawn a better caricature than that priceless photograph or thought up a better caption than his own marvelous words.

Despite this ludicrous notoriety, Dr. Greenspan strode heftily into the conference room where we medical students waited for him, and delivered a rigorous, fiery orientation speech as arrogantly as if he had just won the Nobel Prize. "People are always telling you," he began stridently, "at the beginning of each course, 'This is the most important course you'll ever take.' I'm telling you the same thing about this course. The only difference between me and them is that I'm right. If the decision to go to medical school was right, regardless of what field you go into, medicine is the most important course you'll ever take." More important to the future pediatrician than pediatrics? More important to the future obstetrician than catching babies? But this was not the time or place for questions; I had learned that lesson long before and painfully enough. I simply listened, smiling secretly at the published image of him. His remarks lengthened into a half-hour monologue in which his detachment from our little group—there were only a dozen of us—was studied and effective. As a teacher I knew the situation well. His detachment was of the sort that had no doubt helped make possible the gross fraud perpetrated right under his nose.

He did have one sensible piece of pedagogic advice. He declared that it was absurd to try to read through the textbook of medicine—more than two thousand densely printed, double-column pages—in sequence. This strategy was a fool's errand. If your mind were not a sieve at the start, it would be one long before page two thousand. You could read it endlessly, returning from the end to page one in an infinitely repetitious circle, and the fifth circle through the material would be not much more familiar than the first. Yet this pigheaded approach was exactly what had been recommended to us by the surgery instructor with regard to the almost equally long and dense surgery textbook.

Greenspan, in contrast, drew a map of North America on the blackboard. "Medicine," he said, with an excitement in his eye that for a few minutes transcended his arrogant banality, "is a vast continent. You don't try to march across in some preconceived order. You conquer it patient by patient." He drew a little semicircle, like a nibble out of the land mass, somewhere near North Carolina. "You get a patient with hepatitis, and you read about it while you take care of the patient. You've conquered a little piece of the territory of the liver, and also of that of viral diseases." Now he drew a nibble out of Oregon. "Then you get a patient with myocardial infarction. So you read a couple of chapters on that, and you conquer a bit of the heart. Then you get a patient with liver cancer—so you go back here and make some more progress in your knowledge of the liver.

"You never conquer the whole mass. But you make these little inroads, a patient at a time. You read where you have to read, a chapter here, a chapter there, and one day you turn around and you know a tremendous amount of medicine. But you must read in relation to your patients, or it will just never stick in your mind."

I knew this was wise advice, and I was beginning to soften my opinion when Dr. Greenspan began to tell a story of a medical student some years before. This hapless young man had had the misfortune to share a patient directly with the chief. Some weeks after his rotation ended, Dr. Greenspan ran into him and asked him if he had seen the patient, who was once again hospitalized. "No sir," went the reasonable reply, "I'm on another service now." Dr. Greenspan now looked pointedly grave and shook his head slowly. The pause had its effect. He cast his steely gaze across our little group. "That's just not good enough," he intoned in solemn severity. "I want you all to understand that. That is just not good enough. Your patient is always your patient, no matter what service you happen to be transferred to. I let that student know that he simply was not doing his job."

All this, I knew, was a lie. I was not sure it was a cynical lie—Dr.

Greenspan was doubtless as capable of deceiving himself as he was of deceiving us. But this appearance of enduring concern for patients was phony. His own reputation for remoteness was legendary. His medical students and residents were so brutalized by the pressures he put on them that it was a miracle if they remembered their patients from one day to the next—much less when they were transferred off his service. He might as well have warned us to check for dust on the windowsills and read up on nineteenth-century hospital design. Of course we wanted to care about our patients in that personal way. But he and others like him had set up our training in such a way as virtually to prevent such caring. I did not take kindly to this transparent attempt to shift the blame from himself to us. And it made him ridiculous, like a Charlie Chaplin parody of authority.

At the end he asked, "Any questions?" I clocked a five-second silence, before he turned on his heel and, white coat streaming behind him, sailed out of the conference room. Joan Simon, one of the nicest of the medical students, fell face first on to the table in a simulated faint. The laughter was general, and felt wonderful.

If there is one word that comes to my mind when I think of Sally Brass, that word is *vulgar.* Of all the residents I worked with and under, many of whom were abrasive and difficult, she was the only one who seemed to me abusive. With all the mistakes I saw, with all the incompetence I thought the system could absorb, she was the only one who I thought should not be allowed to be a doctor.

The first time I met her had been some months earlier at the ten o'clock meal—we had been introduced by a resident I was working with on neurology. She had spent ten minutes delineating, with many sordid details, a sex course she had taken at her medical school, complete with unnecessary depictions of the sex habits of the weirdest patients presented, obviously delivered for shock value. She was a small, tightly built, good-looking brunette with short, swept-back hair, who wore tight slacks and three-inch heels—totally inappropriate for either the work or the image of a physician. Her sweaters, too boldly colored for the hospital, generally pulled across her substantial chest. The nurses, always a good barometer of the phony in physicians, detested her.

When I encountered her on my first day in medicine I knew immediately that I was in trouble. She smiled and sneered at the same time. "Do you mind if I abuse you?" she would ask rhetorically, and without waiting for an answer, joking or otherwise, she would proceed to outline my next bit of scut work. Her requests were often reasonable, but the tone was invariably insulting, and there was much that no resident had ever asked me to do before. "Shit slides downhill," she would say, in self-justification, turning her back on another undesirable and uneducational task that she had handed over to me.

As much as I might dislike the situation, I was stuck with her for two full months. We had "long call"—all-night call—every fourth night, and "short call"—staying till ten or midnight to admit at least one patient—on the second of the four nights. We were together approximately one hundred hours a week, under the most obnoxious and stressful conditions. We would be as intimate as two people ever get in a work situation—battlefield buddies possibly excepted—and we disliked each other intensely.

My first day on the rotation was my first night on call. I admitted a patient named Meyer Rosen, an old man who had had his fourth stroke and who looked a decade older than his sixty-seven years. He had suffered from high blood pressure—a classic risk factor for stroke—for many years, but it was now supposedly under medical control. His earlier strokes had affected the left side of his body, more or less transiently, but now he had a new right-sided weakness together with slurred speech, pointing to damage to the left, dominant hemisphere. He was a pleasant man, easy to talk to and unconcerned about his deficit. I was left to speculate whether this was a basic character trait or part of the classic syndrome of right brain damage. His three earlier strokes, causing the right-sided damage, could have blunted many negative emotions and rendered him more or less calm about his illness.

That night I became aware that the admission records I prepared in medicine would be purely an exercise. In surgery and other rotations, the interns had actually relied on medical-student notes, themselves going over the patients only briefly. This made one feel significant, at least as an information gatherer. But in medicine, I soon saw, my notes would be completely ignored as the patient was evaluated first by Sally Brass and then by her second-year resident, who compared their respective findings without reference to mine, and arrived at a conclusion about the patient. Hours later Sally would read my six- or eight-page admission note—she was in the habit, in fact, of reading it and criticizing it in detail, purely as an exercise, at around three A.M., when both of us were in desperate need of sleep. Other than painful, all-embracing sleepiness, I remember virtually nothing from these sessions except humiliating nitpicking. For example, I should use more abbreviations, as if all our notes were not already sufficiently hard to decode, making almost every teacher we had urge fewer of them. At any rate, Meyer Rosen and I were friends. No matter what happened between me and Sally, there would always be the patients, and I could always secure some sort of relationship with them.

On Wednesday, our short-call day, we admitted Marylou Kosinski, a pretty young woman with Graves disease of the thyroid. This had been alleged by some psychiatrists and internists to be a psychosomatic disorder, but that theory was also widely doubted. I was curious, but there was no time to explore this patient's psychological history. She was classically hyperthyroid, with a fast heart-rate, jumpy knee jerks and other reflexes, a tremor in her hands at rest, and a diffusely increased size of the thyroid gland—a goiter. She had the striking, slightly bulging eyes of the hyperthyroid patient—memorable because they give so much the impression of emotional intensity: alarm, or antagonism, or love. You could see a rim of white between her irises and her lower lids, a really classic sign. And when I performed a diagnostic test—asking her to follow a vertically moving finger with the eyes—her upper lids lagged behind the pupils on the downward run. This too was a classic sign. Her thyroid gland function tests were grossly abnormal, and she was expected to come to surgery for removal of much of the gland, since other therapies had already failed.

On Friday I was on again, and we admitted Sophie Hellman, a pleasantly plump, curly-haired old woman with the vividly named disorder crescendo angina. Angina was a distinctive kind of chest pain, often a crushing or tightening sensation under the breastbone, caused by constriction of the arteries supplying the heart, and it frequently occurred during exertion. The pain was often terrifying and of course limited activity; a little bit more constriction might turn anginal pain into a heart attack— the death of a piece of heart muscle starved of oxygen-bearing blood. Sophie—and she insisted that we call her that, in a characteristically pleasant and friendly way—had *crescendo* angina, meaning increasing frequency or intensity of pain, or pain at rest instead of just on exertion, or pain unresponsive to the medicines (usually nitroglycerin) that had previously controlled it. It was also known as "unstable" angina, but "crescendo" seemed to me more evocative and appropriately ominous.

After Sophie was settled in, her cheerful adaptation belied by an occasional bad pain, Friday night was not very busy. By around ten the ward was darkened. The nurses seemed more relaxed, anticipating going home, and grateful to have the daytime bustle of doctors off their backs. Most patients were sleeping. A tiny, shriveled, hunchbacked woman in her nineties needed blood. With soda-bottle glasses in thick black rims, and black, high-soled, stiff, braced orthopedic shoes, Evelyn Laquette made the perfect picture of the cute little old lady. She was the proverbial "L.O.L. in N.A.D."—an infamous, prohibited, and frequently used chart note meaning "Little Old Lady in No Acute Distress."

Of course, L.O.L.'s in N.A.D. had their way of "crumping"—short for trying to die—even after they were buffed to a bright sheen of stable functioning. But Evelyn was a known player, a frequent visitor from her nursing home, with multiple problems none of which was immediately life-threatening. The blood was for prevention of anemia, since she was known to be losing blood in her stool from an undetermined gastrointestinal source. I found my way to the blood bank downstairs, and, in my fatigue, dazzled by the late-night lights, signed for the blood and brought it back to Evelyn. Evelyn was tractable, even helpful, when she was not confused; but on this night she was very confused, and it was a struggle to get an I.V. line started on her. But this was not a struggle that an ace medical student (or for that matter even an average one) couldn't rise to.

After I'd started it and hung the blood on poor confused Evelyn, I turned to see about the commotion in the adjacent bed. A nurse named Susan was trying to put a sweet, somewhat demented black woman named Helen back in bed. Susan, a pert, cute, no-nonsense woman, had worked out a strategy not unlike my wife's bedtime strategy with our children. She climbed into bed with Helen, suggesting that they watch T.V. together. As I was helping her lift Helen into place in the bed, Sally Brass came into the room to find out what was keeping me. I told her that I had hung the blood. As for what I was doing when she walked in, it seemed to need no explanation.

From her contemptuous look, it was evident that she thought I was wasting time. I followed her out, assuming that she had something else for me to do. She did not. She accused me of flirting with the nurses. "Nurses care, doctors cure," was a saying among the nurses, and it certainly seemed to apply to Galen medicine; since nurses knew that doctors rarely cured, the irony was not lost on anyone.

After the ten o'clock meal, which occasioned the most brutal joking by residents about patients that I had heard since leaving surgery, I came back into Evelyn's room to check on the blood I had hung. The blood was fine, but Evelyn was covered with feces, confused, rubbing her hands in it, and bringing her hands to her face. Instead of calling a nurse immediately, I began cleaning her up a bit; I knew a nurse would be along soon. One appeared almost immediately—a new one, whom I didn't know, since the shift had changed. Together we cleaned the mess up and changed Evelyn's diaper. It was a tender exercise that reminded me of changing the diapers on my children, although these were much more foul-smelling. Like a baby, Evelyn seemed baffled but touched by the attention.

When we were finished, the nurse decided to compliment me in front of Sally Brass; this, evidently, had been refreshingly atypical medical-student behavior. Sally interrupted, a look of disgust and impatience on her face. "You know, you don't have to do that," she said, oblivious of the nurse. The implication was clear. I had been through most of my third year: hadn't I learned yet that medical students did not do nurses' work?

The ward was utterly quiet, but I had to stay up for another three hours, until two-thirty, mostly marking time while waiting for Sally to get ready to go over my admission note. I drew a few bloods for her and started an I.V. When she disappeared for a while I read about angina. Finally she went over my note and pronounced it acceptable—reading in front of me while I half-dozed uncontrollably. She suggested a few abbreviations and then we went to bed—in an airless, tiny on-call room in bunk beds at right angles to each other. It took me half an hour to fall asleep, during which I listened to her snoring and thought about the next two months of my life.

Two hours later, at five-thirty, I woke up to the shrill blast of Sally's beeper. "What's up?" I said, as she put down the telephone. She mumbled, ". . . arrest . . . seven four . . ." and was gone. I pulled my shoes on and began running after her. I stopped on each floor starting at the top—for other reasons, that had been my best guess as to where the arrest might be. I checked 874, 774, 674, and 574, to no avail. Then I thought of seven something four and ran back up, finally finding the code spilling out of room 784.

It was Geraldine Feeley, an eighty-two-year-old woman who had suffered a massive stroke that left her aphasic—devoid of language—and generally demented. I remembered her story vaguely from rounds, and I'd thought that she was definitely D.N.R. What was she doing being coded?

But of course, this was not a good question, and I knew enough not to ask it. As soon as I entered the room I was asked to take arterial gases, and this made me feel important—until I realized that I had been offered an opportunity, not asked to help. (I remembered the conversation from neurology, regarding another demented patient who the residents thought should be D.N.R.: *"Is this a slow code?" "This is a medical student code."*) I drilled the femoral artery quickly and smoothly (just luck) and watched the bright red blood pump rhythmically into the syringe. I put it on ice and sent it down with a courier who, magically, had been waiting nearby. Then the intern who had been bagging the patient turned the ambu bag over to me.

I was now wide awake. I began to bag steadily and strongly, breathing for Geraldine Feeley with all my meager skill. I was careful to keep the rhythm steady, careful to keep the mask sealed tightly over her mouth and nose, careful to watch her chest rise and fall with each squeeze of the bag. I really put my heart into it. But I gradually realized that I was missing the subtext. Residents were milling around talking about the code status. Some nurses glared at them in moral indignation while they tried to talk their way out of the code. Finally, after extensive discussion, one of the senior residents went out of the room to call the hospital lawyer.

I did not stop bagging, but I began to pay more attention to the parallel conversations among the residents and the nurses. Slowly, I pieced together the story. Geraldine Feeley had no next-of-kin, no family living with her through this devastating final illness. The only person following her was a lawyer for the nursing home, a man who had never met her. This lawyer had approved a D.N.R. status for her until two or three days before. For reasons that would remain unclear to all of us involved with the case, he had changed his mind about this the previous day.

In other words, if she had had her cardiac arrest a few days earlier, she would have been allowed to die in peace. The resident who had been sent out to the telephone stuck his head in the door and said he had got the hospital lawyer, who in turn had said that he would talk to the nursing home lawyer. I think we all felt that there was something satisfying about these lawyers having to get up before six o'clock in the morning to talk about Geraldine Feeley, since we were all up desperately trying to save her life—a life we did not think we had any business saving.

My hands were getting tired, and I had pains in both forearms, but I went on bagging. The senior resident who was doing the telephoning went out again. Five minutes later he came back shaking his head. "The lawyer says we have to intubate," he said. This they did, later regretting that they had not offered the intubation to me.

I took femoral artery blood for blood gases four times in the next hour and was responsible for bagging her all the rest of the time. All my hand and arm muscles ached. Throughout this time people were joking about her code status, and about the waste of the code and of the I.C.U. bed she would go to. One of the nurses seemed particularly bitter. She chewed on the inside of her mouth as she stared at Geraldine Feeley's chest rising and falling under the pressure of my bagging. She kept shaking her head and saying, "I wish that lawyer could see this. I just wish he could be here to see this."

I kept on with the bagging. Geraldine's pupils were fixed and constricted, as if she were trying to shut out the sight of a strange world. Her eye reflexes were gone. This form of coma was indicative of massive stroke damage to the pons, a part of the brain stem that was essential to all mental and physical functioning. Not only recovery, but life for any length of time, would be virtually impossible. But she would go to the I.C.U. to be kept alive, at great expense—expense that could be translated, somewhere down the line, into care withheld from other, salvageable patients —for a few more painful, hopeless days.

At seven-thirty or seven-forty we had walk-rounds as usual, and we discovered that there had been another, much sadder crisis. Tillie Markowitz, a sedentary eighty-year-old woman who had been admitted for an apparent mild stroke, had suffered a second, serious one. She had come in two days earlier because of a confusional state and a left-sided weakness that proved to be transient. She had also had a puzzling point tenderness in her left breast. But she had clearly been recovering from her stroke.

Now she was completely disoriented and had a much more marked right-sided weakness. As we walked into her bright, new hospital room we saw a plump, gray-haired, toothless old lady with a sweet disposition and bright eyes lying in bed looking up at us, much more confused than she had been the day before. I remembered her chest X-ray. She wore a charm around her neck—it was the Hebrew word "chai," meaning "life," in large gold letters—that had made a stunning symbolic shadow on the skeletal image of her X-ray. Now it hung around her neck, having dismally failed to protect her, as if in accusation of her doctors.

Beside her bed stood the only one of her doctors who was not part of "the A team," the facetious designation our group had for itself. He was Morris Nathan, an elderly internist who looked at us now with tears in his eyes. It was the only time during the course of my medical training when I saw tears of pity in a physician's eyes. Tears of frustration, psychological stress, or self-pity, yes, but tears of sorrow for a patient I would see only once.

"What happened?" he asked us, suppressing a sob. The residents offered him completely blank faces. "I can't understand what happened. She was doing so well."

"The A team" seemed to resent his intrusion, his emotion, and the implicit—if mild—accusation in his question. They did not answer him, at least not meaningfully. They did not engage, confront, comfort, or respond to him in any way. He walked off slowly and sadly, taking away his questions, and his memories of a vital woman he had known as a patient for many years who had now suffered a sudden change that had permanently beclouded her mind.

As soon as he was out of earshot, they began mercilessly to make fun of him. They didn't miss a beat. Between Tillie Markowitz's room and the next, which happened to be on another floor, they exchanged remarks about "gome docs" and "stroked out visits" and had a number of good laughs about Dr. Morris's tears. These exchanges clinched my judgment about the A team. At issue for me was no longer what I could learn from them but whether and how I might be able to survive them.

The following week I admitted a reserved, impeccably mannered old woman for a thorough work-up of a cancer on her left great toe, presumed to be a metastasis of an old adenocarcinoma of the lung. Years had passed, and she had been pronounced recovered after partial lung removal, but this cancer on her toe raised the possibility of recurrence. I wrote a long and detailed admission note.

Once again, beginning at three o'clock in the morning, Sally read and criticized my eight-page admission note, picking at it mechanically even while admiring its thoroughness. I had done a lot that day and night and was in no mood for this exercise. I was fighting sleep desperately. I don't know how she found the resources to go after me so pointlessly at such a late hour, but I am sure I did not show the proper appreciation. I answered a few of her stylized, typical, humiliating questions—as a teacher I knew how easy it was to pose unanswerable questions to any student. Our exchanges became sardonic.

Finally I said, "Look, Sally, I want you to understand something. I am not trying to get a grade of Excellent. I am trying to pass the course. That means I need a grade of Satisfactory. So why don't you tell me exactly what I have to do to get a grade of Satisfactory? Because I don't intend to do any more than that."

This was meant, in part, to insult her, and that was the way she took it. But mainly I meant it as a practical strategy for survival. Of course, I did not really mean, nor did I practice, any form of minimalism in relation to patient care. What I intended and in fact carried out was minimalism in relation to Sally's hazing. She understood this. She and I were now at a standoff. She knew perfectly well that I was far above the line separating Satisfactory from Unsatisfactory, so she had little to hold over me. She did not like this situation, but all she could do about it was to make my life difficult.

All weekend I had to put up with more of Sally's harassment. Whether it was because she was ten years younger than I, or because she did not go home, as I did, to a demanding family situation on our nights off, something made her much more tolerant of sleeplessness than I was. She knew this and made certain that I would not get any sleep unless she did, too. At two or three or four A.M. she would take over the on-call room— the only place either of us could sleep—and dictate her discharge notes for another hour. She could have used any telephone in the hospital, and there were many other quiet places on our floor at that hour where she could have done the work. But she always dictated from the one place I could sleep.

I was therefore slowly accumulating a sleep debt of the sort that makes you irritable, clumsy, foggy-minded, and finally, in my case at least, depressed. In this condition I had to write detailed notes, answer difficult, sometimes trivial questions about patients and their illnesses, and prepare oral reports on many subjects. I was not alone in this, of course; interns, at least, were as sleep-deprived as I was, and the other medical students were not far behind. But I was the only one on this rotation with a family at home who could not "crash"—collapse into bed and stay until I was on duty again. And I was by far the oldest among the medical students, and much older than any of the residents.

Sleep-deprivation had been more tolerable on other rotations, where I got along with the residents and had a genuine interest in the subject— neurology, obstetrics, even surgery. Here it was much harder to bear. To make matters worse, the tooth on which I had had root-canal work done hurt virtually all the time. I was a patient again. I visited the dentist, and when another round of his tinkering failed, I realized that the tooth had to go. This sign not only of aging but of mortality—losing a tiny piece of myself—added to my overall sense of losing ground.

Still, I tried not to lose my sense of humor. I admitted a patient with a fabulous rich Irish brogue and found myself taking his blood while his television blared away. On the tube was a doctor show, and the story centered on a patient with a fabulous rich Irish brogue, being taken care of by an intern with little experience. As I popped the needle into his vein, the television intern was starting an I.V. on his Irish patient, who was saying charmingly, "I just hope you know what you're doin'." My patient didn't make the connection, and I had to wait until I got out into the hall before I burst out laughing.

Comic relief was also provided by Justin Mirsky, an intern on the service who made Sally Brass look silly. He was not exactly the most dedicated physician, but his cynical humor was a breath of fresh air. He was going into neurology, so he lacked that intense straight-arrow fierce competitiveness that characterized Galen internal medicine. He was tall and thin, with a bent nose, and he seemed dapper for an intern. His personal style was cheerful, almost breezy, yet also somehow harried and fast.

He was the one who always brought up the Dubnoff scale during X-ray rounds. This was a scale made famous in the novel *House of God*, for measuring the extent to which the patient's jaw was observed to be descending over the breastbone. Patients were graded from one to a maximum of five. The score was highly correlated with age after eighty or so, and a five was reserved for the patient whose head was sunk way down on his or her chest. A Dubnoff four or five was always good for a laugh.

Sometimes, though, you couldn't quite tell whether Justin was joking or serious. One day after assigning a patient a Dubnoff four point two, "approximately," he said to the staff radiologist, a senior physician in that department, "By the way, are you aware that four patients in the past year have had *major* invasive procedures done on the basis of misreading of X-rays by the radiology intern on at night?" Justin sounded as if he had been personally burned. "I don't think," he went on, "that the radiologist on at night should be an intern."

The radiologist, a graying, impressive-looking man in his fifties, literally looked down his nose at Justin. "This," he said pointedly, "is a teaching institution. You're going to have mistakes. I'm a little surprised to hear that four major mistakes were made this year. But it's a teaching institution and there are going to be mistakes."

Justin then referred to a presumably more enlightened neighboring state where "it's illegal for an intern to be the only doctor who sees someone in the emergency room"; but the older man was clearly not swayed, and Justin finally retreated and gave up needling him.

When I came back on to the ward that morning after X-ray rounds, I found Rosita Mercer, a black woman with multiple illnesses and a difficult personality, crying in the arms of a nurse. None of the nurses or residents really liked her, but crying made her suddenly endearing. Through her tears she was talking about fear—of the breast biopsy she had unexpectedly been scheduled for. She was not afraid of the procedure but of "what they're gonna find." The nurse was simply comforting this difficult lady— touching, talking, saying whatever was necessary, including, at many moments, nothing. Out in the hall, after the patient had settled down, I praised the nurse and said, "I have yet to see a doctor do something like that." She said she had, on occasion, but rarely. She went on to attribute their lack of humanity to the loss of it during the brutal pressures of residency. "I couldn't do it," she said. And she and I both knew that neither of us thought that nursing was easy.

On walk-rounds the next morning a discussion began, for some reason, about the brutalizing pressures of residency. "Does it have to be this way?" I asked.

"No," said Sally, simply and emphatically.

Margaret, the severe, harried second-year resident, said, "It's been this way in every institution I've worked in."

"Why?" I asked, trying to keep the exasperation out of my voice, and risking, as usual, the implicit or explicit censure visited upon those who ask questions.

"Two reasons," Margaret said, without breaking her stride. "Number one, the system is designed so that everybody comes out like Mark Troy." Troy was the chief of house staff at Galen, a position reserved for the most aggressive straight-arrow of all the residents in the previous year's class of chief residents—a group already selected for unrelenting competitiveness. He lectured to the medical students once a week, and his all-consuming achievement motivation—along with something mechanical that could be called dedication—was something to see. If she was right, the system was geared to produce a type of physician that only a few residents could or would become. What would happen to the others, the majority? Margaret, no slouch herself, went on as if reading my thoughts. "You become an automaton," she said rather distantly. "You have so much to do." She spoke the last sentence very slowly, as if it had great meaning for her. She seemed to have forgotten that she was giving us two reasons.

This time, Sally prodded her: "Number two."

"Number two? Slave labor," she said, and strode into the next patient's room.

I finally got the hang of tolerating the time I had to spend with Sally. Early one Sunday morning she came up to me at the nurses' station and said warmly, "By the way, I have some feedback for you on a patient." She was smiling and looked embarrassed. "It's not very positive feedback." I imagined that she was going to tell me that a patient had complained about me, and I couldn't understand why she was handling me so gently. "You remember Mrs. Hellman?" she asked.

"Sure," I said. Mrs. Hellman was the woman with crescendo angina who had been discharged in good condition several days earlier.

"Well, she crumped. She came back into the E.W. with a massive M.I. And unfortunately she died in the C.C.U. the next day."

"Wow," I said, inanely but authentically. I felt myself going pale.

"I don't want you to worry, it's nothing you did wrong." She spoke very quickly now, looking away. "I just wanted you to know what happened."

"Well," I said, trying to collect my thoughts. This was the first patient I had lost who seemed as if she really should have lived. "Could we talk about what we might have done differently?"

Sally was elsewhere. "Ooh . . . ooh . . . that's . . . that's . . . it's a Schubert tone poem." It took me a minute to realize that she was talking about the music on the radio. She began to translate the lyric, obviously proud of her German. She was smiling, leaning toward the radio, and conducting the music with one hand. I too started to get caught up in the translating effort. In a little while the piece was over, and the radio announcer identified it as Schubert's song "The Erlkönig." Sally snapped her fingers and beamed brightly, having more or less scored. We did not return to the subject of Mrs. Hellman.

A short while later I was rounding with her—the Sunday morning version consisted of breezing through the patients' rooms, listening quickly to their chests, asking one or two questions, checking their numbers— temps, blood pressures, any recent tests—and writing brief notes. Sally in particular had no use for dwelling on the problems of other interns' patients, although as the Sunday on-call intern she was responsible for all of them. She expected me to help her write her notes, which I was doing, taking half the patients myself. But when I came to Nancy Wilson, the similarity of her case to that of Sophie Hellman slowed me down.

Mrs. Wilson had the same disease, crescendo angina. There was a brief, barely legible note scrawled by her admitting physician, stating the rather ominous-sounding risks. Had Mrs. Hellman been discharged too early? Had her medications been wrong? Had she failed to understand how to react to her symptoms? I would not, clearly, get any answers to these questions from Sally, but Mrs. Wilson became a sort of minor expiation for Mrs. Hellman. I spent some time talking with her, and she showed me the little scrawled note, asking me to explain what it meant. Our time together stretched to thirty minutes, which did not seem long to me, but Sally had wanted me out of there in something less than five.

I finished rounding with Sally and, ignoring her for a while, spent ninety minutes writing a summary of my conversation with Mrs. Wilson. She had asked me about the risks, and I had been careful about explaining them. I had also been careful in examining her and in questioning her about her chest symptoms during the previous night and that morning. I now feared crescendo angina. And I was also paying a private tribute to Sophie Hellman's memory. I had liked Mrs. Hellman, and I liked Mrs. Wilson. I did not want her to die, too. And I wanted to put the things I had learned in the record. Sally, looking over my note, laughed at me.

Later that day, the senior physician in charge of the ward—and, incidentally, of my immediate education—came in to see some patients. I mentioned Mrs. Hellman to him and asked him if he could go over the case with me. He put me off—reasonably enough, I thought, for a Sunday afternoon. But over the next several days he put me off again and again until I finally gave up asking.

The next time I was on call I admitted a young man with a cardiomyopathy—an obscure disease of the heart muscle that would probably be fatal within a few years. He was being admitted to the research ward, and I spent a good part of the evening on a detailed, complex note about his illness and experimental treatment. When I finished, I looked around the quiet ward. Nothing was happening, and there was little or nothing to do. If I went searching for Sally Brass, she would certainly find some way to make my life miserable, and I saw no reason to hasten that eventuality. If she wanted or needed me, I was wearing my beeper.

The experimental ward was on the same floor of the hospital as the obstetrics unit, although in a different wing. Nostalgic for my happier days delivering babies, I drifted slowly over there, and found my old friend Wendy Feinberg, the resident who was the mother of the Down's syndrome baby. She was now on OB instead of GYN, and she was delighted to see me. Her smile reminded me that some of the residents I had worked with had been wonderful. Timidly, I asked her if there was any chance of my getting a delivery.

"How fast can you change?" she said, smiling more broadly than ever.

I changed fast into my surgical blues, and she shoved me into a birthing room. A Chinese lady who spoke no English was nearing the end of labor. The nurse taught me, once again, the Chinese word for "Push!" and, with the help of the nurse and a fairly calm mother, I delivered a perfect baby boy without a hitch of any kind. The tremendous high that I remembered from my OB rotation of months before was surging through my body. There was no feeling like it in the world. Half an hour earlier I had been sitting in the dark, rather dismal experimental ward, musing on the grim details of a cardiomyopathy and on the discouraging prospect of searching for Sally Brass. Now I was cutting the cord on a new small life, and handing the boy to his mother—to produce that smile I have never seen except in that situation, that takes over the whole of the human face.

A little later, after I changed back out of the surgical scrubs, I passed the baby in the hallway. For convenience, he was lying in an incubator-transport-crib; he didn't need one at all. The nurse who was taking him to the nursery was slowed for a minute by a dense crowd of relatives, at least ten of them, standing in a knot in the hall, pointing, exclaiming, smiling, gesticulating. They hadn't any idea who I was; but they made me feel like the greatest, the most important, and for the moment the happiest person in the world.

The end of the month came, and I asked to be transferred out from under Sally Brass's thumb. This was unusual but within the rules, and although it reflected badly on me I didn't really care anymore. It was a convenient time, since many people were changing shifts, and I was assigned to another intern, Lily Corwin. Compared to Sally she seemed like a fairy godmother. I would have to remain on the same service with Sally, but I would work directly only with Lily. A great weight lifted from my shoulders.

Dr. Gaines, the nondescript attending physician on the ward during April, took his medical students and residents out to lunch on the last day. The talk was entirely of examinations, a caricature of the pre-med syndrome rewritten for a cast of residents and a faculty physician. There had to be exams, of course, at any level, however high, but I couldn't believe these men and women could find nothing else to talk about. As a faculty member myself, I was familiar with occasions like this one. They were important, ceremonious. One tried to be at one's best, to leave the students with something that would be somehow memorable, something that would rise above the petty concerns of the everyday. All Dr. Gaines could think to talk about was one or another national board examination. After lunch, he took aside the two medical students assigned to him and told us that we could have done better. I did not argue with him, or, of course, tell him that I thought that he could have done better, too.

Finally, at my request—unlike his older colleague, who had paid no attention to me—he took us down to the record room to look at Sophie Hellman's record. We went over it carefully. Although Dr. Gaines was careful not to point an accusing finger at her physicians, he seemed critical of how her case was handled, and he seemed to agree that things had not been sufficiently explained to her. She had come into the hospital frightened by the fluttering in her chest, and especially by its increasing unresponsiveness to nitroglycerin. She had left the hospital confident that she had been taken care of, and two days later failed to react as she should have to the same symptoms. The main effect of the hospitalization had evidently been to make her inappropriately complacent. No one had explained to her the most important things she needed to know. So she sat through symptoms that had previously alarmed her, until the extreme constriction of her coronary arteries produced a devastating infarction of heart muscle. And Dr. Gaines accepted my summary of what doctors like to call "the take-home message": *An act of communication can sometimes be a life-saving intervention.* This was my very own "clinical pearl," and I promised myself never to lose sight of it.

13

MEDICINE II

Deathwatches

Later that week I was to attend the dinner for the annual National Book Awards, at which my book would ceremoniously *not* receive the award in the science category. Still, I had been nominated, and I could not forgo the chance to get away from the hospital and taste just a little bit of more or less mature excitement. Being gone from the hospital for thirty hours or so required special permission. No one took any notice of the reason for my absence, except to agree that it was legitimate. Hardly anybody I worked with at the hospital even knew I had written a book, much less one that was considered to be quite good. They greeted this news with a universal lack of curiosity.

Away from the hospital, and spending some time with an old friend, I had time to reflect on my strange situation. After a couple of drinks with him I invented a new syndrome—the one that I now had. R.P.T.A., or Rapidly Progressive Testicular Atrophy was a condition in which the destruction of the ego owing to disastrous role and status change, combined with sleeplessness, humiliation, ignorance, and confusion, led to a cumulative collapse of confidence and pride. I regretted somewhat the seemingly gender-specific designation I had arrived at—I knew perfectly well that there was a female equivalent of R.P.T.A. But it was my own damned syndrome, and I was damned well going to name it as I saw fit. I remembered the books by George Plimpton describing his strange, courageous, hilarious attempts to fill the shoes of top professional athletes in baseball, football, even boxing. Of his first, *Out of My League*— the baseball book—Hemingway had remarked: "The dark side of the moon of Walter Mitty." It was a phrase that lately was often in my mind.

When I returned to the hospital, refreshed by my narrow brush with fame, by having rubbed elbows with the great and near great of the strange world of publishing, I confronted again a total lack of curiosity about what I had been doing. I did not know whether to be impressed by how the residents' complete devotion to their work kept them from wondering about my experience or to be shocked by how little interest they had in anything outside the hospital. Nobody asked a single question. Within minutes I sank back into my medical student persona, resigned to my R.P.T.A.

Lily Corwin, my new intern, was full of kindnesses. She and I understood each other. She was a "rotator"—not going into internal medicine, but rotating through it on the way to her real career in obstetrics and gynecology. She was a small, dark, pretty woman in her mid-twenties with shoulder-length black hair, full lips, and large dark eyes. She did not like internal medicine but she was extremely efficient at it, and she had the intelligence to do what was necessary without suffering openly and without passing the buck. She did not take any pleasure in making my life miserable, and since she did not need to have me take very much off her hands, she assigned me only enough to keep me comfortably busy and to teach me what I could reasonably learn. She was detached from her patients—she said that she had once been "too involved in medicine" and had since learned to detach herself in order to survive. But she was good to them and more than fair to me.

Most of my attention that week was taken up by a fascinating and oddly funny patient called Josiah Brown. Mr. Brown had the Pickwickian syndrome, named for a character in Dickens's *The Pickwick Papers.* It consisted of hypersomnolence in the setting of obesity; and although Dickens had not understood the mechanism he had described it with characteristic vividness. Mr. Brown was a fat black man with a pleasant disposition who fell asleep frequently at any time of the day—while talking to me, while working, even, very dangerously, while driving. The Pickwickian syndrome basically consisted of poor sleep. The obesity caused apneas—breathing stoppages—throughout the night, preventing the patient from dropping very far into sleep, and/or waking him up continually. Sleep was so poor that daytime somnolence ensued, giving scientific validity to the Dickensian image of the fat man who dozes off at the most embarrassing moments. Josiah Brown was at Galen for an experimental treatment that involved a very mild form of machine respiration—this, it was hoped, would prevent apneas, thus permitting normal sleep.

I spent an hour or so a day watching this fat man sleep. He was wired for every conceivable measurement and pumped with oxygen-rich air—continuous positive airway pressure, or C-PAP—throughout his breathing cycle. It seemed to work dramatically on the first afternoon. At least during sleep, the symptom of apnea was improved. But as the days went on the somnolence did not improve. We could show that the excessive carbon dioxide in his blood was being cleared by the C-PAP, and according to the numbers and the chemistry he should have been in balance. But he continued to doze off as frequently as ever. Thus Mr. Brown was a clear case—one among many—of a man whose treatment was successful in terms of medical logic, but who for some reason did not get well.

Although Lily Corwin was my intern now, Sally Brass continued to hand me scut. This was sort of legitimate, since we were all on the same team. One Sunday morning while Lily was dictating discharge notes and I had finished my progress notes and was studying EKG's for an upcoming drill, my beeper rang, and when I called the announced number, Sally asked me, in her usual irritated voice, to administer the "chemo"—chemotherapy—on a patient on the floor. She was busy with another patient upstairs.

"I'm not sure if I know how to do that," I said.

"Come on!" she exclaimed angrily. "We talked about how to do that!" We had not, I knew, talked about it. But I felt chastised and guilty about hesitating, not to mention humiliated. She was accusing me—probably rightly, I thought—of unjustifiable ignorance and inappropriate timidity. *Toughen up,* I thought to myself. *Stop being afraid of your own shadow.*

I walked into the patient's room. He was a thin, dignified, white-haired Irishman in his middle sixties with lung cancer. He was admitted to the hospital every few weeks for several days of treatment with powerful chemotherapeutic agents. This time he was to receive adriamycin—"Big Red," as it was familiarly known—one of the most toxic of anticancer drugs. The nurse stood at the bedside holding up an enormous syringe full of the bright orange-red, potentially life-saving poison. She was in awe of it. I am not a superstitious person, but the physical energy of the room seemed somehow to converge on the fat cylinder of viscous, shiny red liquid.

It was one of the many situations in which the law forbade a nurse from doing a procedure that she could have done better than the medical student who was empowered by the same law to perform it. I had been in them many times—"pushing," or injecting, intravenous drugs was a classic one. Usually the nurse could give me the guidance I needed. Remarkably free of resentment, they walked medical students through this sort of procedure, teaching without humiliating, working with their own brains and the medical student's hands.

But this time I could tell something was different. This was no ordinary I.V. drug. The nurse was afraid of it. She asked me several times if I had ever pushed it before. I never lied in those situations, even when I was encouraged to lie. Finally I caught her fear and retreated. I decided to look up adriamycin.

Through a little reading and talking with this and another, more senior nurse, I discovered that what Sally had ordered me to do had been completely inappropriate. The injection of adriamycin was no "see one, do one, teach one" procedure. It required substantial skill, of the sort that was only gained through supervised practice. Not only was it capable of causing cardiomyopathy and heart failure—things that could conceivably happen no matter how skillful the injection—but it also carried a grave risk of severe local damage to the area around the injection site. A minor ineptness in the intravenous injection could produce extravasation—leakage of the poison into the skin and subcutaneous tissues. Large areas of skin could, without too much difficulty, be destroyed and made to slough off. Limb infection, destruction, amputation could ensue.

In short, that injection was something I could have had no business doing. *Talking* about how to do it, even if we had done so, could not conceivably have justified the order that Sally had given me. She came down herself, furious at having to do something that she had wanted done by me, and I kept my distance from her and the procedure.

Only much later did it occur to me that she had wanted me to do it because she did not feel confident about it herself. That was after I had heard that the patient in question had had extensive damage to his arm caused by extravasation of drug from the injection site.

Events continued to cascade over me at a pace that made it impossible to think about them or put them in order. Stress was the mode of learning, and I could only assume that I was absorbing something, but I had no idea what it was. One day I came home and found three neckties crumpled into the pockets of the jacket I had been wearing. This seemed hilarious, and symbolic of the absurdity of what I was doing. Fortunately it was early enough, and the weather was fine enough, so that I could march off with the children to the park. They at least did not find me ridiculous—or if they did it made me feel good.

I had some more root canal work done on my tooth, a last-ditch effort to save it. The pain was a constant undercurrent of my waking life. I was getting set to give up the tooth, and yet that gesture seemed such a defeat, such a concession to the aging process, such a symbolic victory for the illness all around me, that I felt I could tolerate almost any pain to put off that eventuality. As for sleep, I could not catch up, no matter what I did, and the chronic derangement of my physical and mental state became constant.

There was a new attending physician—a clever, fast-talking, very brilliant woman in her thirties, just a little younger than I—named Nancy Downing. She wore her hair in a severe boyish style, yet affected an out-of-date femininity in her clothing, usually wearing a bright madras or floral print cotton dress with a widely spreading straight or pleated skirt. The skirts spun out from her legs as she wheeled along the corridors, and during sit-down rounds I would sometimes be distracted by her stylish shoes or a glimpse of lacy slip under the cotton skirt. She seemed to me incredibly bright and yet somehow behind in her emotional development —clever problem-solving, of the high school math team sort, seemed to be the activity for which she reserved her highest praise. All in all, she reminded me, uncannily and amusingly, of some girls I had gone to elementary school with during the 1950s. Nevertheless I guessed that I could please Dr. Downing enough to get through the next month. I gave two patient presentations during the first few days she was on with us, and she responded to both of them with praise.

I attempted to cultivate a certain detachment from the situations I was constantly thrust into. Perhaps I was emulating Lily's earned detachment, but more likely I was responding reflexively—and of course, self-protectively. Was I already burning out? One morning on rounds an elderly Yiddish-speaking woman was being questioned by the residents. She understood little English. I knew a few words of Yiddish, and I knew that I could have helped.

But I did not step forward. I was exhausted and discouraged, and I was no longer thinking about what was best for the patient. I kept my mouth shut. To protect my own skin in this bizarre, abrasive environment, I withheld help from a patient who needed it. I betrayed the patient, I betrayed my cultural heritage, and I betrayed myself, and I felt thoroughly ashamed.

Still, there was room for occasional amusement. A new patient named Ida Goldberg, a ninety-year-old suffering from a rare form of arthritis—a rheumatologic curiosity—had been closely befriended by her roommate, Rachel Liebkind. I often saw them sitting in the hall outside their room talking and talking, two frail energetic elderly women in pastel-colored bathrobes with carefully coiffed gray hair. One morning on walk-rounds Mrs. Liebkind, the more talkative of the two—although the contest was close—told me the following story, in a Yiddish-accented, broadly gesticulating style.

She had been advised to anticipate her chest pain by taking a nitroglycerin on waking. This morning she had taken one at four A.M., after waking unusually early. However, she did not really begin to move about until two hours later, at six. At that time Mrs. Goldberg, in the adjacent bed, had had an episode of rheumatic pain. This had caused Mrs. Liebkind to become so upset that she had had chest pain, with the consequence that she would have to stay in the hospital longer. Although this was certainly not deliberate—she certainly wanted to go home—there was instrumental value in this sympathetic chest pain, since it kept the two women together a little longer.

Later that day I had slipped away from the ward to hear a Grand Rounds in neurology, given by my old friend Steve Scoble. Although he was a neurological resident, his rounds were about his trip to Nepal, where he had spent several months doing health surveys and investigating traditional Jhankri healers. They and their patients made a clear and firm distinction between spiritual healers and technical doctors. They thought that both were necessary, and they had no intention of short-changing a patient's access to either. As I listened to this beautiful, crisp ethnological lecture, complete with professional-quality photographs, I looked around me at the residents in the lecture hall, thinking that I could read their disdainful thoughts. They were entertained, and they would say that they were impressed. But they were writing Scoble off as a force of any kind in the aggressive, competitive future of Galen-style academic neurology.

Rounds were made terribly poignant now by the presence of three patients with probably terminal illnesses. One was a forty-two-year-old woman named Sara Norfleet who had a poor-prognosis form of acute leukemia. I first saw her sitting up in bed as the team entered her room. She looked cheerful and in complete command, regal in her elegant nightgown, her dark straight hair pulled back, a broad smile on her lovely, smooth face. She seemed the perfect image of the grown-up American princess, in all the best possible senses. And as if to cap it, she had a note by her bedside, among the usual get-well cards, signed by the president of the United States.

"You're interrupting the birth," she said charmingly, waving us aside with a gentle sweep of her hand. I realized after a moment that she had meant the television behind us, where a baby was being pulled out of a belly by Caesarean section. This was the hospital's closed-circuit network, and the new baby, crying now, was marvelous. Sally Brass and Jack Morgan, the new senior resident, began to talk to her about her chemotherapy, but she continued to try to talk about the birth a little. They complimented her on the way she was tolerating the chemotherapy, newly begun. She graciously acted pleased, if she was not exactly persuaded, by their praise. She was almost completely engrossed in watching a baby being born—or, more exactly, being wrenched well and squealing through a bloody, gaping wound—and she was smiling. She knew that she was beginning a desperate struggle for her life, with at best a fifty-fifty chance.

In the next room Jacob Fine, a skinny sixty-seven-year-old man with a gigantic swollen belly, lay gasping for breath. As we stood in front of each patient's room on walk-rounds in the morning, before going in, an intern or medical student had to present the patient in one or two minutes. Sally's summary of Mr. Fine's condition was "He's well enough to go someplace else to die."

We surrounded his bed and he slowly gained control of his breathing. His oxygen mask was misplaced, swung around at the side of his head. He ignored it. The previous day, he had evidently had a troubling visit from his wife—the residents had talked with her. She felt, and he knew she felt, that his suffering was being unnecessarily prolonged. He began now to speak, very slowly and haltingly, but more than he had spoken in days.

"My wife . . ." He paused for a long time. "I love her very much"—here there was another long pause, with heavy breathing—"and she loves me very much"—another long pause—"this band around my head . . ." Sally pursued this last remark, and discovered that he was referring to the oxygen mask. She put it on him and asked if it was better that way. It was. This served to remind me that Sally Brass had a definite way with patients. It was not my idea of a good bedside manner. It was certainly not gentle. But, however brusque, it was somehow supportive and warm. Some of them loved her.

The third patient was another young woman with terminal cancer. Her name was Judy Grant, and she occupied a double room with one of my own patients. One afternoon Lily and I were drawn to a discussion taking place between two nurses who were talking in hushed tones with looks of extreme concern. I asked what it was about, and Lily looked at Mrs. Grant. "She'll die today," she said.

"How do you know?" I asked.

"She has bad disease," she said simply.

The previous day, I had spent two hours in the double room, at the side of the next bed, working up her roommate, Mrs. Corliano, talking and joking. I had not known that Mrs. Grant, a young mother of two, was dying. The telephone had rung three times—twice for my patient, once for Mrs. Grant. She had struggled to the phone once, but the next time it rang she asked for it to be taken away. No one told me that this young, tired-looking roommate was on her death bed. No one treated her in any special way.

I looked at her now, and shook my head fiercely, as if to rid myself of something evil. Her death was to be as mundane and humdrum as everything else that went on on the ward. The nurses and doctors came and went, checking the numbers, writing their little progress notes—whispering occasionally behind her back, but otherwise talking with her as if nothing special were happening.

After finding out about her I was tempted to stay to see her die, to be near in some way to that obligate, terrifying, solitary experience. But I was not yet callous enough to intrude on her death just to satisfy my curiosity, although this would certainly be urged on me by some. Sally had already lamented that I had missed some poor patient's agonal breathing—the characteristic pattern of the last breaths of life. ("Haven't you heard it?" she had rasped. "You should hear it!")

Instead of hanging around for this spectacle, I left the hospital. I appreciated the afternoon light on the river. I bought myself a badly needed new pair of shoes. I went home and took my children to the park. I commented on my wife's new haircut. I ate a decent meal. And I had a very good night's sleep.

At Grand Rounds the following day, a world-renowned physician and pharmacologist talked about the carcinoid syndrome, a dramatic disorder first described only in 1953. It is caused by a tumor that secretes hormones and other chemical agents that themselves can cause more damage than the tumor. Most clearly implicated is the neurotransmitter serotonin. The symptoms include skin flushes, breaking of small blood vessels in the skin, diarrhea, heart valve damage, and constriction of the bronchial tubes.

To most victims death eventually comes from heart or liver failure.

To illustrate and edify, the lecturer showed a large projected image containing only this poem:

> *This man was addicted to moanin',*
> *Edema, confusion, and groanin',*
> *Intestinal rushes, great tricolored flushes,*
> *And died of too much Serotonin.*

From this lecture I had to run to the dentist to get the bad tooth broken out of my head. The dentist had urged it over a week earlier, and I had finally grown sick and tired—both quite literally—of being in constant pain. I sat down in the chair and was made to recline steeply. An injection of lidocaine was made in the appropriate spot. As I twisted my mouth, waiting for the numbness to overtake the sting of the needle track, two pretty dental assistants hovered rather peculiarly nearby. The dentist smiled, leaning over me, with a pair of what could only be called pliers in his right hand. I wanted to ask him to wait a little longer—the lidocaine had not quite taken—but I wasn't going to risk not being a good patient.

He pried open my mouth and reached in. Now I realized why the two young women had been poised so strangely near me. With amazing deftness, each grabbed one of my arms and pinned me to the chair. I looked up pleadingly, my mouth gigantically open. My tooth was gripped firmly between the teeth of the pliers and with a twisting motion the dentist pulled on it with all his strength. I heard a sickening enormous crack coming right from the center of my head, accompanied by a groan and an involuntary contortion of my body. The pain began immediately. Semi-anesthetized would be the word for what I was. The two women were lifting off, smiling tolerantly like indulgent older sisters. And I was already regretting the loss of the weight of them as my mouth filled with the taste of hot blood.

Shortly thereafter, back at the hospital, we had a ward conference focused on none other than Ida Goldberg, the charming old lady with rheumatoid arthritis whose expressions of pain exacerbated her roommate's angina. Her strange case was presented in every conceivable detail, and the delight of the thirty or so physicians at the marvelous thoroughness of the diagnostic work-up—X-rays, CAT scans, dozens of chemical tests—was not at all dampened by the fact that there was basically nothing they could do for her.

At the end of the discussions one senior physician shook his gray head, sighed, and smiled. "As George Burns says," he mused aloud, "not many people die after ninety." This was to become a favorite remark during morning rounds for the rest of the month, uttered ritually by the residents in chorus, whenever we left the bedside of a patient over ninety. The more hopeless the patient, the funnier the line.

Zelda Levine was not among them, and would not get to be. She was a charming, funny woman in her sixties who had inherited a form of familial tremor—slight frequent shakes in her hands. To control this, so she said, she had begun to drink heavily, and eventually became a lush while trying to chase away the tremor. Her alcoholism had led to multisystem disease—her body was breaking down. She had an enormous liver and spleen, so large that residents came from all parts of the hospital to feel them. Yet she smiled broadly as we stood around her bed. "Don't get old . . . " She made a sweep with her hand. "All you young people . . . Don't die!" she suddenly added. "But don't get old. Someday that'll be possible . . . Don't get old."

Jacob Fine, the gentle man with the big belly, whose wife loved him "very much," had entered in his hospital chart a document of the kind that is usually called a living will. It read as follows.

TO MY FAMILY, MY PHYSICIAN, MY LAWYER, MY CLERGYMAN
TO ANY MEDICAL FACILITY IN WHOSE CARE I HAPPEN TO BE
TO ANY INDIVIDUAL WHO MAY BECOME RESPONSIBLE
FOR MY HEALTH, WELFARE OR AFFAIRS

Death is as much a reality as birth, growth, maturity and old age—it is the one certainty of life. If the time comes when I, Jacob S. Fine, can no longer take part in decisions for my own future, let this statement stand as an expression of my wishes, while I am still of sound mind.

If I am terminally ill or suffering excessively so that there is no reasonable expectation of my recovery, I request that whatever steps are appropriate to ease my pain be taken, but that no excessive or exceptional mechanical or artificial means be used to prolong my life and that I be allowed to die naturally. I do not fear death as much as I fear the indignity of deterioration, dependence, and hopeless pain.

This request is made after careful consideration. I hope that you who care for me will feel morally bound to follow its mandate. I realize that this appears to place a heavy responsibility upon you, but it is with the intention of relieving you of such responsibility and of placing it upon myself in accordance with my strong convictions, that this statement is made.

Jacob S. Fine

Dated April 26, 1985
Witnessed by
Benjamin Fine
Ruth M. Fine

Jacob Fine's signature was not in a steady hand.

According to a note in the chart written by an attending physician, dated April 25, the resuscitation status was discussed with the patient, who proposed to sign a "living will—but this is not acceptable by the hospital." Consequently Mr. Fine's resuscitation status remained unclear.

In any case, and fortunately, given his inclinations, he was found pulseless and cold without respirations at 6:45 P.M. on Friday, May 6. It was the evening of the day in which he had made his poignant, halting statement about his love for his wife and her love for him—his stumbling final speech to the team of residents taking care of him. The Chief Cause of Death, as indicated on the death certificate, was metastatic sigmoid carcinoma, or widespread cancer of the sigmoid colon. His main problems while at Galen during this last illness had been bleeding from the upper gastrointestinal tract, multiple infections, and malignant ascites—the grotesquely swollen belly that Sally and I had one day drained of part of its burden of fluid. Analysis of that fluid had not resulted in a definitive diagnosis, but he was believed to have had two separate reasons for his swollen belly: destruction of the liver by metastatic cancer, backing up the drainage of the abdomen by the portal vein; and seeding of the peritoneal lining of the abdomen by other, smaller colonies of the cancer.

The day Sally and I had painfully drained his belly, I had noticed a copy of Dylan Thomas's collected poems lying on his tray table. I mentioned to him that I was also a fan of Dylan Thomas, but there was little response. By that time he had been thoroughly exhausted, and very nearly defeated, by his illness. Nevertheless he had something weakly resembling a fighting spirit. I could not help imagining that he had perhaps been reading and rereading the great villanelle with the refrain, "Do not go gentle into that good night / Rage, rage against the dying of the light."

On Sunday I was on call, and I ran into a resident I had worked with on psychiatry. His wife was in Galen, having lost a twenty-two-week pregnancy and become infected. The fetus had been perfectly formed. His wife was improving, but I could not help reviewing in my mind the previous month's harrowing experience with Stan and Barbara. Still, they had come through with no trace of illness and with a superbly healthy full-term baby. This young psychiatrist and his wife had to mourn the loss of their mostly developed baby, and battle with postnatal sepsis at one and the same time. They were winning, but he still looked white. Nostalgic for the delivery suite after my sad talk with him, I went up to the OB floor.

A big message scrawled on the labor board reminded me of the holiday I had forgotten: "Happy Mothers' Day" it said, in a strong, cheerful hand.

Judy Grant, the young mother with end-stage cancer, had not died on schedule a few nights earlier. Later that Sunday afternoon I was in the room with my patient, who was still in the adjacent bed. There was a rustling noise behind me as I listened to my patient's chest, and I turned to see that one of the visitors at the foot of Mrs. Grant's bed was fully gowned in a wedding outfit. She was modeling it for Judy—smiling, turning, holding the train bunched up in her arms. Judy weakly told her that it was beautiful.

Out in the hall I asked the beaming, dark-haired bride if she had been married that day.

"Yesterday," she said.

"Congratulations. Are you related to Mrs. Grant?"

"She's my aunt. She was supposed to have been a bridesmaid at the wedding."

Another mother who was, as they say, trying to die that Mothers' Day, was Tillie Hamlin, an eighty-one-year-old woman with an inexcusably far advanced breast carcinoma. This ordinary middle-class woman with a basically sound mind had allowed the whole of one breast and a large part of the rest of her chest to be taken over by an ugly, almost rock-hard yellow-orange growth without reporting it to a doctor. In cases like that most doctors reflexively blame the patient, whereas I always partly blame the doctor—maybe not any specific doctor, but the profession as a whole, at least. Somewhere along the line this woman had so lost trust in medicine that her life could be claimed by a cancer that might have been fairly treatable. We were responsible for that loss of trust.

She "coded" that afternoon. (Making it an intransitive verb helped to put the blame for the event on the patient—only in slang, of course, but to some extent significantly.) A superbly efficient third-year resident ran the code, calling orders out nervously but crisply in the crowded room from her perch at the cardioversion machine that delivered the shocks to the heart. Afterward, in the hall, I heard her talking angrily in subdued tones with two male residents. Tillie Hamlin, all of them agreed, should have been allowed to die that day, but she had an inappropriate resuscitation status. Her daughter had resisted the code status of D.N.R., but the residents laid the blame squarely elsewhere—on the shoulders of Dr. Downing, the attending physician in charge of the case. This pert, cheerful, person was being excoriated for failing even to try to deal with Tillie Hamlin's family. But their rough chat itself stopped when the patient's daughter and son-in-law came within earshot. The residents talked to them, but it was clear that they would only take Dr. Downing seriously —and that she hadn't talked with them at all. In fact, they had barely met her, though in their minds she was their only real doctor.

At the ten o'clock meal the long table was abuzz with more talk about Tillie Hamlin's code. The residents knew that Dr. Downing was busy— with teaching, with writing, with pressing forward the research that might someday secure her a permanent place on Galen's faculty. But these concerns did not cut much ice with them. She had plainly abdicated this major responsibility, and they openly summarized her problem as lack of courage. Because of Dr. Downing's inattention, they were in the position of trying, on Mothers' Day, to convince a daughter that her mother should be allowed to die. They had run an unnecessary, expensive, and painful code. They needed the practice, but this case was too inappropriate even to justify that. And, they knew they might be called upon to go through the same "charade" again and again. It violated their sense of themselves as doctors, and that violation made them angry.

Lily Corwin and I were alone on the ward after the meal, and at midnight Judy Grant, the young woman with end-stage cancer, became the focus of our attention. As the nurses put it—colloquially, as usual, although not very seriously, blaming the victim—"She blew her I.V." I went into the room with Lily and we spent a full ninety minutes attempting to reinsert it. Lily tried over and over again, and I also tried a few times. But Judy had had all her usual veins destroyed by months of treatment; none of them were visible, and Lily and I were blindly stabbing around in places where veins *should* be.

Now, Judy Grant was usually in substantial pain from her cancer. The purpose of her hospital stay was to administer morphine and other analgesics to help her die more comfortably; but, despite the fact that she always had enough morphine on board to blunt her consciousness, she was almost always suffering greatly. She often moaned and writhed in her bed, yet somehow never struck me as a complainer. To the extent that she was conscious, she was polite and gracious. The last thing she needed was to have us poking around in her arms for a couple of hours. She twisted under the needle involuntarily and groggily, but without really putting up a fight.

As often as my status would allow, I kept saying to Lily, "Aren't there people around who are real good at this?" But I knew she was protecting them. Even a medical student should be able to get a needle in a vein, and an intern who woke a resident for that purpose alone might be subject to considerable ridicule. So she was also protecting herself.

Judy continued to squirm under the pain, through the sedation, but what little consciousness she had was employed against her own reflexive response to the pain. "All right," she would say to herself insistently. "All right." And this, for a couple of minutes, would enable her to stop squirming. Holding her hand, and stroking her forehead and her hair, I kept up an intermittent soothing patter, and persuaded myself that this was not worthless.

Finally, to my immense relief, Lily paged the resident on call. He had obviously dragged himself out of bed—it was now nearly two—but was in a surprisingly cheerful mood. In a matter of minutes he secured a line in the right antecubital vein—the usual one for blood-drawing, in the crook of the elbow. This was a bit unfortunate, since it required that Judy's arm be strapped down to an arm-board to keep it from bending at the elbow. But Lily and I had long since stopped giving weight to such relative refinements. We had been trying everything, and we had been failing badly. In a situation typical of one of the major drawbacks of all teaching hospitals, Lily had put off calling someone who was in the event able to solve the problem in minutes. And he solved it without getting angry.

I had one more obligation before catching a couple of hours of sleep, and that was to hang blood for a patient I didn't know. Michael Slater was a mild-mannered man in his mid-fifties who was dying of liver cancer. He obviously wanted to talk, and I did not mind listening. He was cheerful, in a subdued sort of way. He was not unrealistic. He knew that he was dying, but he wanted to keep faith in life. He reviewed his life a bit for me and was proud of the career he had had as a dancer in musical comedies. He had danced, he said, in the movie *Carousel*. But what was important, he said, was the people whom he had loved in one way or another. That was what his life seemed to mean in these last painful weeks.

I noticed that he was wearing around his neck a chain full of gold charms —a cross, a Star of David, a Moslem crescent, and some others I didn't recognize. I asked him about it, and he explained that he wanted the protection of all the religions, but that more than that he wanted to feel a part of them all. He wanted to die with all these symbols hanging over his heart, to die not as a member of a group but rather as a kindred spirit of all of them.

I had hoped I could stay until he was ready to go to sleep, but that did not seem to be coming. Still, I left him in a wakeful sort of calm, remembering what I had once been told about how the dying would help me.

Starting on Monday after a weekend on always seemed a particular trial. On Friday I was ready to say, "Thank God it's Friday." Then I had to show up at the crack of dawn on Saturday, do a thirty-six-hour shift, and be supposedly bright and ready to roll first thing Monday morning. Without hope of a real rest for another five days, I was in a rather unattractive mood.

One of the less cheering yet somehow humorous aspects of life on the ward was the presence of Morris Stern, a ninety-five-year-old demented nursing home patient who was being evaluated for a possible colon cancer, as well as being treated for enlargement of the prostate gland. He lay in a more or less fetal position in his bed, a few wisps of white hair askew on his head, and said over and over again, "Why you do this to me? What I did to you? I never did nothing to you. Why I have to have this? Why you do this to me? What I did to you?" This demented speech, given in common-sense, if distressed, tones, made a constant background refrain in the life of the ward. He delivered it like a mantra, whatever was being done to him: me trying to take a blood sample, a nurse picking at impacted feces, the residents listening to his belly.

He resisted everything. After a failed attempt at both a sigmoidoscopy and a barium enema, on separate days, the note in his chart left by the gastroenterologist read succinctly, "Mr. Stern defies G.I. work-up." His dementia was relatively quiet and sweet most of the time, but he certainly got angry—queerly righteous anger—when anyone tried to do any sort of procedure on him. His peculiar personal variety of dementia thus served as a superb ironic commentary on the doctor-patient relationship, and as an exaggerated symbol of failure of communication: "Why you do this to me? I never did nothing to you."

Dr. Downing, who had still not talked to Tillie Hamlin's daughter—and who had also not become aware of the residents' anger—cheerfully conducted sit-down rounds each mid-morning. First the three medical students would meet with her and present patients we had admitted the night before. Dr. Downing would listen to our presentations, commenting on their adequacy or lack thereof (she liked some of mine but not others), and then would meet with the residents for a more serious evaluation of the patients. The diffusion of responsibility was remarkable. For each patient there was an intern, a second-year resident, a third-year resident, an admitting physician, and the attending physician (this month Dr. Downing), as well as the ward chief, various consulting physicians and fellows, and an assortment of medical students. Each of the three residents, the admitting, and the attending could all be and were on various occasions said to be the patient's real physician. In the case of Tillie Hamlin, Dr. Downing was both the admitting and the attending, so she had double responsibility—her failure was really double. Thus it was not surprising that patients felt, and sometimes said, "I don't really have a doctor here."

After this part of sit-down-rounds was over, we went downstairs for Dr. Downing's favorite exercise, identification of microscope slides of blood and bone marrow pathology. (I remembered that the surgeons, who always spent this part of the morning in the O.R., referred to the whole of internal medicine contemptuously as "ischial tuberosity rounds"—referring to the part of the bony anatomy we sit on.) She gave us unknowns to look at under the microscope and then asked us to guess what they represented.

Like the other medical students, I was usually far behind the residents in this exercise. But one day she said, "This is commonly seen in July," and I knew immediately that she was showing us a physician error; interns begin service in July. When the slide—labeled C.S.F., for cerebrospinal fluid—looked like a normal bone marrow, I knew that it was simply an inept lumbar puncture that had penetrated a vertebral bone and drawn out marrow. I kept my mouth shut for a discreet interval while others guessed wrong, and then offered my correct answer. It was not usual for me to scoop the residents, or even the other medical students in this type of exercise, so I felt good. But it also showed that common sense was in shorter supply among them than textbook learning.

After the slide session, Dr. Downing announced that that week's issue of the *New England Journal of Medicine* carried an article we should all read. I had seen it, and I was amazed that she was assigning it. It was a major statement about humanistic medicine, and the first sentence read, "Something has gone wrong in the practice of medicine, and we all know it." Since Dr. Downing had struck me as being far from critical of medicine, and since she had had no patience with any humanistic concerns that had come up or might have come up in the past couple of weeks, I could not understand why she was taking an interest in this article.

The following day we briefly discussed the article. A few jokes were made. One of the co-authors was a noted cardiologist whom one of the residents knew. The resident thought he would be about the last person in the world who could be expected to be authentically concerned about humanistic medicine, and viewed the article as an example of the worst sort of academic exercise. Aside from laughing at this, Dr. Downing had very little to say. Not knowing the man, I hardly knew what to think, but of course the whole episode was discouraging.

Judy Grant died a couple of days later. It was reported to us at 11:45 A.M., during sit-down rounds, and shortly before we were scheduled to go down to look at slides. Dr. Downing had some sort of minor official responsibility connected with the death, and went out of the room, saying, "We'll be going down to the path lab in a minute." The residents and students filed out of the room, and I took the opportunity to go and see what was happening.

Judy was lying in bed, looking peaceful for the first time. Her husband and a female relative, looking badly upset, were consoling each other nearby. Several nurses were crying. One of them said to me, "I've been here two years, and this is the first time I've seen anyone this young die on this ward." Judy had been on the floor on and off for many months, and many of the nurses were attached to her.

This rent in the human fabric of the ward—dramatically responded to by the nursing staff and the family—was not noted by Dr. Downing. She discharged her minor duty—a signature, it appeared—spun around with her pleated skirt sailing, smiled cheerily, and led the troop of residents and students away to the path lab. There we looked at some tricky unknowns, and Dr. Downing was especially pleased that one of the other medical students got one. Neither then nor at any other time did she mention Judy Grant's death, whether in her capacity as teacher or as doctor. As much as I wanted to hear some discussion about it—even a strictly medical discussion would have been better than nothing—I had developed sense enough not to ask. My concerns, I realized, were idiosyncratic. Nobody wanted to hear about them, not even most of my fellow students. I could simplify my life best by keeping them to myself, and I certainly wanted to simplify my life.

That night I was on call and got only an hour's sleep. I awakened, took a five-minute shower during which I started to doze again, and finally ran enough cold water over myself to be essentially awake. I dressed quickly and stood in front of the mirror to put my necktie on. I got the knot wrong, so I took it off and tried again. The knot was still wrong. The third time I began to concentrate. I could not tie it. By the fifth time, after a rest and several shakes of my head, I was finally able to do it.

Neurological or neurosurgical patients with damage to the right hemisphere of the brain sometimes had what was called a dressing apraxia. This was an inability to remember how to dress, to perform a motor action pattern that had been performed throughout life tens of thousands of times. It was presumed to be the result of damage to the region of the brain that organizes the body in space and directs our acts according to this organized perception. I had had a transient dressing apraxia. I tried hard to guess what had been going on in my brain. An unfavorable flow of blood? A brief and subtle seizure? An anatomically specific wave of nerve cell fatigue? I was only thirty-six years old and I had very briefly lost a critical brain function. I did not know what it was, but I knew that it was secondary to sleeplessness, and I was a bit frightened.

Sick of the emptiness of hospital medicine as I was being exposed to it, I decided somehow to wrench some better experience out of the system. Before morning rounds I caught sight of Dr. Nathan, the older internist who had had tears in his eyes over the unexpected stroke of one of his patients. "Do you mind if I round with you?" I asked him. He seemed surprised, then pleased. I doubted whether this had happened to him many times in the past few years, if ever. He agreed to let me go around with him. I told Lily that I would miss the first half-hour or so of walk-rounds.

We visited the bedsides of four of Dr. Nathan's patients. They were an ordinary lot, and his assessments of their conditions were perfectly routine. He listened to the chests and bellies, studied the nurses' charts, read the progress notes, asked the relevant questions of the patients. He didn't dawdle, and he never said anything mawkish or intimate. He didn't miss a trick medically, and his visits were in that sense equivalent to those of any other doctor on the ward. But there was a warmth in his voice, in his smile, in his hands. His patients believed he cared about them, and for the best possible reason: he did. He was real, that was all. Real. I figured that if I could get mastery of half of what he knew about how to be with patients, it would be worth more than all I could learn from the famous physicians of Galen and their minions.

Every day there were jokes with Sara Norfleet, the elegant leukemia patient, about her looks, her hair, her dress. She initiated them as a kind of good-natured display of wit for the team of residents and students around her sickbed. "I'm losing weight, so I look good. Trouble is, when I lose weight, my bosom gets too small. When I gain weight, my bosom's O.K., but my tummy is too large." I wanted to tell her that her bosom and her tummy were O.K. with me.

One morning we walked in and George Burns was on her television, promoting his book, *How to Live to 100*. Sara was getting a great kick out of him. He pulled on his fat cigar and repeated all his expected, somehow wonderful remarks—the large daily doses of whiskey, cigarettes, and women, the disdain for his doctor's advice. "What does your doctor say about all these habits?" asked the interviewer.

Burns pulled on his cigar again. "My doctor's dead." The book, he said, was dedicated to "the widows of my last six doctors." Sara thought that was hilarious.

Sara was under the assault of chemotherapy, and she had every right to be in a depressed physical and mental condition. Instead, she looked beautiful and maintained a cheerful demeanor that seemed to defy impairment. She knew that she might not live much longer and that the next couple of weeks would tell a great deal about her future. But something inside her insisted on the grace and dignity and happiness of life, an attitude that made life seem more worthwhile for all of us.

Jacob Fine's postmortem took place later the same day, and several of us showed up to see the bad news for ourselves. There were numerous ooh's and aah's about the size and location of the tumor, and about the metastases throughout the abdomen. The belly that Sally and I had drained so carefully a few days earlier was split wide open, and the mysteries that we had mused so long on were revealed. But somehow they did not seem so significant as the remaining mysteries: the "living will," and whether he would have stuck to his claim that he wanted to be allowed to die; his love for his wife, and hers for him, now longing in the void; and his little volume of Dylan Thomas poems, full of secrets, perhaps, about some of his last thoughts.

After Saturday morning I had the rest of the weekend off. My landlady, a sweet, crochety eighty-five-year-old, had a big splinter sunk deeply in her thumb, and she delightedly summoned me to do a job on it. I liked being called in as a doctor by relatives, friends, and neighbors; and I prided myself on not taking on anything bigger than I could handle. This was well within my limited surgical skill, and I sterilized some instruments—makeshift but serviceable—and dug the splinter out. My landlady was not one to fall over herself with gratitude, but her terse respect seemed to me a more than adequate encomium.

After that I was ready to put medicine out of my mind, if only for a day or so. My wife and I went to see a film version of *La Traviata*. Verdi being one of my greatest heros, the cast and production being impeccable, I didn't see how we could lose. And the film was more or less wonderful; but the main problem I had was with Violetta's consumption. I could not experience it except as a medical student. I was trying as hard as I could to banish medical thoughts, and here I was twisting one of my favorite operas into the perspective of the physician, which I could not abandon even for two hours.

14

MEDICINE III

Healing and Hope

Over the weekend I got a call from an old friend saying that he wanted to talk to me about applying to medical school. He was in his early forties, a well-established sociologist with a tenured position at a good university, and he was thinking of leaving all that to become a physician. I agreed to talk with him, and we met in the Galen cafeteria during a not-too-bustling period late on Monday afternoon.

He questioned me to some extent about what it was like, but most of all about how to get in. I tried to find out more about what was behind his decision. He did not have really satisfying answers, and neither did I. He felt, as I had, that he needed a sense of practical purpose in his daily work, a sense that there was more to life than transferring information. He was clearly dissatisfied with his work and his world. But he was a father of two young sons, and in most ways clearly an intellectual. I tried to get him to see how difficult it was, and how it could fail in various ways to live up to his expectations. Practical work that was basically a holding action against a tide of chaos was not necessarily more satisfying than intellectual work that had some hope of making the world a better place. As for his family life, if he went to medical school he could almost bid it good-bye.

But he was not listening. He was looking all around him, distracted by the passing white jackets, by the stethoscopes around the necks of the tired young doctors. He had in his eye the faraway look of those who will not be dissuaded. He was no longer looking for advice about whether to do it, but rather for the strategy and tactics of how. Walking away from him as from a dark mirror, I felt a keen sense of everything I had given up and wondered whether I would end by considering it worthwhile.

That night I was on call and admitted a patient who was to dominate the rest of my stay—six more weeks—on medicine. She was a forty-year-old woman who looked like a half-starved waif. Her name was Charlotte Kaplan, and her main diagnosis was inflammatory bowel disease. This had caused her moderate to severe abdominal pain, along with a number of other symptoms, on and off for fifteen years. All the standard medical treatments and several experimental ones had been so far unsuccessful. She had mild fevers and sweats each night, and woke up "soaking wet." She had a sense of pressure deep in her groin and a feeling of both urinary and fecal urgency. She also had a separate burning pain in her upper belly, sometimes moving from there to her right shoulder.

In addition to all this, she had a severe and active case of the psychiatric disorder known as bulimia, and she had had it for at least eight or nine years. This involved binge-eating, self-induced vomiting, and laxative abuse. In her case the disorder had worsened two years earlier, when she began to consume many thousands of calories a day and to purge by self-induced vomiting several times a day. She was under treatment for this disorder, apparently with some success, by a psychiatrist and an internist working together.

What seemed abundantly clear was that this eating disorder was complicating all efforts to diagnose and treat her bowel disease. The pain in her upper belly was probably the result of damage caused by self-induced vomiting. The loss of acid through vomiting had caused several derangements of her body chemistry. She was apparently malnourished, and she was anemic, which could have resulted from malnutrition or from loss of blood from the inflamed bowel. Last but not least, the standard nonsurgical treatment for inflammatory bowel disease—steroids administered through the rectum—was unacceptable to her because it resulted in the classic steroid side effects of weight gain and bloating, especially in the face. These effects ran right into the thick morass of her psychiatric disorder, which was in essence a disorder of body image.

In the first couple of hours I spent with her I formed an impression of a dependent, even whiny, but somehow likable woman with a marked psychiatric problem that was standing in the way of her needed treatment. As with most patients with emotional problems, my heart went out to Charlotte. I wrote seven and a half pages in my admission assessment of her, and gave a meticulous analysis of her several problems, including the intersection of her eating disorder with her bowel disease. This was all praised, with minor corrections, by Dr. Downing when she read the assessment. At the end I had a page of plans, as required, organized in eight subsections pertaining to various specific problems. As my eighth "plan" I wrote, "This patient appreciates kind attention," an observation that I would not have put down if it had not struck me that Charlotte's reaction to kind attention went beyond the usual response. Dr. Downing red-penciled this statement off my list.

Sara Norfleet's bone marrow biopsy, scheduled for fourteen days after the start of her chemotherapy, came back positive; the treatment was not working. She was told about this, and yet at rounds the next morning she was still cheerful, still eating heartily, still apparently doing well. It was not until the following day that she began to look depressed.

That was also the day on which Tillie Hamlin died. I requested and received from Dr. Downing permission to accompany her to the bedside where she was to talk with the patient's daughter. I wanted badly to learn how such conversations should be handled. As I was often being reminded, this was a teaching hospital. Dr. Downing strode perkily into the room, suppressing her chronic smile with apparent effort. The daughter, about sixty-five years old, was visibly distraught. Her mother lay nearby in the bed where she had died within the last half-hour. She wrung her hands and looked to Dr. Downing for some sort of comfort.

Dr. Downing appeared busy and looked straight at the floor. She spoke —I noticed the time—for just one minute. Her language was curt offi-cialese peppered with medical jargon. Her disapproval of anyone who would allow a cancer to progress so far without aggressive treatment was at odds with her desire for efficiency in communication. But in any case she did not allow herself to be distracted by such an unprofessional reac-tion. She wanted only to do her duty.

In a voice filled with doubt and longing—it had a slight whine and many young Galen physicians would have called it obnoxious—Tillie Hamlin's daughter asked two or three questions about the last steps in treatment. Dr. Downing's impatience with such refinements in a case that, from the outset, had a foregone conclusion was evident to me, although it did not break the veil of her politeness or the rhythm of her perfunctory, awk-ward, ill-chosen phrases. Soon she turned on the heel of one of her blue pumps, having done all that she was required to do. To her back, the daughter said, "She was good. She died on a Jewish holiday." I did a small calculation—I was so tired I hardly knew what day it was—and realized that it must be the holiday of Shavuot, celebrating the giving of the Torah to Moses on Mount Sinai. Dr. Downing turned slightly back, without breaking her stride and still looking at the floor, smiled wanly, and kept on walking.

That week *Time* magazine ran a remarkable story, "Med School, Heal Thyself," describing what was wrong with medical education as seen by some of its most prominent leaders. They decried the reign of technology, the overwhelming memorization tasks, the inhumane behavior of doctors, and the brutality of the whole process of medical education. One of them was the dean of my own medical school. Who's in charge here? I thought to myself and laughed out loud.

I counseled myself patience and cultivation of my garden. "Light your corner," the words of an old friend, came back to me again and again. The light banter with Sara Norfleet on morning rounds lost its spontaneity, but I found excuses to drop in on her to see if there was anything I could do. I did not try to say anything in particular, just to be a friendly face among the white coats.

I was off on the weekend, and before I left on Saturday afternoon, I gave Charlotte my telephone number. She had already formed a strong attachment to me and had told her husband and parents about me in glowing terms. I knew that she was either mildly or moderately crazy, I was not sure which—I did not think she was very crazy. While I was in the hospital she had me paged only occasionally, but when I showed up, her mood brightened visibly. Injections and other procedures that she had rejected in my absence because of her hyperreactivity to pain became possible with my help. The nurses on her floor also came to rely on me. They knew I had a way with Charlotte, and they were increasingly frustrated by her refusals of treatment. Her condition was so marginal that her life might be at stake if she continued to refuse to eat. I was the person most likely to be able to persuade her.

Charlotte never used my home telephone number, and as time went by, I gained from this forbearance a sense of her dignity and self-respect— there were few other signs of it. In a funny way I came to rely on her slender sense of self-worth, the way one can rely on the diffidence of a friend. I knew she needed me, but she did not intrude on my weekend. I had about forty hours off and I spent much of it sleeping—sleep filled with restless, unpleasant dreams about illness and dying.

On Monday morning I woke up sick, with a headache, abdominal cramps, nausea, and vomiting. I began to wonder if I were experiencing sympathetic symptoms, mimicking Charlotte Kaplan. In any case I dragged myself to the hospital and did what I was supposed to do as usual. Charlotte was getting worse, psychologically and, inevitably, physically. She whined almost constantly and refused the most simple procedures, crying over every injection or I.V. insertion or even being put on a bed-pan, as if she were a not very brave six-year-old girl. Most of the nurses gradually turned against her, but a few remained sympathetic, and they continued to rely on me for communication with Charlotte when they could find no other way to gain her cooperation.

Most important, she refused to eat. We all wanted her to avoid surgery for removal of the diseased part of her colon. This could only happen if her gut worked well enough to enable her to gain weight in the hospital. But with her psychiatric eating disorder, there was no way to tell whether her continued loss of weight was the result of her inflamed colon or of her intake failure. She more and more resembled a concentration-camp vic-tim—the bones stood out under a thin veil of skin in every part of her body —and she spent a great deal of time on the toilet chair. Coming into her room at night and finding her sitting on that chair, her body emaciated and her face deformed by a constant look of grotesque, helpless pain— pain that struck everyone as at least somewhat doubtful—constituted a real challenge to anybody's sympathy. Yet for me it was easier, because she saw me as special; and her trust, combined with her nurses' practical reliance on me, made me feel like a doctor.

Her "real doctor," to the extent that she or anyone at Galen ever had one, was Richard Harrison, who was also the head of our course. This meant that I would be under his special scrutiny, and that my relationship with Charlotte would be defined in part by my relationship with him. He had nervous blue eyes and was obviously ill at ease with people. Why he was assigned or accepted the medical-student course as his responsibility I never knew, but students generally found him unsuitable, and it was said that he'd been the butt of ridicule in a novel about Galen published some years earlier.

As a specialist in gastroenterology, Charlotte's case should have been ideal for him. But his real interest was in gastrointestinal tumors, and as for Charlotte's psychiatric problem, he had absolutely no use for it. He was a no-nonsense practitioner of internal medicine, and was known among psychiatric residents as without exception the least psychologically aware of all Galen physicians. Whenever I or anyone else talked with him about her psychiatric problem, he said, "Let's concentrate on her colitis." In Charlotte's entire course of treatment he never grasped the fact, evident to every nurse and resident involved in her care, that her psychiatric problem constantly interfered with attempts to treat her illness. If ever a patient needed a coordinated effort between internists and psychiatrists, Charlotte was that patient. Yet Dr. Harrison consistently refused to approve a psychiatric consultation.

With Charlotte's permission, I talked with her psychotherapist, a psychologist. He had some interesting things to say, but he could not participate in her care since he did not have staff privileges at Galen. I called a respected psychiatrist I knew who was expert at handling patients with simultaneous medical and psychiatric problems, but he too could not become involved unless specifically invited to do so by Dr. Harrison.

In the meantime, Dr. Harrison performed the procedure of colonoscopy on Charlotte, and I assisted him. Or rather, I assisted her. She was in agony the entire time. It was an interesting procedure, and the sight of a great length of her descending colon looking sickly grayish green, and then finally the healthy pink of the upper part of the colon, impressed me with the power of the disease and the immense distinction between this particular form of illness and health. But more than the usual sedation was, as might have been expected, insufficient for Charlotte. I like to think that the sound of my voice helped a little. She squeezed my hand hard enough to hurt me.

I rushed back from the colonoscopy because I was eager to hear a lecture on geriatrics. It was actually the second in a series of two, and the gerontologist had promised, in answer to a request of mine that had been seconded by several other medical students, to devote this next hour to questions of code decisions and D.N.R. These questions were uppermost in the minds of all who dealt with the elderly at Galen, yet we had been taught nothing about them.

In general terms, though, we had been well educated about geriatrics. Another gerontologist who had lectured to us in the preclinical years had been brilliant, outrageous, and funny. He used to shout at us, "You think life expectancy is threescore and ten! You think old people are *supposed* to die! You're lying there at three A.M. in the on-call room and your beeper rings. There's a patient in the E.W. with chest pain. It's an eighty-two-year-old man! You do a lightning calculation. This guy's life expectancy is minus twelve years! You turn over and go back to sleep.

"Well let me tell you something! This guy's life expectancy is not much different from that of a sixty-five-year-old. This guy's life expectancy may not be much different from yours! This guy is a survivor! He's here at eighty-two because he's tough! And he'll be here at ninety-two for exactly the same reason! So get your ass off the cot and down to the E.W. and save his goddamn life!

"Besides which, HE'S THE DEAN'S FATHER!"

This brilliant man had indelibly impressed on us that old people are not sick because they are old. They are sick because they are sick. Our job is to find out what is wrong with them. Age has no bearing on how much someone deserves a diagnosis, and old age is not a diagnosis. Even the slightest shift in expectations, based solely on age, could bias us and become a dangerous, unprofessional, self-fulfilling prophecy.

Our current lecturer was incredibly dull by comparison. Still, he had had some useful things to say about the demography of geriatrics and how treatment of the elderly would constitute an increasing proportion of all medicine, and the majority of internal medicine, for the foreseeable future. He had some useful things to say about dementia and other aspects of physiological aging. But we needed, and had asked for, some guidance through the maze of agonizing ethical decisions that seemed to center on the elderly hospital patient. He promised some, and instead, in this last session, he delivered a standard talk on the classification of dementias—of the sort that we had heard on the subject more than once before. When two minutes were left in the hour, someone reminded him of his promise. "Oh, yes," he said, "I almost forgot," and proceeded to distribute a three-page paper about ethics—it would prove completely banal—after which he dismissed the conference without discussion.

One morning shortly before seven I was rather frantically trying to get the latest test data on my patients out of the computer before rounds. As I got up from the console to give another medical student—or nurse or intern or resident—a chance at it, I noticed Dr. Adams standing nearby. He had been the primary physician of Sophie Hellman, the woman who had been treated for several days for crescendo angina and then discharged in good condition, only to return to the hospital in a couple of days with a massive, soon-to-be-fatal M.I. Dr. Adams, a tall, thin, blond man with an easy laugh, who seemed to be a decent and good physician, demonstrated the computer to a friend. Galen had pioneered the use of computers to store and monitor patient information on a day-to-day or even hour-to-hour basis, and visiting physicians were often interested in seeing the system work.

When his friend left and he got up I said in my most respectful medical-student-to-senior-physician voice, "Dr. Adams, do you mind if I ask you a question?" He stopped but did not turn toward me. "I'm the medical student who was taking care of Sophie Hellman. I was just wondering," I said gently, "if we could talk about what happened to her."

"What happened? She had a massive M.I. and she arrested and she died in the C.C.U." He continued to stand half-turned from me, so that I had to speak to his right shoulder. He spoke matter-of-factly. I began to fumble for words. "Well . . . I was just wondering if there was anything we did . . . that we might have done differently or that I might have done . . . or . . ."

"Sure. She should have been cathed, but she refused. If she had agreed to be cathed, we might have saved her life."

"Oh," I said, "I didn't realize she had refused."

"Sure, she refused to be cathed. It was very unfortunate." He shrugged again, pushed his glasses up on the bridge of his nose, and walked away.

I was musing about the whole problem of patient compliance when I heard the distinctive grating voice of Sally Brass right behind me. I had not even realized she was there.

"What did you say to him?" she demanded very angrily. "Did you— What did you ask him?" There was furious disbelief in her voice.

"I was asking about what happened to Sophie Hellman." Sally's voice was such that my heart was pounding. I knew I had done something wrong, but I didn't know what.

"What do you mean, what happened to her?" she demanded, rasping the words out with no abatement of fury. "You know what happened! She refused to be cathed and she had an M.I. and then she arrested in the C.C.U.! You know, it's very bad form to ask an attending a question like that. Don't you think he feels badly enough? You shouldn't be questioning his judgment!"

"I wasn't questioning his judgment," I said, softly but not timidly. "I wouldn't dream of questioning it. I was just asking him if there was anything we could have done differently."

She shook her head contemptuously. "There was nothing we could have done differently. And there was nothing he could have done differently." She stood up and stared down at me. "Try to have a little respect for other people's feelings," she said and strode away.

I went through morning rounds in a sort of daze, fortunate to be even busier than usual. It seemed very straightforward. If Sophie had been advised to be catheterized—"cathed"—and had refused, then everything possible had been done. Catheterization would have revealed the severely clogged coronary arteries that were soon to take her life and would have in all likelihood led to a recommendation of bypass surgery, a procedure that might well have saved her. In refusing catheterization she was closing the door on this life-saving modality of treatment and could properly be blamed for her own death.

However, I felt uneasy. Sophie had struck me as unusually respectful of doctors. The idea of her being afraid was plausible, but the idea of her adamantly refusing a course of action that had been strongly recommended seemed way out of character. Also, I could not remember any discussion of catheterization. It had been a simple case and I had understood it well, I thought. I had talked with her at length every day, and we had discussed her extensively on rounds. How come I couldn't remember a discussion of catheterization? It crossed my mind that fatigue had made my memory even worse than I thought. I wanted to review the case. As soon as I got a chance—instead of lunch—I went down to the record room and asked to see Sophie Hellman's chart again. I wasn't embarking on any wishful medical sleuthing. I was simply trying to get my own thoughts straight about it. I read her discharge summary carefully. It was dated April 13, and it summarized a hospital course that began with an admission on April 8.

> HOSPITAL COURSE: The patient was admitted with the diagnosis of crescendo angina. She was started on Inderal 10 mg by mouth 4 times a day and put on Nitrol paste every 4 hours. Her potassium was kept above the level of 4. She was given Mylanta alternating with Amphogel for her esophagitis. The patient did well, however, on the morning of the second hospital day, she had an episode of chest pain which was relieved with nitroglycerin. At that time she was started on Diltiazem 30 mg by mouth 4 times a day, and after that initial episode she no longer had any further episodes of chest pain. Her activity level was progressively increased over the ensuing days. She remained free of angina, though able to walk around the room. It was felt that the patient would do well discharged to home on her current medical regimen and might be considered for catheterization in the future if her chest pain proved refractory to medical management. She was discharged to home in good condition on 4/13.
>
> Discharge diagnoses:
>   1. Angina
>   2. Atherosclerotic heart disease
>   3. Hypertension
> Discharge meds:
>   Diltiazem 30 mg by mouth 4 times a day; Inderal 10 mg by mouth 4 times a day; Nitrol paste one inch every 4 hours; nitroglycerin 1/200 sublingual as needed for chest pain.
> The patient has a follow-up appointment in two weeks with Dr. Adams.

The discharge note, undoubtedly dictated by Sally, was signed by both Dr. Adams and Dr. Brass.

I read carefully through the record, reviewing all the notes written by Sally and by me. There were two notes by Dr. Adams. One, undated, was evidently his admit note.

> Attending: A 77 ♀ is admitted c̄ AP of increasing severity when an ecg showed marked ST↓ in V_2-V_4. Plan: Cool off c̄ maximum med Rx and consider an art.

Translated, this meant: A seventy-seven-year-old woman was admitted with anginal pain of increasing severity when an electrocardiogram showed changes indicative of compromised coronary circulation. The plan was to try to control the pain with appropriate drugs and to consider an arteriogram, another term for catheterization.

The second note by Dr. Adams was written on the day of discharge:

> 4/13. Feeling well. No further pain. No angina in free ambulation. Patient is 77 1/2 years old. Will try home activity. If it recurs, will then consider angio since she is vigorous & active.

This meant that an "angio"—angiogram was yet another term for catheterization—was being considered as a future possibility because unlike some other patients, Sophie could not be expected to control her pain by sitting still all the time.

The second note, like the discharge summary, gave a clear impression of distant consideration of catheterization under circumstances that had not yet arisen. Both were far from suggesting the thought that this procedure was considered immediately advisable.

Even more remote was the notion of Sophie's having refused the procedure. I read and reread the entire record several times. There was no evidence in the chart of anyone but *me* having discussed cardiac catheterization with Sophie, as my notes showed. She had not seemed to like the idea, but she had not indicated that she would refuse it if Dr. Adams recommended it. Neither he, Dr. Brass, nor anyone else other than me described any discussion of catheterization with the patient, much less a refusal. From everything I had been taught and had observed in practice about medical record-keeping, the refusal by a patient of an important recommended medical procedure had to be documented with utmost care for the protection of the doctors and the hospital. To fail to do this would be legal folly, and no one in today's climate of constant malpractice litigation would commit such a blunder.

The brief record of the last hospitalization contained the rest of the story. Sophie had returned home on a Wednesday. The following day, Thursday, she had experienced a "fluttering" in her chest throughout the day, with minimal exertion. This had been relieved with three nitroglycer-ins. On Friday there had been more "fluttering," requiring four nitroglyc-erins for relief.

On Saturday morning she had awakened with a heaviness in her arms, pain in both shoulders and in her chest below the breastbone, shortness of breath, sweating, and dizziness. She had taken three nitroglycerins, which relieved most of the pain. But the pain had lasted for three hours, and she finally came to the hospital. Shortly after midnight that night she began to vomit. Her heart rate dropped to 60 and her systolic blood pressure to 80. Then the bottom fell out of the pressure, and an unsuccess-ful code was instituted. She died at 12:55 A.M.

Just as there was no evidence in the chart that she had ever refused catheterization, there was no evidence that anyone, including me, had held a pre-discharge discussion with her of what indications should make her call the doctor or return to the Emergency Room. The "fluttering" in her chest that presaged her death was identical to the sensations she described as having made her call Dr. Adams the day before her initial hospitalization. *It had been the first time she had ever used nitroglycerin,* although she had had it in hand for three years. The effect of her hospitali-zation was to take symptoms that had quite properly alarmed her and transform them so that they no longer disturbed her enough even to pick up the telephone. In fact, she allowed the fluttering in her chest to pro-gress to pain and the pain to become severe before she made a move. The record suggested that she had not had a good explanation of the value of catheterization, but more important, that she had not had an explanation of the symptoms that should worry her.

It was far from certain, but it was at least possible that the appropriate knowledge, the appropriate responses, would have saved her. If so, as I had surmised from my first review of the record, Sophie Hellman died of a lack of communication. Not of a lack of deep emotional contact or of elaborate bedside manner or of makeshift psychotherapy in the midst of the hospital bustle. Nothing so complex or deep. Just a couple of simple conversations. And the defensiveness of those who were supposed to have saved her life spoke eloquently about who was responsible.

Unaware that my beeper had stopped working, I went by to visit Char-lotte late in the afternoon and found the nurses' station bustling with frustrated people. They had been trying unsuccessfully to reach me, since Charlotte had been asking for me as usual. One of her primary nurses had broken down in tears during report. They refused to go any further with Charlotte without a psychiatric consult, and they ordered one behind Dr. Harrison's back—he was away at a colon cancer conference. Since I thought that this should have been done in the first place, I was delighted. When the psychiatric residents came up, I presented the case as I understood it. They visited Charlotte and arrived at their own formulation. Then they invited me to apply to their residency program. This felt good, but it was not helpful to Charlotte. They agreed to see her again, but they were clearly not prepared to see her every day.

Later the same day Dr. Harrison returned from his convention, and he was dismayed at the disarray in Charlotte's care. He called all of us concerned with the case into the conference room. "The situation has deteriorated markedly," he intoned. "I don't like the way things are going." I was ready to hear his observations on the psychiatric aspect of the case, the interaction of the eating disorder with the colitis, the impact of the dependent personality disorder on the nursing staff, something that showed that he knew what was going on. Instead he said, "I don't like the way this patient looks. There's an area of tenderness in the lower left quandrant. I think she has an occult bacterial infection. I want to treat it with chloramphenicol." This impressively strong antibiotic, considered dangerous and restricted for highly specific purposes, was now supposed to be the key to Charlotte's treatment.

The residents, nurses, and students looked at each other and tried to keep from smiling. Charlotte had an exquisite tenderness somewhere in her abdomen all the time. It migrated from place to place. Yesterday it had been in the right upper quadrant. Today it was in the lower left. Tomorrow it would be behind her umbilicus. She also had an exquisite tenderness from time to time in her back, her legs, her neck, her buttocks, and other parts of her body. Her exquisite tenderness in the lower left quadrant was as likely to be evidence of an occult bacterial infection as it was to be evidence of a hangnail.

Dr. Harrison looked around with his intense, nervous eyes—even he didn't seem satisfied with his argument—and got up and left, his hands stuck in the pockets of his long white coat. He had given the order, and we followed it. One of the nurses unlocked the drug room and pulled out a vial of chloramphenicol. The other nurses, the residents, and I were standing around the nurses' station grinning broadly and contemptuously in the wake of Dr. Harrison's performance. The short dark-haired nurse who had been reduced to tears by Charlotte set the vial of antibiotic on the counter, hard, shaking her head disgustedly as she did. The senior resident shrugged his shoulders and snorted a laugh. "It probably won't hurt her too much."

As I watched the antibiotic in the vial tremble and glint in the fluorescent light I was seized by an inspiration. I put a look of mock consternation on my face. "Who *was* that masked man?" I asked in melodramatic tones. Then I turned suddenly and seized hold of the vial, spinning around with it held up catching the fluorescent light. "Look! He left a silver bullet! . . . *chloramphenicol!*" It was the best laugh I got during my three months on medicine.

"You'll do well," said the senior resident admiringly. The release of the general tension was wonderful.

There were many comings and goings that week, since the end of the month was approaching. The head of our ward came back from a trip to the Southwest sporting a grotesque wristwatch combining a Navajo tourist-band made of silver with inlaid jade and one of those cheap digital watches. He showed it off proudly during late-afternoon walk-rounds. "Sort of a combination of old and new," I said, keeping a straight face.

"Huh?" he said. "Oh yeah. I see what you mean. I had the watch from before, but the band is new."

He was aware that I had been an anthropologist, and so he began to lecture me about the Indians of the Southwest. I had spent a month in the most traditional section of the Navajo reservation and knew the other cultures of the region as well as their archaeology and history. As had happened to me many times before, I now listened to a poorly informed disquisition by a doctor on an anthropological subject on which I could have taught him a good deal.

Charlotte's husband, a surprisingly normal person, brought her some dolls from home, and these seemed to brighten her mood. She gained weight briefly—Dr. Harrison no doubt thought it was the chloramphenicol —but soon began losing again. The psychiatrists saw her again, but Dr. Harrison paid as little attention to their recommendations as he had paid to mine.

I left the ward to begin two weeks on the C.C.U.—the cardiac care unit —and I was not at all sorry to move on. The nature and substance of ward medicine as it was practiced at Galen—experimental geriatrics, with interminable hairsplitting conferences, without humane sensibility and without ethics beyond legally defensive medicine—this was not my idea of anything I remotely wanted to do. The arrogance of the residents and the staff physicians was a caricature of the attitude on other services. Dr. Greenspan might think that this was the most important course we would ever take, but for me it had been two months of oppressive waiting. I would do anything in medicine, absolutely anything, before I would train as an internist.

The C.C.U. held some promise of being much more interesting. Such intensive care facilities had sprung up since the 1960s in every major and many minor hospitals; and Dr. Greenspan, pompous figure though he was, had helped lead the way in their design and implementation. It was likely that they were responsible for a small but significant component of the decline in cardiac mortality experienced in the United States in the 1970s. They were simply *there*, with a concentrated, expensive effort, when the heart muscle was injured or began to sputter and fail. In every hospital, they were centers of drama where hairsbreadth lifesaving was a daily job.

My assignment, like those of the residents, was every third night on but with encouragement to leave early on the day after that night. This was supposed to keep us alert all night when we were on. On my first day we were rounding at seven and were at the bedside of an old man who went into ventricular fibrillation and cardiac arrest as we watched his monitor. Mike Li, a senior resident from California, said, "Looks like the Nebraska sign." This meant a flat line on the EKG, like the landscape of Nebraska —no electrical activity at all in the heart. He called for the defibrillator. He pressed the paddles on to the patient's chest, said "Ready," meaning no contact with the patient or with the bed, and shocked him. We watched the green blip on the monitor screen pop crazily out of its flatline and then settle back into the well-known monotonous peaks and valleys of the EKG of a normally beating heart. We waited and watched. It held.

Li turned to me, smiled, and said mildly, "Welcome to the C.C.U."

"Thanks," I said, also smiling and feeling high.

The patient had had the sort of hospital course that made you want to believe either in medicine or God. He had come in four days earlier after a similar arrest, having had to wait ten minutes before C.P.R. was begun. He had been deeply obtunded, unresponsive, with nonreactive pupils and negative cold calorics—a test for any glimmer of brain stem functioning. He had looked as if he could say good-bye to his brain. A day later he had already regained some brain stem activity—his cold calorics were positive. Now his EEG showed, astonishingly, that the projections to his cerebral cortex—the highest portion of the brain—had begun functioning again.

Full neurological recovery now seemed likely. If only his heart could be stabilized, he would do very well.

Alvin Mitchell was much less lucky. He came into the C.C.U. in the middle of the following day, in cardiac arrest. He was coded for two hours, a persistent and depressing effort, before he could finish dying. Then a third patient, Martin Burchette, arrived and arrested in the same bed where Mitchell had just died. It was still warm. Burchette had a parallel code with the same pairs of hands, the same paddles, the same machines for breathing and pumping and monitoring. And he had a favorable outcome.

Sort of. I was assigned to him as my main patient in the C.C.U. I stood by the side of the bed staring down at his limp figure, with lines coming out of both arms and tubes grotesquely distorting his nose and mouth. His wife stood near me, squeezing his hand, waiting for a response that didn't come.

They seemed very poor. Their hair was not well kept, their teeth were in poor repair, and their clothing was shabby. The chart showed that he was an alcoholic, and she looked as if she had put up with a lot. Still, she stood there sadly, full of love and hope. I would gradually learn from her, over the next several days, just how vivid and loyal such hope could be. And from their four grown daughters, whose love of their broken-down father—broken-down, as was clear to all, largely through his own fault— transcended any possible concept of blame.

Suddenly there were "coffee grounds"—the standard description of clotted blood—in his nasogastric tube, and when I told Li I got the job of pumping his stomach. This was far from pleasant, yet it had about it a wonderful workmanlike feeling of usefulness. Years of abuse by alcohol had taken their toll on his stomach lining, and the stress of his cardiac arrest and intensive care was tearing into that lining even further. His stomach in effect had to be washed again and again. No machine could replace my pair of human hands, decisively squirting saline into his stomach and sucking it out again, over and over until the clots disappeared. During the next two or three days and nights, I would spend hours with Mr. Burchette pumping his stomach in this way. He was unconscious, and was never aware, as far as I knew, of anything I did for him. Nevertheless it seemed to me a wonderful form of intimacy.

It was two days after I had left the ward before I visited Charlotte again. I sat with her for a long time, smiling to myself about Dr. Greenspan's lofty insistence that we follow our patients after leaving the service. For him it may have been an offhanded piece of disingenuous pomposity; but for me it was my attachment to her, and my conscience as well. I knew I would be spending a good deal of my spare time with Charlotte.

That day she had been told that she would probably be facing surgery. The team of surgical residents had seen her and left a note in the chart, as had the senior gastrointestinal surgeon. She had been on intravenous prednisone and cortisone enemas for some days now, and this for her was being a very good girl—these were the drugs that she had refused for so long because of the side effects on the shape of her face and body. Nevertheless she was not gaining weight. She was going to be started on hyper-alimentation—the pouring of nutrients through a large-bore needle into a vein—with supplements of a fat emulsion, all geared to put meat on her bones. But no one, especially Charlotte, was very hopeful.

We had a long talk about suffering and the transcendence of suffering—to come out on the other side to enjoy life and to help others. She had worked as a teacher of learning-disabled children, and she was hoping to return to that. I talked to her about Martin Burchette's parallel struggle with his much more threatening illness, and about the concentration-camp experience of a woman I had recently met who had survived the worst that life has to offer. And, incongruous as it seemed, I even talked about my own recent, trivial illness.

All this seemed to calm Charlotte. She was ready to put up with the bloating from the medicine and ready to have the big needles pour the mundane substance of life painfully into her veins. But she was not hopeful.

That week a kindly Jewish woman who was the head of social services for the hospital conducted a talk with the medical students about the stresses we were under. Her well-meaning unpreparedness for what she unleashed was comical—evidently she had not tried this before. She sat at the front of the room with stunned, frightened-looking eyes, trying to say something helpful, while the students delivered one desperate comment after another about the anomic, grotesque, laughable trench-warfare lives we were leading, and about the feeling of complete moral abandonment in the face of a constant stream of new life-and-death experience. She stammered her way at last to some sort of summary statement to the effect that we should confide our feelings to Dr. Greenspan or Dr. Harrison. This advice made us grin in gleeful, cynical disbelief. She finally pulled herself together and got out of the room, no doubt vowing never to try this sort of rap session again.

Afterward, back at the C.C.U., the attending physician in charge that month—he had the improbable name of Lowell Schwartz—gave us an account of a new patient. It was a deliberate, superb instance of life imitating art. Schwartz was enamored of the novel *House of God*, a hilarious, antiheroic account of an internship in internal medicine. Many people at Galen consciously used phrases and jokes from the book. I could not always tell whether the phrases had been in use before they were quoted in the book, but this time there was no doubt. After grilling the students and residents on the details of the case and listing all the relevant symptoms and signs on the blackboard, he wrote at the top, in big block letters, SALVATION on one side, and THE HOUSE OF GOD on the other. "Okay," he said, turning and gazing around at us. "Now that she's in the House of God, how are we going to give her Salvation?" Despite this nonsense, we soon had a plan for the patient that struck me, at least, as better than good.

I walked off with Marty Klein, the C.C.U. intern, a sensible, friendly man who had his heart much more in research on D.N.A. than in his residency. He would sit up half the night in the unit poring excitedly over the latest articles on recombinant methodology, chafing to get back into the laboratory. You could see him sitting there among all the broken bodies, all the failing hearts and lungs, spinning visions of magnificent undreamed-of magic molecules that would put the whole damned messy enterprise of medicine out of business. But at the moment we were finishing evening walk-arounds.

"Lowell Schwartz seems like a bit of a space cadet," I said to him.

"Schwartz? He's a space commandant," he shot back without a pause. "C'mon, let's write our notes and then we can go to pizza rounds."

We calculated the cardiac outputs on a couple of patients and wrote notes on them and a couple of others. We looked in on Burchette, who was "resting comfortably"—a grotesque misnomer for his tube-driven state, yet somehow true. Then I followed Marty to pizza rounds, which turned out to be an informal meal with two other interns and no one else. This was unprecedented, and it made me feel very good. The doctors' lounge had a dingy feel and a locker room smell, but I loved it. Even the cardboard-tasting pizza was a delight. It was a far cry from the time on surgery when I had been sent to "liver rounds"—the weekly beer party—on a floor of the hospital that didn't exist.

On television Walter Cronkite was recounting the life of George Orwell. He gave a disquisition on Newspeak, the language of lies that Orwell had invented for his futuristic society—or rather had extrapolated from the already existing language of lies. Cronkite began listing examples from military language, as in the bizarre reports from Vietnam during the war. Marty said, "We're the worst on this," and the two other interns, stringing mozzarella away from their mouths, nodded awkwardly. As if on cue, Cronkite switched to examples from medical language: "terminal living," which meant dying, was one; "negative patient outcome," meaning death, was another. The laughter in the small, close room was uproarious.

Working closely with Marty Klein and Mike Li, I felt better about medicine than I had in several months. Not that there were no drawbacks. At about three o'clock one morning Marty and I had just gone into the on-call room and lain down when we were called by an excellent C.C.U. nurse. (The nurses there were as good as any I encountered and, if they had been there for five years or more, uniformly better than the residents.)

One of the patients was sitting up in bed with a severe pain on the right side of his chest. It seemed possible that he had had a pulmonary embolism. The nurse was worried, and her concern made sense to me. But Marty did not take the matter seriously, which made the nurses angry and raised a question in my mind about Marty. I liked him because he was smart and funny and intellectual and decent to me. But the nurses questioned his competence, and they knew what they were doing.

My relationship with Mr. Burchette—if you could have a relationship with a man who could hardly acknowledge you, much less speak to you —grew more intense and somehow more rewarding. The stomach lavage was a welcome opportunity to do something of indisputable practical value, forthright and simple, like digging a ditch. My relationship with his wife and family—the daughters and their husbands—was growing, and they relied on me for a strange substitute for communication with him. I was like an interpreter who was partly fluent in "illness," the only language that Mr. Burchette was now speaking.

I liked them a lot. One day when he took a turn for the worse, Dr. Schwartz and I went to the waiting room to talk with them. He sat down close to them, facing the wife directly. He spoke softly and slowly. He looked straight into her eyes. And—an amazing gesture to me, after nearly a year of rotations—he took her hand. She seemed calm for the first time in hours. And I had a new medical hero.

Charlotte lost more weight and was finally scheduled for surgery. Two weeks had gone by, and I was slated to switch again, this time from the C.C.U. to the E.W. I did this regretfully, since the C.C.U. had been the best experience I had had in some time, but I thought I would like another

E.W. stint, this time with medical instead of surgical emergencies. The call schedule was twenty-four hours on, twenty-four off. And we were in charge of any medical problems that happened to walk in off the street, no matter what.

On my first night on call there a textbook procedure came alive. I had learned over and over again that there were pressure receptors in the carotid artery in the neck—right about at the place where the trunk of the common carotid divides, going up toward the brain, the place where you can feel a strong pulse. According to the "storybooks," as some people called the textbooks, a drop in pressure detected there would result in an increase in cardiac activity, increasing the pressure again and thus protecting the all-important brain from lack of blood, the equivalent of a deadly lack of oxygen.

The reverse could also happen; so that if the heart were beating too hard and fast, you could theoretically slow it down by pressing on the carotid sinus. An intern named Rick Naylor walked in on a patient in tachycardia—a very fast heart rhythm—and immediately began massaging the carotids. It was not a benign procedure, since rubbing too hard could stop the heart, but he handled it perfectly and the fast rhythm resolved. It was an elegant thing to watch, not just because it was a textbook tactic that everyone always doubted but because it was so absurdly simple. Hippocrates could have done it. It was a victory over technology, pharmacology, surgery, a triumph for everything simple that had gone out of modern medicine. It was one lone smart doctor against disease and the world.

In the E.W. time passed quickly and not very onerously. The patients moved through the place as if it were a revolving door. There was a short, intense, nervous hemophiliac with bleeding in his joints—a common and exceedingly painful problem. He gave me an education about his condition, and about how patients handle certain problems. He walked in, took over an examining room, ordered his own blood and, under my stunned gaze, his own morphine. He was in great pain, and he had been in the E.W. hundreds of times. He knew much more about his illness than his nurses and doctors, and all of them were eager to learn from him.

An emergency medical technician with asthma also knew how to manage his own treatment. The many medical texts in which doctors thanked their patients for what they had taught them began to take on a new meaning for me. There was a black man with a compressed cervical disc and terrible neck and shoulder pain, whose house had just been broken into, and a slender, pale blond with a neuralgia in her right leg who was wearing underpants with the Playboy bunny stamped all over them. A young black woman came in coughing blood. A grossly obese woman with a swollen ankle, who at first I wanted nothing to do with, turned out to be one of the nicest patients I met. A not very attractive "dancer" in one of the more notorious downtown clubs came in with a goiter, possibly from a grossly inadequate diet. And an elderly woman with a mild stroke on a Sunday, refusing admission, came back on Tuesday with no new symptoms except the most intractable anxiety. These patients were lessons in the sociology of the doctor-patient encounter and of illness itself.

There was an extraordinary couple, Mr. and Mrs. Vilnius, who came in together, each with a serious chronic illness. He was a hemophiliac who regularly bled in his joints and who came in for Factor VIII and morphine. She was the oldest spina bifida patient in the state. Since medicine made survival into adulthood with this condition possible only recently, she was something like a walking miracle. Their tender, pragmatic, lifesaving relationship, observable in the emergency room bay where they were waiting, was remarkable.

As had been the case during my emergency service in surgery, I felt again a temptation to make a career of emergency medicine. I loved the soldier-in-the-trenches aspect of it, the almost constant adrenaline high, the continual clinical surprises, the wonderfully strange people—addicts and alcoholics, prostitutes and convicts, rich people in helpless conditions and poor people with no place to go, I admitted an affection for them all —and, last but not least, the fact that you walked out the door at the end of the day with no further official responsibility on your hands or mind. But people seemed to burn out quickly. The strange hours, the basic abrasiveness of the patient encounters, and the lack of scientific stimulation would eventually get to me. Still, I was romantic enough to feel that it was not out of the question.

I saw Charlotte before she went to surgery, and she seemed less frightened than I'd expected her to be. Nevertheless the underlying agitation ran at an even higher pitch than usual. She seemed to have confidence in her surgeon, as well as continued faith in Dr. Harrison. I never challenged her faith in them, but I wished these two physicians in charge of her case had seen fit to involve the psychiatrists more fully. Their psychological nihilism had been a constant source of frustration. It did not take a genius in psychiatric prognosis to wonder whether the stress of anesthesia and surgery might finally knock out her loose screw. I was proud to be playing amateur psychiatrist but I knew that I was out of my league, especially with surgery now imminent.

When I checked the recovery room to see how she was doing, looking down the row of patients with their many tubes and wires and constant nursing attention, Charlotte seemed strange even from a distance. As I approached I saw that she was in four-point restraint, with a nasogastric tube streaming out of her left nostril, and I.V.'s in both arms. She was writhing pathetically, intensely, incessantly, and fruitlessly.

When she saw me her voice cracked hysterically and she writhed more intensely in the bed. "Come on Mel! Come on! What's going on here? Get me out of here! Mel, I'm serious, get this thing out of my nose. What's going on here? Get me out of here! Come on, untie me, get me out of here, I'm going home. What do they think they're doing here? What are they doing to me? I'm getting out of here!" She pulled at the wrist restraints and tried to reach for the I.V.'s and the nasogastric tube.

I tried to talk with her, but she only continued to repeat the same sentences. She thought she was being tortured. She had no understanding that she had just come out of surgery, or indeed of her illness in general. According to her nurses, she had repeatedly torn the tubes out of her arms and nose and climbed over the railing of the bed. It had taken several people to hold her down and get her into restraint. All the while she had repeated incessantly the same pathetic uncomprehending persecuted phrases.

This was a classic postoperative psychotic break. These are well described in the literature, although it is not clear whether the main cause is an idiosyncratic reaction to the anesthetic, to the stress of surgery itself, or to some other related cause. They are usually transient, but they are unpleasant and dangerous and may herald the onset of a long psychotic disease. In Charlotte's case, I thought, the break had been quite predictable and, correspondingly, preventable, with a little intelligent effort in the psychiatric realm. Her internist and her surgeon had made a mistake as serious as if they had failed to take adequate precautions against wound infection, with the result of serious bacteremia. Yet they would never have to face any awkward consequences, not even learn a lesson, because their ignorance of psychiatry was a source of manly medical pride not only to them but to many of their peers.

A few days later, my next to last on the service, was both the day the new interns arrived and my fifteenth wedding anniversary. The interns were fresh and scared and bumbling, and I was glad at the chance to watch them on their first day of true responsibility as physicians. Predictably, they did not automatically experience a major increase in knowledge between their last day as medical students and their first day as physicians. There was no such magic for them, and there would be no such magic for me.

As they and the residents and even some of the younger faculty chatted about dates and parties and casual encounters, I realized yet again how out of phase my life was with theirs. I had been married for fifteen years. (My wife and I used to joke that we had three-year contracts, which we had to renew deliberately or else our marriage would theoretically automatically lapse. We were renewing our contract that day for the fifth time.) I had two children. I'd had a career teaching students some of whom were now farther along in their medical careers than these residents were.

I went to see Mr. Burchette in the C.C.U.. He was still trached—tracheotomized—and unable to speak, but was now alert and expressive. His wife was standing next to his bed, holding a pen and paper that he had evidently tried to use. He took them now in his trembling hands. "Please I'm going to die," he wrote, awkwardly and slowly, showing the words to me. I shook my head from side to side hopefully, and took and squeezed both their hands. Yet it was not at all unlikely.

Charlotte recovered gradually from her postoperative psychosis and fortunately had no memory of it or indeed of the surgery. On my last visit to her she seemed as well as she had been in weeks, pale but calm. The surgery appeared to have been the right therapeutic choice for her, and she had the highest regard for both Dr. Harrison and the surgeon. It was one of the ironies of medicine that patients could worship doctors who had been clumsy in handling their cases, as long as things came out all right in the end.

We had a pleasant talk. She then tried to give me a check for fifty dollars, made out by her husband, "a token," she said, "just for you and your wife to go out to dinner." I refused this firmly but I did not feel insulted—in fact it was nice to have some acknowledgment of my effort. She also gave me a rather nice pen, which I accepted. And I extracted one further promise of payment: she was to write to me and let me know the first time she played tennis again.

I was scheduled for a fifteen-minute meeting with Dr. Harrison, who would report to me in person the evaluation I would receive for the course. As a teacher, I was impressed with the courage involved in such a confrontation.

I needn't have been. Dr. Harrison sat, without looking at me as usual, and read verbatim from his written summary of my performance. I had been "near excellent" in the C.C.U. and "satisfactory" in all other areas. "Obviously," he said, "you are above average in the psychological aspects of patient care." His tone was unmistakably contemptuous. "But you could do better in terms of medical diagnosis and treatment."

The "fifteen-minute" session had gone on for five minutes and was clearly about to end. I made a quick calculation. I wanted badly to say something about Sally Brass, even though I knew it had to reflect unflatteringly on me. I had no interest in justifying my performance, and the appearance of trying to improve my grade with any sort of argument was abhorrent, but I did not want to pass up the chance to register a complaint. Too much was at stake—future students, patients, and now interns who would be working under her as she entered her second year.

"You remember," I said respectfully, "I did get off to a bad start with the intern who supervised me during the first month—"

He cut me off immediately. The interview was over.

I was taking a brief nap in the E.W. on my last day when I woke up to a phone conversation between Marty Klein and a lawyer. I pieced together some of the story from his end of the conversation and he filled me in afterward on the rest. The lawyer was a twenty-six-year-old woman "wrongly" brought into the hospital by the police a few days earlier. She had telephoned the E.W. to ask how many Sominex would result in death. Marty had been the intern on duty and had talked with her. Something about the way she asked the questions—an edge of hysteria that struck him as if it might be a suicidal person's not very subtle call for help—had led him to send the police to her apartment. She had taken some Sominex, but not enough to kill herself. Now she was angry, and was taking off after Marty with all the legal ingenuity at her disposal. He was, quite rightly, concerned.

Coincidentally, that evening, a taxi driver brought a beautiful blond young man into the E.W., unconscious. He was dressed in a T-shirt and shorts, and had nothing in his pockets except his green plastic Galen hospital card. The driver had been passing by the park and had seen the young man stumbling, adrift on a bizarre, circuitous path on a busy sidewalk. He had watched as the young man finally fell and had gone over to examine him. Taxi drivers often served as monitors for the lonely ill. When he found the Galen card in the young man's pocket, he brought him immediately to the E.W.

I was to spend the next twelve hours or so with this man. I checked his heart rate, respirations, and blood pressure, all of which were adequate. It was expected, however, that he would deteriorate, and he did. He had apparently ingested something, and whatever it was was sitting in his stomach slowly but surely leaking into his bloodstream. He lay on the table unconscious, naked except for his short shorts—an Adonis, really. It was extraordinary to see this shapely well-muscled body, this unusually fine face, and to know that despite the temporarily stable vital signs, he was unmistakably, in both senses, trying hard to die. And that he might still do so.

I took a blood sample and sent it out for toxicity screening. Then I intubated him nasogastrically and began pumping charcoal into his stomach. Time was important, and I worked steadily and quickly. Marty checked in on me frequently but had his own emergency, and saw that I was doing about as much as anyone could.

Finally the young man returned some stomach contents through the tube, and they contained something bright pink that could only be pills. But many pills were red or pink, and we couldn't figure out what he had taken on the basis of this. Still, at least we knew we were right about the ingestion, and that we could probably forget other theories about how he might have become unconscious. His hospital chart, which finally came down from the record room, confirmed that he had had previous suicide attempts and that there were no chronic medical illnesses, such as diabetes or liver disease, that might cause this collapse. However, the chart showed that he was an epileptic, which suggested the pills he might have taken, as well as raising an alternative explanation for his collapse. But there was no evidence of a pattern of past seizures that could have resembled the picture he now presented.

Most of all, we knew that we were getting some of the poison out of his stomach. Those pink globs in the brown and gray mush were among the poisons that might have killed him, and I had pulled them out with an enormous plastic syringe and squirted them into a metal bowl on the table. I was pumping and pumping, washing the charcoal in and the stomach contents out, and with every cycle I felt that the chances of his death were diminishing.

Finally, after about three hours, he began to regain consciousness, and admitted, in a drowsy, helpless voice, that he had tried to take his life.

Over the course of the next hour, he said that he had drunk two bottles of champagne and taken most of the pills he could find in the house. These included fifty to seventy Dilantin, his antiseizure medication (which was colored red and purple), and a small number of the analgesic Dalmane, as well as possibly some phenobarbitol.

The more he recovered consciousness, the more he chatted, pleasantly but sadly, about his psychiatric history and his suicide attempts. He was thirty-five years old, gay, and under long-term psychiatric treatment. He worked as a waiter in a dining car on a train. He had been hospitalized for a month for psychiatric treatment seven years previously. I found him gentle and intelligent and began to like him a lot.

Then he began to talk about leaving so he could get to work in the morning. He was probably not in really grave danger, but all the E.W. residents agreed that there would be no excuse for discharging him. He would have to be observed overnight. He now began to express some resentment at this. He was talking thickly and was unsteady even in a sitting position. If he were discharged, he could be dangerous to himself in a dozen different ways, only one of which was another attempt at suicide. And of course, there was no assurance that further absorption of drugs from the small intestine would not yet increase his blood levels to a potentially lethal range.

A psychiatry resident reviewed the chart quickly and took in what I told him about the case without much comment. "Let's go see him," he said.

He began to interview the young man, and the answers were now beginning to be surly. The advice was clear: the medical and psychiatric situations were life-threatening, and he had to stay in the hospital. But the patient had no intention of doing this. At one point a truly hard edge crept into his voice, as he said, "Do you think you can lock me up in here? You better not think you can do that," and he leaned forward suddenly. The psychiatry resident took a step backward. Suddenly I felt that I was in the presence of a potentially dangerous man, whose remarks became steadily more surly as he became less drowsy. The psychiatrist and I left the room.

"He's a worm," said the psychiatrist matter-of-factly.

"What?"

"Forget about him. He's a worm."

I did not forget about him, but the psychiatrist was right. The more persistently I tried to explain the importance of his staying in the hospital, the more mean and surly he became toward me. I had saved his life, and he was returning that kindness with remarks as nasty as any that had ever been directed at me. His face was contorted into such ugly expressions, such grotesque reflections of a sick, twisted soul, that I could not believe that I had found it attractive, even asleep. As he had risen through the levels of consciousness, from coma to stupor to drowsiness to semialertness, he had gone through a personality change more dramatic than any I had ever seen.

The psychiatrist had deemed it unfeasible to attempt a civil commitment. The young man was free to go. He climbed down from the table with difficulty and began walking unsteadily, like a very drunk man exerting tremendous control over his movements, out of the room and down the corridor. I followed him at a newly respectful distance. He looked around at me with immense resentment. But nothing could stop me from following him to the front door of the hospital, and I did this, despite the fact that he was out of my jurisdiction as soon as he left the E.W.

He turned and gave me a bitterly sardonic smile as he stepped across the threshold. I stepped after him; leaning in the doorway, taking in the cool night air, I watched him progress down the steps and down the long walk to the sidewalk at the edge of the busy street. Beside me at the top of the steps, the statue of Galen stared stonily down. *This,* it seemed to say, *is not Medicine. This is not my sphere of responsibility.*

The young man walked like a drunk taking a test for sobriety, holding himself comically almost steady, yet never dropping the grotesque hateful expression from his face. He turned left, walked a few paces, and then turned completely around and took off in the other direction down the sidewalk. He continued walking in that direction, looking back only once, and I watched him until he disappeared into the warm night.

15

THE FOURTH YEAR

Highlights and Heroes

If the third year of medical school represents a sort of sink-or-swim immersion, fraught with continuous anxious transformation, the fourth offers something akin to coasting. The student is not a doctor in most important senses of the word, but the elemental skills are in place, and a surprisingly high proportion of critical events have been experienced or at least observed closely. The goal of the fourth year is to develop the skills, under conditions of blissful nonresponsibility, before the assault of internship brings responsibility with a vengeance. Much of the program is elective, and the student can choose to sample freely among medical disciplines, or concentrate on a future field of specialization, or some combination of the two. It is a time—a last time—for consolidation, exploration, and thought.

One of the first things I determined to do with my elective time was more inpatient psychiatry with John Brandt and his radical pharmacologizing. I knew his approach had limits, but I also knew that it represented the hard core of scientific psychiatry as it was likely to be practiced for the near future. It was something I could get hold of, something I could learn to do, an island of proven value in a sea of hypothetically effective psychological interventions. After learning it I could think it over, see its limitations, somehow get beyond it. But first I wanted to learn it, and learn it well.

I also wanted to be with Brandt. Before entering medical school, I had had years of experience with soft psychiatry and psychology. I had been in psychoanalytically oriented psychotherapy, and I had read at least a dozen of Freud's books. As an anthropologist, I could not avoid being influenced and instructed by the psychodynamic theorists. But Brandt's persistent "Just show me any kind of evidence!" applied not only to patient care but to psychodynamic interpretation generally. My main experience in trying to use it in anthropology had been—after a period of seeming illumination—one of confusion and disappointment. Yet when I was with Brandt, I invariably defended it. Perhaps because of my own experience in psychotherapy; or because in some sense, like many people I viewed and reviewed my own life as a sort of psychodynamic odyssey. Perhaps it was only because the weight of European literary and philosophic tradition, which I revered, needed no evidence to declare the child the father of the man. For whatever reason, part of me was and is committed to this view of the mind and of human life experience.

Brandt had got into psychoanalysis because it was the thing to do if you aspired to leadership in psychiatry. But by the time he reached mid-career the psychopharmacology revolution had been so successful that psychoanalysis was in retreat, and the once essential didactic analysis no longer mattered.

We shared three patients, and each was a revelation to me. Stephen Riggs was a tense, wiry, thirty-year-old who could command a diagnosis of schizophrenia even from Brandt. To Brandt schizophrenia was almost a ruse; it belonged in quotation marks. After removing from the category every case that deserved the rediagnosis of affective disorder (manic-depressive illness for the cyclical "schizophrenias," depression with psychotic features for some of the chronic ones) what was left was a wastebasket category, "residual idiopathic non-affective psychosis." ("Idiopathic" is one of at least five euphemisms in medicine meaning "We don't know what caused it" or, in plain English, "Huh?" The others are "cryptogenic," "essential," "primary," and "functional.") These idiopathic psychoses, according to Brandt, were caused by a variety of anatomical brain malformations—subtle perhaps, but outside the category of genetically and physiologically meaningful psychosis.

I first saw Stephen Riggs in a white room bare except for a mattress without sheets. He sat on the mattress looking disheveled and filthy and talked in circles about his thoughts. Brandt stayed with us for a while, and then left us alone together. I sat on the floor not far from his mattress and tried to give him a mental status examination during the first of our many conversations.

His mental status was bizarre—even in a ward full of people with bizarre thoughts. He did not describe paranoid notions or voices or strange ideas about his influence on the world. His thoughts were not racing, he was not euphoric and he was not depressed. He was simply obsessed with his own thoughts. He talked about them in a way that was difficult to understand, not because it was incoherent but because it had so little content. He spoke very slowly, without emotion of any kind. "It's not better today. I really can't control them. I'm trying very hard to control them. I'm afraid they're going to get away from me. I keep going over and over them. Maybe if I keep going over and over them I'll be able to control them."

"Them?" I asked.

"The thoughts," he said impatiently. As far as I could tell the thoughts were not about anything except the difficulty of keeping them under control.

Stephen had experienced a steadily deteriorating and chronic impairment since the last year of high school, when he flunked out. His older brother had committed suicide not long before that. His parents were able to support him through a dozen years of increasing disability—some education here, a religious commune there, once in a long while, very briefly, a job—with occasional significant contact with the apparatus of psychiatric care. Both his flatness of affect and his chronic isolation suggested schizophrenia, and so did the relentless course of his illness.

After a few days he came out of the bare room and got a room of his own on the ward, a pleasant dormitory-style hall. He said he was feeling better, and so he was able to keep notes on the problems he was having with his thoughts. The notes, written with painful care on tiny pieces of paper, were no more informative than his conversation. If the basic distinction between people and animals is that people are conscious of their own mental functions, then Stephen had carried this consciousness to a bizarre extreme. He was the ultimate solipsistic self-reflective intellectual, the most self-conscious person I ever met.

Frank Snell was a fast-talking hustler in his late twenties who did not quite seem to belong in the hospital. On two or three occasions over the past few years he had gone to Saudi Arabia, where he had vague plans for making a lot of money. None of these plans had worked out, but he was still hopeful about them and about some newer ones. On the last return home he stayed with his parents, argued with them, and in a fit of rage began throwing furniture—including one chair through a window.

This was the extent of his symptomatology, and that fact made me very uncomfortable. He seemed like a wild young man with a lot to learn about life; but that described a great many young men outside the locked doors of Burdick. Snell was inside, and on lithium, one of the most powerful of psychiatric drugs. From the moment of his arrival, every time I saw him, he continued to insist on his normality and the unfairness of his being locked up. He blamed his parents, who didn't share his confidence in himself and were "trying to prevent him from making good."

I thought of Soviet "mental hospitals" where diagnosed dissidents suffered "treatments" for "mental illnesses" that were such only in the minds of politically motivated psychiatrists. Frank Snell seemed reasonable. His conversations with me were always completely rational, and his resentment of his parents seemed reasonable. His speech was pressured—difficult to interrupt—but in academic life I had known worse on that score. O.K., so he got angry and threw a chair out the window. So he had some unsuccessful wacky-sounding business ventures. Did these behaviors merit hospitalization?

The third patient was Carrie Jonquil, a former nurse. At the age of twenty-two she had had a depression ostensibly precipitated when one of her patients, an elderly woman in a deteriorated condition, died shortly after Carrie gave her an injection. The injection had been routine—an appropriate dose of a sedative—and no one had suggested that Carrie had been in error, or that the injection had anything to do with the woman's death, which in any case was expected. However, Carrie had gone into a long, profound depression in which the main theme had been obsessive thoughts about this death and her responsibility for it. After some months she had received an inappropriate diagnosis of schizophrenia, her obsessive guilty thoughts being deemed a "first-rank symptom" of this disorder. She was placed on a drug of the phenothiazine class. Her depression gradually improved—as depressions often do spontaneously—and although she was seen repeatedly she was not taken off the drug.

After two years of treatment she developed a now classic, dreaded side effect known as tardive dyskinesia. This disorder affects a substantial proportion of patients treated for many years with antischizophrenic drugs. In Carrie's case it developed unusually early and was, as is often the case, permanent. Because of the drug's damage to the brain, her arms, hands, mouth, tongue, and to a lesser extent other muscle groups involuntarily twisted and contorted, sometimes jerkily, sometimes sinuously, in movements that neurologists call by the Latin words for "dancelike" and "changeable." She received every available treatment for the condition without effect, and more than enough time had passed to ensure that she would not be among the lucky sufferers from tardive dyskinesia who recover spontaneously.

She was now twenty-five years old, intelligent, pretty—with dark hair and dark eyebrows framing a strong face—and trapped in a body with a humiliatingly damaged nervous system that rendered her the virtual antithesis of grace. Her depression was more or less under control, since an appropriate new drug regime had been instituted—ironically, since her brain damage gave her every reason to be depressed—and she was now completely dependent on doctors, who as a class were responsible for wrecking her brain and her life.

She did not like to be interviewed, but she was tolerant of me. I was hoping against hope that some neurological magic might bring her back from her crippled state. I was hooked on her. I went to the library and pored over all the latest papers—thousands of people like her were being studied all over the world. I arranged for her to be seen by a visiting neurologist, as if he might have some special insight that the lesser neurologists and psychiatrists who had already seen her had failed to have. Brandt encouraged me; he must have thought it was worth the lesson.

Neither my library doggedness nor my great-physician fantasy produced any results. I'd had sense enough not to say anything to raise her hopes, so there was no letdown; but the intensity of my desire to find some way to help her must have communicated itself to her. In any case she allowed me to hang around her a bit, a privilege she granted very few. Most of the time she sat in her room, not moping exactly, but glad to keep her deformity—an active, aggressive one that insisted upon itself continually—out of human view, even if this meant almost complete isolation.

I touched her, perhaps, but I did not make her feel much better, which John Brandt certainly did. I don't know exactly how he did it, but he would come into her room and within a few minutes she would be laughing. It was partly that he refused to treat her gingerly. He recognized her deformity as the central fact of her life, talked about it openly, even joked about it. This strength of his, this boldness in crossing the terrible boundary that seemed so formidable to others, endeared him to her. In any case, she had a sort of crush on him, and he used it like a medicine. Each of his visits was a warm brusque cheerful pass through her realm of isolation, and I would watch it work on her like a pep pill. I looked forward to these visits myself; it felt so good to see a smile appear for a time on that resigned, pretty, contorted face.

During that rotation I went to see the head of the hospital, a psychiatrist with important connections in Washington. I'd sent him a copy of my book about human nature, and I wanted to get his reaction to it and to my prospects for integrating my previous work with the practice of psychiatry. But the most interesting thing we talked about was Brandt, whom I went out of my way to praise. I praised his teaching, his way with patients, his mind, his clinical acumen.

"Yes," said the head of the hospital with a big diplomatic smile on his face, "yes, but he's not wise." I considered this extraordinary statement for a moment, and did a quick mental cost-benefit analysis of pressing the point. But against my better judgment I proceeded to sing John's praises again. The head of the hospital looked across at me—we were surrounded by lavish paneling, comfortable Scandinavian furniture, large intricate plants. "Yes," he said, with the same tone of voice, with exactly the same smile on his face, "but he's not wise." I knew enough about the habits of important men to know that such a precise repetition meant that the point was not open to discussion.

John Brandt seemed wise to me. Maybe not diplomatic, not eclectic, not political, maybe not even right—but wise in his core, in his heart, in his bones. Did he close his eyes to some of the complexities of psychiatric disorder? Unquestionably. Did he limit his challenges to patients who he thought might have a classic response to lithium, avoiding such things as character disorders, alcoholism, and drug addiction? Yes, but he had a right, on the frontier of knowledge, to focus on a treatment he could define and make work. Manic-depressive illness had once been a deadly disease, with most patients ending as suicides. Even now it was among the riskiest of psychiatric disorders. His goal in life was to manage it, and he was fulfilling that goal well.

I was glad he was in the world, with his relentless funny skepticism of unproven theories accepted by everyone else. I was glad he was always there to say, "Just show me any kind of evidence." I thought he could help keep the proponents of unproven theories honest. I even thought, with a crowning irony, that his continual ribbing might force them to produce the evidence that would lay his skepticism to rest forever.

As for the patients, they were usually on his side, or at least their cases usually followed his predictions. For several months Stephen Riggs continued to be obsessed with his thoughts about his thoughts about his thoughts about his thoughts, and then for some reason he showed marked improvement. Brandt laughed at himself then: the one patient he had been willing to accept as an incontrovertible chronic schizophrenic was showing signs of a possible cyclical disorder; so much for tolerance for the enemy.

Frank Snell stabilized on lithium, and his talk and behavior changed subtly but markedly. His speech was no longer pressured, his plans for the future were more realistic, and the sense that he was on the edge of a violent outburst disappeared. He seemed to regain control of himself. Something a little glorious in his character had disappeared, too, but lithium gave him back the ability to live—a fair trade, to my mind, for his unwieldy, reckless, and finally unhealthy sort of glory.

As for Carrie Jonquil, her very presence, her every contorted posture and forced graceless movement, proclaimed to anyone who paid attention that the cost of diagnosing schizophrenia where there is none is unacceptably high. If trying to prevent this outcome is not wisdom, I don't know what wisdom is. In the meantime she had to deal with her depression, to recover from it, to come out of her isolation, to live. John Brandt helped her. His smiles, his bad bold jokes, his unmistakable awkward tenderness made life better for her, just as if she had been a patient in neurosurgery with unavoidable permanent brain damage. He fulfilled his own precept of being good to his patients in the way that his surgeon father had been good to his. There was no talking cure for tardive dyskinesia—or even, as far as he was concerned, for depression—but there was all that can be gained from the healing voice and touch—laughter, gentleness, dignity. That was as much wisdom as I needed to see in a doctor, and to me John Brandt was a hero.

So, beyond a doubt, was Johann Ringler. He was another person I had singled out from the third year, someone I knew I wanted more exposure to. A month with him on the pediatric endocrine service was a revelation. The patients were children and adolescents with abnormalities of growth, of genital development, of the pacing of puberty. He sat there with that twinkle in his eye, holding his pen up to one teenager or another, saying, "If this pen would be a magic wand, what one thing would you change . . . or would you rather keep that a secret?" They always told him, although sometimes they had him kick their mothers out first. They were confronting their abnormalities in that strange moment of life when comparing oneself to others is the only rule one knows, and the comparison was unfavorable. He knew it, and they knew he did, and they soon trusted him not to belittle their feelings. He talked to them gently, or directed them with a warm strong paternalism, or edged over next to them and put his arm around their shoulders. Unfailingly, he knew how to make them feel at ease and how to make them listen.

These gestures were healing in almost every case. That is, they made a difference in the choices the patients made, in the way they conceived their futures, in the way they felt about themselves. But with two categories of patients Ringler's bedside manner could be a matter of life and death. The first was the juvenile diabetics whom I had seen him work so well with during my third-year pediatrics rotation. His magic made them "good" diabetics—compliant with their diets and insulin regimes, however difficult it might be in the course of a teenage life.

The second was anorexics. These in a strict way were not even his business. I had always encountered anorexics in a psychiatric context—except for Charlotte Kaplan, who suffered so terribly because she was prevented from getting psychiatric help. The psychiatrists could certainly stabilize the disorder and reduce the 5 to 10 percent mortality rate to something more acceptable. But they laid no claims to having solved it, and they usually shook their heads sadly and acknowledged how intractable a disorder this was.

Ringler responded to anorexics with his usual magic. They came his way when the referring physicians considered these teenage girls as having primarily metabolic rather than psychiatric disorders. This placed the emphasis in the wrong place, considering the consequences of the disorder rather than its etiology. But Ringler accepted the windfall and took the patients figuratively and literally in hand. Arm around their shoulders, he made simple and crystal-clear deals with every one of them.

"You will come here every Monday and Thursday, to be weighed on my scale there. You will gain one pound a week or I will put you in the hospital. You agree to that now, or I will not take care of you. One pound a week. And don't forget, I know all the tricks—hiding pieces of metal here and there, loading up on water before you walk through the door, all of them. The metal trick won't work at all. The water trick will work for one week. Am I making myself clear?"

He produced this stern monologue for the benefit of Peggy Ferguson, a sixteen-year-old blond, tastefully made up and stylishly dressed, who sat quietly across the desk from him while her parents sat nearby, listening with a different kind of attentiveness. They had pressured her to come in, but that might not have been enough in itself. Fortunately there was also a boyfriend who was concerned about her health and who had sense enough to know that her dietary habits were off the scale of normal.

"I know you are sitting there thinking you can fool me. You can't, but you will try anyway. I know more about you than you know about yourself. I am not like the psychiatrists, who wait around and talk back and forth on and on as the weeks and months go by while you keep losing weight. I am setting the goals, and I am going to hold you to them rigidly. You are not in charge now. I am in charge from now on. You will gain weight, according to my schedule, or I will put you in the hospital."

Peggy's eyes had that clear superior look of teenage confidence that says, Yeah, tell me about it, I'm not afraid of you.

"Chances are you will come into the hospital. When you are in the hospital you will not leave your bed, even to go to the bathroom. If I let you go to the bathroom you would vomit. So you will stay in bed and use a bedpan. You will be watched constantly. And you will eat. The only reason you will get out of the bed will be to get on the scale. You will gain one pound a week. And if you don't, I will feed you intravenously. Then you will gain weight, and then after that you will gradually learn to eat again."

When Peggy was about thirteen she had had a period of being very overweight. This had so unnerved her that when she lost weight, she never stopped. The interesting thing about her was that she was not an advanced case. Ringler had dealt with many anorexics successfully, both early and late in the course of illness, but he obviously much preferred to intervene early. What was unusual was his insistence upon hospitalizing them *before* there were medical indications for doing so—before the appearance of such life-threatening consequences of starvation as slowing of the heartbeat and breathing, low serum potassium, and low body temperature. Ringler put his patients in the hospital before any of these things happened, a strategy that sometimes involved a struggle with the hospital administrators.

But Peggy had all the signs and symptoms of the psychiatric disorder, and at least one medical consequence, cessation of menses. (According to one theory an unconscious goal of anorexia is to deny reproductive maturity.) That was enough for him. In any case, he hospitalized her for the reason he gave her—she failed to gain a pound a week.

In the hospital she tried all the tricks, just as he had predicted she would. Like many anorexics, she was horrified by the prospect of intravenous feeding; the concern with body image that is at or near the center of the syndrome was absolutely outraged at the thought of tubes running into veins in both arms. In Peggy's case, the combination of that threat, plus Ringler's visits—we visited her together at least once a day—sufficed, under conditions of restricted movement and closely observed eating, to make her begin slowly to gain weight.

It would have to be said that Ringler treated her like a child. He patronized her, gave her orders, behaved paternalistically, and all in all performed perfectly the role of the Central European Father (he had four children of his own). But he *was* a pediatrician, and his patients were not adults, even the ones who, like Peggy, were on the verge of adulthood and liked to think of themselves as adults. It might be said that he was playing into their illness. They wanted to be treated like children—they had no menses, their bodies returned to a prepubescent state, they engaged in a constant childish struggle with their parents, whose efforts to make them eat invariably recalled an earlier stage of childhood. But by treating them like children, he gained a certain admission into their quite disturbed world that was denied to others who insisted on respecting them as adults.

In short, his approach ran against much psychological theory, or at least ignored it, and it worked. Peggy gained weight more or less steadily, and was discharged from the hospital after two weeks. She did not exactly have a smile on her face—she resented being brought back from the brink of self-starvation, and like all anorexics she resented losing the battle with her elders about how much she should eat. In Ringler's program of outpatient follow-up, she joined several dozen other patients whom he had followed long enough to establish that they had outgrown anorexia. Not that there was no backsliding—occasionally there was even a second hospitalization. But his rate of success was remarkable. I discussed it with a psychiatrist I had worked with in Galen's eating disorders unit. He knew about Ringler's approach and was impressed. "The damn trouble is," he said, "you have to be Ringler to do it."

I tried to picture the psychiatrist throwing his arm around one of Ringler's teenagers as she stepped down off the scale. I tried to picture myself doing it. "I see what you mean," I said.

One of the gratifying things we did that did not depend on Ringler's personality was the treatment of hypothyroid newborns. These were infants with congenital absence, malplacement, or inadequacy of the thyroid gland. They came to the pediatric endocrinology clinic because their parents got a letter from the state telling them of the disorder. That letter stood between their children and the syndrome of severe mental retardation that gave the world the word "cretin"—an irreversible condition with abnormalities of the face and body that stigmatizes the victim as being mentally retarded from the specific cause of hypothyroidism in early life.

Whenever one of these infants came in—the one in several thousand newborns who had been picked up by the state-sponsored screening program—I thought of the man who wrote those letters, who in fact had developed the program and put it in place. He was the public-health specialist I had met at an elegant brunch two years before, the doctor who had claimed that there was no real purpose to medicine; that medical practice was a complete waste of time. In the thyroid screening program, he tested a spot of blood on a card provided by the parents of every newborn infant in the state. With this effort, he was convinced, he'd done more good in a few years than he had in his entire previous career as a practicing physician.

Of course, without Dr. Ringler or someone like him to give the thyroid hormone replacement therapy that saved the infant's brain, the program wouldn't work. But the key step was to pick the vulnerable infant out of the crowd. One could then confirm the diagnosis of hypothyroidism, try to determine the cause of it, and institute treatment. As long as this was done before the patient was three months old, the child had an excellent chance of growing normally.

While examining one of these babies I looked up at the parents and realized I was looking into a familiar face. The father was Sjogren, the big, bearded, rough-edged Norwegian resident I had encountered on surgery —the arrogant one who had referred to pediatric burn patients as "crispy critters" and who had said of a woman with clogged carotid arteries, "She might shoot some cookies into her helmet." Now he was more subdued— not only, perhaps, with fear for his newborn daughter, but because with his specialty fellowship the pace was more humane and the work more thoughtful.

He, his wife, Ringler, and I looked at the thyroid scan. The uptake of radioactive iodine showed that the baby girl had only rudimentary thyroid tissue. It was located in two places—one tiny bit in the normal location in the neck, another in an abnormal location at the base of the tongue. This was in the gland's path of embryological migration to its normal place; in this case the migration had been incomplete.

As the father of two children, my heart went out to Sjogren, but I couldn't help thinking of the irony of this turn of events. Here was the proponent of surgical intervention as the acid test of real-man medicine; the man who called medical doctors fleas and neurologists "the worst fleas in medicine—the last to leave a dying body." Not only was he now in the hands of Ringler, an undoubted flea; but—worse, by far—his child's life, or at least mind, was going to be saved by nothing more than a screening program—not even medical action, just prevention. And I couldn't help wondering what sort of clever remark he might have made, before this, about the man who gave up the practice of medicine to measure levels of thyroid hormones on blotting paper with little spots of blood.

The Sjogrens' second visit took place late on a Friday afternoon. I'd been looking forward to getting home to my wife and two children, and it looked as if I might get out of the hospital by six o'clock. Then Ringler's beeper rang. It was the emergency room, and I began trying to mimic his long strides as we made our way down there.

He was almost always in the hospital until late in the evening, and I had asked him once, while striding somewhere else, what his motivation was. The smile on his face had been winning. "It's a chance, or maybe a feeling, that you might be able to beat the odds. That if you give that extra hour, or two hours, you might be able to make the difference, to beat an illness that might otherwise have won."

This time the message delivered between the strides was a specific one. The patient was a three-year-old boy with congenital adrenal hyperplasia. There were several forms of this enlargement of the cortex, or outer part, of the adrenal gland. This boy's was based on a genetic defect in one of the enzymes involved in hormone synthesis in the gland, eleven-hydroxy-lase deficiency, which had two dangerous consequences—hypertension and loss of salt. He had to be managed with exceptional deftness on relatively new and only erratically effective hormone replacement therapy. No matter how carefully his doctors and parents monitored his salt and fluid and blood pressure fluctuations, there would be frequent inevitable crises, times when he would go out of control, and have to be admitted to the hospital for restabilization. Such crises were often life-threatening.

Ringler's eyes were wide, his kind face glowing excitedly at the prospect of beating the odds again. The pediatric section of the E.W. was quiet, and it took us a while to find the right examining room. It was a small, dingy one, with paint peeling off the walls, and in the center there was a stretcher holding a slender, pale boy. Two residents and a nurse hovered over him, an I.V. was in place, and in a moment of instantaneous silent communication the senior resident conveyed to Ringler that the situation was basically under control. He examined the boy briefly and asked the senior a few questions about the treatment. He nodded at the answers in a satisfied way. "O.K.," he said. Then he looked around to find the mother. Only a minute or so had passed since we walked into the room.

The mother's frail-looking body was an adult version of the boy's. She was very pale, with short dark straight disheveled hair and on her face a look of the most terrible anguish. Her body was tense and bent, as if she were trying to protect her chest and belly. She looked up at Ringler with a gaze of abject supplication. I realized that Ringler did not know her, but he knew the boy's syndrome, and so he knew exactly what the mother was going through. He began to speak. "He's O.K. It's frightening, I know. But these things have to happen. He's stable now, it's all under—"

Then something clicked in his wonderful intuitive, born-clinician's mind, as he recognized the particular anguish she projected. He paused for a long moment during which he met her eyes. The question burst out of him: *"Do you blame yourself?"*

Her nod was automatic, repeated again and again, as she began to cry. They almost fell toward each other, and in one motion he folded her in his arms and sat her down beside him on the chairs against the wall. In a voice full of strength and tenderness, welling up with the most spontaneous honesty, and with more than a little anguish of his own, he said, *"I can't stand it when you blame yourself."* These words broke down whatever defenses were left in her, and she sobbed and shook in his arms until there were no more tears.

One of the things I did in the fourth year that I should have done sooner was a rotation in diagnostic radiology. This established as familiar a hundred strange images and shadows, each a key to the recognition of a disease, each pointing vaguely toward a path leading out. I have never been a very visual person, yet there was something sufficiently satisfying about seeing *through* people, about the concrete anatomical representation of their pathologies, to elicit my interest and make me do well. The rotation was set up to provide a grounding in general radiology during the first two weeks, followed by two weeks of specialization. By the end of the second week I had committed to memory so many shadows of chests and guts and skulls and limbs that I glided through the examination—twenty unknowns snapped onto the viewing boxes—enjoying the various puzzles.

Then I was given the option to specialize, and from long-standing interest, I opted for two weeks of neuroradiology—imaging of the disorders of the brain. Here I spent day after day gazing at the shadows of brains and spinal cords—mostly radiographs of the skull and spine and CAT scans of the soft tissue enclosed by them. N.M.R.—nuclear magnetic resonance, also known as M.R.I., or magnetic resonance imaging—was then only at the investigational stage at Galen; although I saw a few, they were not routine. They were expected to be better for imaging tumors of the cerebellum and brain stem, because these were heavily surrounded by bone, where CAT scans were subject to glare. They were also valuable in such diseases as multiple sclerosis, which cause the deterioration of white matter, because they imaged the difference between gray and white matter so well. Still, the old-fashioned bony X-rays and especially CAT scans spoke eloquently about many neurological disorders.

The unit was dominated by two young faculty members. One, Betsy Sinclair, was a serenely competent and brilliant Southern woman in her early thirties with whom I immediately half fell in love. Her soft, curly brown hair set off big alert brown eyes in a large-boned elegant face; her lips were sensuous and her skin an unblemished milky beige, here and there suffused with pink. Her voice was so musical and soothing that I found it sometimes difficult to concentrate on what she was saying. She might be saying "craniopharyngioma" or "transphenoidal hypophysectomy" or "Schedule the next angiogram at four," but I could look into her eyes and imagine her saying "Ashley, honey, don't you just *love* the magnolias?" Of course, this was partly a male defensive reaction against her brilliance. She was not only a fine young clinician but a well-published scientist. The chief of neurosurgery, never a friendly man, would come down, grin broadly at her, and say "Here's the Queen of the Pituitary."

In contrast to Betsy Sinclair was Barry Goldfarb, a basically good-natured but foul-mouthed and vulgar man who hailed from my own home town, Brooklyn. Every time he opened his mouth I was wrenched back to my childhood, and I half expected to get slammed in the head with a stickball bat while desperately trying to slide home to a sewer. Against the background of Betsy's polite, elegant drawl, Barry's voice would rasp like a belch, and every fourth or fifth word was "shit" or "fuck" or "piss." *"What the shit are we gonna do if this fucker bleeds into his brain stem?"*

There was an art to this, I remembered from Brooklyn, which involved continual creativity in the placement of those forbidden words, a sort of dirty syntactic imagination. But of course, there was always your basic "What the fuck are you doin', you schmuck, you call that contrast enhancement?" which could be thrown at a resident or medical student at will. Then Betsy might say, "Barry . . ." with her peculiarly Southern mild brand of impatience, and I could close my eyes and hear Scarlett saying "Tara."

"Beauty and the Beast," I called them, obviously, when Henry Benson and I—he was the resident I worked most closely with—watched them discuss a case. We both chuckled softly. Henry was kind to me and in general gentle to a fault, and Barry made his life utterly miserable. Still, Henry kept his sense of humor. After one dose of invective that had contained as many "schmucks," "drecks," and "schmecklachs" as the more obviously harsh American street words, I said to Henry, "Barry is the kind of guy who makes me ashamed to be a New York Jew."

"He's not so bad," Henry said, and turned back to a CAT scan. Henry was from a small town in the Midwest, and had done the first year of his residency in Toledo. He spoke quietly and unpretentiously.

I said, "Well, I bet in Toledo you didn't get cursed out in Yiddish."

"Oh, no?" he said, without looking up from the scan.

Betsy and Barry were both expert at cerebral angiography, one of the most sophisticated, difficult, and risky techniques of brain imaging. This procedure basically involves injecting a radio-opaque dye into the vasculature of the brain and then making a skull X-ray; not only the bony structures but also the dye makes shadows, and so the brain's blood vessels can be visualized. However, the dye cannot simply be inoculated into the general circulation—it would dissipate before it could be of use in demonstrating the vessels of the brain. It has to be introduced into the brain's own circulation.

This is done by an exquisitely deft procedure. The patient is anesthetized, and a special catheter is introduced into the femoral artery, at the groin. From here the catheter is slowly snaked up the great arterial tree, past the beating heart, to the common carotid artery. Then it has to be advanced, with much greater difficulty, up the narrowing and branching portion of the arterial circulation for the brain. At critical branching points a bit of test-dye is released, and a machine, at the bidding of a pedal, produces a fleeting image of the part of the tree that has just been injected. If it is off, the catheter will be drawn back and re-advanced, and another image made, until the tip is ideally situated. Then, finally, a series of cerebral angiographs, or permanent vascular pictures, are made.

For these procedures Betsy Sinclair wore a lead apron with a yellow paisley print on its plastic cover, looking for all the world as if she had just stepped out of the kitchen. With her hands at the groin of a patient, holding the end of a long, carefully positioned catheter, she could poke around safely in his brain, governing its integrity with the gentlest motion of her wrist. And with the pedals under her foot she could deliver the subtlest injection of dye, the most discrete (and discreet) dose of radiation. Barry was good at this too, but I knew who I would have wanted poking around in my vessels. Concentrate as I might on the thing as a medical procedure, I could not help feeling that this process by which she snaked her catheter around in the patient's vascular tree was somehow erotic.

On some occasions it was almost explicitly maternal. She specialized in the visualization of infants' and children's brains, and more than once I went with her to the pediatric wing of Galen to see a follow-up on a successfully treated case of congenital hydrocephalus or a child going blind with an optic nerve glioma. She was at her gentlest bending over an anesthetized baby whose brain she had to image with angiography. Once I noticed an anesthesiologist with a button on the chest of his surgical greens. I leaned over the body of an unconscious toddler to read it: "Come near me and I'll kill you." I drew back instinctively, at the same time enjoying the joke: the anesthesiologist did not look dangerous. Still, the contrast between his crazy button and Betsy Sinclair's *gentillesse* was more than a little compelling.

The procedure was not without risk. Clots could form at the catheter tip, break off, and travel through the vascular tree, lodging in some vessel. Excess dye could cause a spasm, constricting an artery that could choke off a piece of the brain. The procedure was therefore not done lightly or without trepidation. But Betsy, with her serenity and confidence, seemed about as safe with it as anyone could be.

She and Barry were also helping to pioneer an unprecedentedly invasive form of radiology. While poking around in the brain vasculature for diagnostic angiography, some neuroradiologists had come upon the idea of doing something in there besides imaging. Within a few years, a burgeoning field of manipulative neuroradiology had grown up in diagnostic angiography suites. Vascular malformations—such as the one that had caused some of the terrible headaches and abnormalities of vision I had observed in neurosurgery—were being treated by introduction of a catheter and injection of what was basically a glue instead of a dye. They could sometimes be cut off by this procedure and benignly destroyed, relieving the symptoms without surgery.

Another technique was the introduction of a balloon catheter to cut off an abnormality in the blood vessels of the brain. For example, there was a dangerous condition called a carotid-cavernous sinus fistula—an abnormal open flow of blood from the carotid artery in the region of one of its larger sinuses. My 1981 textbook of neurology (the leading one) said that it had to be treated by surgery, but radiologists were now, in 1984, introducing balloon catheters into the cavernous sinus and blowing up the balloons. When it worked well, this procedure solved the problem without surgery. There, practically under the sign that read, "The only way to learn neurosurgery is to open up people's skulls and practice," the radiologists were taking away cases from the surgeons, solving them with a bit of wire introduced in an artery in the groin. One neurosurgical resident assigned to the neuroradiology service spent his rotation there working on his tennis game. That was the only way he could deal with the fact that radiologists—*radiologists*, the most genteel and hands-off people in medicine—were solving major neurosurgical problems without opening up people's skulls.

Barry's coarse humor was never more in evidence than in one of these procedures, and in this respect he out-surgeoned the surgeons. But to give him credit, he was on the frontier of the field, and was pioneering procedures that might well one day become standard. He had a healthy rivalry with the surgeons, of course, but also with neuroradiologists at Galen and other hospitals who were pioneering this and other procedures. The world center for this type of work was Paris, and to his dismay he had to rely on French balloon catheters. He only hinted at the obvious sexual joke.

I watched while he did what was to be the eighth balloon catheterization of a carotid-cavernous sinus fistula at Galen. The lead apron I was wearing weighed a ton, and sweat was appearing almost everywhere on my body, but the procedure was so impressive I hardly noticed. Barry, muttering more or less all the way, passed the catheter up to the brain with perfect skill. He made his series of trial images. These were spectacular, popping by on the screen like a series of semiabstract still images on television—a pattern of leaf veins, say, or a river delta seen from a great height. Finally, he situated the balloon exactly in the cavernous sinus, at the base of the brain. When he squirted the dye at this point, you could see the puff of dark liquid churn out of the vessel at the leak. There was the normal channel of the arterial tree, clearly bounded with the blackish shadow within it. Suddenly there was the ominous black cloud billowing out of the leak.

It was now necessary to inflate the tiny balloon. This was a time and place where grave damage could be done. But Barry was in command of the situation. He inflated the balloon without incident. This trickiest part was done perfectly. With two quick moves of the foot pedal he squirted the dye and imaged again. Now the leak that had been so impressive before was completely gone. The occlusion had worked. The channel was whole again, and the vascular tree would anastomose—grow in around— the blockade left by the balloon. All Barry had to do was detach the catheter, leaving the balloon in place, and he and the patient were home free.

Unfortunately this was not so straightforward as it was supposed to be. Barry began to tug gently on the catheter in the prescribed manner, expecting it to detach easily from the balloon. His usual muttered din of curses rose to a higher pitch, and those of us who were watching—two medical students, an anesthesiologist, and two nurses—realized he was having trouble.

"What the fuck is this?" he said. He stomped on the pedal a couple of times, producing momentary images of the problem on the screen. Finally he gave up waiting, pulled harder, and imaged again.

The screen showed the balloon in place, but with a short tail of catheter line bobbing around in the vascular flow. Instead of detaching at the point of connection to the balloon, the line had torn a couple of centimeters away from it. This was a disaster. There could be no leaving it in place.

Slowly the line was withdrawn and when it came out of the femoral artery Barry held up the torn end, dangling it pathetically in the air. He was a furious bundle of nerves throughout the next part of the procedure, which had to involve deflation and removal of the balloon. He did this very skillfully, with a new hook catheter.

When he was finished he held up the two torn ends—one still attached to the balloon, the other part of the free line—and approximated them to each other. For a moment he was uncharacteristically silent. Then with one sweeping motion he slammed the torn device down on the dirty instrument table while at the same time sliding the lead apron off his shoulders. He looked at the catheter, disgusted, contemptuous, and said loudly and clearly in his broadest Brooklyn accent, "Send that piece of shit back to France."

My last two rotations took place in Galen II, a branch of the hospital located in the city's worst slum. It was surrounded by a half-burned-out neighborhood where almost the only remaining establishments were liquor stores and pawnshops. Prostitutes paraded brazenly on streetcorners, and a dense population of derelicts and bag ladies lived in the surrounding streets. There had been assaults on nurses, medical students, and doctors. On the first night I went there, as I drove up to the hospital lot, a foot-long rat ran across my path in front of the car.

In this context the Galen II Emergency Room—a thoroughly horrible place, full of sickness and suffering—was a haven in a vast roiling ocean of constant misery. I later met a dedicated couple who ran a shelter for derelicts, committed ideological radicals who had no use for any "establishment" institutions; yet they looked upon Galen II as the one place in the city that was almost completely benign, the one place where their people would never be turned away.

The medical section of the Emergency Room was like a circle in hell peopled with almost eternal sufferers. The patient overload was ludicrous. The waits were often three to five hours, and many patients left without care. Most of the patients were black, and most of the doctors were white.

When we ascertained a patient's name, we often had to leave the Emergency Room area to try to find the hospital record on the dumbwaiter down the hall. Although the hallway was crowded and dirty, I always felt it was an island of sanity that I could go to for a minute or so—before coming back through the swinging doors to chaos and devastation. Coming through those doors you would see a six-hundred-pound woman being moved from a stretcher to a bed by a machine called "The Mobilizer"; an alcoholic having seizures; a young man clutching an infected arm; another yellow with advanced hepatitis; a row of people against a wall, each attached by an intravenous line to a plastic bottle on a pole; and many others waiting patiently with less than obvious ailments.

These would be only the immediately visible sufferers, the ones overflowing the examining rooms and lining the walls. There was also a room full of asthmatics with eerie green masks over their faces and I.V. lines in their arms, trying desperately to catch their breath. Many examining rooms had patients undergoing more invasive procedures. And there were the two resuscitation rooms in which patients in one or another kind of cardiopulmonary crisis were pounded and rubbed and injected and sampled and breathed for while they hovered on the brink of death.

There was also the room way in the back where the famous Mal Goodman, director of the Emergency Room, received nonplussed visitors and did his local television grandstanding. Goodman was a genius—in teaching, in emergency medicine, in supervision—and one of the funniest men I have ever met. He was from the Bronx, and took pride in his New York accent. He studied the great comedians, especially the Jewish ones, and evidently worked on his routines.

And he loved the Emergency Room. He had come to Galen II to take over an impossible situation, and the more impossible it was the better he liked it. He had posted little three-by-five cards at every desk and station, and every few feet on the walls, giving his home phone number, his beeper number, and the message: *In the event of a disaster I must be called immediately.* This referred to a major fire or accident or epidemic bringing many critical patients to the emergency room at the same time. He let it be known in no uncertain terms that if he were not called in such a situation every resident on duty would be fired. He was in the Emergency Room before seven-thirty each morning, and he stayed there for at least twelve hours.

He hardly left it except to go to "metabolic rounds"—breakfast, lunch, and dinner, a few minutes each—although his body was so thin and muscular that it was puzzling to know where he put the food. At breakfast he would rush past the line of people waiting on line and grab a couple of boxes of high-fiber cereal—"Purifies the body," he would say, with intense mock-seriousness—and then sit down with colleagues to discuss the previous day's cases. But by that time he had put in three hours of work. At seven-thirty he was lecturing to the residents and medical students, twitching his moustache, bouncing and turning jerkily, scrawling on the blackboard a few key words, and above all grilling the residents and students—not without humor, but without mercy.

"Now, Rick, I'm just a dumb Emergency Room doc. I'm not smart like the guys upstairs in cardiology. That's why they keep me down here, because I'm dumb. But it seems to me—correct me if I'm wrong—it seems to me that if you did that the patient would die." No one would dare correct him because he was rarely wrong.

"Sylvia," he would say, enunciating with exaggerated care, "what do *you* think?" Whereupon Sylvia would desperately try to come up with something that would not cause the patient to die.

He had an international reputation in emergency and disaster medicine because he had a forceful, simple, and usually unchallengeable approach to whatever was likely to come into the Emergency Room. His job was the immediate and temporary prevention of deterioration and death. He was not concerned with the niceties of long-term stabilization or cure. He knew perfectly well that many of the people he saved and sent upstairs in good shape were likely to go downhill and die—through no fault, usually, of the upstairs physicians. But it wasn't his job to think about that. His job was to prevent them from dying *now,* in the crisis. And, if possible, to get them out of pain.

Some people found it difficult to learn from him, but I found it wonderfully easy. I understood and liked his humor, I tolerated his ribbing well, and I appreciated his no-nonsense pragmatic style. Not because I was anti-intellectual—hardly that; but because the Emergency Room was not the place for musings, or for the endless deliberations of internal medicine sitdown rounds. And because it was good to be able to do something that had to be done fast and under pressure, without advanced technology and without a lot of tests. He lectured in a deliberately manic style, and he would frequently stop, look up, grin crazily, and say, "Oh this is wonderful, this is so good, isn't this wonderful?" or, "Where's my lithium? Who took my lithium?"—this being the drug for the alleged treatment of his alleged mania. We met in a room right next to the incoming ambulance ramp, and whenever one came in he would invariably stop, cock an ear, grin especially broadly, and after a perfectly timed pause say, "Don't you just love sirens?" He loved to imitate the higher-ups at the hospital, and he claimed he was applying for a sabbatical to perfect his imitation of the chief of medicine at Galen I.

The early morning pressure-cooker sessions were a decision-making, problem-solving laboratory. A recent patient was usually at the center of the discussion. There were five causes of everything. For example, a patient had come in with a leg hurting and swollen. "Ralph," Mal would say, "what are the five causes of a leg that's hurting and swollen?" Not Ralph alone, but everyone together, eventually came up with the causes: deep vein thrombosis, superficial vein thrombosis, cellulitis, trauma, fracture, and ruptured Baker's cyst—a burst accumulation of fluid behind the knee. Sure, there were six; but that didn't matter, because there had to be five causes of everything. Five causes of syncope, or fainting: vasovagal, due to increased abdominal pressure; heart or lung malfunctions (such as arrhythmias or pulmonary embolism); central nervous system problems (such as seizure or stroke); metabolic (such as hypoglycemia or salt loss); peripheral nerve problems; and psychiatric abnormalities. Six again, but who was counting?

In the differential diagnosis of shortness of breath, there were really five: heart attack or angina; pneumothorax (air in the chest causing partial collapse of a lung); pericarditis (infection of the membrane around the heart); pulmonary embolism (a clot thrown into an artery supplying the lung); and pneumonia or another accumulation or space-occupying process. To make this diagnosis one had to remember this alphabet soup: SOB = EKG + CXR + ABG—shortness of breath equals (requires) electrocardiogram plus chest X-ray plus arterial blood gases. These were a few of the many catechisms Mal Goodman drilled us in.

But the most important, the ones he absolutely insisted on, were the protocols for treatment of cardiac emergencies. The eight or so full-page protocols had to be completely and exactly committed to memory. For example, in asystole, or absence of heartbeat, you had to give two ampules of bicarbonate by intravenous push injection, and then five cc of epinephrine (1:10,000 dilution) the same way. These would combat acidity and stimulate the heartbeat. The epinephrine had to be repeated in two minutes if there was still no heartbeat. Then one milligram of atropine—another, indirect method of stimulating the heartbeat—had to be given by the same route. An Isuprel intravenous drip would then be instituted—a one-milligram ampule in 250 to 500 cc of distilled water with 5 percent dextrose—and the drip would be run quickly. An ampule of bicarbonate like the first should be given every ten minutes. In the face of continued failure of the heartbeat the patient should be shocked (at 360 amps), epinephrine should be repeated, and four other options—electrical pacing and three further drugs—should be considered.

This was one of eight protocols we had to learn at at least this level of detail before the end of the month—while taking care of scores of emergency patients, going to lectures and rounds, reading to prepare ourselves for Mal's morning grilling, and preparing and giving oral presentations at least once a week. And it was known that the slightest omission would result in having to take the test over again, and again, and again, as necessary. Finally, the problem was presented not in the form of an oral question but in the form of an EKG tracing on an oscilloscope monitor. We had to identify the eight rhythms accurately before reciting the protocol.

Of course, the excitement was that our memorization of the protocols was interleaved with events in the Emergency Room that required their accurate use. Medical students were called on only to assist, not run the resuscitations, of course. But every day we could see the logic of the protocols saving lives or, at worst, nearly saving them. And we not only could but had to get our hands very dirty indeed. I was frequently in the middle of a code myself, taking my turn again and again at compressing the chest or bag-breathing, listening to the shouted commands (a controlled-hysterical version of the protocols), trying to place what was going on in the logic of cardiopulmonary dynamics, and watching the monitor tracing for hopeful signs of a change in the electrical messages let out by a failing heart.

I certainly grew accustomed to death. One morning I was compressing the chest of a middle-aged man seventy times a minute or so, with the intense activity of a crackerjack medical team swirling all around me. The code was being run by a third-year resident who was considered one of the best around. After forty-five minutes he said, "I'm calling it," and all our intense activity suddenly went slack. That was the extent of the difference between life and death. For forty-five minutes we had expended all the human and technological resources of modern emergency medicine without stinting for anything, and when the words "I'm calling it" were spoken, although no physiological or medical change had taken place—merely the passage of time—the man on the table crossed the sociological boundary between life and death.

I leaned back reluctantly, yet glad to take the pressure off my hands. I looked at them, and at the patient's chest, now by definition cadaverous instead of suffused with official hope. It was yellowish, immobile, fleshy, hard, cool. I washed my hands, let the muscles in my arms relax, exchanged some casual phrases with the two or three other medical students, and went off to "metabolic rounds"—to breakfast, and an enjoyable one—without another thought.

There were many cardiopulmonary emergencies, but these made up only a fraction of the work. If there were only time, each patient could have been an education. One young man came into the emergency room with his sister, who explained that he had a history of psychosis and that over the past few days he had been showing signs of slipping out of control. He looked around constantly, and his eyes were wide with intense fear. He spoke little, invoking God's help for his pain and confusion. He and his sister waited for a long time in a couple of hard chairs against the wall of the crowded hallway—much longer than they should have.

Then, while my back was turned—I was going to the desk to call psychiatry again, to find out why they hadn't come down—he suddenly began to shout, calling on the Lord. He dropped to his knees and shouted, "Now, Lord, now! This is the time, Lord! Come down and help me, Lord! Come down and help me now!" The posture and tension in his body were so authentic, his voice was full of such a passionate intensity, that I for all my atheism (and for all my training in psychiatry) was deeply, emotionally taken in. My eyes were moist and my heart beat fast as I secretly hoped for him: *Yes, Lord. Come on down and help him, Lord. Now.*

I put the phone down mechanically and was on my feet beside him. I and two nurses were grabbing hold of him. His sister was saying, "I told you. I told you he was getting bad." I wanted to tell her that I was on her side, that the system was awful, that the crowd of patients around us in the hallway deserved better than what they were getting, that it was not my fault.

Her brother was resisting being stood on his feet. He tried to keep his hands together and kept on with his praying, intensely and movingly. "Help me, Lord. Help me, Lord. Help me now. Please Lord."

A cheerful, hard-bitten nurse said, "He needs some Vitamin H." This was a reference to haloperidol, or Haldol, the usual drug of choice for the immediate first-line treatment of acute psychotic breaks. It was a useful drug, and the right one under the circumstances, but the circumstances shouldn't have arisen. And in any case the phrase "Vitamin H" contained a world of cynical judgment about the condition: that it was inexplicable and permanent, that Haldol fit it like a glove, that this artificial, completely unnatural compound was so perfect for the ailment that it might as well be a vitamin—a benign natural substance the absence of which constitutes a deficiency state. The phrase was as charged with irony as a Leyden jar with lightning.

One of the other nurses snapped the top off the Haldol ampule and drew the drug into a syringe. A resident took the first nurse's advice and nodded to the second. We all held the young man down while the nurse found a hunk of muscle in his upper arm to slip the needle into. He continued to keen and pray while we held him. The drug gradually took over from our restraining hands, but by that time he had been locked into four-point restraint in a narrow steel stretcher, all the while poignantly calling on the Lord.

Another patient crossed my path at a moment when I was particularly ready to do the right thing for her. She was a seventy-eight-year-old woman named Eleanor Kiley, and her complaint was of a vague abdominal discomfort. Mal had sternly lectured us on the obscure presentation of certain abdominal crises in the elderly. In a young person, there is almost no mistaking a "hot belly"—caused by a ruptured appendix or a twisted, infected loop of bowel. The pain is usually excruciating, and the "chandelier sign" in response to pressing on the abdomen or to sudden release of the pressure—the patient screams and jumps up onto the chandelier—leaves little doubt as to the existence of a crisis. In the elderly, however, similarly dangerous and disruptive events in the abdomen can present without any severe pain or tenderness. Often the sensory nerves to the viscera are dulled by alcohol or diabetes or merely aging, and the result can be that only a mild nausea or sense of fullness signals an impending disaster.

Since Mal had just been hammering away at us on this subject, I thought the worst when I met Eleanor Kiley. She half-sat, half-lay on a stretcher in a corner of the hallway just inside the emergency room doors. She looked calm and patient, and she was sucking or chewing on a piece of candy. I took her pulse, blood pressure, and temperature, all of which were normal. She spoke comfortably, and described vague abdominal discomfort beginning the previous evening. She rubbed her belly with an unpleasant look on her face. Something about her made me raise a red flag, and so she had a radiological evaluation of her colon—a plain X-ray of her belly followed by a barium enema study.

I did not hear of her, and forgot about her, for several days, when I got a chance to see the report. She had had a perforated sigmoid diverticulum: an outpouching of the lower part of the colon had become infected, formed an abscess, burst, and caused a diffuse peritonitis. The events were parallel to those of a ruptured appendix in a child or young adult, and the implications were similar. After the radiological studies, she had had an exploratory laparotomy—an abdominal surgical fishing expedition—which led to a draining of the abscess, a lysis of adhesions, and a colostomy. I saw her some days after the surgery. She was calm and patient looking still, but the vague discomfort was gone. She scarecely knew it, but Galen had saved her life.

One feature of Mal Goodman's style that annoyed some people but delighted others was his enthusiasm for ethnic and racial jokes. Most people admired, even loved him enough so that nothing he could say would be offensive. Like most comedians who are successful at this sort of thing, he attacked himself and his own group—Northeastern Jewish mamas' boys squirming under the thumbs of domineering wives—more savagely than he did any others. But he did go after others—hilariously, I thought—and he didn't take on anyone who was really vulnerable. Since there was quite a range of ethnic representation among the residents and students, he could have a field day. For instance, one of the brightest residents was a Puerto Rican named Julio. Mal would not allow him to answer the easy questions, and would refer the hard ones to him only after everyone else had given up.

"Well, Julio," he would say in his most exaggerated style, "what do *you* think?" More often than not Julio would thoughtfully produce a superb answer while Mal tapped his foot and nodded nervously. Everyone knew that the answer was excellent, and that Mal thought it was excellent. But Mal always held back praise. "O.K., Julio. That's an acceptable answer. In fact it's not a bad answer at all. In fact it's a good answer. A very good answer. Thank you, Julio." By this time everyone was waiting for the punch line. Julio was smiling wryly, watching Mal expectantly. Mal, with his usual good timing, turned back to the blackboard and began writing as if to continue the lesson.

Then suddenly he turned on his heel and pointed at the hapless Puerto Rican with his chalk: "But listen Julio," he fired sternly and rapidly, "if there's one hubcap missing in the parking lot today, I'm talking just one, you're finished, you know what I mean? You're out of here."

Chuck was a black third-year resident who was known to be among the best in the service. His commanding authority had struck me when I watched him not only running codes but in his role as physician-in-charge of the emergency paramedics when they radioed the Emergency Room desk from the ambulances to request advice or permission to institute one treatment or another; it was remarkable to watch him make an assessment within a few exchanges and determine what should be done to prevent the patient from being dead on arrival.

Since Chuck was very big and had a big booming voice, Mal—who was shorter than average and thin—used to call him "Hurricane." He used to love to contrast himself with Chuck physically, and never missed a chance to put himself down by means of the contrast. "I'm afraid that if I disagree with him over this patient, Hurricane will squash me like a bug. Nevertheless I have to do it."

But there were also the rewards. One morning Chuck had been on duty all night and had had a particularly difficult patient come in with a cardiac arrest. He had worked on the patient for hours, and now he looked exhausted but satisfied.

Mal, as he often did with interesting cases, grilled him intensively on his step-by-step interventions. "Well, Hurricane, did you have any interesting cases last night, or did you just hang out and deal cocaine? I realize I'm taking my life in my hands when I ask you this."

Chuck smiled tolerantly and described the patient's arrest. "O.K., Hurricane," Mal overenunciated. "So what did you do?" Chuck described his first intervention, while Mal stood up front with knit eyebrows and arms folded over his chest, tapping his foot. "And *then* what did you do?" Chuck described the next intervention. "And *then* what did you do? And *then* what did you do?"

This went on and on with no change in Mal's expression or tone of voice, and without hesitation on Chuck's part, until the patient was out of danger upstairs in a warm bed. Everyone knew from the initial symptom picture and the first few responses to treatment that this patient had no right to be alive. Chuck seemed to grow larger in stature with each successive response. "And *then* what did you do? And *then* what did you do?" The rest of us were in awe while Mal listened with brows furrowed. He did not even nod. When Chuck was finished he turned to the blackboard, and then away from it to look back at Chuck again. With his usual perfect timing—and no use of the name Hurricane this time—he said, "Chuck, some people would call what you did brilliant, heroic, and magnificent. But me being who I am, we'll just let it go." He turned back to the blackboard. All eyes turned to Chuck, whose face had relaxed into a great, broad smile that stayed there for at least half the morning.

For my last elective rotation, and my last clinical experience in medical school, I wanted to deliver more babies. There was a very small chance that I would switch gears and decide to go into obstetrics, though I really felt too old and tired for such a difficult course. I had done some research on human reproduction, and everything connected with it still commanded my interest. But more than the research interest, and in spite of how tired I was, the exhilaration of deliveries had remained vivid in my mind. I selfishly wanted the O.B. high. And the best place to get it most often was on the floor of Galen II devoted to service—read "poor"—obstetric patients: Simson 4.

"The woman about to become a mother, or with her newborn infant upon her bosom, should be the object of trembling care and sympathy wherever she bears her burden or stretches her aching limbs. . . . God forbid that any member of the profession to which she trusts her life, doubly precious at that eventful period, should hazard it negligently, unadvisedly, or selfishly!" These words of Oliver Wendell Holmes were inscribed on a homely plaque hung on a wall behind a nurses' station on Simson 4. If sententious and overwritten, they were certainly sensible; and they served to inspire the nurses and residents, more or less. But trembling care and sympathy would not be exactly appropriate terms to describe the efficient mass processing of deliveries that characterized Simson 4.

The ward consisted of one very long hallway—about the length of a football field—half of which had labor rooms on both sides, and the other half of which had delivery rooms on both sides. Here, although women were not given general anesthetics to put them to sleep, neither were they encouraged to have anything like natural childbirth. Anesthesiologists were always on hand to give an epidural or some cocktail of narcotics and other pain killers. The women were not of the same subculture or social class as most of the women in my third year O.B. rotation, and they had not been exposed to the concepts and arguments of the natural-childbirth movement. They were simply young women—or, quite often, girls—who wanted to get their babies born. They did not have an exaggerated respect for physicians—this was in some cases putting it mildly—but they had the idea that here were people who could get their babies out, and they were willing to go along half-skeptically with anything those people recommended.

One of the things they recommended was that medical students do every possible normal spontaneous vaginal delivery, and some others as well. I took this recommendation and ran with it. Unlike every other rotation I was on, O.B. gave me the impulse to become the kind of medical student the residents tolerantly called "an animal"—a hyperaggressive go-getting type who insists on doing procedures himself, takes over the residents' own work, and learns an inordinate amount, by doing. On day one, when I walked onto Simson 4, I was ready to do a delivery, and everything seemed to conspire against me. A group of third-year medical students was competing with me. Protocol was cumbersome. And to complicate matters further, the same day was the first day of the introduction of a midwifery service to Simson 4.

Here was a test of my convictions. I believed in midwifery, and I knew that for normal deliveries this was the best route for many of the patients of Galen II. They needed the attention, the care, provided only by midwives with their hour-after-hour *attendance*—that old-fashioned tried and true formal term—at the labor. They did not need medical-student deliveries, which typically consisted of a clinical version of the wham-bam-thank-you-ma'am sexual encounter: a how-do-you-do at full dilatation, a perfunctory good-bye at the closing of the episiotomy, and another notch on the ace medical student's delivery belt, with, somewhere along the way, a baby.

My convictions flunked the test. I was an animal. One part of my mind watched in disbelief while I complained bitterly that the midwives were taking away deliveries that were rightfully mine. I unwittingly instigated an argument between the attending physician in obstetrics to the head of the new midwifery service, under the watchful eye of the chief of obstetrics, over medical students' rights to normal deliveries. *"Medical students'* rights!!??" my better judgment was shouting over my shoulder. *"Medical students'* rights!!??" But my better judgment was losing to my desire to practice and learn.

I figured that I might be able to solve much of the problem by taking the night shift. There would be no other medical students and only one or two midwives. I showed up at midnight one night and began to anticipate a delivery as keenly as a meal after a fast. As luck would have it, there were only two normal deliveries that night. The first was taken by a midwife. The second was taken by a doctor who fainted.

One of the staff obstetricians had a friend, an internist, who was soon to go to Zaire as a missionary physician. Normally I would have revered her for her willingness to do that, and I knew that what she would do in Zaire would be more important to more people than almost anything done by a Galen doctor. But when I found out that she was coming over at the last minute to take away the delivery I had been working and waiting for, laboring with the mother all night, I was furious. I suspected that the hospital's insurance would not cover this situation, and I was not above resorting to mention of this. I protested to the staff man who had brought her over, and to the residents, to no avail. She was getting my delivery.

At least I could watch. I was looking forward at least to *seeing* the baby come into the world. That was not a substitute for delivering one, but it was the next best thing. Nothing untoward happened. The head crowned, and the usual smelly mess made up of amniotic fluid, blood, urine, and feces was dripping off the table onto the floor.

Suddenly the internist was looking pale and wobbly. Then she was rubbing the sweat off her brow onto her sleeve while apologizing. Then she was on the floor. Her friend the obstetrician was obviously torn between the desire to help her and the need to take care of the mother, who was on the brink, and the baby, who was about to be expelled into thin air. I was of course hoping against hope that the obstetrician would turn to me to get me to finish the delivery, while attending to his friend himself. But he stepped in to control the baby's head and sent a nurse for a resident, who was soon there managing the delivery emergently.

Meanwhile, I was kneeling at the side of the fallen internist, taking her pulse, getting her legs raised a bit, watching her revive, and talking with her about her symptoms and her mental status; she would be fine. But her absurdly embarrassing failure released a flood of satisfaction in me after my resentment at being deprived of my delivery. I still admired her intention to go to Zaire, and my bedside (floorside?) manner was courteous, but I was positively gloating.

I assumed correctly that she would not show up on O.B. for a while. The night was mine. So each evening I got in my car at home around eleven and was in surgical blues and at the labor board by midnight. The board was usually full, there were no other medical students, and the midwives, who were in any case fighting for approval, could not handle more than two patients a night. I began to get one delivery after another.

Many of the patients were unwed and many of them, wed or not, were teenagers. I assisted at the induced premature birth of a stillborn fetus to a twelve-year-old who had been impregnated by her father. Her mother, who was calm, helpful, and even wise, and who would have been a grandmother had the fetus come to term, was twenty-eight, ten years younger than I. I delivered the fifth child of a twenty-year-old woman. When I passed her in the recovery room she was talking with a friend, the two looking for all the world like a couple of college girls chatting about their social lives. Her chart said that after each of her deliveries she had been given advice about birth control; the first child had been born when she was fourteen.

One night it was a bit slow and we were standing around waiting for something to happen when the elevator doors opened and a surgical intern wheeled out a plump sixteen-year-old girl on a stretcher. She and her mother, who was walking beside the stretcher holding a hand to her face and shaking her head from side to side in disbelief, had spent the past few hours in the surgical emergency clinic. They had come there to investigate an obscure but intense abdominal pain. To the surgical residents' credit, it did not take an exploratory operation to figure out that the girl was in labor. The mother was stunned, which was not surprising, but the girl as well claimed complete lack of knowledge of her pregnancy. I talked with her at length and became convinced that she might be telling the truth. "Well, I knew that my periods were irregular, but—" I delivered the baby, easy for the mother and one of the easiest of the month for me.

Tom Swazey, my favorite resident that month, smiled tolerantly and was not surprised. He had seen many of these. "The all-time prize for denial," he said, "goes to one I delivered precip in the ambulance on the ramp downstairs. She kept saying she couldn't be pregnant. She was conscious, the baby was out and crying, the cord was not yet cut. She pointed down at the kid, with the umbilical cord trailing from the kid's belly into her vagina, and she screamed, 'That's not my baby!' "

Swazey was terrific, calm, knowledgeable, easygoing, and perfectly competent. When there was a need for urgency he was on the stick with the best of them, but when there wasn't, he thought it was wrong to be the least bit on edge. In high school he had run for school president; "Don't be crazy, vote for Swazey!" had been one slogan, but the other had been "For a more mellow leadership." If Swazey were president of the United States, the chance of nuclear war would be greatly reduced. As a second-year resident in O.B., he correspondingly reduced the chance of psychological disaster on Simson 4. Labor is one time in life when the mind-body problem has a clear and simple solution: a "bad head" can easily give the mother a bad labor. He lowered the likelihood of such an outcome by being, staying, and spreading calm.

That meant calm in relation to medical students and other residents as well as in direct relation to patients. When he was supervising one of my deliveries I felt comfortable and confident. He seemed to have a sixth sense about when I could be left alone and when I couldn't, and he always left me alone when he could. Sometimes he left me alone when I thought he should have stayed, but he turned out to be right, and the result was an important advance in my knowledge and competence.

Under his guidance I went from strength to strength. I stood at the foot of the delivery table and commanded the brightly lit, nervously quiet room—the mother, the father or other companion, the nurses, even the anesthesiologist—giving mild-mannered and polite but clear and decisive orders: when to push, stop pushing, bring the mother a blanket, move her down the table, show her the baby, run the oxytocin drip. Tom would stick his head in the door occasionally—once during crowning of the head, say, and once during the sewing of the episiotomy cut or tear. But basically he was busy himself and I was on my own. Of course, the system was buffered against my stupidity. If I were to give a dumb order the nurses would correct me, reverse the order, or refuse to carry it out.

Once I called for the oxytocin prematurely—it is supposed to cause the uterus to contract and prevent bleeding after completion of the delivery. The anesthesiologist smiled and asked indulgently, "Don't you want to deliver the placenta first?" Not to do so, I remembered, could cause the disaster of a retained placenta. After appropriate momentary embarrassment I said, "Oh, yeah, sure," tugged gently on the cord, delivered the placenta, and then asked for the oxytocin again.

But for the most part I coordinated all the events of the delivery and carried out a large proportion of them myself. I wheeled the bed down the hall to the delivery room, I talked the mother through the last stages of labor, I controlled the baby's head as it came through the birth canal, I cut the episiotomy, I suctioned the mucus out of the nose and mouth to allow breathing to start, I clamped and cut the cord, I placed the baby under the lights, I delivered the placenta and checked it for abnormalities, I asked for the baby to be brought to the mother and father, I sewed the tear or cut, I filled out the numerous forms, and I congratulated the parents. I was in charge from start to finish, and it felt wonderful.

In vivid contrast to Swazey's calm was the constant tension created by Henry McCormick. He was an intern who was arrogant way beyond his knowledge and skill. Not that that was unusual, but his character was such as to turn every situation into a crisis. He would pop into my delivery room and begin pacing around and giving anxious directions. These ordinarily were basic imperatives that I was already following, as could have been seen from a real look at the situation. Or, in some cases, they were urgings to invoke an intervention that was clearly unnecessary. I would not have relied on my own judgment about these things, but there were enough instances when Swazey or another resident looked in on the same situation that McCormick had just evaluated, and pronounced his judgment wrong and mine right, so that I eventually transferred my confidence from McCormick to myself.

One night in the prep room McCormick introduced me to the practically hysterical concern that obstetricians have about litigation. Patients came off the elevator and sat in a row of chairs in the hallway until they were seen by a nurse and doctor. They told their stories to the people who saw them—here the waits were on the order of minutes, not hours—and if they were judged to be in labor (strong and regular contractions, or rupture of membranes) they would be assigned a stretcher in one of the preparation rooms for further evaluation pending admission. If they were well dilated and moving quickly they might be put in a bed and sent right back to the delivery suite. Our job was partly to make these decisions—triage—and partly to conduct the initial history and physical.

I did many of these myself, including getting all the details of the presumed labor, checking the urine and taking blood samples, locating and measuring the fetal heartbeat, gloving up and measuring cervical dilatation, and making a recommendation. As on all other services, the details of the findings had to be carefully recorded in assessment notes. I faithfully recorded the time of onset of contractions, their frequency and intensity, the rupture or intactness of membranes, the history of prior births, pregnancies, and abortions, the presence of complications in this pregnancy, and so on, in addition to the results of my physical examination.

One night we were about to send away a patient whom we deemed to be not yet in labor. This happened frequently. Patients came to the hospital early for a variety of reasons, were examined, reassured, and sent home with clear instructions as to the symptoms that should bring them back in. In this particular case the patient had had only occasional contractions, but she had had a flow of some fluid from her vagina earlier in the day. Her membranes appeared to be intact, and when we tested the fluid in her vagina for ferning—the characteristic fernlike microscopic pattern that would prove it was amniotic fluid—the test was negative. No ferning, no amniotic fluid, no rupture of membranes, no hospital admission: simple.

Suddenly McCormick was flashing his angry eyes at me, saying, "Come outside, I need to talk to you," in as stern and loud a voice as he could allow himself in front of a patient—more so than most doctors would have allowed. In his hand was the blue sheet on which I had written my findings. He waved it in the air and banged on it with his other hand. "Why did you write this? Don't you understand what's going on here? What are we gonna do if the hospital gets sued?"

When he stopped waving the paper long enough to let me look at it, I saw the words "I had a lot of water" in quotation marks after the letter

"S:," meaning "Subjective." As I had been trained to do, I had written down the chief complaint in the patient's own words. This excellent tactic was designed to protect everyone, and to allow all other health professionals reading the sheet to encounter first the patient's words rather than my interpretation. This time, so McCormick argued, I had placed him, myself, and the hospital in jeopardy.

"What if she gets an infection?" he asked with intense anxiety. "What if she crumps? Do you want her husband's lawyer to see that we sent her out with that as the chief complaint?"

"Maybe we shouldn't send her out."

"Do you think she's ruptured her membranes?"

"No. No ferning, no rupture."

"Well if you want to send her out, you don't send her out with that kind of thing in the record."

"I thought I was supposed to write down what she said."

"Not in a case like this. Don't do it again, for Christ's sake."

McCormick was giving me a lesson in the new defensive medicine that had grown up because of relentless, often frivolous malpractice litigation, directed against obstetricians as much as against any other group and more than most. Seven out of ten obstetricians had been sued, and many doctors were giving up delivering babies. It was not because they were worse than other doctors, but because in this situation people expect perfection. They start out well and they expect to end up well. When the inevitable occasional untoward event occurs, they sue. Still, to falsify the record by omission of crucial facts? Not only what he was recommending but the way he spoke to me made me wary of his orders. I steered clear of McCormick as much as I could, but unfortunately he frequently brought his tense pushy manner into my delivery room.

I tried to make Swazey my constant companion. We used to sit around in front of the labor board talking about the cases and trying to make predictions, or quizzing each other mercilessly about every detail of obstetrics and gynecology. The residents that month were studying for a qualifying exam, in default of which they would be dropped from the program. So the mood was one of spirited, tense camaraderie. I liked to spend time with the laboring women, talking with them, watching their monitors, trying to stay alert for fetal distress—demonstrated by a baby's heart rate, always depressed by a contraction, failing to bounce back into normal range after the contraction ended. These late decelerations, or "late decels," were the language in which the fetus called for help. Three of them within sixty seconds could result in an immediate Caesarean section. I disliked finding them, but I did.

Mostly I just talked with the women, who were sometimes cheerful but often confused, sometimes brave but often exhausted, sometimes calm but often in pain, and almost always poor. Their ignorance of the labor process, of contraception, and of medicine and surgery in general was great. They were quite capable of courage and fortitude, and we often saw it, but for the most part they wanted to close their eyes and get it over with.

As for me, it didn't matter how tired or depressed I was. If there was a lull between deliveries of several hours during a given night, I would check all the patients three or four times, and sit around and chat for a while, but then I might start to sulk a bit. Sleep deprivation can be depressing; I could almost hear the clock tick as I passed through early middle age. Then a voice announcing a delivery or a section would crackle over the loudspeaker, or a bed would be rolled down the hall toward delivery surrounded by nurses, and I would be on my feet in a fraction of a second. Sleep fell away like water shaken off by a dog and melancholy abruptly became a totally foreign word. I was moving under that strange combined energy of natural process and medical responsibility. I was ready; I was on. The efficiency of my sleep-deprived body was surprising enough, but the high was druglike, astonishing. During the delivery, I felt I could do anything. After it, for a couple of hours at least, I was in an altered state of most remarkable consciousness. An old friend who knew me well said, "Why don't you go ahead and devote your life to this? I've never seen you doing something that made you feel so good." I began to wonder myself why I didn't.

I delivered twenty-six babies that month, bringing my lifetime total to thirty-six. During the last few days I was consciously aiming for thirty-five, and on the last day following the last night I stayed until mid-afternoon. What I thought was my last delivery—the thirty-fifth—was that of a twenty-one-year-old woman having her second baby. The mother defecated about half a liter of a smooth white substance during the delivery. "She eats a lot of clay," the father said. He was a wonderful man who created a fine mood in the room and rhapsodized about what was going on: "I had to be here. I wanted to experience it." He and I had a good relationship, and at one point he asked a nurse, "Has he ever done this before?"

"Thirty-four times," I said smiling. I had reached a plateau where I felt so comfortable with my basic level of competence that a joke about it was no sort of threat. The episiotomy did not extend and was easily sewed. The baby, a boy, weighed over seven pounds, and was born in the very pink of health.

I walked out of the delivery room feeling wonderful, and was on my way home from Simson 4 for the last time. My last delivery had been excellent. But as I walked down the corridor a bed was rolling toward me, and the nurses were offering me one last last delivery. I was exhausted, but I couldn't resist. I did not even stop to think, Don't push your luck. The mother was a pleasant nineteen-year-old with a lisp. She was wearing gold earrings—unusual in the delivery room—because there hadn't been time to take them off.

There was no anesthesia, not even the smallest pain pill, and there was no injury of any kind whatever. There was a moment in which a lip of the cervix had been in the way of full dilatation, and McCormick and another resident had answered my call for help. Neither of them had been able to resolve it. After they left I applied gentle pressure and resolved it myself. Otherwise, the delivery was the most perfect of all the ones I had managed, and the baby, a seven-pound girl, was a match for that perfection, blinking her lids over bright brown eyes.

That delivery seemed somehow to have been sent to me, and I stayed with the mother and baby for quite some time. In the recovery room I found the mother exceptionally sweet and gentle, holding her baby with great tenderness. She told me that she had one other child, a girl with Down's syndrome of mental retardation. She loved the child very much, but it was so wonderful to have a second, perfectly normal baby. Her smile was not quite the usual postpartum grin, but something altogether other-worldly.

I went to my locker at last, and took off my surgical blues, stuffing them into the laundry bin with keen regret. In my street clothes, my obstetrics text under my arm, I stood in front of the nurses' station and looked down the corridor for, now, really the last time. Tom Swazey happened by and we repeated our good-byes. "Make sure you have your performance here recorded in a letter in the department file. In case you decide to do it after all." I looked at him. He was the only resident I had worked with who was older than me—in fact exactly the age I would be if and when I got to my second year of residency. Like me, he had been in academia first. Like me, he had been interested in psychiatry, and he had even done a year of a psychiatric residency.

He seemed to be living proof that I was not too old yet; and that encounter, combined with the luck of my marvelous last, unexpected delivery, seemed to insist that I keep an open mind. But the thought of all those years of sleepless nights, of all that subordination to people like McCormick, of all that separation from my children during their one and only childhood—those thoughts intruded themselves even on my delivery high.

16

CONCLUSION

Healing Artisans

In the preceding pages, I have attempted to give an objective account of what I experienced, but I have not pretended that it is an objective account of what happened; on the contrary, I have tried to describe all events in the light of a full and frank subjectivity: my subjectivity as an anthropologist; as an educator; as a husband and father in his middle thirties; and as a medical student and future physician. Among my classmates I shared the first with none, the second with one or two, the third with a handful, and the fourth with all.

As an anthropologist I tried to see behavior—acts and speech—accurately, to appreciate the behavior involved in learning, training, and care against the background of social structures and institutions; and, too, to understand medicine in the context of human nature—which I, but by no means all anthropologists or physicians, believe in in a specifiable way. I understood the social constraints surrounding modern medicine and something about how they came to be. Because of them, as well as for purely intrinsic reasons, there have been great transformations in the doctor-patient relationship, with inevitable consequences for the medical teacher-student relationship. I tried to see such changes not in a shallow context of recent American history, but, however uncertainly and for whatever it is worth, against the length and breadth of human cultural variation.

I also, ubiquitously and reflexively, made reference to what I had seen and experienced during my two years in Africa, not as a romantic standard of comparison, but as a marvelous mirror that transforms as it reflects our own institutions. There I was able to see human beings at their most unprotected in the battle with disease; to see social structure at its simplest; and to see an elementary civilization crystallize around a ritual of healing—its central religious experience—even to the point of apprenticing myself for a while as a ritual healer in training. These experiences conditioned me to revere, really revere, the technical capability of modern American medicine and to scorn naive critics who belittle it. But they prepared me equally to question the supremacy of technique that has, in the eyes of some critics, rendered American medicine a spiritual wasteland and its practitioners impotent to confront matters of life and death other than with a test or drug or scalpel.

As an anthropologist interested in the biological basis of behavior, I had knowledge in certain basic science areas relevant to medicine: brain structure and function, human reproduction, infant and child growth and development, and mind-body interaction. I tried throughout my training to squeeze out of my clinical encounters knowledge and experience relevant to my concerns—psychiatry, neurology, obstetrics and gynecology, and pediatrics related to growth, development, and behavior.

I usually had more knowledge of the basic science underlying these fields than did residents who were not specializing in them, but I learned how and when to keep my opinions to myself. When I could choose my teachers, I made every effort to go to the best. Rarely did I work with anyone who had nothing to teach me clinically; although there were several whose abrasiveness was such as to make it almost impossible to learn from them. Finally, I often knew more than my teachers about matters pertaining to public health and about the social and cultural aspects of health and disease, but they usually viewed this knowledge as almost wholly irrelevant.

As an educator, I knew something about teaching and learning. I had taught undergraduates and graduates for years and my courses were viewed as challenging and valuable; judging by the enrollment numbers, they were successful. I knew how to supervise students in difficult and sometimes dangerous research enterprises in field settings and to help them learn to do accurate and worthwhile research, publishable in the most competitive journals. I had also taught hundreds of premedical students, and I knew their situation and their character. So I thought that I had a right to some opinions about how teaching goes on in the preclinical years of medical school, and to a more qualified sort of opinion about how it goes on in the clinical years.

The mundane portion of my opinion is now widely held: too many facts are being taught too thoughtlessly in too short a time. In the clinical years, this vast array of memorized fact is purportedly reorganized in analysis of cases, but this is not real analysis. It is rememorization of facts, this time in the form of decision trees rather than mere lists. This kind of training favors prodigious memorization above or even to the exclusion of all else; and it is only recently that medicine has come to emphasize this dismally narrow ability, as the knowledge explosion has left medical educators bewildered as to just what can be safely left out. But what is left out inadvertently is least expendable: a sense of balance and judgment about what is important, and strategies and tactics for arriving at such judgments, for independent learning, and for weighing the value of the new.

Of course, medical school cannot resemble graduate school, since these two institutions have diametrically opposite purposes. The graduate school must produce a unique product: the student must not only go as soon as possible beyond what has been taught, but must actually create knowledge and then teach it to his or her teachers. The medical student must on the contrary end by being as similar as possible to every other medical student, must master as much as possible of the body of knowledge that is taught, according to a process that leaves no room for originality. At the end of study, all fifteen thousand graduating medical students, given the same patient, ideally should perform the same examination, write the same assessment, and formulate the same options for treatment.

As far as I can tell, really no one thinks that the mass of facts delivered by medical-school faculties can be learned, and everyone agrees that it must be cut down. But no one has had the courage to start cutting. In this sense the problem is like that of the federal budget deficit: everyone agrees that spending must be cut, but no one is prepared to take up the ax. And sadly the political forces at work in maintaining the style of medical-education-as-assault-on-memory are not unlike those that maintain federal government deficit spending.

Just as the advance of science has in some sense caused this problem, it may soon help to solve it: the age is approaching of the hand-held medical library, organized around the same decision trees that are now the focus of so much human brain-wracking. A whole category of successful medical students and physicians—the ones who have great memories but lack much else—may come to be set aside by machines. Ironically, a silicon microprocessor chip may be one of the keys that reopens the door to the humanistic medicine of the past.

Which brings me to my second point about medical training: the models to which students are exposed are largely wrong. The process of modeling by teachers is a ubiquitous, if unmentioned, aspect of training in any field. In the clinical years of medical school this process is explicit, and is the lifeblood of the program. But there is more to it than meets the eye, more, that is, than learning hands-on procedures that cannot be taught any other way. The physician's attitudes, mind-set, moral stance, and the hour-by-hour decisions about how to use one's time—all these and many other subtle matters, even including how and what and how much to feel, are observed by the student and imitated assiduously. Even where the explicit message is "Do as I say, not as I do," the implicit message is "Do whatever you think is right, but if you want to survive in this world you'd better be like me."

The models are doctors whose qualifications as physician-teachers are unknown; the residents have been chosen because of their ability to perform well in school, and medical educators freely and formally admit that one cannot predict how well such students will do in future clinical settings. More important, the residents are under the greatest pressure they have been or will ever be under. They are outrageously overworked, sleep-deprived, overburdened with responsibility, bewildered by a barrage of ever changing facts, and oppressed by the medical hierarchy, of which they are on the lowest rungs.

For reasons of expediency, the residents have most of the responsibility for the presentation of physician-models (and of physician-teacher-models) to medical students in the clinical phase of training. If the medical students like them, as they frequently do, that is partly because they are so alike—people selected in the same way a few years apart, after exposure to very similar life experiences. But it is equally because the residents are teaching the students survival skills in a world that is not going to change before the students themselves are swept up in it. Whether these skills have much to do with being a physician—in the larger sense that some of us would still like to believe in—is not known.

It was in my third persona—that of thirty-five-year-old man, husband, and father—that I experienced my greatest disharmony with the pattern of medical training. I was physically more vulnerable than most of my fellow-students—less tolerant of sleeplessness, lack of exercise, and poor and irregular diet. I could not participate effectively in the supportive fellowship of students experiencing the same stresses together and commiserating with each other after hours. I went home to a family who loved me, and some of my fellow students rightly envied me that; but I envied them the absolute quiet of their rooms, and their freedom to go to the library or the bedside or the swimming pool or the local bar exactly as the need or even inclination arose. I envied them the ability to think about almost nothing but their training, with survival as the bottom line and excellence as the unmistakable goal.

Yet I felt—perhaps in self-defense—a certain not quite salutary superiority. Walking and singing my infant son to sleep, or soothing my four-year-old daughter in the middle of the night, or even talking with my wife about mundane family business, I felt I had something over most of my student colleagues. I had been changed by these experiences, as most of them had not yet been. Also, I was more aware of my own mortality. I had begun to meet up with the aches and pains of middle age, and my parents were elderly. I thought about everything important in medicine—nurturance, pain, fear, sex, love, loss, death—in ways subtly but significantly different from theirs. The difference was most evident in some specialties —obstetrics, pediatrics, and psychiatry for example—but was present everywhere.

And it didn't do me a lot of good. I often wished for less consciousness. In dozens of situations where my fellow students seemed to act first and think later, I usually thought and then acted, in an often hesitating or qualified way. To the limited extent that I was a "doctor" this did not impair my functioning—situations that depended on a medical student are rare enough, and in them I was always able to act, and act quickly. But it did impair my functioning as a student. I should have focused more on my education and less on the social or psychological or ethical dimensions of patient care. The informed consent signed by patients in a teaching hospital cleared the consciences of my fellow students as to what should be done by whom to whom. I wish I had had the youthful élan to do what I had to do less reflectively.

As an ordinary medical student, I experienced some typical transformations. I did become socialized to the habits of more or less reflexive action. As hundreds of clinical encounters turned to thousands, I gradually overcame the normal social inhibitions that keep us from intruding on another person's "space." The intrusions that had at first bothered me—questions about personal habits with alcohol and sex; speaking paternalistically to adults my age and older; giving orders to disrobe, to assume a grotesque or embarrassing posture, to open to scrutiny every private place; touching and poking and pressing without embarrassment; deliberately inflicting pain; and making incisions in the protective envelope of the skin—all these and others became not just intellectually but deeply, emotionally, acceptable.

I have developed the impatience with ethical discussions characteristic of most house officers. It isn't that I don't consider them important, it's just that I don't consider them my job. I follow the rules laid down by the hospital—meaning, the rules laid down by society. Tell me in plain English what the Do Not Resuscitate order means and exactly whom it applies to, and I will carry it out. Tell me which fetuses you want saved and which thrown away; to the best of my technical ability, I will comply. Tell me what sort of craziness warrants involuntary commitment and I will know which patients to keep off the street. Tell me the rules—define them as strictly as you can—for taking the heart out of patient A and putting it into patient B, and I will go on with that dazzling technical miracle; I won't have pangs of conscience, which I really don't need and which only make my work harder.

Of course, the time comes, the residency years having receded, for a reawakening of interest in such questions—even for a certain territorial defense of one's right to answer them. But medical school suppresses them, so as to keep the fiercely difficult postgraduate training years relatively free of such concerns.

To a lesser extent, I have been absorbed into the "teamness" of medical training. During my last few months on the wards I tried to be decent to the patients, but my bonds, my emotional energy—what the psychoanalysts call cathexes—were all with doctors and medical students and, to a lesser extent, nurses. Authentic human feelings flow among members of a team, and these create and stabilize the social organization. It is the job of this organization to deal with the patients, but the patients are outside of it. Relations with them should be smooth, cordial, and efficient, but they are certainly not personal. And increasingly as one's training goes on, one feels quite protected by the fact that their dependency, their frightening, unpredictable involvement with you, is dispersed among the team members. In Martin Buber's terms, the relationship with a fellow team member may be an "I-Thou" involvement, but the relationship with a patient is at best "I-You" or, to be precise, "We-You."

Disloyalty to the team is always dangerous, and it can be remarkably subtle. Too great an involvement with patients can in itself be sufficient to suggest it. This works not because you have "gone over to the enemy," to put it crudely—after all, the patients are not the enemy—but rather through an implied accusation leveled against the other team members: I care more than you do for patients, therefore you do not care enough. Avoiding this implication helps to suppress at least some nurturing impulses toward patients.

Hewing to a standard of behavior toward patients is part of a much

larger process of practicing medicine according to the norm. In the norm
there is safety. This is true in the ultimate legal sense: a judge will rule on
alleged error or negligence contingent on the local standard of practice.
If you do what is commonly accepted, not in the medical journals or in the
leading hospitals but in your local medical community, then you are probably safe.

Psychologically, the safety of the norm is even more important and
ubiquitous. You *feel* safe, not just legally but morally, to the extent that
you do what everyone else is doing. Here the complexity of everything
you learned in medical school becomes almost irrelevant. The training
process involves mastering routines. These are relatively few in number,
and they must become reflexive. "Diencephalic" was the way a neurologist friend of mine described his thought processes in handling a new
patient. This refers to the part of the brain below the level of the cerebral
cortex which, he implied only half-jokingly, was unnecessary after a certain point in training. In a human endeavor as fraught with moral jeopardy
as medicine, the spiritual comfort the practitioner derives from keeping
to ritualistic routines, held firmly in common with other practitioners, is
difficult to exaggerate.

And of course, last but hardly least, I now tend to see people as patients.
I noticed this especially with women. It is often asked whether male
medical students become desexualized by all those women disrobing, all
those breast examinations, all those manual invasions of the most intimate
cavities. I found that to be a rather trivial effect. What I found more
impressive was the general tendency to see women as patients. This clinical detachment comes not from gynecology but from all the experiences
of medicine. I described a time during my medicine station when, on a
bus, I noticed the veins on a woman's hands—how easily they could be
punctured for the insertion of a line—before noticing that she happened
to be beautiful. And, too, I tend to see the flaws, in the most lovely women:
the slight asymmetry of the face, the mild problem with the complexion,
the tired eyes, the pain in the back or feet from the high-heeled shoes.

Of course, this is also aging. In I. B. Singer's story "A Friend of Kafka,"
the title character says rather hilariously that seeing the flaws in a woman
first, which he had begun to do, *is* impotence. But medical school ac-
celerated this process and gave it another dimension—something between curiosity and caring. I see the flaws not just because the veil has
been torn from my eyes by everything from the anatomy lab to the
gynecological surgery suite, but because I have come to think first of what
is wrong. Where is the pain? What is the problem? How can I help you?

My stance toward people—not just women—now has a large component of a desire to find out what is wrong—*something* is wrong with everyone —and to try to make it right. It is not the only thing I think of, but it is always in the back of my mind. Call it patronizing, call it a grotesque distortion of human relations, call it a transparent psychological defense; nonetheless it is real, and I suspect it is common.

I noted that while I was taking Basic Clinical Skills it appeared that I might be "medically accident-prone," running into situations where medical help was called for, and where I felt responsible but inadequate. This still happens, but I know and can do a good deal more. Friends and relatives often ask me medical questions, and I rather enjoy that. I always carefully describe my limitations and then give an opinion—usually a referral or a corroboration of someone else's opinion. At the least, I have information to give, and that is frequently helpful and comforting.

By one of the coincidences that are as memorable as they are strange, on the very day I was awarded my M.D. degree, a radiologist friend and I, driving across town, passed an accident. "I guess we should stop," he said.

"I guess so," I agreed. We found a man with a head injury sitting on the sidewalk. In a minute or so we established that his heart rate, respiration, and blood pressure were normal enough; that there was no clouding of consciousness; that pressure was not rapidly building inside his skull; and that there were no other major injuries. Then the ambulance arrived, and we were happy to turn the case over to the paramedics. I certainly don't feel ready to handle absolutely anything, but I feel ready for a lot.

For the time being I have returned to research and teaching. I haven't ruled out a residency; the continued appeal of doing one is great. Clinical medicine is one of the experiences—like falling in love, or parenthood, or (I am told) war—the appeal of which is difficult to appreciate from the outside. Years ago, when I was thinking of going to medical school, I asked our pediatrician what he thought of the idea. His answer, which seemed strange at the time, was, "It gives you a certain power." This, I now know, did not mean sociological power. It meant the surge of almost spiritual energy that accompanies the successful clinical encounter—the excitement of the danger, of the need, of the cure. There is no substitute for it; it is wonderful.

And yet it is also somehow false. One of the most interesting people I met in the course of my medical training was a scientist who had graduated from medical school but had not done a residency. He had wanted to be a doctor, he said, because as a child with polio he had seen a great deal of doctors, and they were the only people who spoke softly to him. But as a man, still limping from his encounter with the virus, he had experienced in medical school an inevitable disillusionment. One event stood out in his mind. Early in his fourth year he had been involved in the care of a middle-aged Italian man who successfully survived a life-threatening illness. One day when he was at the man's bedside the patient grabbed his hand and kissed it. He accepted the thanks and, he said, walked out of the room and down the hall on cloud nine.

Suddenly he brought himself up. "You schmuck," he said to himself. "What the hell do you think you—or anybody—did to deserve anything like that?" His distaste for the patient's gratitude and, more important, for his own pleasure in it—for what he saw as the illegitimacy of his power —clinched his decision not to become a practitioner.

In a wonderful piece in the June 27, 1985, *New England Journal of Medicine*'s "Occasional Notes" column, titled "Cost Containment by a Naval Armada" two academic physicians argued that the greatest benefit of our invasion of Grenada was the closing of its medical school. Since we have a glut of physicians, preventing the production of more can save society vast sums of money. They estimated the cost to society of each physician at "$450,000 per annum (income, overhead, hospital care, drugs, and amortization of capital costs)." They further state that "health care costs are related not to the amount of illness but to the number of practicing physicians" and that "in industrialized Western nations, there is no demonstrable relation between the health of the population and expenditures for health care." They recommend such measures as paying medical schools a large sum of money for each student they refrain from training, and paying already-trained physicians $100,000 a year to refrain from practice.

By this standard I am saving society a very large sum of money for each year that I refrain from practicing medicine. In the meantime, since (among other subjects) I write about and teach preventive medicine and health, I might actually prevent some illness. If I get lucky I might find something in my research that saves the economy even more. So I should not feel guilty about not practicing medicine. I should, on the contrary, feel guilty that I am still tempted to do so.

As for the education of the doctors of tomorrow—whether or not we can afford them—I am still puzzled. There is great ferment in medical education at present. I have already alluded to an article on medical education that appeared in *Time* magazine, in which the dean of the Harvard Medical School was quoted as saying, "Medical education is not in optimum health," adding that "there is little agreement on the diagnosis or treatment." The dean of the Johns Hopkins School of Medicine was quoted as saying, "We would like to reverse the trend toward early specialization and overemphasis on science as preparation for medicine." The president of the American Association of Medical Colleges referred to the process as "brutal." Lewis Thomas, the noted physician-author and then head of Memorial Sloan-Kettering Cancer Center, was quoted as saying that the curriculum in the first two years should be "cut in half." The dean of the Columbia College of Physicians and Surgeons was quoted as indicating a need for instruction on "how to deal with the patient, the patient's family and his whole life, rather than 'the third bed on the left with a coronary.' " And finally, the dean of the Boston University School of Medicine reportedly made the following sensible statement: "If we want our students to be compassionate, we as faculty and administrators have to be compassionate too."

In 1984 an official panel on the General Professional Education of the Physician of the Association of American Medical Colleges produced a report with a similar thrust. The report described a need for "fundamental reappraisal of how physicians are educated." It recommends (among other things) modification of admission requirements, with deemphasis of test scores; reduction of scheduled time and lecture hours in medical school; promotion of independent learning and information skills; and supporting and counseling medical students as individuals. This formal appraisal by the body officially responsible for American standards of medical education, like the informal canvasing in *Time*, corresponded to my own assessment of the machinery of medical training as I was, so to speak, being ground through it.

Why am I then not optimistic?

Partly because these pieties have been uttered so often before. It is no accident that Franz Kafka and the sociologist Max Weber were near contemporaries. Weber analyzed the diffusion of power and authority in the complex institutions of the modern industrial state and showed the lumbering independence of bureaucracies from outside or internal influence, even from the top. Kafka meanwhile traced, brilliantly and often hilariously, the plight of the individual lost among those interlocking webs of authority. In the *Time* article, men who were the bosses of the bosses of the bosses of my bosses at the hospital were decrying the sort of things that went on among their underlings but were bewildered as to what might be done. It was as if K. were to read in a newspaper that the head of the Castle was disturbed by the inability of individuals in the town to communicate with it and its functionaries. This news would be hard to believe—and, of course, maddening.

Partly, too, my skepticism stems from the nature of their suggestions and the responses they make to each other. One can sense the institutional autonomy and diffusion of authority described in their different ways by Weber and Kafka. The suggestions for change, which are continually being implemented in various medical schools, are then heavily criticized by officials at other medical schools, who in turn try other changes to reach allegedly similar ends. In fact, most of the experiments have already been tried somewhere. They are introduced with fanfare, tried for some years without dramatic success or failure, and replaced at length with a new system introduced again with fanfare. As often as not the proposals for change substantively alternate, so that *plus ça change, plus c'est la meme chose* is the only sensible thing you can say about them. A medical school dean once said, "It's easier to move a cemetery than to change the curriculum," and this ponderousness makes even trivial movement seem significant.

There are good reasons for the glacial pace of change, of course. These same heavily criticized medical schools have given us, for scores of years, the best medical care to be had in the world. Conservative medical educators understandably feel that they must be doing something right. But a more vocal, equally experienced group has now gained ascendancy, and that group is calling attention to defects not in the technological but in the human aspects of care. In the cool realms of technology (they seem to be saying) we may have succeeded beyond our fondest dreams; now we can afford to, and must, turn our attention to the relatively neglected realms of humanistic medicine. Some of them are saying that in a larger, philosophic sense, the enterprise is foundering. I doubt this, but if it is so, then the relatively minor tinkering with medical education that goes on all the time amounts to a rearranging of deck chairs on the *Titanic*.

What little research there is is not encouraging. High grades in college predict high grades in the preclinical first two years of medical school, but neither predicts any component of later performance. Medical students have been shown to be unusually obsessive and compulsive and to be narrower in their interests, less adaptable, and less comfortable with other people, than other students their age. Patterns of adaptation to medical school have been shown to include, most commonly, emotional constriction, fierce concentration on grades, manipulation of others to get ahead, and high anxiety. Between 20 percent and 46 percent of medical students require psychiatric assistance. Summarizing fifty-three articles and books in 1966, LeRoy Levitt wrote in the *Chicago Medical School Quarterly,* "The rapid technological advances and social demands constantly increase the stress and inexorably produce emotional turmoil in every student." Subsequent studies have confirmed this again and again. Other studies have shown that cynicism increases during the four years of medical school, though not during nursing school or law school. The medical sociologist Donald Light has noted that the process of selection and training runs counter to virtually all descriptions of the ideal physician, ancient or modern.

Change will be slow in coming, if it ever comes, because consumers—patients, all of us—are as conservative as the most staid medical educators. We too place the highest value on technical prowess. In certain areas where things are safe, where potential problems are minor, or where interventions don't really matter, we are willing to consider alternatives. Thus, the rise of family medicine for relatively minor primary care, of the alternative childbirth movement for uncomplicated deliveries, and of hospices for the terminally ill who have little to gain from hospitals. Care in these settings can be provided by nonphysicians such as nurse-practitioners, who have assumed their roles after an entirely different process of selection and training.

Most Americans are, so far, unwilling to sacrifice scientific and technical perfection even in these limited realms, believing, perhaps mistakenly, they will fare better by sticking it out in the great hospital-palaces, however cold and forbidding. For the treatment of most illnesses, for which technical knowledge and prowess make a difference, we seem to prefer a cold or even disturbed physician with full command of current medical science, to the most sensitive and compassionate bumbler. Psychologically, we seem to tolerate anything, so long as the doctors make the pain go away, so long as we leave the hospital alive.

There are other inertial forces at work. I have said that the most important influence on training in the clinical years of medical school is the eventuality of internship and residency. First and most significantly, medical students are trying to become, not physicians, but house officers. House officers are their models, the men and women whose shoes they will soon be filling. Although students cannot experience the residents' stress of responsibility, they can and do share all other aspects of stress—overwork, sleeplessness, isolation from the outside world, impairment of normal social relationships, poor diet, frequent patient presentations, lectures and seminars, and relentless cross-examination by superiors about everything.

The usual answers to the obvious question "Why must it be this way?" are unsatisfactory. One, provided by house officers, is "Slave labor." According to this theory interns and residents work on the bizarre schedules they do so that senior physicians can make a fortune and hospitals can make ends meet. The hourly wage of house officers (they work as much as a hundred hours a week or more for an annual salary of about $20,000) is obviously very low indeed. But this is simplistic—house officers could be exploited with equal ruthlessness and work shorter shifts than thirty-six hours.

A second common answer is, "They had to do it, so we have to do it." According to this theory (almost as paranoid as the first) the senior physicians require young people to go through the same terrible stress they did because they wish to repeat the suffering, and arbitrarily withhold certification until the new generation has jumped through the same hoops. (In fact, some doctors say that training used to be harder—an absurd claim based only on the number of hours per week on call and ignoring both the much longer current course of training and the exponential increase of medical knowledge.) It is certainly true that rituals of training perpetuate themselves. But this, too, is only part of the answer.

A much more interesting justification claims that all this is necessary. As the famed turn-of-the-century clinician William Osler said, "Live on the wards." Once I was brought up short at a dinner party by a physician-teacher who remarked, "You have to live with disease. You have to be there to follow its course, to really become intimate with everything about it. How would you feel about an anthropology graduate student who wanted to come home from his field work every evening?" There is something compelling in this analogy. The two sorts of trainee are both under great stress, both cut off from normal life, both in a total immersion with their subject. There are things you see by following a patient for thirty-six continuous hours, by being on a ward for a hundred or more hours a week, that you would not otherwise see. And it is surely true that the sheer number of hours in a residency program enlarges the range of what the resident is exposed to. How many removals of parotid gland tumors? How many patients with rare slow viruses? How many lung cancer patients who actually respond to adriamycin? This pressure to be exposed to as much as possible during training is one of the main reasons that residents do not clamor for shorter hours.

But there are more, and darker, reasons. A psychiatrist friend of mine argues that stress and sleeplessness are essential in the making of a doctor.

He characterizes the barrier between the physician-in-training and the acts he or she must eventually perform as not merely formidable but insurmountable. No normal person can cross it; no normal person can assume such responsibility, do such bizarre things to people, inflict such pain, make such heavy decisions. So the person must be temporarily rendered abnormal. When your beeper wakes you after two hours' sleep (having not let you rest for thirty hours before that) and you roll out of your cot and rush to the bedside, you will be faced with decisions no person should have to make—decisions on which life will depend but which in their nature cannot be carefully considered. The fatigue and stress make you care a little less; they enable you to make the decisions. You do it in a daze. And after doing this hundreds and then thousands of times, they are no longer deliberate or even confused, but reflexive. You have learned to bypass existential moralizing and to grapple with a grotesque pragmatic reality that cannot be ignored. Eventually, you do this even when you are well rested and not under any stress. And when that happens you have become a doctor.

It is obvious from what I have written here that the stress of clinical training alienates the doctor from the patient, that in a real sense the patient becomes the enemy. *(Goddamit, did she blow her I.V. again? Jesus Christ, did he spike a temp?)* At first I believed that this was an inadvertent and unfortunate concomitant of medical training, but I now think that it is intrinsic. Not only stress and sleeplessness but the sense of the patient as the cause of one's distress contributes to the doctor's detachment. This detachment is not just objective but downright negative. To cut and puncture a person, to take his or her life in your hands, to pound the chest until ribs break, to decide upon drastic action without being able to ask permission, to render a judgment about whether care should continue or stop—these and a thousand other things may require something stronger than objectivity. They may actually require a measure of dislike.

In the end, we all—doctors, patients, hospital staff—have a sense that the doctors are doctors, and can be allowed to do what they do, *because of* the rigors of the training. Because we view it as painful, stressful, life-distorting, and terribly long, we allow it to justify the remarkable power we give the doctor over us. The doctor has paid for the power with suffering.

Among the !Kung San (Bushmen), of Africa's Kalahari, there is a very moving healing ritual. Women sit in a circle around a small fire, clapping in complex rhythms and singing in a yodeling way. Men with rattles strapped to their legs dance around in a circle behind them, always in one

direction, steadily, monotonously. Through a combination of dance, concentration, listening to the music, and practice, some of these men enter
altered states of consciousness—trances—in which healing by the laying
on of hands is believed to be possible.

In these trances the men take great risks and experience great pain—
especially when they are learning. Their souls may leave their bodies
never to return. Injury, pain, and death are part of the expected risk of
learning to heal. Physically, while in trance, they may injure themselves
by running at full tilt into the pitch-dark savannah, or by pouring glowing
red coals over their heads. Furthermore, the medicine itself is said to boil
up in the flanks of each healer, and this effect, essential for healing power,
is said to cause a pain like no other. Spiritually, they believe that their souls
leave their bodies when they are in this state. As mature healers, they can
use this phenomenon to advantage, arguing in the spirit-world on behalf
of the ill person.

The best insurance against the risks is the support of the community of
healers. Trusting in your fellow-healers, especially your teachers, you can
let go psychologically and spiritually; they will pull you away from the
coals or prevent you from running into a tree; they will teach you how to
turn the pain in your flanks into healing power; they will slowly bring your
soul back to your body. You can count on them, more or less. But you
cannot avoid the risks or the pain. The risks and pain are what give you
the power to heal. As a sometime apprentice in both systems—the !Kung
and the American—I can say that the confidence to heal comes in part
through the pain; that you feel justified in exercising such terrible power
over your fellow human beings to the extent that you have suffered to get
the power; and, last but not least, your patients feel it too.

For myself, at least for the moment, I have said good-bye to all that. I
view the clinical training enterprise as a powerful bureaucracy with which
I have some fascinating, valuable but not usually pleasant encounters.
Much of the unpleasantness had to do with my own flaws; but much had
to do with the culture and social structure of the healers, which I have
been privileged to observe at close quarters.

This social structure comprises a vast army of people, mostly young, who
show, at least for a time, a uniformity of spirit. They are tough, brilliant,
knowledgeable, hard-working, and hard on themselves. They are reliable
and competent in situations ranging from eighteen-month-long management of cancer chemotherapy through eighteen-hour-long brain surgery

to emergencies in which life may hinge on what they can do in eighteen seconds. Without exception they have endured great challenges, and they have done so without entirely losing their sense of humor. They have experienced many things that are closed to others. With very few exceptions, they are professionals.

Perhaps they have earned the right to arrogance; they certainly feel that they have. But one wonders if they can see the self-serving aspects of their behavior. They are extremely unreflective, criticizing each other relentlessly for any slight delay during which some real thought about what they are doing might take place. No habit is so quickly extinguished as that of "wasting" another physician's time. They smile at their patients, when they can, in something like the way flight attendants smile at their passengers. At its best, it is a passable, even good bedside manner, but I doubt that it is compassionate. Behind the patients' backs hostility is ubiquitous, with a frequent reliance on gruesome humor. Sympathy for each other, emulation of and gratitude toward their teachers—exactly as demanded in the Hippocratic Oath—have primacy in their emotional lives, next to the absolute primacy of survival. They are authoritarian in a satisfied, calm —not shrill—way, but their discipline is nonetheless ironclad.

Doctors resemble army officers in several interesting ways. They are in charge of matters of life and death, and are in a relentless confrontation with dangerous and intractable enemies. These decisions, usually made under pressure and always subject to legal scrutiny, must be made according to rules and must follow a chain of command. The most vulnerable person is the one who becomes separate, either psychologically or morally, from the group. In the training process, as in the day-to-day functioning of the hierarchy, stress and abrasiveness are considered not merely acceptable but salutary. They help to prepare the members of the hierarchy for uncertain and perilous encounters with the outside world, toughening them up and weeding out weaklings. But of course the function of an army is supposed to be destruction and killing, while the purpose of medicine is healing.

As the Hippocratic Oath candidly recognized, the physician must look first to the relationship with other physicians and physician-teachers. Young physicians rely on each other for support, and the resulting teamwork is frequently beautiful to see. But it risks making them self-congratulatory, and despite the emphasis traditionally placed on breadth of general knowledge, the modern young physician is usually very narrow unless he or she is either iconoclastic or brave.

Even after their training is over, doctors do not seem to broaden very much. This is partly because the habit of arrogance now becomes a burden, and it is hard to get free of. In general conversation, they become frightened because of their narrowness, and their ignorance contrasts with their medical competence. So, whatever the subject, they tend to talk rather than listen—a habit strengthened in their peer interactions, in the stance they take toward nonphysicians, and in their attitude toward their own patients.

To them, the world consists only of doctors and nondoctors. They inevitably drift, on their sturdy boat of medicine, farther and farther away from the shore of common human experience. Even the superb body of experience to which they are exposed in their daily work is somehow largely lost to them as a source of existential growth. Despite their impressive experience and heavy responsibilities, they often remain eternal adolescents, sadly locked in a thrilling and important but somehow still collegiate sort of enterprise.

As I watch my fellow medical students drift from the shore I feel a twinge of regret—for the loss of that excitement, urgency, responsibility, and the feeling of belonging to a disciplined, winning team. But more than regret I have the "good-bye-to-all-that" sort of feeling, a preparedness to make my separate peace.

And yet, to have that thrill of waking up suddenly in the middle of the night, to have the weight of sleep fall away in a matter of seconds and to have that sense rise up from your arms, from your chest, from your bowels, that you are desperately needed, that your personal flaws and problems do not matter, that, right here and now, for the next hour, you have a perfectly clear purpose in your life . . .

Obviously, I still admire much of what they do and are—their spirit, their intelligence, their memory, their endurance, their competence in emergencies, their calm in the face of pain and death, their technical facility and power. But I also long to see them gain some greater understanding of the human situations they deal with, understanding not just of renal tubular exchange ratios and digoxin dosage regimes but of the fear, the loss, the dependency, the emptiness, the pain.

I do not believe in God, or in an afterlife, or in any insubstantial component of the spirit. Yet I know—and this is increasingly being proved—that there is a nonphysical aspect to healing, which I am prepared to call spiritual. It relates to heart and mind, hope and will, love and courage, values and ideas, social and cultural—including religious—life. In the hospital, I learned to keep my thoughts to myself about all such matters. There the pretense is that everyone knows about them, and it is unnecessary to talk of them. In reality, everyone "knows" about them but practically nobody cares, except insofar as finding them the source of a good laugh. Such cynicism, which increases during the medical school years, deeply affects the young physicians' view of life—not just of illness but of the whole of human experience. They have trained themselves to participate just so far and no farther with, say, a terminal cancer patient in his or her search for personal meaning; but then they cannot simply slough off this habit of diffidence when it comes to their own search for meaning, when they contemplate the course of their own lives.

It is less than appealing, what this makes of them; yet I love them in some crazy way. I have worked with them, roomed with them, argued with them, learned from them, gone through emergencies and sleepless nights and a dozen other kinds of crises with them, breathing the same stale antiseptic-laden air. I know what they can be and do and it is very impressive. In some sense many of them will remain among my heroes, and I will think of them wistfully in a recurring daydream of serene competence and fabulous technical power. But then I will think of the price they pay. If I had it to do over again, I suppose I would still do it. Yet in making that choice for myself I would not want to make it for someone else. For my daughters or son I would be frightened of the stresses—whether the traditional stresses intrinsic to medical training or the new economic and legal ones stemming from the world outside—that make life so difficult for doctors.

Yet of course, when I am in trouble—and notice that I do not say "if" —I will go to them, and they will improve my chances.

Life is short and the art long, the occasion instant, experiment perilous, decision difficult. And yet, healing is possible—indeed, it is ubiquitous. It goes on in every creature every day. And among our privileges as the most sentient, most clever creatures on this planet is the ability, occasionally, to perform acts in aid of it. In a spiritual as well as in a technical sense— not just for the sake of healing but for the sake also of meaning—we would do well to take that privilege seriously.

A Glossary of
House Officer Slang

The language house officers—residents and interns—use expresses their unique world view—their concepts, their categories, their defenses, their humor. If it seems frequently brutal and egotistical, we should consider the circumstances that produce it and remember that it is a revealing body of expression that may well be essential to their survival. In any case it is central to their socialization and training.

I heard all the words and phrases listed here used by house officers in the normal course of everyday hospital life. Some of the slang is widely used throughout the United States; some of it has more local or personal application. Some of the words and phrases are in general usage among young people, but seemed to me to be worthy of inclusion here because of special connotations in the hospital context. I am unfortunately not able to identify the geographical distribution of the words, and it is likely that there are significant linguistic subcultures. (I can more easily identify the distribution of some of the words and phrases by medical specialty.) The hospitals in which I worked drew house officers from all parts of the United States, and it was clear that some of them imported slang usages that were new to the local physicians. Some of these were rapidly taken up into local parlance. More intriguing, there were conscious references to and repetition of slang words that appeared in *The House of God*, a hilarious and touching satire of medical internship—a clear case of life imitating art.

Slang is in rapid and continuous flux. This list is only a small fraction of a changing and growing lexicon, and suggestions for augmentation or correction will be gratefully received.

allergic salute   Typical gesture of a child with nasal allergies; rubbing the nose upward with the palm of the hand; produces the allergic crease, a characteristic wrinkle in the nose.

A.M.A.   Against Medical Advice; a way of leaving the hospital; this designation constitutes important protection for the house officer and appears prominently in the charts of such patients; all the letters are pronounced, as in the physicians' organization, although the latter is rarely mentioned by house officers.

A.M.F.   Occasionally written in a patient's chart in place of A.M.A.; "Adios Mother Fucker."

animal   Clinically, in relation to invasive procedures, an extremely aggressive medical student; "They let her do a herniorrhaphy as a third-year student. She started out, she was afraid to put a needle in a patient, but by the end of the rotation she was an animal."

appy   Appendectomy; removal of the vermiform appendix.

ass time   Time wasted sitting around; said of internal medicine by surgeons, and of psychiatry by internists.

Aunt Minnie   In radiology, a case you can recognize only if you have seen it before; while looking at the film or scan, the radiologist says, "That's an Aunt Minnie." "What's that?" "Did you ever see Aunt Minnie?" "No." "Well, if you did, you'd know her."

bag   Verb meaning to breathe for the patient artificially using a hand-operated device called an ambu-bag, something like a bellows; as in, "Here's the cardio-verter, so why don't you stop bagging her for a second and we'll *zap* her."

bag of worms   Ventricular fibrillation, the most serious cardiac arrhythmia; named for the appearance of the EKG.

Band-Aids   Derisive or at least belittling reference to treatments that are pallia-tive at best, having no curative power.

barbies   Short for barbiturates, a class of sedative drugs.

baseball stitch   Type of skin closure, resembling the stitch on a baseball.

B.F.I.   Big Fuckin' Infarct; a massive myocardial infarction (heart attack) or stroke.

big G   In obstetrics, a grand multigravida; a woman who has had many babies.

Big Red   Adriamycin, a highly toxic chemotherapeutic agent for cancer; bright red in color; dangerous to give, dangerous to work with.

bite the bullet   Noun-phrase used when anesthesia doesn't work; "This is the second C-section we've had to do this week with bite the bullet for anesthesia."

blow   To destroy a vein while trying to insert an I.V.; "That medical student's already blown every vein in both arms."

boarders   Patients from other services occupying beds on the team's ward or floor; usually unwelcome.

bones   Orthopedics; the surgical subspecialty in which injury and disease of bone are treated; probably the most lucrative medical specialty, and frequently as-sociated with the games and playgrounds of the idle rich.

boogie   To move patients along quickly in a clinic or emergency room; "Let's boogie!"

bounce   Patient comes back after an unsuccessful turf; as in, "I tried that turf to Ortho, but it only worked for about two days, and she bounced back."

box   Verb meaning to die; as in "This is a guy who's trying to box," which does not imply anything intentional, merely that he is dying; the connotation is that he needn't.

brainiac   Brain; as in "If they do bizarre things, it means their brainiac's acting a bit funny"—a reference to children with high fevers.

buff   Verb meaning to make a patient better, or at least look better, by the signs and by the numbers; an improvement, but by no means necessarily a cure; "I've got that pneumonia the surgeons *turf*ed us so buffed they'll never recognize him when I turf him back;" or, to polish oneself or one's student in preparation for an exam or grilling by a superior.

buggy   Of a patient, full of bugs; not the germ kind of bugs necessarily, but the kind you find in an automobile or computer program; flaws; in as, "I want that charming *gomere* buffed and *turf*ed back to her nursing home before she goes buggy on us."

bug juice   Antibiotic; as in, "We better shoot some bug juice into this guy or we're gonna start a micro lab right here in his room."

bugs   Germs; as in, "What kind of strange bug is in this lady's throat?"

bump   To increase the level of something, usually suddenly; as in "that diabetic bumped her sugar today" or "Dr. Allen decided to bump the digoxin."

buzz   To order and/or administer X-ray therapy (XRT) for cancer treatment; to irradiate.

buzzing   Of a patient; "hyper" or manic.

cabbage   Pronunciation of C.A.B.G., for Coronary Artery Bypass Graft; increasingly popular corrective surgery for atherosclerotic heart disease during the past decade; some of its uses now controversial.

call   1) Night or weekend duty at the hospital; now used as much with the verb to have ("I have call") as with the preposition on ("I'm on call"); also, "call night," "call schedule," etc.; 2) Short for judgment call; decision in which there is no clearly right answer; "It's a call."

carbon-based protoplasm   As in "Dr. Schwartz is definitely not from carbon-based protoplasm;" equivalent to calling him a space cadet, or even a *space commandant;* head in the clouds; strange.

catch   To deliver a baby; since there are always at least two pairs of hands around in a modern hospital delivery, the delivery is "credited" to the person who actually "catches" the baby as it emerges from the womb; as in, "And we guarantee that every student in this rotation will get to catch at least ten babies."

chandelier sign   Local physical tenderness great enough so that after pressure is applied, the patient has to be removed from the chandelier; a relatively sure indication that the patient is not malingering.

chassis   Skull, as referred to by some radiologists; as in "This chassis is perfectly kosher from stem to stern."

cheap case   Easy case to figure out and diagnose.

check out   Verb meaning to die; as in "Mr. Goodman finally checked out this morning;" not to be confused with discharge.

Christian   A believer, in relation to the value of a rule or the severity of an illness; what you become after a particularly scary experience with a patient.

C.I.C.U.   Pronounced "kick-you;" acronym for cardiac intensive care unit.

code   To use full emergency measures to resuscitate a patient who has suffered a heart or breathing stoppage; implies a great flurry of activity, the most exciting moment in nonsurgical practice; or in some cases the most disturbing, as in "We'd damn well better get an official *D.N.R.* on this patient, because I don't want us to have to code her again;" also, a noun referring to the process.

C.O.L.D.   Chronic Obstructive Lung Disease; pronounced as individual letters, but when written inevitably and ironically implies the common cold, a somewhat less severe respiratory ailment (C.O.L.D. is usually eventually fatal).

cookie   A clot or other solid object traveling through the bloodstream, likely to block small arteries and cause damage; as in "She might shoot some cookies into her *helmet.*"

crash   To intubate a patient in a hurry, in an emergency; "I hate to crash these laboring women for C-sections."

crepe   See "hang crepe."

crispy critters   Children chronically hospitalized due to third-degree burns over most of their body surface; among the saddest cases in medicine; also known as "toasted toddlers."

crit   Hematocrit; the percentage of whole blood comprising red blood cells; vital measure in a patient with blood loss, a blood or fluid disorder, and many other conditions.

crock   Patient with nothing physically wrong; appears to be short for "crock of shit," but the latter full phrasing is never heard; a hypochondriac or somatizer; candidate for "psychoceramic medicine."

cruising   Patient who is stable; not quite a *"rose,"* but on the way.

crump   Verb meaning to decompensate or fall apart (of patients); threaten to die; die.

C.T.D.   Circling the drain; said of a patient who is dying.

cut   To perform surgery; or, in reference to a specific operation, as in "If you get a lady in labor, in any kind of trouble, I don't care what it is, you'd better get ready to cut her," a reference in this case to Caesarean section.

C.Y.A.   Cover your ass; an injunction referring to the increasingly necessary (in a legal sense) defensive medicine; or simply to good practice.

deep sea fishing   Exploratory surgery (fishing expedition) with particularly little to go on.

defenestration   Throwing oneself out the window; a solution feared for some patients, wished for for others, and threatened by house officers, for their patients or themselves.

Dig   Pronounced "dij;" short for digitalis, one of the most frequently used, oldest and most effective heart medications.

dirtball   A chronic alcoholic, drug abuser, bag lady, or other street person who rarely bathes, has frequent infectious contacts, and is likely to be a walking colony of dangerous microorganisms; a very common emergency room usage.

dixie   Verb meaning to voluntarily disappear from the hospital against doctor's orders; probably from D.C., the acronym for discharge; as in "Mr. O'Neill dixied again tonight, and that's it for me, I'm through."

D.N.R.   Do not resuscitate; a designation unofficially or in some places officially given to patients who are not to receive heroic measures (not to be coded) in the event of breathing stoppage.

D.O.A.   Dead on arrival; of a patient brought into the Emergency Room.

doc   The most affectionate and respectful way a house officer says "physician"; as in "Good doc!"

dribble off the court   A patient is said to do this when the illness gradually but steadily destabilizes; as when a patient with heart failure drifts out of control. "I had to *bump* Mr. Allston's digoxin 'cause he was starting to dribble off the court."

drones   Derogatory euphemism for medical students on the service.

Dubnoff scale   A measurement developed by a legendary Galen Memorial Hospital house officer; on chest X-rays, the extent to which the mandible is seen to have descended over the chest, on a scale of I to V; highly correlated with age after eighty; a source of much hilarity during X-ray rounds.

dud Patient with no interesting findings; less strong than "crock," which implies blame for the patient.

dump Noun or verb referring to an unwelcome transfer of a patient; see also *turf.*

the dwindles Of an elderly patient; fading away; "Well, I'm afraid poor Mrs. Morgan's got the dwindles."

epidoodle Epidural anesthesia; often used in childbirth or Caesarean section.

eyeball To examine; "Marty, would you eyeball this rash for me, I can't figure it out."

Eyeball Nickname for a large and respected eye hospital and clinic.

filet How surgeons open up a kidney to remove the stones.

fishing expedition Exploratory surgery, frequently abdominal, with no specific goal except to find out what's wrong.

flail Something like *horror show,* but with a connotation of total helplessness of surgeons or physicians in an emergency.

fleas Derogatory term for medical doctors used by surgeons; refers to their presumed tendency to be "the last to leave a dying body"; as in "Neurologists? They're the worst fleas in medicine." See also *mopes.*

fleas and lice A euphemism for two separate intercurrent disease processes; said in order to justify a departure from the standard diagnostic rule that whenever possible all symptoms and signs should be accounted for by a single disease process; as in "Don't forget it *is* possible to have fleas and lice."

F.L.K. Funny Looking Kid; on a pediatric service, a child whose facial or other physical characteristics suggest the possibility of genetic or chromosomal disease.

Fly sign Patient lies with mouth wide open, allowing flies to enter and leave at will; ominous.

The Four Hundred Club Patients with blood alcohol levels above 400 mg% who are "still walkin' an' talkin' "; said with a certain admiration.

Galen rule of learning "See one, screw one, do one." (Modification of the Rule of Learning, "See one, do one, teach one.")

Galen Warrior Patient with lots of metal implanted in the course of prior treatment.

gall bag Cholecystectomy; gall bladder removal; also, the organ itself.

garbageman A baby born with serious defects; "The thing about forceps is if you're not careful with them you can end up with a baby that's a garbageman."

go down Go to sleep; "With a fourth year medical student around you ought to be able to go down for the night."

go in To perform surgery; as in, "I think we'd better go in."

gok As in, "This is a clear case of gok"; pronunciation of the acronym G.O.K., for God only knows.

gome Short for *gomer.*

gome docs Elderly incompetent physicians (as viewed by house officers) still practicing; usually in affiliation with *Mount Saint Elsewhere;* or, a doctor of any age who specializes in gomers; *gome,* short for *gomer,* is otherwise only applied to patients.

gomer Acronym for Get Out of My Emergency Room; refers to an old, decrepit, hopeless patient whose care is guaranteed to be a thankless task; usually admitted from a nursing home.

gomere Female *gomer;* pronounced "go-mare," as if it were a feminine ending in French; which, through an ironic sort of gentility, gives the old demented woman a sort of touching respect while allowing the house officer yet another level of mockery.

gonzo   Of a patient, discharged or dead.

goober   Small metastasis, or distant colonization by a cancer, usually found in groups; as in *"Unclear medicine* says his brain is full of goobers;" contrast the larger *"gumba."*

G.P.   General practitioner; implies little or no training beyond the internship, an option once common but now almost impossible; although a need for this kind of doctor has now produced the family practitioner, who has had years of residency training but in general medicine and surgery.

gork   Verb meaning to sedate someone heavily; or, noun referring to a patient with severely impaired mental functions (in common parlance, a vegetable); a related usage is "gorked out."

go sour   Decompensate; deteriorate; *"dribble off the court."*

groinecology.   Derogatory term for gynecology.

gumba   Tumor metastasis, usually large, as in "a big gumba in the left cerebral hemisphere;" related to *goober.*

gunner   An aggressive medical student in an uncomplimentary sense (contrast "animal"); reads the text before the first day of class, scoops fellow students, "guns" for grades.

hand-holding   Psychological support of a patient, either because of a special need or because little else can be done; usually resentful or derogatory.

hang crepe   Important verb phrase meaning to lead patients to expect the worst; it being always better to change the news from bad to good; "Given Mr. Stern's condition, I want you to hang crepe when you talk to the family."

heavy chain disease   Refers to a patient brought to the Emergency Room in handcuffs; a play on the real diagnosis of the same name, a disorder of antibody formation, where the reference is to a chain of molecules.

heavy hammer   Especially strong pain killer; "When a patient is that hypersensitive, you might have to bring out the heavy hammer."

helmet   Skull or head; as in, "I think the new player in Room 2 has a cracked helmet.

hematomato   Hematoma; an accumulation of blood where it doesn't belong.

hit   Verb meaning to give medicine, radiation, or other treatment; as in, "I think we better hit him with the roids."

hit   Noun meaning a newly admitted patient, or more specifically the procedure —taking an hour or more—required of a house officer who is "doing an admission;" as in, "Would you believe I got eight hits last night? Eight? Eight? That's got to be the record for the year."

HO   Pronunciation of the initial letters of house officer; sounds as in Santa's laugh, but with an occasional distinct slide toward the southern word " 'ho,' " a drawled version of "whore."

horror show   An extreme mess in which either 1) one mistake after another leads to a relentless, intractable, and usually very ugly deterioration; or less commonly 2) the patient's condition itself leads to the same sort of result.

hors d'oeuvres   Orders; as in, "I can't take a consult now, I have to write the hors d'oeuvres on this patient."

hot belly   Surgical abdomen; an abdominal pain or condition requiring immediate surgical intervention; as in acute appendicitis, or a ruptured colonic diverticulum.

hypocritic oath   Hippocratic oath, set forth by the Greek physician Hippocrates and sworn to at the conclusion of training by his disciples and other physicians for centuries. No longer in use in its traditional form in most medical schools in the United States.

ice On a nuclear scan of an organ, a very "cold" spot, meaning no uptake of the radioactive isotope; may indicate death of that area of tissue.

imminent Soon to die; as in "They're transferring Mr. Jones to the private patients' ward because he's imminent."

insult Synonym for consult, an assessment requested for a patient on another service who has developed a concurrent problem in one's bailiwick; as in "I can't go to dinner, I'm writing up an insult."

ischial tuberosity rounds A derisive reference by surgeons to the ubiquitous and lengthy "sit-down rounds" of internal medicine; ischial tuberosities being the surfaces of the pelvic architecture that one sits on; the clear implication being that these rounds are unnecessarily protracted and pseudo-intellectual, arising to fill time in which the surgeons are really doing something—namely surgery.

jug Pronounced "joog;" short for jugular vein.

kiddie Affectionate term for pediatric patients.

kosher Either normal, when said of an organ or test result; or abnormal in a standard way, when said of a disease process or symptom picture that had seemed strange; or proper, when said of a medical or surgical procedure.

lac Laceration; "You mean you still haven't learned to sew a lac?"

lipstick sign Some days after an operation, a female patient will begin to feel well enough to put on lipstick; a relatively good sign of recovery, although it is also seen as a brave gesture in terminal patients.

L.M.D. Local medical doctor; the patient's town or neighborhood physician; usually condescending, often frankly derogatory.

L.O.L. in N.A.D. Letters are all pronounced ("ell-oh-ell in enn-ay-dee"); little old lady in no acute (or apparent) distress; an abbreviation frequently found near the beginning of admission or clinic notes of elderly female patients, except where a senior physician has expressly forbidden its use; sets the reader's mind at ease that there is no major illness or trauma, although some treatable illness may well be present; contrast "crock," "gomer"—which, incidentally, no one would dream of writing or even abbreviating in a chart.

lytes Electrolytes in the blood, including among others ionized sodium, potassium, and chloride; among the most important and most common laboratory measures, and one of the first diagnostic strategies after the history and physical.

M. & M. Morbidity and mortality; weekly conferences reviewing recent severe illness or death on the service; interesting cases, occasionally mistakes; pronounced as in the candy.

mashing Pressing, as part of the physical examination; "Don't mash too hard on that now, or you'll get the *chandelier sign.*"

MDeity Reference to physicians' arrogance.

meat Biopsy tissue; as in the saying "No meat, no treat," meaning, if you don't confirm the pathology with a biopsy, you won't know what treatment to go ahead with.

metabolic rounds Breakfast, lunch, dinner, snack; "Hey, it's time for metabolic rounds," that is, stabilizing the metabolism of the doctor.

M.I. Myocardial infarction; death of a part of the heart muscle due to blockade of a coronary vessel; commonly called a "heart attack;" pronounced as individual letters ("emm-eye").

M.I.C.U. Pronounced "mick-you;" acronym for medical intensive care unit.

Minor scourge Minor surgery clinic, one of the toughest of all hospital assignments for a house officer; minimum of interesting cases, maximum of pressure and insults from patients, no sleep.

mole Exceptionally hard worker; plodder.

money changers   Private physicians, especially successful group practices, whose work cannot be trusted because of the profit motive; "O.K., let's see what the money changers thought this CAT scan was."

mopes   Pronunciation of the acronym M.O.P. for medical outpatient; not a reference to the patients but to the medical doctors who take care of them; derogatorily, by surgeons; mopes are nonsurgeons who take care of trivial conditions with slow and uncertain methods under no pressure; see also *fleas*.

Mount Saint Elsewhere   General designation for the lower class of hospitals, from big nasty city ones to charming, inept community ones; definitely derogatory; sometimes abbreviated "Mt. St. E.;" the nickname long preceded the television program with a similar name.

Mudd-Fudd   Humorous pronunciation of M.D.-Ph.D.; used to refer, usually respectfully these days, to individuals who hold both degrees, and who are likely to achieve power and prominence in academic medicine.

M.U.O.   Marginal undesirable organism; see *dirtball* and *worm*.

N.A.T.   Acronym for "not a trooper;" scrawled on the labor and delivery board by the name of a patient who is seen as particularly uncourageous in her handling of labor.

Nebraska sign   flatline electrocardiogram, indicative of total cessation of even the slightest electrical activity in the heart muscle; known in Europe as the Holland sign.

negative patient outcome   Death.

negative wallet biopsy   Designates an indigent patient, unable to pay.

negatory   Cute synonym for "negative," as in a test result.

neuron   A neurologist; as in, "I think we better get a neuron to do a *roadside consult* on this one."

N.G. cowboy   Used in reference to interns or students who have to get astride a patient to put down a nasogastric (N.G.) feeding tube.

N.I.C.U.   pronounced "nick-you;" acronym for neurosurgical intensive care unit.

no-hitter   A full night on call with no patients to admit; "Can you believe it? Miller got a no-hitter last night! And here he is complaining!"

N.T.B.   Acronym for "not too bright"; scrawled on the labor and delivery room board by the name of a patient who is judged by the nurses to be inaccessible due to sheer native stupidity.

N.T.D.   Nothing to do (on a patient, at least for now); the house officer's dream abbreviation.

O.B.G.Y.N.   Obstetrics and gynecology; pronounced as a string of letters, "oh-bee-gee-wye-enn;" in England, "Obs-'n-Gynie" (hard G) like a sort of vaudeville team; looked down on by surgeons as semiskilled labor and by the radical alternate birth movement as legalized torture.

O.D.   Overdose of drugs; as in the common usage; noun or verb.

offending rounds   Attending rounds; rounds with the attending physician for the month.

oops!   Designation on the labor board; out of pelvis; the baby's head is not engaged and the labor has not really begun.

O-Q shift   Change from *"O sign"* to *"Q sign;"* ominous.

O.R.   Acronym for operating room.

orbit   Waiting for certain highly popular surgical procedures for which there are long queues (for example, the coronary artery bypass graft, or CABG, pronounced "cabbage"); may be due to geographic maldistribution, legally imposed maximum bed count for a given hospital, or other causes. As in "We've got people now dying in orbit."

orchid in the arctic How small premature babies have to be treated.

orthopod Orthopedic surgeon; also "ortho," for the field.

O sign Moribund elderly patient with mouth open and tongue inside; contrast "Q sign," tongue out, considered worse; and "O-Q shift;" all humorous.

O.T.D. Out the door; of a patient who has been discharged; "gonzo."

outfield Patients on wards or floors other than the team's main working location; highly undesirable, since they require much extra walking and climbing, lengthening rounds and otherwise interfering with efficiency. See also "boarders."

Oversight Ward The overnight ward, an observation unit for Emergency Ward cases that probably do not need admission but need to be watched for twenty-four or forty-eight hours.

oy, inspiratory and expiratory Two sounds made by Jewish nursing home patients, humorously considered a significant distinction.

pac-man To eat away at a fresh clot with a catheter that squirts streptokinase; "So you sort of pac-man your way down this vessel with streptokinase, dissolving clot as you go."

P⁵T Piss-poor protoplasm poorly put together; more extreme version of "triple P."

P.I.A. Officially, pregnancy-induced anxiety; unofficially, pain in the ass.

pick-up To identify a disease from a routine examination, without prior suspicion; "Hey, a melanoma! What a great pick-up for a medical student!"

P.I.C.U. Pronounced "pick-you;" acronym for pulmonary intensive care unit.

Piss-Poor Protoplasm See "triple P."

Pit Short for Pitocin, a drug for inducing labor; also, a verb meaning to use the drug; as in "I can't stay here all weekend; if she doesn't get moving I'm gonna Pit her;" "Vitamin P."

Pit Common derogatory reference to the hospital Emergency Room; as in "Who's *Twit in the Pit* tonight?"

player Patient on the ward; as in "Who's this new player Sylvia Johnson?"

poke To perform a needle aspiration biopsy; "If her temp stays up I'm gonna poke her;" also "tap."

polypharmacy So many drugs given to the same patient that it's almost impossible to understand the overall effect; "Well, Freddy's really ridin' the roller-coaster of polypharmacy, and I don't know what's doin' what to what."

poop Give birth rapidly or precipitously; after the child's word for defecation; "If you want that delivery in Room 3, you'd better move; she's gonna poop that kid right out."

pretzel Pelvis; "This lady's pretzel is cracked in three places."

psychoceramic medicine Treatment of "crocks;" the phrase ridicules a category of patients and a category of physicians (including the whole profession of psychiatry) simultaneously.

Puerto Rican forceps Two nurses on stools, on either side of the delivery table, pushing on the fundus of the uterus with all their might. (Several other ethnic groups may be insulted using the same phrase.)

punt What you do when you don't know what to do; "I know exactly what I'm gonna do with Mrs. Feldman. I'm gonna punt."

pushy Refers to a woman in the second stage of labor, after full dilatation of the cervix, when active conscious pushing by the woman is recommended; no derogatory connotation intended.

Q.N.S. of the C.N.S. Q.N.S. is an acronym for quantity not sufficient, a designation with which some samples come back from the lab; dreaded by house officers, since it means drawing the blood (or whatever fluid it was) all over again; C.N.S., central nervous system, the whole phrase simply means unintelligent, a reference to a patient; see also *N.T.B.*

Q sign   Moribund elderly patient with mouth open and tongue hanging out to the side; worse than "O sign;" see also "O-Q shift."

Rays   Radiology; the medical subspecialty in which radiation is used for visualization or treatment; considered intellectually challenging but otherwise shamefully easy, not at all the typical endurance test for students and house officers.

R.D.   Real doctor; said variously by radiologists, pathologists, psychiatrists, dermatologists, even obstetricians, when in trouble; "Hey, this lady needs an R.D.!"

real case   Serious emergency; "I'm sorry I can't take care of your father right now, I've got a real case."

res   Resident physician; house officer beyond the internship or first year of training; may also be called simply the "junior" or the "senior" depending on which year above the first he or she is in; see also "tern."

resurrectene   A drug that resurrects the dead, or at least the near dead; the only suitable treatment for some patients; see also "zippola."

retrospectoscope   Instrument for Monday morning quarterbacking; as in the statement at a surgical mortality conference that begins "I can see through my retrospectoscope that what we should have done was to . . ."

roadside consult   Unofficial consultation on a patient between physician friends; nothing in writing, nothing binding.

rock & roll   Leave the hospital or intensive care unit. As in "Mrs. Moscogliani is ready to rock & roll."

roids   Steroids; widely useful group of drugs, for many different situations, but not used lightly.

roll   To leave the ward or hospital; "Ready to roll;" see also *rock & roll.*

rooter   A drunk who hangs around the hospital; from their habit of rooting for ambulances as they drive in up the ramp; *rooter royale:* an especially egregious example of the type; *piney rooter:* a rooter from a backwoods area.

rose   A patient who is completely "buffed;" not necessarily well, but ready to roll.

Rule of learning   "See one, do one, teach one." (See *Galen rule of learning.*)

scoop   Figure out the case first; "Any medical student who's worth anything sooner or later will scoop a resident."

scrip   Prescription; "Let me teach you how to write a scrip, so you can do some for me in clinic.

scut   Routine daily ward work, sometimes dirty but often just paperwork, of which there is a vast amount; done by the lowest person on the totem pole who can legally do it, and who can be trusted not to do it so badly that he or she creates more work instead of doing some of it; sometimes ironically interpreted as "some clinically useful training."

scut-monkey   Medical student who is good at, and/or likes, scut.

S.I.C.U.   Pronounced "sick-you"; acronym for surgical intensive care unit.

sieve   Opposite of *"wall"* (q.v.).

sign out   See *"check out."*

storybooks   Textbooks; "You've got to get out of the habit of believing it just because it says so in your storybooks."

suck points   Brownie points; gained by deliberate ingratiation with one's superiors.

supratentorial   Above the membrane separating the higher part of the brain from the lower; colloquial for imagined or psychosomatic pain; "Really it's supratentorial; she's got nothing."

T.   Trauma; injury, accidental or otherwise, as opposed to disease; in this context always physical; also, "multi-T."

tank up   To give fluids to a patient who is dehydrated; "Mr. Yarrow's lips are dry; you'd better tank him up a bit."

terminal living   Dying.

tern   Intern; first-year resident physician; the designation of a house officer in the first year of training after the M.D. degree, the year that leads to licensing; see also *"res."*

tiger country   Parts of the body with a density of delicate and important structures; dangerous to enter with a needle or scalpel; as in "You'd better watch it there, that's tiger country." Said in the *O.R.*

toasted toddlers   Synonym for *crispy critters,* which see.

Tonto   Nickname given to the author by a resident; medical student sidekick, from "The Lone Ranger."

toxic   Sick; a reference to a child who simply strikes you as really ill, in a way that goes beyond the usual childhood illnesses and beyond the mother's anxiety; the house officer's intuition that must be relied upon sometimes for hospital admission.

train wreck   Total medical disaster, but (unlike "horror show") not from physician error; patient with multiple trauma, or simply with several superimposed illnesses; not a hopeful designation.

triple A   Abdominal aortic aneurysm; balloonlike bulge in the abdominal segment of the descending aorta; rupture or threat of rupture constitutes a surgical emergency and is life-threatening.

triple P   Piss poor protoplasm; refers to the overall problem in a patient who keeps getting different serious illnesses and can't seem to get well; not based on any scientific concept, but nevertheless viewed by house officers as somewhat more than a joke.

triple ripple   Three-way acid-base disturbance; derangement of the body's all-important balance of blood electrolytes, but in this case coming from three separate abnormalities, superimposed on each other simultaneously; quite unusual, very difficult to interpret and treat.

tube factor   Humorous mathematical estimate of how likely a moribund patient is to survive, based on how many tubes are connected to various bodily cavities; "Don't forget, life expectancy is inversely correlated with the tube factor."

tune-up   Patient with a chronic illness that cannot be cured (e.g., congestive heart failure, kidney failure) comes in to be checked and *"buffed."*

turf   One of the most common and important verbs used by house officers; to transfer a patient, as quickly and permanently as possible, to another service, to the street, or (when all else fails) to the morgue; viewed in the minds of some house officers as a flashing neon sign: TURF TURF TURF.

turn sour   "She was a rose for two weeks and now she's turned sour on me;" see *"go sour."*

Twit in the Pit   House officer assigned to the Emergency Room, or pit.

Unclear Medicine   nuclear medicine. The subspecialty that uses advanced nuclear imaging techniques, viewed more skeptically by other physicians, to reveal tumors and other tissue abnormalities.

virgin case   A diagnosis just now picked up, with no previous record of treatment; the medical student gets to see it fresh and make the whole formulation.

visit   Physician with visiting privileges at the hospital; not part of the paid staff but empowered to admit patients (or rather, to pressure house officers into admitting them) and then to participate in their daily care; usually, though not always, looked down on by house officers and staff.

Vitamin H   Humorous name for the antipsychotic drug Haloperidol; implies that the patient is suffering from a deficiency of it; "Let's give him some Vitamin H."

Vitamin P   Humorous name for the labor-inducing drug Pitocin; see *"Vitamin H."*

wall   A house officer on service in the Emergency Ward who knows how to prevent unnecessary admissions or to *"turf"* them somewhere else; opposite of *"sieve."*

waltz-in clinic   Walk-in clinic, where residents see patients without appointment.

whip   Remove surgically, especially quickly; as in the surgical sayings "When in doubt, whip it out" and "Whip that mother dog out through a smokin' hole."

white worm   An appendix that, on removal, proves to be uninfected, meaning that in some strict sense the surgery was unnecessary; up to twenty percent in major hospital populations; without which many infected appendixes would be missed, leading to rupture, peritonitis and, frequently, death.

widowmakers   Certain patterns of occlusion of the coronary arteries with poor prognosis, more or less irrespective of symptom picture.

with the program   Refers to a severely ill patient who is improving; as in "Mr. Goldman seems more with the program;" frequently refers to a patient with mental status impairment, but not exclusively.

worm   A hateful, threatening, or dishonest patient.

zap   Verb meaning to use electric shock paddles to convert a patient's heart out of an abnormal rhythm; or, to give a particularly dangerous medicine, or a very large dose; or to irradiate; see also *buzz.*

zebra   A rare medical condition almost never found except in books; frequently "identified" by medical students who dream of fame and then face the embarrassment of being taught to recognize one of the old standbys in a slightly new guise; from "He heard hoofbeats outside the hospital window and he naturally surmised that it was a zebra."

zippola   Nothing, with emphasis; the amount that can be done for some patients.

FOR THE BEST IN PAPERBACKS, LOOK FOR THE

In every corner of the world, on every subject under the sun, Penguin represents quality and variety—the very best in publishing today.

For complete information about books available from Penguin—including Penguin Classics, Penguin Compass, and Puffins—and how to order them, write to us at the appropriate address below. Please note that for copyright reasons the selection of books varies from country to country.

In the United States: Please write to *Penguin Group (USA), P.O. Box 12289 Dept. B, Newark, New Jersey 07101-5289* or call 1-800-788-6262.

In the United Kingdom: Please write to *Dept. EP, Penguin Books Ltd, Bath Road, Harmondsworth, West Drayton, Middlesex UB7 0DA.*

In Canada: Please write to *Penguin Books Canada Ltd, 90 Eglinton Avenue East, Suite 700, Toronto, Ontario M4P 2Y3.*

In Australia: Please write to *Penguin Books Australia Ltd, P.O. Box 257, Ringwood, Victoria 3134.*

In New Zealand: Please write to *Penguin Books (NZ) Ltd, Private Bag 102902, North Shore Mail Centre, Auckland 10.*

In India: Please write to *Penguin Books India Pvt Ltd, 11 Panchsheel Shopping Centre, Panchsheel Park, New Delhi 110 017.*

In the Netherlands: Please write to *Penguin Books Netherlands bv, Postbus 3507, NL-1001 AH Amsterdam.*

In Germany: Please write to *Penguin Books Deutschland GmbH, Metzlerstrasse 26, 60594 Frankfurt am Main.*

In Spain: Please write to *Penguin Books S. A., Bravo Murillo 19, 1° B, 28015 Madrid.*

In Italy: Please write to *Penguin Italia s.r.l., Via Benedetto Croce 2, 20094 Corsico, Milano.*

In France: Please write to *Penguin France, Le Carré Wilson, 62 rue Benjamin Baillaud, 31500 Toulouse.*

In Japan: Please write to *Penguin Books Japan Ltd, Kaneko Building, 2-3-25 Koraku, Bunkyo-Ku, Tokyo 112.*

In South Africa: Please write to *Penguin Books South Africa (Pty) Ltd, Private Bag X14, Parkview, 2122 Johannesburg.*